Blackening Britain

Global Critical Caribbean Thought

Series Editors:
Lewis R. Gordon, professor of Philosophy, UCONN-Storrs, and honorary professor, Rhodes University, South Africa
Jane Anna Gordon, associate professor of Political Science, UCONN-Storrs
Nelson Maldonado-Torres, associate professor of Latino and Caribbean Studies, Rutgers, School of Arts and Sciences

This series, published in partnership with the Caribbean Philosophical Association, turns the lens on the unfolding nature and potential future shape of the globe by taking concepts and ideas that while originating out of very specific contexts share features that lend them transnational utility. Works in the series engage with figures including Frantz Fanon, CLR James, Paulo Freire, Aime Cesaire, Edouard Glissant and Walter Rodney, and concepts such as coloniality, creolization, decoloniality, double consciousness and la facultad.

Titles in the Series
Race, Rights and Rebels: Alternatives to Human Rights and Development from the Global South
Julia Suárez Krabbe
Decolonizing Democracy: Power in a Solid State
Ricardo Sanin-Restrepo
Geopolitics and Decolonization: Perspectives from the Global South
Edited by Lewis R. Gordon and Fernanda Bragato
The Existence of the Mixed Race Damnés: Decolonialism, Class, Gender, Race
Daphne V. Taylor-Garcia
The Desiring Modes of Being Black: Literature and Critical Theory
Jean-Paul Rocchi
Decrypting Power
Edited by Ricardo Sanín-Restrepo
Looking Through Philosophy in Black: Memoirs
Mabogo Percy More
Black Existentialism: Essays on the Transformative Thought of Lewis R. Gordon
Edited by danielle davis
A Decolonial Philosophy of Indigenous Colombia: Time, Beauty, and Spirit in Kamëntšá Culture
Juan Alejandro Chindoy Chindoy
Blackening Britain: Caribbean Radicalism from Windrush to Decolonization
James G. Cantres

Blackening Britain

Caribbean Radicalism from Windrush to Decolonization

James G. Cantres

ROWMAN & LITTLEFIELD
Lanham • Boulder • New York • London

Published by Rowman & Littlefield
An imprint of The Rowman & Littlefield Publishing Group, Inc.
4501 Forbes Boulevard, Suite 200, Lanham, Maryland 20706
www.rowman.com

6 Tinworth Street, London SE11 5AL, United Kingdom

Copyright © 2020 by James G. Cantres.

All rights reserved. No part of this book may be reproduced in any form or by any electronic or mechanical means, including information storage and retrieval systems, without written permission from the publisher, except by a reviewer who may quote passages in a review.

British Library Cataloguing in Publication Information Available

Library of Congress Cataloging-in-Publication Data

Library of Congress Control Number: 2020945998

ISBN 978-1-5381-4354-4 (cloth)
ISBN 978-1-5381-4840-2 (pbk)
ISBN 978-1-5381-4355-1 (Electronic)

To Amita and Radha—two warriors.

Contents

Acknowledgments ix

Introduction: *More English than the English?*: Claims-making and Contestations in Britain and across Empire xi

1 From Small Islands to a Small Island: The Caribbean Background and Interwar Migration 1

2 The 5th Pan-African Congress, Manchester 1945: Black Internationalism in the Context of Britain 17

3 After 1948: Existentialists in Exile: Intellectual Responses to Racialized Realities 45

4 "We're Here, and We're Here in a Big Way": West Indians Respond to the Notting Hill Race Riots 65

5 Diasporic Artist-Activists and Imperial Reckoning: Academic and Grassroots Responses to Notting Hill 93

6 British Caribbean Independence and the 1962 Commonwealth Immigrants Act: Meanings of British Nationality 115

7 Black Publishers and Revolutionary Epistemologies: Radical Knowledges and Black Post-Nationalism 169

Conclusion: Beyond Britain: Black Liberation Dreams 209

Coda [Crisis]: *Windrush* at 70: The Hostile Environment	215
Select Bibliography	221
Index	229
Author Biographical Note	239

Acknowledgments

This project was possible because of the support of many people and institutions. Thanks are due to Lewis Gordon for his encouragement in developing this study. Jane Anna Gordon has my never-ending gratitude for helping me to move this work from a lunch conversation to a book. I also want to thank editors Scarlet Furness and Frankie Mace at Rowman-Littlefield.

Michele Mitchell has been a steadfast mentor and guide. Through his mentorship and unflinching commitment to the highest standards of intellectual inquiry and research Professor Michael Gomez has helped to shape my scholarly trajectory. Quincy Mills supported my burgeoning interest in diaspora studies, watched me fall, and continued to support me. Ada Ferrer, Joshua Guild, and Sukhdev Sandhu saw an early iteration of this project and I am grateful for their insights and suggestions. Thanks also to Terence Keel, Gaye Johnson, George Lipsitz, Aisha Khan, and Roberto Strongman. My high school History teacher Laura Arcuri told me when I was fifteen that I would write a book someday—you knew before I did.

I want to thank the archivists who facilitated my research: Marie, Arlene, and Victoria in the Asian and African Reading Room at the British Library; Sarah Garrod and Emily at the George Padmore Institute; Rhoda Boateng and Abigail Wharne at the Black Cultural Archives in Brixton, Anya Edmond-Pettitt at the Institute of Race Relations, and Lorraine Nero in St. Augustine.

This work has been supported by assistance from the Research Foundation of CUNY, CUNY Mellon Faculty Diversity Career Enhancement Initiative, Faculty Fellowship Publication Program, and the Dean's and Provost's Offices at Hunter College. The Association for the Study of the Worldwide African Diaspora and the Caribbean Philosophical Association have been tremendously supportive in fostering intellectual communities to which I am proud to belong.

I must acknowledge deep gratitude for intellectual exchanges with my friends and colleagues Laurie Lambert, Shauna Sweeney, Max Mischler, Tyesha Maddox, Jonathan Square, Ebony Jones, Njoroge Njoroge, Reynolds Richter, Daniel Rodriguez, and Gregory Childs. I also want to thank Beatrice Wayne and Lars Dyrszka for felling a tree and building me the desk upon which this book was written.

Thank you Darrayl Cummings, Luke Parker, Nic Riley, and Nabanita Pal who are both friends and family to me. Thanks to Lesia Ruglass, Dana Asbury, Cresandra Corbin, Alex Wynn, Viki Rasmussen, Jeremy Glick, Guy Ortolano, Chiké Edozien, and Jerome Teelucksingh.

Zainab Abbas has been a light and mum to me across the Atlantic, extending warmth, graciousness, love, and Sunday roasts that powered me during research trips abroad. The Goklanys welcomed me into their home and supported me in crucial ways from the day we met. Thanks my brother W. Christopher Johnson for holding me accountable—you have been a partner in the archive and a true friend.

To my parents, Gladys and Jimi Cantres who did not ask too many questions about what one does with a PhD in History but rather trusted in me and I thank you. Thank you my Cantres, Harper, and Manghnani families.

Finally, to Amita Manghnani Cantres for your gracious ferocity and resilience.

Note: Chapter 3 is derived in part from an article published in *African and Black Diaspora*, March 2018, copyright Taylor & Francis, available online at tandfoline.com/African and Black Diaspora: An International Journal.

Introduction: *More English than the English?*

Claims-making and Contestations in Britain and across Empire

On June 21, 1948, the steamliner *MV Empire Windrush* arrived at the port of Tilbury, England, carrying 1027 passengers.[1] Leaving from Jamaica, the *Windrush*'s arrival marked the beginning of a period of rapid migration from the Caribbean to the United Kingdom after World War II. *Windrush* passengers were transported to Clapham, southwest London, where they were housed in a World War II air-raid shelter. Over parts of the next three decades, migrants from the Caribbean were met with both contempt and patronage from native Britons. West Indians developed distinctive patterns of recognition and consciousness, and as a result new patterns of identification among the migrant community in the United Kingdom emerged, spurred by significant historical events and processes of racialized politicization in Britain. Notions of estrangement from Britain were crucial to the development of patterns of identification that West Indian migrants utilized while negotiating British society. The placement of the arrivals in a subterranean shelter ensured they were literally out-of-sight in London and presaged the often-tenuous relationship between migrants and British-born citizens. The hostile environment in London shocked migrants and their collective struggles in the capital upset the salutary perceptions Britain projected as the "mother country." The pursuit of social and economic belonging for West Indians characterized much of the next three decades of their histories in Britain.

For Citizens of the United Kingdom and Colonies, arriving in Britain represented opportunity, but once in the metropole, migrants encountered a sobering reality, resulting in a new identity formation centered upon a migrant, pan-West Indian consciousness.[2] Severely limited economic opportunities within the Caribbean, wherein most black and brown citizens had access to employment only on the large private and internationally owned sugar and fruit plantations, provided the impetus for migration to metropolitan Britain. The period of this study marks the ethnogenesis of pan-West Indian collective identification in the United Kingdom, informed by the West Indian background but forged as a response to the constraints of life as migrants of color in the metropole.

Although the arrival of the *Windrush* marks the symbolic genesis of West Indian migration to Britain, it is one event within a dynamic and nuanced period. In this study, three different microeras mark the radicalization and changing patterns of identification among West Indian migrants in London during the twentieth century. Those stages were the interwar years through 1948: marked by West Indians and Africans arriving for study and arguing against the color bar through efforts at integration and tolerance; 1948–1962: when the British Nationality Act brought more migrants, more racialized discrimination and the 1962 Commonwealth Immigrants Act encouraged the struggle for civil rights and potential sovereignty abroad; and 1962–1971: distinguished by further radicalization, Caribbean and African independence, black power exemplified by unorthodox organizing and black presses and the emergence of black post-nationalism coinciding with the passage of the highly restrictive Immigration Act in 1971. Scholars have written about these periods separately but insufficiently reckon with their vastly nuanced interconnectedness and ultimately privilege an Anglo-centric notion of progress at the expense of Afro-Caribbean identifications traversing space and time and emergent in the particular nexus of late imperial Britain.

Blackening Britain interrogates the ways West Indian activists, intellectuals, political actors, and artists conceived of their relationship to Britain. Ultimately, this work shows a move away from British identity and a radical, revolutionary consciousness rooted in the West Indian background and forged in the contentious space of metropolitan Britain.

In the present study, identification refers to what Stuart Hall termed, "the process by which groups, movements, institutions, try to locate us for the purpose of regulating us; try to construct us within symbolic boundaries in order to locate us, to give us resources, or take resources away from us . . . as part of a conversation around social positioning at any time."[3] Hence, identification is an ongoing and dynamic historical process rather than the limited categorization that "identity" implies. In regard to his own experience, Jamaican-born Hall asserted that "nobody from the Caribbean came here in the 1950s thinking of themselves as West Indian . . . I discovered I was West Indian in London . . . and never completely, because one also always remained partly Jamaican . . . island jealousies were also maintained alongside the discovery of a kind of pan-Caribbeanism, the location of which was primarily Notting Hill or Brixton."[4] The experience of Caribbean migrants in London facilitated an awareness of a particular West Indianness developing in the imperial

Introduction: More English than the English? xiii

center rather than inherited from the islands. These conceptions of identification shape this analysis of West Indianness with respect to the migrant experience and historical events that informed these changes.

Although cultural studies' frameworks provide a departure point for investigating the experiences of black Britons, they nevertheless suffer from an ahistorical rendering of identification, geography, and political consciousness. Caribbean people were not simply Caribbean in the West Indies and British in the British Isles but rather their ideas, symbols, politics, and epistemologies reflected ongoing entanglements of historicized engagement in various contexts within the British Empire.

Blackening Britain considers the complex structures of colonial societies and understands West Indians as historical actors shaped and informed by a confluence of factors, experiences, and historical relationships. At the onset of World War II, the Great Depression spurred widespread labor unrest in the British Caribbean. Banana farmers and dockworkers in Jamaica went on strike in 1935 and through the rest of the decade labor resistance spread throughout the British Caribbean.[5] By 1943 the People's National Party and the Jamaica Labour Party were established, and in 1944 the first elections under universal adult suffrage were held. Jamaica, with the largest population and political economy, was but one constituent unit of the British Caribbean. Trinidad, Barbados, and Grenada also developed political sovereignty movements concomitantly. *Blackening Britain* follows an important era when West Indians began to participate more fully in electoral politics, served in the British armed forces in World War II, and expressed their discontent with the political economy and governmental structures in their homelands.[6]

West Indians, by their own direction, transformed the metropolitan British state by coloring the very precept of a "British" identity. What distinguishes this work is that rather than focus on British citizenship, *Blackening Britain* is oriented around the emergence of post-national diasporic consciousness within the metropole, informed by the Caribbean background and based on developments regarding racialization in the capital as well as in apartheid South Africa, the United States, and sites of decolonization in British Caribbean and African spaces. This work narrates the changing patterns of identification that developed among the Caribbean migrant community in the post–World War II metropole culminating in articulations of "black post-nationalism."[7]

HISTORIES ACROSS ERAS

Kennetta Hammond Perry's work illuminates specific ways West Indians and other black or nonwhite citizens in Britain asserted their sense of national belonging and appealed to the state to experience the fullness of their rights and privileges. Minkah Makalani details the many ways black women and men from Africa and the Caribbean moved in and out of spaces like London, Paris, and Berlin radicalized by Marxism but also motivated by a deepening racial consciousness. Kathleen Paul offers an analysis of British legislative policy and its racial undertones especially after World War II. *Blackening Britain* contributes a narrative linking these three periods more seamlessly and suggesting the eventual demise of British identity among the most fervent activists and intellectuals. In *Black Empire,* Michelle Ann Stephens posits the notion of "transnational blackness" in the context of the work and lives of Marcus Garvey, Claude McKay, and C. L. R. James once arrived in the United States—this study considers how the activities that transcended the American nation-state by British-Caribbean radicals reflected their background in the Anglophone Caribbean and had important ramifications in the British metropolitan space.[8]

Perry argues that "the politics of race effectively imped[ed] Caribbean migrants of African descent from fully realizing their right to belong in Britain as citizens."[9] Her descriptive approach illuminates the meaning of blackness and its seeming irreconcilability with British identity.[10] *Blackening Britain* addresses the historical legacy of a cadre of radical thinkers who were impacted by the phenomenon of "unbelonging" in Britain and reoriented their identification away from the specific categorization of "Britishness" and their ensuing novel political orientation best characterized as black postnationalism. They were the vanguard of cultural and intellectual production in London at the turn of the 1970s without belonging to Britain due to racial prejudice and exhibiting a substantive connection to the newly independent former colonies of their births. Rather than belonging or making claims on membership, they instead transformed British culture as migrants informed by radical principles of Caribbean thought.

Blackening Britain emphasizes a different conceptualization of identity within the British imperial and decolonizing idiom. Although many West Indians made claims to a British identity, it was not necessarily their sole identification. The "statist modalities" of the black Atlantic were upended by the multifarious ways that Caribbean people conceived of and expressed themselves. British culture became cosmopolitan in spite of British provincialism through the innovative renderings of identity and their complementary cultural formations informed by the West Indian background.

The postwar period marked an important era for West Indians in London who negotiated British society and collectively reoriented their consciousness as racialized alien citizens in the metropole. Interactions between West Indians and the native British population exacerbated differences of race, class, culture, and conceptualizations of the British national community and produced particular identity reconfigurations within each group, contributing to the growth of a novel collective consciousness among various sectors of West Indian migrants. As historical actors whose social and political consciousness developed over decades in London, West Indian migrants were agents of a process that involved both a negotiation of British society and burgeoning patterns of mutual identification among the migrants. The particular subjects of this study were industrial workers, students from the British Caribbean, and migrants active in community and professional associations. Of these groups, there was a high concentration of Jamaican workers[11] and a number of influential political and cultural figures who maintained correspondence with friends and relatives in the Caribbean. In addition, Barbados and Barbadians occupy an important position, due to the cultural significance of Barbados in the British national imagination. The reputation of Barbados as "Little England,"[12] had a major impact on the cultural consciousness of West Indians prior to and after their arrival in metropolitan England. Migrants from Trinidad and Tobago also constituted a large portion of the migrants in London and were instrumental in the intellectual and artistic life of the community.[13]

Windrush-era migration to the United Kingdom changed metropole–colony relations, highlighting notions of race, citizenship, Caribbean political imagination, and identification within the British Empire. Rapid migration to London was a response to the lack of employment opportunities in the Caribbean and the perceived abundance of jobs in Britain.[14] Despite arriving from the Caribbean, migrants did not necessarily politically align with one another. The ways that West Indian migrants translated localized identities across the Atlantic, however, may be an insufficient retelling of their experiences in Britain.[15] *Blackening Britain* transcends the scope of legal parameters for citizenship and nationality and interrogates how racial difference operated in the everyday lives of West Indians in Britain. How West Indians fit themselves into the larger British imperial polity is crucial, as is recognizing how migrants from different islands came to associate with one another as a collective within London.

Novel West Indian consciousness and identification can be categorized into four major processes: organic collective action, political mobilization, manifestations of shared consciousness, and patterns of communication. These mechanisms developed concomitantly alongside escalating racialized consciousness that emerged from the experience of alienation and discrimination in Britain. Organic collective action refers to loosely organized political activity among Caribbean migrants whether facilitated by formal organization or garnering participation primarily from interested individuals. Political mobilization suggests the development and propagation of clearly articulated racialized politics in the United Kingdom. Shared consciousness is a component of identification exemplified by representation of the experience of life in London among migrants. Common examples include reportage, narrative, or memoir. Manifestations of shared consciousness are fluid and distinct—revolutionary epistemology manifest in the radical scholarship and arts production of intellectuals, and artists. Self-identification and consciousness are categories that help to explain the historical developments of migrant communities in London. The Caribbean literary tradition was transplanted to the metropole and underwent a significant change in content, later focusing closely on the experiences of migrants alienated in Great Britain.[16]

Patterns of communication among migrants and their friends and families established networks extending from Britain throughout the West Indies, maintaining ties between the colonies and metropole. Sustained contact between migrants and the West Indies suggests that the Caribbean as home lingered in the consciousness of the migrant community. Channels of communication were the practical component of what constitutes West Indian migrant consciousness. *Blackening Britain* investigates how networks of communication between migrants and their families and friends in the colonies contributed to vigorous political radicalization through relationships which developed with peoples in British colonial Africa, newly independent South Asia, and the United States. Radicals in Britain had a political consciousness encompassing more than local, regional, or national perspectives—they were concerned with racial justice across national boundaries and throughout the global South. The political consciousness of these people was born out of localized experiences in Britain though were far from provincial—they were the most cosmopolitan persons in the metropole.

The alienation and unbelonging West Indians faced engendered a desire to create innovative notions and conceptualizations and complimentary spaces of belonging, liberation, and social cohesion in London. By the end of the 1960s, their radical politics reflected not only a desire to belong to Britain but focused on fostering elements of liberatory politics despite the restrictive conditions in the former colonial mother country. Their race-first perspectives in many instances emerged from scholarly, spiritual, and mythological renderings of Africa and the Caribbean as the center of their outlook.

BEYOND "BLACK BRITAIN"

Applying U.S. race relations scholarship to another context cannot tell the history of migrants of color in mid-century Britain. The present study appraises political machinations of late imperial Britain and the status of Caribbean-born citizens in relation to metropolitan Britain. Although CUKC status allowed for the free entry and exit of citizens from Caribbean colonies, it is imperative to examine the disconnect between metropolitan politics and the reality of social and economic conditions in the West Indies. Stark racial and ethnic differences between the Caribbean and Britain impacted residents of each region in critically dissimilar ways. Caribbean migrants, aware of their home islands' relationships to Britain, were commonly substantially more cognizant of the interplay between colony and metropole, subject and citizen, than were their metropolitan counterparts. Caribbean migrants, especially the educated classes, held more sophisticated worldviews than their metropolitan British interlocutors.[17] Caribbean social and ethnic heterogeneity—coupled with the constant influx of news from the United States and the United Kingdom—imbued migrants with a cosmopolitanism largely absent in the British Isles outside of London or parts of Cardiff, Liverpool, or Manchester.

Histories of twentieth-century West Indian migrations sparingly address the multiplicities of experiences migrants endured, especially with regard to the earlier periods of mass immigration. Academic studies from the 1950s and 1960s particularly focus on the demographic trends in London after the influx of new migrants from the Caribbean. More recent scholarship, including ethnographies and archive-based historical scholarship, often make specific events or developments their subjects rather than viewing the process of radicalization and West Indian identification as significant historical processes.[18]

There is a tendency to conflate the study and histories of blacks in Britain with African American history,[19] though this study argues against oversimplification and a complementary misappropriation of terminologies and methodologies. Racialization emerged and developed according to particular contextual realities with respect to the United States and Britain. Caribbean migration to Britain, though largely the product of poor working, living, and social conditions in their home region with respect to the perceived opportunities in the metropole, was largely chosen. Furthermore, the very notion of "black Britain" is fraught within the context of emergent political blackness.

Regarding social structures, the premise that "community" and "society" are in Britain separate and perhaps mutually exclusive social group categorizations is an important distinction to note. Only Britons of certain class, racial, ethnic, and national background are eligible for membership in British "society," whereas other groups always constitute distinctive "communities" and are forever viewed as interlocutors within British "society." The fact that West Indian migrants were foreign-born compounded the notion that their lives and social formations in Britain could be perceived only at the level of "community" and never understood as making up part of the national society. Dealing with multiple levels of exclusion, black migrants were among the most visible residents in mid-century Britain, though were perceived as the class most estranged from the predominating notion of "society" in Britain.[20]

Circumstances of migration emerged from the dearth of employment opportunities in the Caribbean, and the paucity of higher education prospects in the region; exploitative labor practices in the primary industries and throughout the agricultural sector were also decisive factors. Many migrants held salutary notions of the metropole and claimed their rights based on CUKC status. Thus, West Indians were not tied to Britain as a physical or historical home but sought an articulation of an actualized relationship of belonging to British imperial culture. The prevailing notion that Caribbean migrants, Indians, Pakistanis, Ghanaians, Kenyans, and others were not concerned with the tangible claims on Great Britain but rather pled for a symbolic, theoretical belonging in the British imperial formation, is striking. The different histories of these groups and their black American counterparts are therefore obvious. *Blackening Britain* shows how patterns of colonial Caribbean migration were particular and distinct to British social relations, imperial politics, and the rapid radicalization of Caribbean peoples in the metropole.[21]

The present study offers interventions into African diaspora migration history, British cultural studies, and black British history. African diaspora literature related to Britain is quite expansive, with a focus on transnational and migration histories in Europe.[22] Cultural studies contributions have been significant, though without always providing clearly historicized notions of the development of social and cultural formations.[23] The disparate historiographies informing this work can be effectively addressed in a novel way that utilizes both the theoretical insights of cultural studies and the historical patterns of migration, negotiation, and racialized identification—an ethnogenesis of West Indian migrants in postwar London. By the 1970s, however, this identification was radicalized by select individuals whose political outlook and action can be described as black post-nationalism—transcending the nation of Britain and even the collective West Indian identity. This innovation marked a pivot toward a global notion of black radical solidarity.

Literature on black Britain is customarily concerned with residential patterns, difficulties of assimilation, and the legal components of migration and settlement.[24] Mike and Trevor Phillip's work has been influential in framing popular discourse on contemporary British race relations. Kathleen Paul addresses the changing legal conditions of colonial citizenship during the decline of the British Empire although without further complicating race relations outside the realm of legality. This project presents a rendering of British social relations beyond citizenship and subjecthood, primarily through charting social relations between native and migrant Britons and the subsequent patterns of identification that emerged.

African diaspora frameworks have been useful for migration histories, in charting how African descended peoples have identified themselves in varied contexts. Racial formation, subjugation, and oppression have been significant themes in many places, though various lacunae with regard to historical scholarship and diaspora in Britain persist. Diaspora scholarship on migration in other European contexts, however, provides a variety of methods and approaches, ranging from ethnography, oral testimony, to studies of cultural production, and the histories of transnational and pan-Africanist intellectual movements in twentieth-century Europe. In addition to diaspora literature on Europe, histories of migrants and their community and social formations in United States abound. These often examine the changing social and cultural formations of migrant populations and emphasize cultural retention as well as modes and methods of assimilation in new political circumstances.[25]

IDENTITIES AND IDENTIFICATIONS

Migrant self-identification has been an element of British race relations scholarship, and how migrants viewed themselves—as members of the British national community, the empire at large, or as marginalized outsiders negotiating within their new environs—remain essential in the present study. Negotiating public space—as individuals and members of a racialized group—was central to migrant experiences and their activity was highly scrutinized because of the visibility of black migrants in British society. For example, the Notting Hill Carnival remains an important event wherein West Indians make claims on public space in Britain while asserting their Caribbean identities. Gilroy locates the utility of identity in the way it "can be traced back toward its sources in the institutional patterning of identification . . . memory and ritual."[26] Retaining the Carnival tradition enables West Indians to reproduce their cultural forms in new environments while remembering its origins. A host of institutions designed and initiated by West Indians reflect the public nature of their claims to multiple threads of identification.

Hall's work on identity is mediated largely through the notion of articulation. He suggested, "articulation is a metaphor used 'to indicate relations of linkage and effectivity between different levels of all sorts of things' . . . the unity which they form is thus not that of an identity . . . the unity formed by this combination or articulation is . . . a 'complex structure' . . . in which things are related as much through their differences as through their similarities."[27] Identification among black migrants in Britain was based on relationships among migrants and between the migrant community and native Britons. Both difference and similarity informed the relationships between group members and Hall's intervention allows for investigation of historically specific accounts of the development and progression of the politics of articulation. This study suggests various mechanisms of identification operated *through* differences all the while acknowledging and reckoning with them. The revolutionary and epistemological movements that grew out of a radicalized migrant consciousness developed precisely out of a recentered and reoriented consciousness of migrants of color.

Racial conflict and citizenship are themes that have complicated notions of transnational cultural formation, particularly in the cultural studies framework.[28] Transnational tropes may be inadequate to describe the cultural forms of migrants to Britain. The ways black migrants viewed themselves had much to do with their national origins and though not restricted by national boundaries, commonalities were located in race and racial belonging. This study regards transnationalism as conditional—the translations and exchanges between black migrants and black Britons outside of internationalisms because of the presence of the empire. However, because Great Britain was the predominant nation-state model at the time of decolonization, colonial subjects needed to reckon with their own identity against that of metropolitan Britain's. Furthermore, the affiliations and networks developed and maintained by migrants in London were a mechanism that contributed to and reflected their black post-nationalist consciousnesses. Politically active migrants sought not only to advocate and mobilize for island-based nationalist movements but also theorized and conceptualized a radical and racialized diasporic politics by the close of the 1960s. Despite London's metropolitan position, the turn toward sovereignty and decolonization allowed persons from around the Commonwealth to refute the old imperial connections and build politics around belonging to a racially conscious and egalitarian network of peoples.

Different methodologies and conceptual approaches in the historiography of modern black Britain provide perspectives on the historical development of communities of color in the late imperial metropole. Twentieth-century Caribbean migration to the United Kingdom was starkly different from other historical diasporas that emerged from the large-scale importation of Africans via the transatlantic slave trade such as the United States, the Caribbean, or Brazil. More specifically, postwar migration was marked by two essential factors unavailable to slaves: citizenship and freedom of movement. Postwar migrants had CUKC privileges and despite conditions in the Caribbean and the paucity of job opportunities in Britain, West Indians were not forcibly removed from their island homes and taken to England as chattel despite historically having been brought to the Caribbean in that manner. In some cases, the British recruited West Indian laborers to rebuild after the war. Britain thus existed in the political and social imaginaries of Caribbean peoples as an aspirational site. Caribbean colonials understood Britain as the center of the empire and wished to live in the metropole largely due to notions of egalitarianism, fairness, justice, and equality associated with the British national reputation. Within the Caribbean, British iconography dominated, whether by the corporate signage on major plantations or the Union Jack flying over government buildings. Contrary to the lived reality of the prevalence of racial bias in hiring practices and little opportunity for social ascendance within the Caribbean, migrants hoped to enjoy their extensive privileges and citizenship rights in the capital.

In *Melancholia Africana*, Nathalie Etoke reframes the possibilities of Africana solidarity and affinity through a uniquely innovative rendering of the pursuit of recovering what was lost in slavery, colonization, and dehumanization for African and diasporic people. West Indians in mid-century London occupied multiple places of unbelonging—in the Caribbean where they had been taken as slaves or in the colonial "mother country" pulled by the incentive of possible economic improvement.[29]

The rapid decline of the British Empire—concomitant with rebuilding efforts in Great Britain after World War II and the rise of the United States and the Soviet Union as global superpowers—meant that migrants were journeying to a substantially different metropole than the one which controlled and dominated a vast empire just decades prior. Brown, drawing on Gilroy's emphasis on national specificity, in her study of black Liverpudlian culture suggests, "Black American exceptionalism marginalizes Black Britons and other Black Europeans from what their American counterparts myopically constitute as 'real' Blackness."[30] Britain reemerged from the ashes of war no longer at the pinnacle of the international hierarchy. Tensions that developed between migrants of color and native white Britons had at their core contestations over belonging in Britain and consequently the availability and value of Britishness. Antagonistic Britons sought to assert themselves as inheritors of a once indomitable empire and the influx of Africans, West Indians, and Asians in the metropole represented the decline of historically glorious Anglo-Saxon civilization.

Caribbean migrants, shocked by the reality of racialized discrimination and injustice in Britain, were largely unprepared for the vitriol directed toward them. Their naiveté was rooted in the dominant role Britain played in their everyday lives. Rather than colonized consciousness, which under the weight of British imperialism's hegemonic influence constantly exerted over all aspects of Caribbean social, political, and economic lives, the migrants carried *colonial* consciousnesses with them. The political and imperial consciousness of Caribbean peoples would be best understood as fundamentally different than the metropolitan perceptions of the colonies. Migrants did not necessarily harbor complexes, but essentially different self-conceptualizations than the European one. Migrants often were well aware of the constitution and nature of the empire though not entirely beholden to the enterprise so that they were unable to see themselves in any way contrary to what was told to them by Britons. The various violent and microaggressive encounters students and workers faced were surprising precisely because the colonial perspective valorized notions of egalitarianism and West Indians were therefore unable to indict the metropolitan establishment for violating its own fundamental ideals. Because everyday experiences of life in Britain were profoundly different than predominant notions of British metropolitan society transmitted throughout the empire, many colonial migrants had more clearly articulated perspectives on the idealized image of British society and culture. The practical influence Britain exerted over the Caribbean, through its control over schools, courts, businesses, and the police forces, was so widespread that the prevalence of political consciousness valorizing and championing the gospel of British imperialism was virtually unavoidable. For the purposes of this study it is imperative that the distinction between colonial and colonized consciousness is articulated.

Colonized consciousness suggests an allegiance to imperial authority expressed by its oppressive, hegemonic functionaries. Colonial subjects, unable to envision and unable to develop a politics outside the realm of consciousness established by colonizing powers because alternate realities would never be in their interest, can be said to have colonized consciousnesses. On the contrary, colonial consciousness is marked by the inability to envision alternate realities not for want of other perspectives, but because the hegemonic influence over epistemological traditions and practical life were so dominant that alternative consciousnesses have no metaphysical space in which to develop. This project suggests Caribbean migrants had distinctly colonial, rather than colonized consciousness; they were frustrated and angered by the fallacy of British social norms in comparison to the ideals of British imperial culture but often unable to act effectively against the hegemonic structures operating in the metropole. This colonized mentality was described by Frantz Fanon in *Black Skin, White Masks*, as the "so-called dependency complex of colonized peoples."[31] This project contends that by the 1970s, the most radical West Indians in Britain were engaged in black post-nationalist movements, identifying primarily on the basis of racialized class consciousness, national origin notwithstanding.

In addition to the burden of colonial consciousness, West Indian migrants reacted to and acclimated to visible iterations of racialized hegemony upon arrival in Britain. Like subjects throughout the empire—discriminated against and disenfranchised to varying degrees, but spontaneously consenting (or being coerced) to the will and influence of London—Caribbean migrants at home found themselves subject to the influence of colonial officers. When abroad, migrants directly encountered the specter of inequality and subordination of the British enterprise. The ubiquity of the British imperial project was imposed so thoroughly in the lives of its subjects that Caribbean peoples could not escape its impact in labor, governance, and social structures. Gramsci's initial notion of hegemony is thus useful for this study. His contention that the social hegemony dominant groups exercised throughout society and its dual component of state domination, whereby the command over subordinate groups is carried out by state apparatuses of law and juridical government, held true for the case of the British in the Caribbean, even in its last stages of formal empire.[32]

Gramsci's notion of "spontaneous consent" is appropriate in this analysis as Caribbean migrants impulsively assented to the impulses of British imperialism even in their home islands. The historical component of this consent is clearly present: British imposition and dominance over the region had roots centuries prior to World War II and remained commiserate with the metropole's relationship to the colonies in both position and function. From the seventeenth century, Britain controlled the political economy and government of the colonies and utilized its own industrialization to manufacture and finish the wealth of goods from the region through to the late colonial period. Once in Britain, Caribbean people were confronted with the reality of totalized domestic hegemony, as unwelcome interlocutors in the seat of power over millions globally. The state's coercive power, which was omnipresent in the Caribbean for West Indians, was exacerbated in the metropole because of racialization in the social life in the capital.

The durability of British ideals and images that were present in the everyday life of people in the Caribbean is one component of the hegemonic influence London cast over the West Indies. Another was the material reality of British and multinational corporations dominating the islands' political economies; Parliament directing state governance; court systems made up of lawyers and magistrates educated in metropolitan Britain; and the sobering reality of young Caribbean men serving in the volunteer armed forces of Great Britain, defending the metropole, in wars halfway around the globe.[33]

The psychological and epistemological impact of British imperial hegemony on Caribbean subjects cannot be understated. In addition to the material domination exerted on West Indian peoples, the metaphysical trauma on consciousness, closely linked to essential notions of citizenship and subjecthood, pervaded the historical development of colonial consciousness among British Caribbean peoples. British Caribbean subjects, though not formally expressing an inferiority complex, had to contest with Britons' superiority complex upon arrival in the metropole. Their own identifications diverged in fundamental ways from that of the average Briton's view.

Epistemologies prevalent in the Caribbean—despite valorizing British ideals—were also responsible for the initial fertilization of revolutionary and anticolonial sentiment among migrants in the metropole. As David Scott has outlined, C. L. R. James's classic study *The Black Jacobins* was rooted in "anticolonial Romanticism," and undoubtedly influenced generations of scholars and intellectuals' understanding of a particularized political imaginary. Scott argues that this radical scholarship was unabashedly commemorative of racialized revolution in Saint Domingue and critical of European racialism and economic and humane exploitation.[34] James's work can be read as informed but not wholly beholden to the metropolitan episteme.

With respect to the British imperial project, consciousness has been a central concern of scholars for decades. In their study of impact of English missionaries on the Southern Tswana people, Jean and John Comaroff suggest "colonized peoples . . . frequently reject the message of the colonizers, and yet are powerfully and profoundly affected by its media . . . that is why new hegemonies may silently take root amidst the most acrimonious and agonistic of ideological battles."[35] While the presence of missionaries may not have resulted in widespread conversion, colonialism infiltrated Southern Tswana culture to the point of transgression. Colonialism operated on a number of fronts in Southern Africa, from the religious and spiritual to the colonial political system and its entrenchment in education ensured a colonizing presence in the lives of subject peoples. Religion, the major motivating force of the missionaries, was merely a constituent part of a larger, multilayered colonizing process and structure. Influenced by Fanon and his understanding of the debilitating and transformative aspects of colonial domination, the Comaroffs' use of consciousness as a frame to study the Tswana is apt. Their argument for a pervasiveness of colonial and colonized consciousness within the missionary campaign underscores the ubiquity of British hegemony through multiple forms of social and cultural imposition. Furthermore, the Comaroffs highlight the inconsistencies between British and Tswana conceptions of societal norms and political relationships. Politics and administrative policies the British assumed would readily be understood were interpreted in completely different ways by the Tswana, whose ideology and epistemology was formed by a specific set of historical circumstances, distinct from those that shaped English political consciousness.[36]

Blackening Britain explores the problems of assimilation and integration West Indian students and workers respectively faced upon entry into the United Kingdom. The trajectories of Trinidad-born Eric Williams and C. L. R. James traveled follows, moving through periods in the Caribbean, Great Britain, and the United States, and reflections on how these routes allowed them to develop particularly sophisticated notions of racial formation and colonial subjugation in numerous national and imperial contexts. The notion that peoples of African descent were oppressed, whether by colonial systems in the case of the British West Indies or disenfranchised as in the American Jim Crow South, was especially useful in the burgeoning of a distinct anti-racist African diaspora perspective. Williams, along with James and George Padmore, all participated in conferences and conventions that theorized race, racialization, and colonialism, with the objective of fomenting dialogue and discourse on the elimination of racial prejudice. Caribbean student articulations around racial bias and the meaning of Britishness reflected the continuing development of novel political consciousness.

An analysis of West Indian responses to the Notting Hill Race Riots chronicles the violent outbursts in summer 1958 and places these episodes in a larger context of British racial violence. *Blackening Britain* casts the responses of West Indians to the riots as groundbreaking in their political radicalism and fundamentally challenged predominant racial attitudes in Britain. After Notting Hill, radicalization of the postriot generation is highlighted including intersections with movements toward anticolonial progress throughout the Caribbean territories. This narrative concludes through revisiting the history of diasporic West Indian radicalism throughout the first two-thirds of the twentieth century, emphasizing the central role Britain played both as a site of contestation and as an incubator of the progressive and far-reaching revolutionary politics of the anti-imperial vanguard.

West Indians in London developed distinct conceptualizations of race that had roots in the social and political environments of the West Indies. If West Indians had experienced racialization at home, the specificity of British racial formation was unexpected to the migrant population. The responses of the literati and intelligentsia were unprecedented in Britain and reflected the specificity of their experiences as colonial citizens in the metropole.

Many scholars have written about pan-Caribbeanization of migrants from the region resident in Britain during the second half of the twentieth century.[37] *Blackening Britain* uncovers how these people transformed the social, political, and cultural fabric of metropolitan Britain as well. If the *Windrush* made Jamaicans and Trinidadians into West Indians, West Indians in turn blackened (through cultural, intellectual, and political expressions) the crucible of racist Britain. Priyamvada Gopal's work on locating the origins and crucial articulation of British dissent in the colonies and among the colonial arrivants in Britain is especially useful considering the ways West Indians transformed British notions of freedom and anticolonial politics.[38] Christopher Gair and Shalini Puri have respectively offered notions of "post-national" frameworks that situated the postcolonial era in ways that do not privilege the so-called success of nation-state formation after decolonization. Black post-nationalism here refers to racialized radical politics in Britain to emphasize the unique and particular condition of black diasporic histories.[39] Africans and diasporans living under conditions of forced migration, slavery, colonialism, and within the confines of Eurocentric borders and economic structures had never fit within the simple order of the nation-state. The histories of British colonialism in the Caribbean withheld belonging to the nation-state from its black subjects and the political radicals of the post-*Windrush* generation later rejected the British nation. Refused belonging for so long, the most progressive and revolutionary radicals ingeniously moved beyond British nationality once it was made available to them.

The radicalism of post-national Caribbean activism in Britain extended beyond the limits of the structures of postcolonial societies in the West Indies. The reality of postcolonialism was limited by adhering to a global order from a position of disadvantage while the radicalism of metropolitan residents threw off those very configurations. Rastafarians, black power activists, and "cultural" Marxists in the metropole exemplify black post-national radical sensibilities. They happened to be in Britain but their ideas were by no means bound by Britain or by the nation-state model.

Blackening Britain regards the spaces and institutions established by Caribbean people as black and brown in their design, background, and conception and often particularly not-British in their reception and reputation. British popular, political, and legal cultures were not colored in official manners but rather despite the rejection of racialized vanguardists. The meaning of "black British" must be qualified further through the disaggregation of what is both black and British and what is black and happens to have emerged or iterated in metropolitan British spaces. British imperial identification did not wholly transform colonial subjects nor did it make them British in the ways racialized whites were. British cultural and political institutions were colored black precisely by those who were thought and treated as though they were foreign and who resisted the particularities of British racial formation. By the 1970s British citizenship was ancillary to the radical goals of the black and brown people who colored political action and epistemology in Britain, Africa, and the Caribbean.

NOTES

1. Of this figure, 802 passengers gave their last place of residence as a country or territory in the Caribbean. Estimates suggest 492 passengers boarded in Jamaica. Contemporaneous news reports variously announced the arrival of between 400 and 500 Jamaicans disembarking. Passengers from the Caribbean were not alone on board the *Windrush*—the ship's passenger list included Mexico, Scotland, England, Wales, Burma, and Gibraltar as the last country of residence for other travelers on board. According to reports by the BBC and *The Guardian* some of the arrivals in June 1948

had boarded the *Windrush* in Mexico, including Poles who had been resettled during the Third Reich to various locations in Latin America following World War II.

2. The British Nationality Act 1948 created the status of "Citizen of the United Kingdom and Colonies" (CUKC) as the national citizenship of the United Kingdom and its colonies. CUKC status extended to people born or naturalized in either the United Kingdom or one of its colonies.

3. Stuart Hall, "Politics of Identity," in *Culture, Identity, and Politics: Ethnic Minorities in Britain*, eds. Terence Ranger, Yunas Samad, and Ossie Stuart (Aldershot, England: Avebury, 1996), 130.

4. Ibid.

5. See Colin A. Palmer, *Freedom's Children: The 1938 Labor Rebellion and the Birth of Modern Jamaica* (Chapel Hill: University of North Carolina Press, 2014); Thomas Holt, *The Problem of Freedom: Race, Labor, and Politics in Jamaica and Britain, 1832–1938* (Baltimore: Johns Hopkins University Press, 1992); Ken Post, *Arise Ye Starvelings: The Jamaican Labour Rebellion of 1938 and its Aftermath* (The Hague/Boston/London: Martinus Nijhoff, 1978).

6. See Bridget Brereton, ed., *General History of the Caribbean, Vol. V* (London: Macmillan; UNESCO Publications, 1997); Stephan Palmie and Francisco A. Scarano, *The Caribbean: A History of the Region and Its Peoples* (Chicago: University of Chicago Press, 2011); Harvey R. Neptune, *Caliban and the Yankees: Trinidad and the United States Occupation* (Chapel Hill: UNC Press, 2007).

7. I consider the work of Benedict Anderson in *Imagined Communities* and suggest that the postcolonial era in British Empire was marked not only by the desire to create nation-states out of constructions of "national culture" but that in the case of the former British West Indies—the infrastructure of nation-state development was usurped by more radical visions of racialized uplift that transcended the framework of the nation-state. I also draw on Jurgen Habermas's notion of the bourgeois public sphere excepting that in this study, the nature of public discourse and contestations over identity, belonging, and racialized politics also operated outside the realm of the bourgeoisie. Other authors such as Nancy Fraser have offered similar critiques. I contend that the public spheres black radicals moving through spaces of British influence were manifest in the infrastructure of organizations but also in the raising of transnational and post-national conceptualizations of emancipatory racialized politics. Jurgen Habermas, *The Structural Transformation of the Public Sphere: An Inquiry into a Category of Bourgeois Society* (Cambridge: Polity, 1962, 1989 trans.). Nancy Fraser, "Rethinking the Public Sphere: A Contribution to the Critique of Actually Existing Democracy," *Social Text* No. 25/26 (1990), 56–80.

8. Michelle Ann Stephens, *Black Empire: The Masculine Global Imaginary of Caribbean Intellectuals in the United States, 1914–1962* (Durham: Duke University Press, 2005).

9. Kennetta Hammond Perry, *London Is the Place for Me: Black Britons, Citizenship, and the Politics of Race* (New York: Oxford University Press, 2015), 5.

10. See also Rob Waters, *Thinking Black: Britain, 1964–1985* (Berkeley: University of California Press, 2018).

11. Jamaica was the geographically largest and most-populated of the British Caribbean territories.

12. For the longer history of Barbados as "Little England" see Kortright Davis, *Cross & Crown in Barbados: Caribbean Political Religion in the Late 19th Century* (Eugene, OR: Wipf & Stop, 1983).

13. See O. Nigel Bolland, *The Birth of Caribbean Civilization: A Century of Ideas about Culture and Identity, Nation and Society* (Kingston: Ian Randle, 2004); and *The Politics of Labour in the British Caribbean: The Social Origins of Authoritarianism and Democracy in the Labour Movement* (Kingston: Ian Randle, 2001).

14. See Rosemary Brana-Shute, *A Bibliography of Caribbean Migration and Caribbean Immigrant Communities* (Gainesville, FL: University of Florida Libraries, 1983); Ceri Peach, *West Indian Migration to Britain: A Social Geography* (London: Institute of Race Relations/Oxford University Press, 1968); George Gmelch, *Double Passage: The Lives of Caribbean Migrants Abroad and Back Home* (Ann Arbor: University of Michigan Press, 1992); and Franklin Knight, *The Caribbean: The Genesis of a Fragmented Nationalism* (New York: Oxford University Press, 1978); Michael Banton, *The Coloured Quarter: Negro Immigrants in an English City* (London: Jonathan Cape, 1955).

15. See Paul Gilroy, *The Black Atlantic: Modernity and Double Consciousness* (Cambridge, MA: Harvard University Press, 1993). *The Black Atlantic* is a foundational text for analysis of cross-Atlantic African diasporic connections, especially with regard to the United Kingdom. Gilroy emphasizes the transnational nature of relations between West Indian groups and the British metropolitan population, suggesting that identification across and transcending national identities was preeminent in the development of a West Indian consciousness in Britain. He notes the peculiarity of the West Indian experience as a minority group in Britain and subject to white nation-state ideology and policy. Gilroy's reference to "statist modalities" of European ideologies is a critique of the limited perspectives of a strictly nationalist view of political and social influence.

16. See Sukhdev Sandhu, *London Calling: How Black and Asian Writers Imagined a City* (London: HarperCollins, 2003); Onyekachi Wambu, *Hurricane Hits England: An Anthology of Writing About Black Britain* (New York: Bloomsbury, 2000).

17. See Bernard Porter, *The Absent-Minded Imperialists: Empire, Society, and Culture in Britain* (Oxford: Oxford University Press, 2004).

18. Mike and Trevor Phillips, *Windrush: The Irresistible Rise of Multi-racial Britain* (London: Harper Collins, 1998), is a foundational ethnographic study of the first generation of migrants after World War II. British sociologist and ethnographer Michael Banton produced two studies in the 1950s, *White and Coloured* and *The Coloured Quarter*, exploring racialization in contemporaneous British society. Along with Ruth Glass and Ceri Peach, much of the British social science scholarship avoids the historical components of the West Indian migration and conceptualizes the ensuing climate as a strictly sociological problem.

19. Paul Gilroy in *The Black Atlantic*, Hazel Carby in *Cultures in Babylon: Black Britain and African America* (London; New York: Verso, 1999) and Jacqueline Nassy Brown, *Dropping Anchor, Setting Sail: Geographies of Race in Black Liverpool* (Princeton: Princeton University Press, 2005) compare the experiences of blacks in

the United States and United Kingdom. This study does not aim to compare these experiences though Perry and Joshua Guild both offer thorough comparative interrogation of patterns of affiliation and urbanized claims-making among West Indians in London and New York. See Joshua Bruce Guild, *You Can't Go Home Again: Migration, Citizenship, and Black Community in Postwar New York and London* (PhD diss., Yale University, 2007).

20. This notion of "community" versus "society" in Britain is taken from a talk given by Andrew Flinn, at New York University's Archives and Public History Program, "Underground Archives, Hidden Archives, Community Archives," April 15, 2011. The division between community and society run deep and have a certain mutual exclusivity, in popular and official parlance the two are never discussed concomitantly.

21. Although South Asian and African migrants also engaged with West Indians and among themselves in London, they are not the focus of this study. I note their interactions but focus this analysis on the West Indian migrant group. They remain, however, important in discussions of political blackness.

22. For the African diaspora in Britain see Brown, *Dropping Anchor, Setting Sail*; Edward Pilkington, *Beyond the Mother Country: West Indians and the Notting Hill White Riots* (Boston: I. B. Tauris & Company, Limited, 1990); Nancy Foner, *Jamaica Farewell: Jamaican Migrants in London* (Berkeley: University of California Press, 1978); Gmelch, *Double Passage*; Clive Harris and Winston James, *Inside Babylon: The Caribbean Diaspora in Britain* (London; New York: Verso, 1993); Darlene Clark Hine, Tricia Danielle Keaton, and Stephen Small, *Black Europe and the African Diaspora* (Chicago: University of Illinois Press, 2009); Hakim Adi, ed., *Black British History: New Perspectives* (London: Zed Books, 2019).

23. See Paul Gilroy, *There Ain't No Black in the Union Jack: The Cultural Politics of Race and Nation* (Chicago: University of Chicago Press, 1991); John Solomos, *Race and Racism in Britain* (New York: St. Martin's Press, 1993); Dennis Dworkin, *Cultural Marxism in Postwar Britain: History, the New Left, and the Origins of Cultural Studies* (Durham, NC: Duke University Press, 1997); Stuart Hall, "Cultural Identity and Diaspora," in *Identity: Community, Culture, Difference*, ed. Jonathan Rutherford (London: Lawrence & Wishart, 1990); Homi Bhabha, *The Location of Culture* (London: Routledge, 1994); Avtar Brah, *Cartographies of Diaspora: Contesting Identities* (New York: Routledge, 1996).

24. See Kathleen Paul, *Whitewashing Britain: Race and Citizenship in the Postwar Era* (Ithaca, NY: Cornell University Press, 1997); Mike Phillips, *London Crossings: A Biography of Black Britain* (London: Burns & Oates, 2001); Mike and Phillips, *Windrush: The Irresistible Rise of Multi-Racial Britain*; Perry, *London is the Place for Me*.

25. See Irma Watkins-Owens, *Blood Relations: Caribbean Immigrants and the Harlem Community, 1900–1930* (Bloomington: Indiana University Press, 1996); Philip Kasinitz, *Caribbean New York: Black Immigrants and the Politics of Race* (Ithaca: Cornell University Press, 1990); Winston James, *Holding Aloft the Banner of Ethiopia: Caribbean Radicalism in Early Twentieth Century America* (London; New York: Verso, 1998); Tina M. Campt, *Other Germans: Black Germans and the Politics of Race, Gender, and Memory in the Third Reich* (Ann Arbor: University of Michigan Press, 2005).

26. Paul Gilroy, "British Cultural Studies and the Pitfalls of Identity," in *Black British Cultural Studies: A Reader*, eds. Houston Baker, Manthia Diawara, and Ruth Lindeborg (Chicago: University of Chicago Press, 1996), 229.

27. Stuart Hall, "Race, Articulation, and Societies Structured in Dominance," in *Black British Cultural Studies*, 38.

28. Paul Gilroy, *Black Atlantic*; *Black British Cultural Studies Reader*. The most prominent lacuna in *The Black Atlantic* is Gilroy's omission of Africa as a point of departure for studying the diaspora. Although West Indian migrants left the Americas, the sense that they had somehow overcome Africanity permeates Gilroy's contentions. Within the text, the lack of references to Africa suggests a disjunction between the histories of the Caribbean and Africa despite their inherent links through the slave trade and the British Empire. Even as Gilroy notes that the "culture and politics of black America and the Caribbean have become raw materials for creative processes which redefine what it means to be black, adapting it to distinctively British experiences and meanings," he omits the place of Africa in the conceptualization of cultural forms in Britain and he maintains the primacy of Britain in the process of cultural formation. Rather than allowing for the possibility of distinguishable migrant cultural forms, Gilroy characterizes these forms as products of adaptation to the British experience.

29. Nathalie Etoke, *Melancholia Africana: The Indispensable Overcoming of the Black Condition*, trans. Bill Hamlett (London: Roman & Littlefield, 2019).

30. Brown, *Dropping Anchor, Setting Sail*, 41.

31. Frantz Fanon, *Black Skin, White Masks* (New York: Grove Press, c2008), 64.

32. Antonio Gramsci, *Selections from the Prison Notebooks of Antonio Gramsci*, eds. Quinton Hoare and Geoffrey Nowell-Smith (New York: International Publishers, 1971), 12–13.

33. See Richard Smith, *Jamaican Volunteers in the First World War: Race, Masculinity, and the Development of a National Consciousness* (Manchester: Manchester University Press, 2004); Michael S. Healy, "Colour, Climate, and Combat: The Caribbean Regiment in the Second World War," *The International History Review* 22, no. 1 (2000): 65–85.

34. David Scott, *Conscripts of Modernity: The Tragedy of Colonial Enlightenment* (Durham: Duke University Press, 2004).

35. Jean Comaroff and John Comaroff, *Of Revelation and Revolution, Volume 1: Christianity, Colonialism, and Consciousness in South Africa* (Chicago: University of Chicago Press, 1991), 311.

36. This is especially important to consider Africans and Africana people in relation to British colonial incursions.

37. See James, *Holding Aloft the Banner of Ethiopia*; Makalani, *In the Cause of Freedom: Radical Black Internationalism from Harlem to London, 1917–1939* (Chapel Hill: University of North Carolina Press, 2014); Marc Matera, *Black London: The Imperial Metropolis and Decolonization in the Twentieth Century* (Berkeley: University of California Press, 2015).

38. See Priyamvada Gopal, *Insurgent Empire: Anticolonial Resistance and British Dissent* (London: Verso, 2019).

39. See Christopher Gair, ed., *Beyond Boundaries: C.L.R. James and Postnational Studies* (London: Pluto Press, 2006); Shalini Puri, *The Caribbean Postcolonial: Social Equality, Post/Nationalism, and Cultural Hybridity* (London: Palgrave MacMillan, 2014).

Chapter 1

From Small Islands to a Small Island

The Caribbean Background and Interwar Migration

Five hundred pairs of willing hands grasped the rails of the Empire Windrush as she came alongside the landing stage at Tilbury early yesterday morning . . . 500 Jamaicans, every one of whom was eager to work in Britain . . . 204 West Indians who have friends in Britain have been given travel warrants to wherever they want to go, the 52 Forces volunteers will be accommodated in a Colonial Office hostel, and the remaining 236 were taken by special coaches to the Clapham South shelter.[1]

Plantations dominated Caribbean societies in the twentieth century, structuring political economies that were dependent on Britain or the United States and where wages were insufficient and underemployment was widespread.[2] British colonial histories in the region illuminated exactly why. Beginning in 1655, Jamaica became a British colony after a military invasion. Sugarcane and coffee cultivated by slave labor imported from Africa drove the colonial economy from the mid-seventeenth century. The experiences of slavery and the plantation system, implemented by England and other European nations throughout the Caribbean, were the fundamental historical processes in the development of the region through the twentieth century. Plantation slavery shaped the social structures, economic organization and political histories of all the West Indies.[3]

The economic component of the colonial relationship made a complex system of political administration and policymaking a necessity in order to fully maximize the profitability of Britain's West Indian holdings. Continued association between peoples in the colonies and administrators abroad persisted only because of the profitability of the land and resources in the Caribbean. The inception and growth of the transatlantic slave trade then provided for centuries the manpower to cultivate the land in the West Indies.

The large-scale production of raw materials coupled with the rapidly developing industrial sector in large British cities, the thriving sea trade hinged on the success of ports such as Liverpool and Bristol, and the world's most efficient and armed naval forces allowed the British imperial economy to grow exponentially beginning in the seventeenth century. Importing Africans to the West Indies to supplement the dwindling and quickly eviscerated native Arawak and Carib populations was facilitated by English military innovation and long histories of business relations with Arab and African traders on the west coast of Africa.[4] Prior to emancipation, Caribbean territories were central to Britain's empire, providing enormous supplies of goods and requiring very little free labor. Furthermore, slave populations held no formal legal rights, thus making the British Caribbean colonies extremely exclusive in terms of popular official political rights. Lawmakers and administrators were white Englishmen and often born abroad in the metropole only to administer the colonies after schooling and colonial appointments in other regions throughout empire. The electorate excluded essentially all nonwhite peoples, though there were some limited, albeit to varying degrees throughout the islands, rights for free people of color. Colonial legislatures were made up of wealthy planters and their families or other British born and educated men with no representation from the majority population on any island. This allowed for the super-exploitation of the black masses in the region. There was no legal political space for blacks to access in the West Indies, and official crown colony status sustained black disenfranchisement, subordination, and oppression even through the transition from slavery to apprenticeship and later full emancipation.

Thomas Holt's work has provided a useful lens for understanding the antagonistic relationship between many West Indian colonies and Britain since the end of slavery in the nineteenth century.[5] Emancipated British West Indian societies, as Holt has argued, inured fear among British administrators, legislators, and politicians for over a century by the time of the *Windrush's* arrival. The threat of revolt in the West Indies intensified in the aftermath of the Morant Bay Rebellion and the implementation of martial law in that period only served to draw battle lines in what was perceived as an island-wide race war. Indeed, the long history of British colonialism in the region was consistently intertwined with the unsettled and pernicious reality of racial inequality and the threat of black rule.

Holt in conjunction with Kamau Brathwaite's work on creolization, allows us to understand the complicated social and political structures of the Caribbean which in turn were sustained into the mid-twentieth century.[6] Brathwaite's notion of creolization is useful for this study as it highlights the distinctive characteristics of the social and political institutions of the Caribbean informed and shaped by the interplay of Africa, European, and indigenous influences. *Windrush* arrivants varied greatly from the British population who received them. Brathwaite's exploration of both the external colonial relationship and Jamaica's internal social structure and problems provided an outline for understanding the complicated nature of Caribbean societies.

Holt and Brathwaite both emphasize the codification of racial strata in Caribbean society and illustrate the fundamental role race played in the social and political histories of the Caribbean and Britain. The dichotomy of freedom/enslavement legally correlated precisely to white/black, forming the basis for the social structure in the colonies and guiding the colonial relationship for centuries. The migrants of the *Windrush* generation inherited these histories and nevertheless ventured to the metropole in the hopes of realizing the promises of modern metropolitan life.

There is a connection between the historical memory of English abolitionism and the migration of people of color in the mid-twentieth century that merits serious investigation. Prior to the conclusion of the World War II, small numbers of Africans, Asians, and Caribbean colonial subjects resided in metropolitan Britain. The roots of the strict racial segregation in colony and metropole had origins in the history of British abolitionism, dating to the late eighteenth century. British imperial relationships maintained social, political, and moralistic components in official government policy and administration as well as in the everyday lived reality of subjects and citizens, slaves and masters. As Christopher Leslie Brown noted in his assessment of the abolitionist tradition, "the campaign had its roots in a distinct and distinctive moment in British imperial history, a moment that presented both unfamiliar challenges and novel possibilities to those preoccupied with the character and consequences of overseas empire."[7] The maintenance of Britain's growing empire in the eighteenth century, despite the loss of some North American colonies, competition from other European nations' plantation enterprises in the Caribbean, and the development of social and political identities that constituted their domain, coalesced at the time of the burgeoning abolitionist movement in Britain. Rather than a genuinely conceived moralist movement, Brown argued that abolitionism was the product of converging historical forces with little regard for the well-being of enslaved populations.

West Indians were often aware of the political developments in Britain from thousands of miles away. Britain loomed large in the consciousness of its West Indian colonial citizens and migration to the metropole occurred prior to the influx of West Indians in the mid-twentieth century. The lack of institutions of higher education in the West Indies necessitated travel to the United Kingdom for those seeking post-secondary degrees. Because the industrial sector of Caribbean economies lagged behind those of the United States and Great Britain, the islands' workforces were relegated to plantation labor or menial service work. The legacy of slavery in the region was compounded with the material reality of foreign-owned plantations, poor education, and a lack of well-developed industrial and economic infrastructures from island to island. Though multinational corporations were enriched, West Indian working classes labored but barely sustained themselves. Among those with some financial security, education was an option, though often also required state-sponsored scholarships to Britain. Opportunities for economic progress in particular were severely limited throughout the British West Indies and thus migration to the mother country often indicated the impulse to attain greater educational, economic, and social gains.[8]

Imperial Britain's long history of dominance over West Indian affairs stagnated the potential of West Indians to manage and administer their homelands. A political class of wealthy landowners in the region, coupled with the clout of London-based colonial policies excluded native black and South Asian–descended subjects from the highest levels of regional politics. Britain's stronghold on Caribbean affairs, maintained primarily through the Colonial Office, stifled the development of nationalist movements or any kind of recognized political participation for the better part of two centuries. The end of World War II would provide the impetus for important advances spurred by decolonization.[9]

Prior to 1948, West Indians also migrated in large numbers to the United States, much closer geographically to the Caribbean and a destination that contained a wealth of educational and employment opportunities.[10] Earlier in the twentieth century, migrant workers from throughout the British West Indies were recruited to work on building the Panama Canal. Large numbers of Jamaicans, Barbadians, and Grenadians traveled to Panama to work in the building of the Canal from the late nineteenth to early twentieth centuries.[11] The cultural dominance of Britain in the West Indies was an effective lure for many migrants in later years. Strong associations with Britain persisted through both world wars, especially as West Indian servicemen comprised significant contingents in the Allied war effort under the auspices of the Royal Air Force and other branches of the British military. West Indians had a history of direct participation in British military campaigns, which reflected the relationship with the so-called mother country, despite living an ocean away and not enjoying the full privileges of British citizenship.

Cultural connections between the West Indies and Britain, as a product of Britain's hegemonic relations with its colonies, subjugated and disempowered West Indians. Many West Indians so closely identified with Britain, not necessarily out of affinity or admiration, but rather because they recognized the ubiquitous influence of Britain and pervasiveness of metropolitan policies and cultural forms in their everyday lives. The Union Jack flew over government buildings, the post offices, courts, and schools, and royal holidays were commemorated and celebrated throughout the islands. Local British politics received regular coverage in the West Indian press, despite the distance between people in the region and these proceedings in the metropole. The notion that West Indians were members of the British national community, however, did not always resonate in the metropole. Rather, the valorization of Britain served to deepen the divisions between colonies and metropole. Britain was referenced as the ideal within empire, further suggesting the deficiencies of life throughout the colonies. West Indians were forced to conceptualize themselves perpetually in relation to the capital, so their understanding of British life was as thorough as their knowledge of their own islands. The British Broadcasting Corporation's Empire Service (renamed the Overseas Service in 1938), began in December 1932 and was transmitted through Britain's colonial territories. Among the programming was *News from Britain*, an hourly update on happenings in the metropole. Jamaican Arthur Curling remembered his grandmother, "would listen to the radio at six o'clock every evening in the West Indies, World Service... whatever was said there had to be gospel... it was said by the BBC and it was from England, therefore it was right."[12] Britain diffused its news and culture throughout empire, constantly reinforcing and reproducing the metropole's position in relation to its colonial subjects.

Quotidian transmission of information regarding Britain to the colonies represented the ubiquitous presence of the mother country in the lives of colonials. BBC broadcasts developed and reaffirmed the notion that Britain was closely connected to its colonies by regularly projecting powerful symbols and representations of British culture through mass media. Curling explained, "we were always British... in Jamaica... we hadn't our own identity... I can remember when it was the Queen's birthday... the Coronation, everything was done the way Britain wanted us to."[13] Alienated from formal political participation, West Indians were nevertheless engaged directly with the cultural politics of metropolitan Britain.

The British West Indies were supportive of metropolitan war efforts, even as its citizens lacked the formal political rights of those in Europe. The Anglo-American Caribbean Commission was founded in March 1942 with the express purpose of "encouraging and strengthening social and economic cooperation between the United States of America and its possession and bases in the Caribbean and the United Kingdom and the British colonies in the same area."[14] The goal of this collaboration between two powers was military defense, as each sought to protect their interests in the region. The West Indies' dependence on the import of foodstuffs was combated by colonial governments' leasing land to those willing to cultivate food crops, financial stabilization of the local food crop markets, and undoing the notion that the plantation system was the only viable political economy structure possible in the islands. The government initiatives ameliorated but did not eliminate the general production shortages in the region.

Questions of self-determination and the promise of increased sovereignty through indirect rule circulated in British imperial discourse. Britons acknowledged the difficulties West Indians would face upon decolonization. Furthermore, British officials expressed a cynical view of colonial populations, referring to the possible independent Caribbean as a cauldron of "serious confusion in all of our colonies through the impact of Western civilizations on backward peoples . . . the situation will become progressively worse."[15] For many Britons, independence in the Caribbean was unthinkable because colonial peoples were regarded as incapable of self-rule. An uninformed British public underestimated West Indian political capability and were unaware of West Indian political development. The racialized logics of sovereignty regarded nonwhite, non-Europeans insufficiently civilized to rule themselves.

MONTEGO BAY 1947

Before the arrival of the *Windrush*, West Indians envisioned establishing and codifying notions of affinity among the citizens of disparate islands in the Caribbean. The Conference on the Closer Association of the British West Indian Colonies, held in Montego Bay, Jamaica in September 1947, reflected this goal. Two years after the end of World War II, secretary of state for the Colonies Arthur Creech Jones posited the idea of federation and shared this with representatives from the British Caribbean colonies. Jones suggested to the Conference that the "Federation . . . need not interfere with the identity and individuality of the separate Colonies. It need not be derogatory of . . . the legitimate authority . . . in the individual territories."[16] In terms of gaining and maintaining self-government, Jones regarded the individual islands too small to do so successfully. In the decades prior to formal decolonization and independence, colonial officials were aware of the particular constitution of the West Indian islands in relation to one another and to the respective communities of people on each island. Conference delegates viewed the colonial relationship as an unsustainable one and the question of federation or total independence was one that would shape Caribbean politics in the next two decades.

While conference attendees acknowledged the primacy of Britain and metropolitan policies on the political economics and social relations in the Caribbean, Jamaican politician and labor leader William Alexander Bustamante was among the first to indict Britain as culpable for exploiting and indoctrinating colonial citizens. Bustamante insisted, "I have become

suspicious about the motive relative to the formation of this federation
... most of us West Indians have been asking for self-government we are told that self-government for the time being is really not good for us and the thing we deserve is federation."[17] Dissatisfied with Jones' motivations, Bustamante argued against following policies devised and implemented by imperial executives, seeking instead to pursue West Indian self-determination. Bustamante's objections to the proposed federation critiqued the history of British colonialism in the region, attempted to steer the islands away from continued exploitation, and to utilize independent nation-states to provide for the citizenry, which in his estimation, had been victimized by the British colonial apparatus for centuries. Bustamante's denunciation of British policy continued through his rendering of the purported closeness of Britain and the West Indian territories. He offered ironic oratorical alms to Jones, when he explained, "anything I have said regarding England—regarding the slums she keeps us with... the Governors she sends here... is not meant that I have any ill-feelings towards the English. I have no ill-feelings towards strangers."[18] Despite the belief that Britain was intimately connected to colonial possessions, Bustamante, in the presence of Jones, emphasized the exploitation and estrangement of West Indians within the imperial body politic. His view was later corroborated and explicitly supported by a number of other delegates including Trinidadian unionist, politician, and writer Albert Gomes, and Barbadian labor leader Grantley Adams.

The refutation of Federation by West Indian delegates was important for a number of reasons: West Indian leaders conceived of each island as having a distinct identity, geography, particular availability of tillable land, and skilled workforce, which contributed to variation among plans for economic structures. Federation, from their perspective, would conflate peoples in the West Indies as a uniform group and continue their characterization as a singular entity, which Bustamante criticized as a political formation that would be more amenable to manipulation by the British colonial apparatus. High-ranking party leaders in the Caribbean were frustrated with relationships dominated by Britain and they abhorred the premise of consolidating their resources and identities for metropolitan benefit. Dissent among colonial representatives was eloquently articulated, suggesting that despite the hegemonic relations Britain reinforced with the West Indies, many leaders were not loyal to the imperial project and actively campaigned against it. Britain had already dominated the politics in the region and stifled the fuller political development of their colonies, Bustamante imagined that continued association with Britain would prolong the patterns of exploitation. Ironically, Chairman Jones expressed his desire as the colonial official to remain quiet at the beginning of each day's proceedings ceding the debate floor to the West Indians.

Although Bustamante remarked against the proposed federation, other delegates, from Jamaica and elsewhere, offered optimistic and supportive commentary on the prospect of an official, closer relation between Caribbean territories. Jamaican F. A. Pixley and Bustamante's cousin Norman Manley supported the Federation, citing the promise of a united Caribbean front that would maintain and honor the respective affairs of the individual constituent islands. Manley insisted, "Federation will enlarge the area of action and enlarge the possibilities of winning that prosperity which we West Indians alone . . . must create for ourselves."[19] The fact that delegates from Jamaica disagreed over Federation and independence illustrates the complicated and sophisticated political consciousness and public discourse in Jamaica. Caribbean colonials did not hold uniform views on sovereignty and autonomy within the region, discrepancies existed even between the political leadership within individual territories. Despite their estrangement from participation in metropolitan politics and position as peripheral colonial subjects, the delegates at Montego Bay offered nuanced self-conscious political aims. Furthermore, their close understanding of British imperial policy was a product of their condition as colonial subjects and their awareness of the motivations of the colonial enterprise. As more than eyewitnesses or bystanders in the region, the Montego Bay delegates were among the most knowledgeable representatives throughout the entire colonial realm.

CARIBBEAN LABOUR CONGRESS, KINGSTON 1947

Weeks before the conference in Montego Bay, a Caribbean Labour Congress Conference was held in Kingston, though the two symposia shared few common delegates. W. A. Crawford, founding member of the Barbados Labour Party, suggested that labor conference attendees were unwelcome at the Colonial Office proceedings. Crawford explained that in Kingston, "the opinion was expressed that the true voice of the people in these Colonies would not be heard at this Conference . . . the question inevitably arises, 'Why were steps not taken to ensure that the true voice of the West Indies be heard.'"[20] Unlike the Labor Conference, the Montego Bay Colonial Office meetings involved officials only from the Caribbean political elite and excluded many trade-union leaders. The Montego Bay Conference emphasized the role of colonial administration in the Caribbean without the insights of those outside of specific political offices. Rather than challenging the imperial status quo, Montego Bay was an opportunity to reorient and reframe the debates on the West Indies, with a focus on the colonies in place of London. However, Crawford insisted the exclusion of important local labor leaders limited the conference's trajectory and prevented the advancement of more radical political agenda. British colonial policy was so embedded in the political projects of West Indian leaders enabling the Colonial Office to organize this gathering of the political and intellectual vanguard. Furthermore, its everyday proceedings were administered and chaired by Britons rather than West Indians. Debates over Federation acknowledged the probable continued influence of Britain in the region. Just as the West Indies were alienated from metropolitan policymaking, Crawford's objection suggested another degree of estrangement within Caribbean social and political structures, between labor leaders and working-class citizens on one hand and colonial administrators and local politicians on the other.

Divisions between trade unionists and colonial officials persisted throughout the Caribbean from the early twentieth century with numerous general strikes and work stoppages orchestrated from island to island in many of the significant industrial sectors.[21] Influential labor organizers, such as Trinidadian Uriah Butler, also carried radicalized politics to metropolitan Europe and the United States, and recruited large followers as they gained prominence as spokespeople against colonial exploitation and racial subjugation.

In 1938, Jamaican laborers struck at the port of Kingston and on sugar estates throughout the island. On May 12, workers at the Kingston wharf struck for an eight-hour workday and increased pay. A mass march of unemployed persons gathered at a proposed road-building site in the hopes of gaining employment in the project the same afternoon.[22] The next day, police fired on striking workers at the Frome sugar estate. A jury found no one including the Captain General Sir Edward Denham criminally liable for the deaths.[23] That June, police shot and killed two and wounded two others in St Mary's Parish. They opened fire on groups of workers, though the popular press generally categorized the victims as "looters" and "mobs."[24] The Jamaica government took the threat posed by the striking workers seriously, even as the police force was "fully supported by the military."[25] Jamaica Governor C. C. Woolley ignored the economic basis for the strikes, instead characterizing them as "riots" and attributing labor activism to "the work of a criminal element."[26] On June 5, police opened fire in the "Islington District of St. Mary ... rioters were looting shops ... one rioter aimed a shotgun at the sub-officer in charge ... the rioter was shot dead before he pulled the trigger ... three other members of the mob were killed and one wounded."[27] Despite reports that "demonstrators say they do not wish to give the police trouble; their only object is increased pay,"[28] Woolley nonetheless ordered attacks against the strikers. The prospect of strike action was met with military retribution by the Jamaican government. On May 30, troops were sent to the interior of the island in fear, "that trouble will spread in the district west of Mandeville."[29]

Simultaneously, in Kingston there were no disturbances but "armed patrols ... [were] still on duty."[30] The Colonial government hastened to invoke the full scope of its power, suppressing the protesting labor class ad nauseam. Colonial functionaries characterized political and economic dissent as riotous behavior.

Norman Manley, the head mediator of the negotiations over waterfront labor, after meeting with 2000 workers in May 1938, presented Governor Woolley the demands of the workers: uniform 1/- an hour wage.[31] At the close of the meeting, Manley led the dockworkers "as loyal British subjects, in the singing of the National Anthem."[32] Jamaican seaside workers were agitating against unfair economic practices while remaining loyal to the British Empire. On their behalf, Manley argued for increased wages and made the governor agreeable to "an undertaking ... [in which] the representations of the labourers regarding wages will be put forward."[33] Despite the violently repressive response of police and military in Jamaica against the dockworkers, they nevertheless were able to formulate a campaign for negotiation and improved labor relations through Manley's negotiations.

In 1938, Walter Guinness, 1st Baron Moyne, was appointed chair of the West Indies Royal Commission to investigate the living conditions in the West Indian colonies after the extended labor unrests of the 1930s. The Moyne Commission revealed various troubling characteristics of life in the British West Indies during the period immediately before World War II. The Moyne Commission[34] provided a critical look into the Caribbean at the outbreak of World War II and the poor conditions workers faced. With regard to education, it was reported that "there is not nearly enough accommodation for the children who attend schools ... accommodation is frequently ... in a chronic state of disrepair and insanitation ... teachers are inadequate in numbers ... not well paid ... training is largely defective or non-existent."[35]

In terms of housing, the Moyne Commission found, "in the poorest parts of most towns and in many of the country districts a majority of the houses is largely made of rusty corrugated iron ... the original floor has disappeared and only the earth remains."[36] The decrepit foundations of many Caribbean dwellings were matched by the lack of "sanitation in any form ... the environment gives rise to malaria, worm infection and bowel diseases, leaking roofs, rotten flooring ... the spread of tuberculosis, respiratory diseases ... and, to a certain extent, leprosy."[37] Unsatisfactory conditions for citizens in the Caribbean created an underclass majority that was underfed, ill, and could scarcely afford to provide for themselves. In Jamaica, a hurricane in 1944 rendered 15,000 people homeless and only served to exacerbate the desperate conditions for many on that island.[38]

MOVING TO BRITAIN

West Indian assimilation into British society was daunting and virtually impossible to anticipate. After 1948 many West Indians, aware of their legal status and cognizant of the role that metropolitan Britain played in their economic and social lives, identified with British imperial norms. Despite close and complicated understanding of British culture and politics, many Caribbean migrants arrived underprepared for everyday life in the United Kingdom. Small, private interest groups, such as church organizations, as well as colonial governments in the Caribbean, designed and circulated informational pamphlets to equip prospective migrants for life in Britain. These circulars often provided basic advice regarding the West Indian's general well-being such as advising migrants to carry warm woolen coats, gloves, and thick socks. Other packets were more detailed in their descriptions of the common social mores of native Britons. The leaflets demonstrated that West Indians anticipated the possibility of being viewed differently by the general public in Britain. Rather than interrogating how British racial and social attitudes developed, the pamphlets described them matter-of-factly. It was deemed important to inform the migrants of the contemporaneous British social context but, little effort was made to actively receive the incoming citizens. West Indians, though unfamiliar with the nuances of everyday life in Britain, were nonetheless subject to different forms of racialization, specifically in the cities where they settled. Renting rooms in London for instance, proved difficult for black migrants in most areas of the city due in large part to the long-standing de facto color bar.[39]

As a symbolic representation of imperial achievement and the home of the intellectual and cultural traditions that predominated public life in the West Indies, Britain was the ideal destination for colonial migrants. The educational and employment opportunities in Britain were unparalleled in the Caribbean colonies. Britain's position as imperial center and common West Indian consciousness including awareness of the Caribbean as peripheral in relation to London induced migration. The hegemonic nature of British colonialism ensured that within the political imaginary of the islands' best and brightest, most introspective and most radical, the metropole predominated. In a profound way, Britain occupied a conceptual space for imperial subjects who were formulating identities based on their conceptualizations of Britain, rather than the Caribbean islands, as their home. Britain was desirable because of the opportunities available but also due to the relative paucity of opportunities in the West Indies. Caribbean political economy was less diversified than its metropolitan British counterpart; foreign-led multinational corporations and holding companies dominated agricultural economics. Higher education options were severely limited; no-post secondary institutions existed anywhere in the Anglophone islands. The reputations of elite British universities lured the brightest minds from the region as well as from around the former empire, to the halls of the most prestigious institutions in the nation. White Britons trained the most accomplished scholars of and from the West Indies at the time in the metropole. The overwhelming influence of British culture in the West Indies was undeniable.

Although it is difficult to provide a totalizing depiction of West Indian consciousness (because that suggests a uniformity which never existed), it is useful to consider how West Indians conceptualized themselves in relation to Britain to understand the impetus for migration to the metropole. It is necessary to deal directly with notions of race and ethnicity that are particular to British culture and politics. West Indians were viewed as outsiders because of British (and oftentimes specifically English) renderings and characterizations of blackness and foreignness but also because of characterizations of whiteness and Englishness that Britons created and reproduced about themselves. Jamaican Euton Christian, despite having served in the Royal Air Force and fighting in Japan during World War II, remembered "this country [Britain] doesn't like strangers . . . foreigners . . . that was the message."[40] These identities, at once relative and adversarial, were reinforced with the influx of migrants from the Caribbean. Despite the popular belief that England itself represented a pure "Englishness," the geographic space was also subject to the influence of imperial politics and relations between metropole and colonial territories.[41] Ultimately English identity was the product of mixing and disparate, sometimes competing influences. As Ian Baucom has argued, "Forged by the conquest of others and forging itself for foreign conquest, England . . . is both a rose garden and a frontier . . . because like the imperial frontier with which it is coincident, [England] is an eternally shifting, eternally contested space of struggle."[42]

England and Englishness are concepts that exist in relation to characterizations of peoples and places described as explicitly "foreign," "alien," or "not-English." The metropolitan center of empire was shifting based on the changing relationships forged through the administration of empire. The arrival of West Indians in unprecedented numbers transformed the capital on a local, sociopolitical level while also influencing larger discourses on imperial politics and the nature of British citizenship and nationality. Baucom pushes this notion further: "Englishness, like Britishness, has been, and continues to be subject to a global reformation."[43] The interplay between colony and metropole necessitates a reading of English and British identity that considers the remaking and reordering of metropolitan society, politics, and patterns of identification. Just as the scores of citizens throughout the colonies were subjected to the influence of the metropole, the British themselves were never exempt from the influence of colonial social and cultural formations. British identity was refashioned by those whom it intended to convert, which in turn transformed notions of the British nation itself. If racial formation was distinct in varying contexts within the British Empire, race and racial differences were significant and constant categories throughout the British realms. In the West Indies and Britain, subjects contended with specific racialized politics. Although the racialized component of social structure in the Caribbean was more clearly pronounced and the promise of civic and social equality espoused in London, the historical reality was a pointedly virulent and omnipresent negative characterization of blackness and valorization of the conflated symbols of whiteness and Britishness.

NOTES

1. "Five Hundred Pairs of Willing Hands: the Jamaicans Land in Britain," *Daily Worker*, Wednesday, June 23, 1948, 3.

2. Gisela Eisner, *Jamaica, 1830–1930: A Study in Economic Growth* (Westport, CT: Greenwood Press, 1974); Philip D. Curtin, *Two Jamaicas: The Role of Ideas in a Tropical Colony* (Cambridge, MA: Harvard University Press, 1955); Orlando Patterson, *The Sociology of Slavery: An Analysis of the Origins, Development and Structure of Negro Slave Society in Jamaica* (London: MacGibbon & Kee, 1967); Orlando Patterson, *Slavery and Social Death: A Comparative Study* (Cambridge, MA: Harvard University Press, 1982); Edward Brathwaite, *The Development of Creole Society in Jamaica 1770–1820* (Oxford: Clarendon Press, 1971); Mavis C. Campbell, *The Dynamics of Change in a Slave Society: A Sociopolitical History of the Free Coloreds of Jamaica 1800–1865* (Rutherford, NJ: Fairleigh Dickinson University Press, 1976); Richard Sheridan, *Sugar and Slavery: An Economic History of the British West Indies, 1623–1775* (Kingston: Canoe Press, 1994); Elsa Goveia, *Slave Society in the British Leeward Islands at the End of the Eighteenth Century* (New Haven: Yale University Press, 1965); Gordon K. Lewis, *The Growth of the Modern West Indies* (New York: Monthly Review Press, 1968); Bridget Brereton, *History of Modern Trinidad 1783–1962* (Kingston; Exeter, NH: Heinemann, 1981).

3. Edward Kamau Brathwaite's notion of the "inner plantation," the social and political structures of the slave Caribbean extant outside the purview of the planter class, is discussed at length in his seminal *The Development of Creole Society in Jamaica*.

4. Michael A. Gomez, *Reversing Sail: A History of the African Diaspora* (Cambridge, UK; New York: Cambridge University Press, 2005); John K. Thornton, *Africa and Africans in the Making of the Atlantic World, 1400–1800* (Cambridge; New York: Cambridge University Press, 1998); David Eltis and David Richardson, *Atlas of the Transatlantic Slave Trade* (New Haven: Yale University Press, 2010).

5. Holt, *The Problem of Freedom: Race, Labor, and Politics in Jamaica and Britain, 1832-1938* (Baltimore: Johns Hopkins University Press, 1992).

6. Brathwaite, *The Development of Creole Society in Jamaica, 1770–1820*.

7. Christopher Leslie Brown, *Moral Capital: Foundations of British Abolitionism* (Chapel Hill: Omohundro Institute of Early American History and Culture, Williamsburg, Virginia; University of North Carolina Press, 2006), 2.

8. Lloyd Braithwaite, *Colonial West Indian Students in Britain* (Barbados: University of the West Indies Press, 2001); Viv Edwards, *The West Indian Language Issue in British Schools: Challenges and Responses* (London; Boston: Routledge & Kegan Paul, 1979).

9. Colin A. Palmer, *Freedom's Children: The 1938 Labor Rebellion and the Birth of Modern Jamaica* (Chapel Hill: UNC Press, 2014); Colin A. Palmer, *Inward Yearnings: Jamaica' Journey to Nationhood* (Mona: University of the West Indies Press, 2016).

10. Nancy Foner, *Islands in the City: West Indian Migration to New York* (Berkeley: University of California Press, 2001); Irma Watkins-Owens, *Blood Relations: Caribbean Immigrants and the Harlem Community, 1900–1930* (Bloomington: Indiana University Press, 1996); Mary C. Waters, *Black Identities: West Indian Immigrant Dreams and American Realities* (Cambridge, MA: Harvard University Press, 1999); Winston James, *Holding Aloft the Banner of Ethiopia: Caribbean Radicalism in Early Twentieth-Century America* (London; New York: Verso, 1998); Ransford Palmer, *Pilgrims from the Sun: West Indian Migration to America* (New York: Twayne Publishers, 1995).

11. Shalini Puri, *Marginal Migrations: The Circulation of Cultures within the Caribbean* (Oxford: Macmillan Caribbean, 2003); Lara Putnam, *Radical Moves: Caribbean Migrants and the Politics of Race in the Jazz Age* (Chapel Hill: University of North Carolina Press, 2013); Watkins-Owens, *Blood Relations*.

12. Interview with Arthur Curling, *Windrush*, 12.

13. Ibid.

14. "West Indies Collaboration with the US in the Caribbean," British National Archives: CO 318/452/2.

15. "British Colonial Policy," *The Times*, Tuesday, May 14, 1946, 5.

16. First Plenary Session, Montego Bay Conference Report, *Conference on the Closer Association of the British West Indian Colonies* (London: H.M. Stationery Office, 1948), 9.

17. Ibid., 21.

18. Ibid., 27.

19. Ibid., 61.

20. *Conference on the Closer Association of the British West Indian Colonies* (London: H.M. Stationery Office, 1948), 69.

21. The British West Indian Labour Unrest of 1934–1939 began with labor agitation in British Honduras in February 1934 and included sugar rebellions in Trinidad, Saint Kitts, and British Guiana, oilfield strikes in Trinidad, protests in Jamaica, rioting in Saint Lucia and Barbados over the next half-decade. Many of the influential strikers and labor organizers were involved closely with Garvey's UNIA. See O. Nigel Bolland, *On the March: Labour Rebellions in the British Caribbean, 1934–39* (Kingston: Ian Randle Publishers, 1995); Palmer, *Freedom's Children*.

22. "March by Unemployed," *The Times*, May 13, 1938.
23. "The Jamaica Riots," *The Times*, May 14, 1938.
24. "Two Killed in Riot," *The Times*, June 4, 1938.
25. Ibid.
26. "Jamaica Disorders: Warning to Lawless Elements," *The Times*, June 6, 1938.
27. Ibid.
28. Ibid.
29. "More Jamaican Strikes," *The Times*, May 31, 1938.
30. Ibid.
31. "Cruiser Reaches Jamaica," *The Times*, May 27, 1938.
32. Ibid.
33. Ibid.
34. See Palmer, *Freedom's Children*.
35. *Report of the West India Royal Commission, 1938–1939* (CMD 6607), 32.
36. Ibid., 34.
37. Ibid.
38. "Distress in Jamaica," *The Times*, October 27, 1944.
39. There was no legal basis for racial discrimination nor were there any legal protections against race-based exclusions. Migrants did not necessarily carry uniform notions of racialization in the capital—in fact their experiences with prejudice in London were particular to the environment in the metropole.
40. Interview with Euton Christian, *Windrush*, 52.
41. Bernard Porter, *The Absent-Minded Imperialists: Empire, Society, and Culture in Britain* (Oxford; New York: Oxford University Press, 2004); Robert Young, *The Idea of English Ethnicity* (Malden, MA: Blackwell Publishing, 2008); Robert Young, *Colonial Desire: Hybridity in Theory, Culture and Race* (London; New York: Routledge, 1995); Kim F. Hall, *Things of Darkness: Economies of Race and Gender in Early Modern England* (Ithaca: Cornell University Press, 1995); Raymond Williams, *Culture and Society, 1780–1950* (New York: Columbia University Press, 1983).
42. Ian Baucom, *Out of Place: Englishness, Empire, and the Locations of Identity* (Princeton, NJ: Princeton University Press, 1999), 37–38.
43. Ibid., 40.

Chapter 2

The 5th Pan-African Congress, Manchester 1945

Black Internationalism in the Context of Britain

Africans and people of African descent, especially those who have been poisoned by British imperialist education, needed a lesson . . . Every succeeding day shows exactly the real motives which move imperialism in its contact with Africa, shows the incredible savagery and duplicity of European imperialism in its quest for markets and raw materials. Let the lesson sink in deep.[1]

Prior to the arrival of the *Windrush*, many West Indians, Africans, and South Asians had traveled to England for education and employment by virtue of their homelands' colonial relationship with metropolitan Britain. In particular, the intellectual tradition of West Indians living in the United Kingdom cannot be ignored. The legacy of scholarship, specifically theorizing race, identity, and conceptualizing the status of racialized subjects and citizens was particularly important in understanding perceptions of racial formation in Britain prior to 1948. Trinidadian Eric Williams, for instance, made invaluable contributions to Caribbean history and transformed the contemporaneously extant historiography of West Indian political economies and their relationship to colonial metropoles with his seminal 1944 study, *Capitalism and Slavery*. Writing against the prevailing notions of traditional British historiography, which attributed abolition to the benevolence of morally enlightened figures in nineteenth century British politics like William Wilberforce, Williams suggested that slavery ended because of the economically viable alternative of opening new markets in the Americas rather than maintaining British plantation economies which were not as productive nor profitable as their French counterparts. Williams completed his doctorate at Oxford in 1938, and later produced a number of other works that sought to reorient

Caribbean historiography and dispel commonplace attitudes with regard to slavery, racialization, political economy, and empire.

RECONCILING RACE IN THE CARIBBEAN AND BRITAIN

Britain's substantial history of black radicalism dates to the late nineteenth-century. Trinidadian-born barrister Henry Sylvester Williams convened the first Pan-African Conference in London's Westminster Hall in 1900. The League Against Imperialism, West African Students' Union, and the League of Coloured Peoples were all active in the 1930s. Jamaican physician and social justice advocate Harold A. Moody was a co-founder of the League and his politics of integration and co-racial collaboration marked the tone of League activities for decades.[2] While chairing the London Missionary Society, Moody penned *Freedom for All Men*, part of a series of "triple jubilee papers" in commemoration of the Society's sesquicentennial in 1945. Moody argued for a test of British intentions, as he noted "Britain has the largest coloured Empire in the world. There are more Africans under the British flag than under any other . . . Britain however, has not found it possible to give to any African the opportunity to rise to any . . . position within her vast Empire." He was dismayed at the notion that "Britain has invited a number of skilled technicians and trainees to come to this country from the West Indies and elsewhere . . . one would have thought that they would have been received over here with open arms . . . In many cases places of amusements and of social intercourse have been denied to them."[3] Moody articulated rather moderate and integrationist perspectives on inclusion and freedom. He advocated for the presence of people of color I more positions of leadership within British society and institutions.

Moody regarded himself as a trailblazer in raising the issues of racial inequality and the possibilities of race prejudice in Britain. His lecture at St. Luke's College in 1945 entitled "Colour Bar" publicized the pervasiveness of racialized discrimination in Britain. Moody explained that he, "was among the first to deal with this subject [colour bar] in a public manner and to bring it out in the open, and many of our . . . leaders . . . looked upon me with a certain amount of suspicion."[4] Moody arrived in Britain in 1904 to attend King's College in London where he "was accepted with no more formality than if . . . born in Britain and had attended an English public school" only to witness "this attitude completely change with the influx of a large number of students from India" culminating in "a 10% quota . . . on all overseas students" following the end of World War I.[5] The quota system operated in favor first, "of Dominion students, then European, and finally the coloured student [who] could only secure places if any were left . . . usually there were none."[6]

Moody was especially aware of how "the Colonial status is another big element in the Colour Bar . . . a means whereby certain sections of the population of the Colony-owning power, have been able to exploit the areas and peoples concerned and to exercise the English desire for domination."[7] He described structural and historical inequality regarding race and argued that colonial citizens carried these inferiority complexes with them to Britain. As a loyal British subject, Moody located the origins of British racial biases outside of the metropole. He argued that because "the English . . . are zealous devotees of the Cinema [and] . . . 70% of the pictures shown are of American origin" the portrayal of "the black man in some menial position or as a buffoon or as a semi-nude savage" was a product of American-originated ideals rather than British ones.[8] Moody noted the international release of feature films whereby American culture could have a major impact on the attitudes of British people and therefore excusing racial bias as an American export to metropolitan British society.

Although Moody indicted American racialized views for influencing Britons, he nevertheless hoped to ameliorate racial tensions in Britain through interracial collaboration. Moody argued that the first task for Britons was "to re-orient, to reconstruct our thoughts and ideas about other people" teaching citizens in order to "help the people in Britain . . . [through] educating them on inter-racial questions."[9] Moody suggested reeducation and the promotion of fairer, more accurate knowledge regarding black and brown people in order to undo the stereotypes about them predominating among white Britons.

Moody believed the problems of acclimation for people of color could be solved through their own initiative and diligence. He excused Britons as, "woefully ignorant and mighty slow to appraise a new situation," but noted that "that once they take it in fully they do give themselves thereto wholly and completely . . ."[10] Moody encouraged "overseas students . . . during their vacations, to go about the country lecturing . . . groups and . . . spreading necessary information about the Colonies." Moody obliged the colored colonial student class to travel and teach white Britons so that "integration, will . . . solve this problem of the Colour Bar and [Britain's] future status in the world."[11] The integrationist principles of the L.C.P. rang true in Moody's assertion that integration was the antidote to race prejudice.

Integration and interracial amity were central to the League's activities and Britons lauded Moody for his openness and efforts toward cooperation. David Vaughn, minister at Camberwell Green Congregational Church where Moody attended, had such reverence for the physician that he wrote a biography of him, *Negro Victory: The life story of Dr. Harold Moody* in 1950. Vaughn explained his distinct "privilege to live with the spirit of

Harold Moody . . . to be counted amongst his friends during his life-time."[12] This commemoration of Moody suggested the significant impact he had on his British interlocutors. Vaughn's lauding of Moody was oriented around his resistance to color bias and his prolific work in medicine, race relations, and the labor structure in Britain. The book's title illustrated what those who venerated Moody thought—he was a remarkable person but a "Negro" nonetheless. Moody believed perhaps in the irrefutable British identity that had no space for blackness. He was included in Britain through eschewing of the particular realities of their racial classification. Moody hoped to be British and in British minds that meant he could not perhaps continue to be African or Jamaican.

Henry Sylvester Williams worked against the colour bar in British society that negatively impacted nonwhite colonial subjects, their professional status and academic qualifications notwithstanding. Williams and his organization, the African Association solicited opinion and expertise from racialized others in Great Britain. Through the convening of over two dozen representatives from Africa, the Caribbean, and the United States in 1900, Williams inaugurated the Pan-African Association—perhaps the very first articulation of the language of "pan-Africanism."

The work of early twentieth century Caribbean intellectuals in Britain predated the mass migration of the post–World War II period but nonetheless carved out the conceptual space for West Indians to negotiate British society and provided the foundational ruminations on what it meant to be a person of color in the metropole as well as providing the basis for anticolonial struggle which would dominate the political history of the long twentieth century. Despite the presence of working-class migrants, who articulated their political awareness in other ways, the work of these intellectuals provides the frameworks of analysis for understanding the plight of the migrants. The experiences of Eric Williams, George Padmore, and C. L. R. James in particular, as activists and intellectuals, illustrate that their scholarship also had roots in the working-class migrant experience.

THE FIFTH PAN-AFRICAN CONGRESS

In 1945, the Fifth Pan-African Congress met in Manchester, bringing together intellectuals, artists, activists, and labor organizers from throughout the African diaspora to design political campaigns to ameliorate the plight of diaspora populations due to various forms of racism and racialization in the Americas, Europe, and Africa. Manchester was chosen to host because of the significant number of British-based organizations that contributed to planning the meeting.[13]

On October 15, the opening session, "The Colour Problem in Britain," featured a number of prominent organizers. The panel suggested that racialization in Britain was a central concern for Congress leadership and postulated the notion that race relations in Britain had implications for other sites of diaspora. Diaspora consciousness figured in symbolic ways for the Congress organizing committee who decorated Chorlton Town Hall, the meeting site, with the flags of Liberia, Haiti, and Ethiopia. Amy Ashwood Garvey, Jamaican pan-Africanist, U.N.I.A. leader and former partner of Marcus Garvey, chaired the opening featuring: Peter Milliard, president of the Pan-African Federation, E. J. Duplan of the Negro Welfare Centre, A. Aki-Emi, a representative from the Gold Coast, A. E. Moselle of the United Committee of Coloured Peoples' Association, De Graf Johnson of the Edinburgh Coloured Peoples' Association, Peter Abrahams the South African representative of the International African Service Bureau, S. O. J. Andrews, a representative from Grenada, and E. P. Marke, of the Coloured Workers' Association in London.

Milliard championed W. E. B. DuBois's role in organizing the previous four congresses and for drawing connections between diaspora populations. Originally from the Gold Coast, Duplan recounted the recent history of people of color as laborers and soldiers in defending Britain during the World War I. He reiterated the integral role played by these groups on Britain's behalf in World War II. Aki-Emi, also from Gold Coast, supported Duplan's report and noted that the increasing presence of people of color in Britain was due to the pervasiveness of imperialism in their home countries. Moselle provided social and demographic context to the discussion, noting the large colored population in Cardiff, attributing the trend to Cardiff's position as the leading coal port in the United Kingdom and the restrictions on colored seamen, relegating them to employment only on coal-carrying steamships.[14] Moselle also reported on the possibility of repatriation of black and mixed-race children of black seamen and white British mothers to Africa. De Graf Johnson corroborated these points with regard to the problem of racial discrimination in Britain. He identified students' estrangement from the general black population. Abrahams cited the high incidence of racialized violent police practices throughout the country. Andrews however, optimistically imagined the prospect of African peoples banding together in a struggle against racial injustice and colonial exploitation. He reemphasized the imperial connections between Britain and her West Indian colonies and reconfirmed the sacrifices colonial citizens made for Britain.

Andrews reminded the Congress of the burdens black people shouldered for Britain during the world wars, "Negroes from all over the world have died for freedom and are prepared to die for peace."[15] E. P. Marke commended the presenters and attendees for their engagement with issues of racial justice and their commitment to cooperating in a campaign against exploitation and inequality in Britain and abroad.

DuBois chaired a panel, "The Problem in the Caribbean," which outlined and analyzed the challenges facing West Indian political economies. Ken Hill, from the Jamaica Trades Union Council, emphasized that politically progressive West Indians were interested in and often engaged directly with the political affairs of Africans. Panelists accentuated the need for greater West Indian sovereignty in their local economies, the end of Crown rule, and the promise of self-government. They emphasized the growing disconnect between the colonial administrators and local politicians from the concerns of the working classes and the labor union leadership throughout the region.

Greetings were extended to black Americans during the Congress, underscoring global diasporic consciousness among the conference participants. The Congress endorsed "Afro-American opposition to unequal distribution of wealth . . . the conduct of industry solely for profit . . . [and] believes that the successful realisation of the political, economic and social aspirations of the thirteen million people in the United States is bound up with the emancipation of all African people, as well as other dependent people and the working class everywhere."[16] Diaspora solidarities permeated many of the presentations that made specific reference to peoples of African descent throughout the world as a collective. T. E. Sealy of the Jamaica *Daily Gleaner* emphasized, "respect will come to us Negro peoples, fully, only when we have won the fight for political self-determination wherever we may be. Where we are numerically in the majority we must have a correspondingly preponderant influence and power in a self-governing authority. Where we remain a minority, we must have protection and privileges equal to those demanded by and afforded to the dominant majorities."[17]

George Padmore's 1949 work, *Africa: Britain's Third Empire*, originated from a request from the previous 1945 Pan-African Congress in Manchester to shed light on colonial problems in British Africa. Padmore focused on the economic, political, and social tribulations affecting indigenous Africans across Britain's continental empire. Padmore thanked Malcom Joseph-Mitchell, secretary of the League of Coloured Peoples and other Congress colleagues for their help in his research. Diasporic Africans relied upon and encouraged one another to mobilize around anti-imperialism across the United Kingdom and in various communication networks across the Americas and Africa. Padmore's *Africa* was testament to the enduring connections forged only a year after the arrival of the *SS Windrush*.

Padmore's survey of British imperialism in Africa was comprehensive and attenuated to the specific problems afflicting native Africans across colonial environments. Padmore provided detailed historical accounts of the precolonial and colonial eras of British African territories, stressing the size and scope of the changes in each context. He also noted the dominant industries and systems of political economy in territories as varied as South Africa and British West Africa. Furthermore, Padmore examined the various methods of colonial administration, ranging from indirect rule to direct rule to in the case of South Africa, colonial fascism.[18]

BLACK THOUGHT IN THE TWILIGHT OF WORLD WAR

In addition to *Capitalism and Slavery*, Eric Williams' 1962 work, *British Historians and the West Indies*, argued against the traditional characterizations of the West Indies in British historiography, from the early nineteenth to mid-twentieth centuries. Williams' work centered the experiences of West Indians in the plantation economy rather than utilizing only metropolitan records and official statistics in order to emphasize the role of West Indians in the development of the colonial enterprise. From a West Indian perspective, Williams argued that race and racialization were defining components of the colonial relationship between the West Indies and Britain. He argued, West Indians had a particularized racial consciousness that stemmed from their interactions with and knowledge of systems of colonial governance and their subjugated roles in the political economy. Racial consciousness among West Indians in London did not originate in the metropole though racial formation in the West Indies and Britain operated in different ways.[19] Williams cited efforts of earlier thinkers like Trinidadian John Jacob Thomas who was among the first generation of educated West Indians in the period of emancipation.[20]

Williams' 1969 autobiography, *Inward Hunger: The Education of a Prime Minister*, offered a detailed discussion of the way colonial and British metropolitan education informed his political development. He noted how his predilection for Latin and academic diligence earned him the respect of his peers and the faculty at Oxford. By 1947, Williams expanded his research interests beyond the West Indies, focusing on political developments in Kenya and Nigeria in addition to studying the ramifications of race-based segregation in the United States. By the end of World War II, Williams had a broader notion of racialized colonial subjugation especially with respect to a number of sites within the British empire. Furthermore, his interest in colonial problems throughout Africa and Asia led to his involvement in the establishment of the Institute of Colonial Affairs at Howard University in Washington, DC.[21]

After the publication of Williams' first book, *The Negro in the Caribbean*, in 1942, "a joint African-West Indian group in London sought and obtained permission from the publishers . . . to bring out a separate edition in

England."[22] Prior to the *Windrush* era West Indians and Africans in London were concerned with the particular role race and racialization had in the history of the Caribbean. The African Progress Union was active from 1918 to 1927. At the close of World War I, the Union requested that the Government include a black delegate at the peace discussions in Versailles. They also subsidized legal counsel Edward Nelson, who defended blacks on trial after the Liverpool riots of 1919.[23] The Union participated in the Paris Pan-African Congress in 1919 as well as the London congresses in 1921 and 1923. The APU also developed contacts with the Anti-Slavery Society and organizations in France and the United States.[24]

Though Williams served on the Caribbean Commission, a union between the United Kingdom and the United States from 1943 until 1955, he offered prescient critiques on the makeup of the committee and highlighted the exclusion of West Indian members among its ranks. He remembered, "in appointing the first Deputy Chairman of the Research Council, I as a West Indian who know the West Indies was passed over for a British representative who knew nothing about them . . . he was a returned officer from the administrative service in an African territory . . . he had just stepped off in Washington . . . and landed a job in the West Indies."[25]

Williams monitored the state of education in the Caribbean while drawing connections between formal education and the political imaginaries of activists and intellectuals. Because educational opportunities were severely limited in their home region, British political philosophy and epistemology were the only intellectual tools many Caribbean folks obtained through their formal school years.

Egyptian Duse Mohamed Ali began *African Times and Orient Review* in London in July 1912 as the first political journal produced for and by black people in Britain. The periodical reported on atrocities from around the colonies including nude public floggings in Nigeria. It also promoted the accomplishments and political campaigns of prominent diaspora individuals. Ali's paper carried the British debut of Marcus Garvey as well as the Ghanaian philosopher and nationalist Kobina Sekyi.

Oswald Denniston, a Jamaican who arrived on the *Windrush* at age 35 and later operated a stall in Brixton Market, remembered his schooling in the Caribbean. He expressed surprise "that the average working-class English person knows very, very little about the colonials . . . things we learn at school, it's ridiculous when you come to think about it."[26] Denniston also retold a common child's song he remembered hearing and reciting while in school:

The rich man's son inherits lands and piles of brick and stone and gold
He also inherits soft white hands, tender flesh that fear the cold,

Nor dare to wear a garment old
A heritage, it seems to me, one would wish to hold in fee
What does a poor man's son inherit?
Stout muscles, sinewy heart, a king of two hands
A heritage, it seems to me, one scarce would wish to hold in fee[27]

Denniston recalled the distinctions drawn between the landed, white, wealthy classes in Jamaica and the poor, black, working class masses.

Williams noted that within the British Caribbean schools, "not more than three-fifths of the population . . . [was] enrolled . . . compulsory education exists—on paper . . . expenditure per child is one-sixth of the sum spent in England."[28] The poor educational funding in the region prevented the majority of West Indians from attaining adequate formal schooling. Williams explained that the curriculum in West Indian schools was based primarily on English history and literature, and science. Scholarships from Trinidad to secondary schools and universities in England were based on the following subjects: English political history, European history, Greek history, English colonial history, English economic history, Latin, Roman history, French, Spanish, and Shakespeare.[29] The emphasis on British history, along with special attention to European and classical traditions in the standard curricula for Caribbean students placed the metropole squarely at the center of West Indian consciousness from childhood.

School curricula were one component of Caribbean societies where British imagery and influence predominated. Britain's ubiquity impacted the material opportunities, epistemological foundations, and the political imaginaries of Caribbean peoples throughout their lives. As Williams noted the literal scarcity of schools in the Caribbean, he explained "the majority of schools . . . are located in the urban centers, few in the rural areas where they are most needed."[30] The number of young West Indians with no access to educational institutions contributed to the dearth of possible candidates to travel to the metropole for post-secondary education. Williams also criticized the foreign opportunities for wealthier black Caribbean students. Scholarships for local students were limited to those with close affiliations with prestigious British universities. Because these scholarships emphasized social status, nonwhite pupils, whatever their academic achievements, were generally dissuaded from applying or had their applications ignored.

Williams critiqued metropolitan training for tropical medicine, agriculture, and geography. He scoffed at the notion that with "no university in the . . . British West Indies, future doctors go to the School of Tropical Medicine and Hygiene in London . . . to be taught the control of malaria and typhoid by men who may never have seen a case of either."[31] Students were traveling thousands of miles from the tropics to Europe in order to study the diseases of their homelands. The paucity of higher education in the region maintained the tradition of young West Indians traveling abroad to further their formal schooling and in turn to increase their employment opportunities, whether in the United Kingdom, the United States, or islands such as Cuba and Puerto Rico.

The lack of Anglophone universities in the Caribbean necessitated young people traveling to further their formal education, simultaneously depleting the British West Indies of many of its sharpest, most ambitious minds. C. L. R. James's work identified the endemic problems of Caribbean education—lack of funding, inadequate facilities, and color bias within scholarship competitions. Williams's memoirs corroborated many of these frustrations and critiques. The problems of unequal and wide-ranging discrepancies in education across the region would prove to be significant for generations of young people during the mid-twentieth century, spurring many of them to go to Britain for university or employment.

Trinidadian James was a prolific historian, social critic, playwright, and political radical whose travels through the West Indies, Europe, Africa, and the United States informed his own political consciousness in exceptional ways. Educated in classical Greek and Latin literature and history, James was aware of the significance and influence of the Western canon on the cultural formations and venerated figures of the Western world and theorized race and racialization in innovative ways which departed from typical characterizations of non-Europeans as backward or uncivilized. His *Black Jacobins* retold the story of the Haitian Revolution, the only successful slave rebellion in the New World and suggested that the political consciousness of the slaves in Haiti was as sophisticated as and nearly analogous to the claims Jacobins had made against the aristocracy during their revolution in metropolitan France. *The Black Jacobins* portrayed the Haitian revolutionary leadership, especially L'Ouverture and Dessalines as important historical actors whose claims for freedom and independence derived from their sophisticated and complex understanding of the plantation economy and the implications of the Declaration of the Rights of Man and Citizen. According to James, the revolution in Haiti went far beyond the scope of a rebellion as it had been previously characterized.[32]

In addition to that groundbreaking study, James's semi-autobiographical account, *Beyond a Boundary*, utilized an analysis of the sport and culture of cricket both in Trinidad and in England, and provided unique insights into how popular cultural formations represent complex systems of power, social relations, class, and race. During his youth in the town of Tunapuna, James was aware of how cricket reflected attitudes and social mores of colonial British society. He remembered the racial divisions in the cricket clubs on the island, each club consisting of men of the same phenotype and class background. This was particularly insightful regarding racial formation in the Caribbean, as migrants carried with them cultural baggage reflecting local iterations of colorism to Britain. Furthermore, social position, though observable throughout the island, did not override perceptions of certain men's cricketing abilities. The sense of fair play in cricket and by extension in British society persists throughout *Beyond a Boundary*, though James complicates this notion because of the problematics of racial formation in the West Indies and metropolitan Britain.[33] James long recognized the significance of racial distinction and contemplated its mutability, from the West Indies to Britain and the United States.

James lived in Britain from 1932 until 1938, theorizing and reorienting notions of historical contingencies of empire and their effects on Caribbean sensibilities and patterns of identification. Like Williams, James's historical structuralist approach claimed that larger transatlantic historical developments such as the slave trade, the plantation system, and the struggles of postcolonial nation building via neocolonial economic market system, largely informed his understanding of the epistemological development of Caribbean societies and the large role British ontology and epistemology played in migratory experiences throughout its crumbling empire.

Despite African-descended peoples making up the majority of the British West Indian population, Caribbean scholars recognized the pervasiveness of racialization in their home societies before witnessing or experiencing these patterns in the metropole. In advocating for West Indian sovereignty, James noted the problematic specter of colorism within Caribbean societies, where differences in complexion acted as inhibitors to national unity and social egalitarianism. He explained, "The [coloured population] find it difficult to combine."[34] Color and ethnicity informed relationships within the islands and James suggested a number of hypothetical situations in which complexion trumped qualifications or even hereditary advantages within Trinidad. He explained, "a dark-skinned brother in a fair-skinned family is sometimes the subject of jeers . . . fair-skinned girls who marry dark men are often ostracized by their families . . . it is not too much to say that in a West Indian colony the surest sign of a man's having arrived is the fact that he keeps company with people lighter in complexion than himself."[35] James also attributed colorism to middle class status. "[T]he people most affected by this," he wrote, "are . . . the middle class who, lacking the hard contact with realities of the masses and unable to attain to the freedoms of a leisured class, are more . . . given to trivial divisions and subdivisions of social rank and precedence."[36] The intra-racial rivalries, which existed since the era of emancipation, apprenticeship, and Indian indentureship, prevented Caribbean societies from developing coherent and unified national independence movements until the mid-twentieth century. The material and cultural domination of these areas by

British capital and imperial legal culture as well as the continued suppression of peoples in the Caribbean thus remained unchallenged through the early twentieth century.

Even as *The Black Jacobins* presented a revolutionary epistemological rupture in Caribbean historiography by crediting African leaders of the Saint Domingue revolution with overthrowing French slavery and establishing an independent nation in the former colony and thus seeing through radical ideals of freedom and agency, James nevertheless attributed a great amount of the revolutionary sentiment to European radical politics of the contemporaneous period. His research relied on the opinions and observations of European witnesses in Haiti. Much of James's own understanding of the significance of the revolt was based on perspectives of Europeans and their concomitant renderings of the revolutionary warfare happening in Saint Domingue. European ideals held a prominent place in the political and historical makeup of citizens and subjects in the Caribbean, to the point that even James's pioneering work were at their original composition, greatly informed by European perspectives and paradigms of knowledge.

The longstanding material and metaphysical dominance of the Caribbean colonies by Britain intensified when a number of prominent artists and intellectuals from the region traveled to the metropole for school and work. James and Williams were inundated by the durable extensive British academic tradition and consequently its insufficient renderings of race, class, gender, and national origin. Whereas James could identify and admire the sublimity of William Makepeace Thackeray,[37] he also identified and lamented the lack of serious analysis of nonmetropolitan, nonwhite culture and its impact on the culture and politics of empire. James also rejected notions that race was not a primary component of historical systems and processes such as the slave trade, the plantation system, and ultimately the revolutionary overthrow of these systems in favor of new Enlightenment-based precepts of freedom and equality in Saint Domingue.

James envisioned West Indian self-determination and independence. His ideal required deconstructing the fabric of the British empire, which he characterized as a wicked system which, "permit[ed] a privileged few to work their will on hundreds of thousands of defenseless people . . . the West Indian of any ambition or sensibility has to see positions of honour and power in his own country filled by itinerant demigods who sit at their desk, ears cocked for the happy news of a retirement in Nigeria or a death in Hong Kong; when they go and others of the same kind take their places."[38] James's scathing critique of British imperialism was multilayered and unrelenting. He was aware of the colonial offices throughout the empire and the British born and educated administrators who traveled from one place to the next depending on post availability. James noted that it was not uncommon for an official in

Trinidad to leave for Hong Kong, Bombay, or Lagos in the event that a similar position became available in any of those respective colonial capitals. The essence of the imperial enterprise, in James's estimation was the exploitation of masses by a tiny administrative elite seeing out the directives of Parliament throughout Africa, Asia, and the Caribbean. Dismayed by the absentee domination of the colonies by Britain, James instead advocated for a politics wherein the Caribbean "people . . . should be free to make its own failures and success, free to gain that political wisdom and political experience . . . otherwise . . . we remain without credit abroad and with no self-respect at home . . . a feckless conglomeration of individuals inspired by no common purpose, moving to no common end."[39] James's anticolonial political philosophy inspired generations of scholars and activists to work for decolonization and independence throughout the twentieth century.

James theorized a revolutionary category of "creative universality" which interrogated and emphasized the contributions of writers as central to new ontological and epistemological traditions of the African diaspora. James's work is best described as formative part of Afro-Caribbean historicism.[40] His research and analysis of the Haitian Revolution coupled with his engagement with European socialism made James a primary figure among international black intellectual agitators.

GEORGE PADMORE

Trinidadian Padmore also contributed to the development of a transnational consciousness among blacks living in the metropole. Padmore was involved in the Comintern, attending meetings in Moscow where he and other black Communists debated the prospect of forming their own black International. From Hamburg, Padmore edited the International Trade Union Committee of Negro Workers' (ITUCNW) periodical, *Negro Worker*. As early as March 1930, when Padmore began his role as editor, the *Negro Worker* reflected an ambitiously globalized perspective. Under Padmore, *Negro Worker* coupled stories on labor demonstrations in Jamaica and political struggles in French West Africa with reports on Japanese imperialism in Korea and clashes between police and revolutionaries in Nicaragua. Padmore elevated issues of racialization alongside class-based struggles that predominated the Communist platform. As Padmore attempted to hew closely to the Communist Party line, *Negro Worker* kept African liberation at its core. For Padmore and other black Communists, Russia remained the revolutionary example, though *Negro Worker* turned significant attention to revolution in Africa, Asia, and the Caribbean. Padmore was especially concerned with the treatment of native Liberian workers by the Firestone Rubber Company in the

1930s. He placed the Americo-Liberian elite alongside American imperialists in Cuba, Puerto Rico, and the Philippines.[41]

To disseminate *Negro Worker*, Padmore drew on his connections from the ITUCNW and black sailors traveling across oceans and continents. By 1922, Cyril Briggs's Crusader News Agency aided in distribution through their offices in New York, Cape Town, and Paris.[42] C. L. R. James noted the reach and influence of *Negro Worker* as critical in the political development of many diaspora Africans. James suggested *"Negro Worker* gave to hundreds of thousands of active blacks . . . the consciousness...that they were part of an international movement . . . men in Mombasa, Lagos, Port of Spain, Port au Prince . . . read and followed with exceptional concern the directives which came from the trusted centre in Moscow."[43] *Negro Worker* established a network of black workers, far exceeding any institution or organization previously connected to the Comintern. In Hamburg, Padmore received requests from black workers from around the globe to aid in their organizing.

Padmore's short career leading ITUCNW coincided with his move from Hamburg (after the rise of the Third Reich) to London where he found himself among African and Caribbean anticolonial radicals. Reginald Bridgeman, the head of the League against Imperialism's British Section introduced Padmore to Barbadian Communist Arnold Ward, who headed the Negro Welfare Association in London during summer 1931. Ward urged Padmore to go to London to aid in organizing black workers there which brought him into close contact with a number of important black London figures in the early 1930s. In London, Padmore reunited with childhood friend James and officially left the Comintern to focus on independent organizing efforts. The Comintern was the last predominately white political body Padmore would ever hold membership in while James conversely became more engaged in the operations in the Communist movement. Padmore nevertheless dedicated himself to the radical black tradition of revolutionary struggle.[44]

Communists in Britain mobilized support from colonial migrants and sought to integrate them into their political platform. Although Padmore traveled in elite circles among black Communists in Europe, the London-based Stepney Communist Party operated on a grassroots level, recruiting newly arrived migrants. The Party addressed *The Colonial Worker* to "those citizens of Stepney whose native lands are tied down and exploited by foreign capital . . . we extend our greetings to their fellow countrymen in Africa and the Caribbean . . . who are . . . taking up the struggle against the savage rule of imperialism."[45] The Party's call to colonials was distinctly localized and critiqued, "Colonial House . . . [as] an insult . . . in Stepney" arguing that, "it should be knocked down and a really fine building put up for our coloured visitors . . . British people should invite these coloured men into their homes."[46] The Party decried the state and condition of the residence for colonials and implored native Britons to extend hospitality to newly arrived migrants. British Communists were aware of the latent racial biases in Britain and sought to emphasize these attitudes in order to garner more support from the West Indian arrivants.

Antonio Gramsci's notion of organic intellectuals would recognize James, Williams, and Padmore's influence because their theorizing of race in the Caribbean and the British empire, the United States, and European colonial holdings in Africa, reverberated throughout other classes subjugated by British imperial state domination. As Gramsci suggested, "The function of organizing social hegemony and state domination certainly gives rise to a particular division of labour and therefore to a whole hierarchy of qualifications in some of which there is no apparent attribution of directive or organisational features."[47] The West Indian intellectual class in Britain contested with a state apparatus that made designations based on labor classification and which these intellectuals interrogated on multiple levels in order to draw connections between other racialized black peoples based on race and ethnicity rather than solely on their positions in the British political economy.

Padmore located class-consciousness within a notion of the centralized role racialization played in the modern world. In his 1931 pamphlet *The Life and Struggles of Negro Toilers*, he sought to "set forth . . . the conditions of life of the Negro workers and peasants . . . enumerate some of the struggles which they have attempted to wage . . . to free themselves . . . and to indicate . . . the tasks of the proletariat in the advanced countries so that the millions of black toilers might be better prepared to carry on the struggle against their white imperialist oppressors."[48] Padmore articulated his vision for ending the economic and social exploitation of the millions of black workers around the world. He conceived of mass mobilization of black workers, informed by the knowledge of systems of exploitation and oppression throughout Africa and its diaspora. Padmore charged European imperialists for their domination of black workers in Africa, emphasized the ramifications of slavery on blacks throughout the "New World," and charged the United States with extending its imperialistic yoke across the hemisphere after abolition. Padmore's tract was published under the auspices of the Red International of Labour Unions (R.I.L.U.) soon after its tenth anniversary. R.I.L.U. was a militant organization of the world-trade union movement and Padmore's involvement stemmed from their recognition of the Negro workers as "the most exploited, the most oppressed in the world."[49]

Padmore's critiques of imperialism indicted exploiters of laborers worldwide. He included a section on "Black Soldiers of Imperialism," criticizing the European capitalist nations for forming black armies. He noted that the French had mobilized "one of the largest black armies in Africa which could be brought to Europe and used as shock troops when the war begins . . .

African troops are being freely used in suppressing colonial revolts both in Africa and in Asia, as well as strikes in France."[50] Padmore noted the 200,000 Africans who served in the French Army during World War I and traced the longer history of French military recruitment and enlistment in West African colonies beginning in the nineteenth century. He criticized the King's African Rifles in British East Africa, made up of over 4000 native African troops between the world wars and the British colonial ban on native military forces. Padmore criticized black African troops conscripted into colonial military enterprises where native forces were not established. He noted that in the British West Indies, males between eighteen and forty-five years old were all still subject to possible conscription. European military control was comprehensive and extended into the politics of the colonies, creating societies in which natives had neither sovereignty nor autonomy over their own defense forces. Padmore argued that racial exploitation was only exacerbated by the conscription of black soldiers into colonial armies and militias.

THE LEAGUE OF COLOURED PEOPLES

The League of Coloured Peoples, formed on March 13, 1931, in a London YMCA, advocated for black civil rights in Britain and the amelioration of racial prejudice throughout the world. The inaugural executive committee consisted of C. Belfield Clark of Barbados, George Roberts of Trinidad, Samson Morris of Grenada, Robert Adams of British Guiana, and Desmond Buckle of the Gold Coast. By the close of World War II, the League worked to expose racial discrimination in Britain and abroad. In January 1945, the League had new offices in Westminster, placing them in close proximity to the corridors of British political power. The League developed a "Charter for Coloured Peoples" which identified major impediments to racial equality and reemphasized their mission to eliminate discrimination and injustice. The *League of Coloured Peoples' Review* functioned as the organization's mouthpiece for pertinent issues in the United Kingdom and the West Indies. *The Review* reported on the political developments throughout the Caribbean including the first free elections in Jamaica in 1944.

President of the League, Harold Moody, wished to establish a center to house their activities. The League conceived of the center as a space that would be founded through the efforts of Africans from around the world. L.C.P. sought to appeal to diasporic Africans in order to fundraise with the stipulation that the center was also for them. In April 1945, Moody expressed desire to engage "the assistance of Negro America and of Negroes throughout the world" in order to ensure the center would "become the Mecca to which our people would come from every quarter of the globe."[51] The League's

Newsletter contained a section called "News Notes" that featured articles from around Africa and the diaspora related to issues of race and race consciousness, including reference to periodicals such as *Race Relations, The Times, Nigerian Eastern Mail, Bulawayo Chronicle, The Gwelo Times, Cape Standard, The Comet (Nigeria),* and *West African Pilot.*[52] The references to African periodicals highlighted the L.C.P. and Moody's continued engagement with the possibilities of dialogue between the continent and its diaspora.

In 1945, Moody emphasized the ongoing exchange between the metropole and colonies when referencing the return of the League's General Secretary John Carter home to British Guiana to "take up practice at the Bar in that Colony."[53] A British-trained barrister, Carter had served the League for three years. The League closely watched and reported on events in the Caribbean to their metropolitan audience. L.C.P. viewed enfranchisement in the colonies as an important move toward empowering subjects within the framework of limited colonial sovereignty. The League praised the first general election in Jamaica in December 1944 allowing every person over the age of twenty-one to vote as "a great step forward . . . in British Colonial Affairs."[54] An unprecedented development, the Jamaica Constitution established "a House of Representatives, a Legislative Council and an Executive Council," while also authorizing the Governor to "appoint the Legislative Council." Unlike Crown Colony status, the constitution's provision for the Executive Council of ten members, five of whom were appointed by the House of Representatives, represented a move toward more power for the "representatives of the people." While the League supported this progress, they noted that after "Secretary of State for the Colonies, Colonel Oliver Stanley [finished] . . . touring the Bahamas, British Honduras," he would "be present at the opening of the Jamaica Legislature."[55] Stanley's arrival in Jamaica concomitant with the passage of the new Constitution was a move away from direct rule but also reflected continued predominance of local affairs by agents of empire.

Moody enjoyed tremendous success as a doctor and public figure but his pursuit of a Cultural Centre for the L.C.P. involved negotiating and collaborating directly with private white citizens and government officials. He believed his professional proximity to white administrators would ameliorate racial prejudice. Moody however, was likely acceptable because of his exceptional status. A London-trained doctor who contributed to the civic health of the metropole, Moody's distinctiveness in the eyes of Britons was clearly articulated in his obituary. Memorialized with near messianic praise, Moody's approach to allaying race relations on behalf of nonwhites was lauded in multiple quarters. It is no surprise that the L.C.P. drew comparisons with the American-based N.A.A.C.P. whose multiracial leadership often took an assimilationist tone in working to rectifying race discrimination and inequality.

Other League leaders such as Trinidad-born cricketer and barrister Learie Constantine also chose collaborative strategies for integration and imagined alliances between black and whites in Britain. Constantine led a gathering of the Anglo-Negro Fellowship in Liverpool in January 1945. He commended a white member, "Eileen Minnitt . . . for her contribution to the cause of Racial amity." He celebrated the Anglo-Negro Fellowship as an organization which, "had done so much, within its limits, to help remove Race barriers amongst the technicians who had come to this country to assist in the war effort." General Secretary Carter was also in attendance and said of Minnitt, "if there were more families like hers we would not have Colonial problems, nor would there be any need for the League of Coloured Peoples."[56]

Moody encouraged interracial cooperation and the League pursued the recognition of colored people in Britain. In March 1945 Moody lauded the "warm reception which was given to this Bill [Colonial Development and Welfare Act] in the House" and urged members for "the need for an enthusiastic and practical acceptance of our project for a Cultural Centre in the heart of Empire." L.C.P. advocated enfranchisement in the colonies but were also unashamed of their relationship to formal empire. Moody believed, "Britain really needs us," noting "many of our boys and girls are in the Forces or in munition factories doing excellently . . . they are all having a good time and are well treated."[57] Moody alluded to racial bias and issues within the armed forces by servicemen of color but yet remained hopeful.

At the Fourteenth Annual General Meeting of the League at Memorial Hall in Farringdon, London in March 1945, Moody emphasized the "need for . . . a [cultural] centre" noting the success of the "establishment of a chain of hostels and centres up and down the country . . . [which] have done much to ease the situation created by the war."[58] L.C.P. engaged the Colonial Office to collaborate in the acquisition of a cultural space and boarding house for colonial migrants. Moody stressed the burgeoning collaborative efforts between Parliament and colonial subjects of color, and he acknowledged, "the new interest awakened in Parliament and in the country . . . about the Colonies and Colonial Affairs."[59] He also argued for the central role of Caribbean people in the British war effort, according to Moody, "these . . . poverty-stricken areas, provided money at the rate of one million pounds a month during the first 30 months of this war."[60] Moody reminded the audience of the sacrifices made by colonial people in their labor and military contributions.

After World War II, L.C.P. issued a manifesto, on *Africa in the Post-War World*, which according to Moody, "stirred up a good deal of interest among African Groups in this country and overseas." The African Peoples' Organisation of South Africa sent a supportive cablegram along with "backing of all groups of African peoples in Britain,"[61] encouraging Moody to present "a *United Front*. . . so far as our peoples are concerned." Moody linked the struggles of continental Africans to those of the diaspora and black people in Britain. In the immediate aftermath of World War II, black activists in Britain were developing notions of political blackness and a consciousness unbound by the confines of the state.

In 1948, the League reiterated its objectives through editorials in the *Review*. The leadership maintained, "one of the main functions of the League is to combat manifestations of racial discrimination involving either the individual or the collectivity . . . the fears and prejudices of British employers and workers are being intelligently tackled, and employment has been secured for many coloured persons, especially those being released from the service."[62] Ex-servicemen constituted a significant portion of West Indian arrivals and the League acknowledged the necessity of providing veterans with jobs upon arrival. Noting difficulties many West Indians faced in gaining employment, the League emphasized commitment to advocating equal treatment for all members of British society. Their offices in Westminster provided them greater visibility and enabled the League to organize meetings and activities in public venues throughout central London. On March 7, 1948, the League organized a procession from Russell Square to Trafalgar Square protesting the shooting of unarmed, peaceful protesters from Gold Coast by London Metropolitan Police. At Trafalgar Square, speakers including Padmore and Gold Coast nationals spoke out against the violence. In addition to participating directly in the organization of events in London, the League's *Review* reported on the activism and political mobilization of other groups in the city.

In May 1948, the *Review* reported on the founding of the Seventy-Seven Club in London's West End. Named after 77 Wimpole Street, the address of the Coloured Servicemen Hostel where it was founded, the club connected West Indians throughout Britain during their stay in the country. The Seventy-Seven Club invited prominent guests to present on issues affecting men of color in Britain. The arrival of the *Windrush* was an important moment for the League and the organization provided many of the ex-servicemen on board with accommodation. The *Review* also reported on the securing of jobs for twenty passengers and the negotiations between the League and trade union officials on the prospect of attaining employment for many more of the new arrivals.[63]

In 1948, the League boasted of Grantley Adams, president of the Barbados Workers' Union, appearing at a United Nations session in Paris as a member of the United Kingdom delegation. It was the first time a West Indian "had been invited to be a member of the Imperial delegation."[64] Adams was also president of the Caribbean Labour Congress and represented the official voice of the labor movements throughout the region. The League reported, "Colonial peoples throughout Africa and Asia, as well as West Indians, looked to Mr. Adams to put their grievances, their hopes and aspirations before the representatives of 52 nations."[65] The League promoted an internationalist outlook, recognizing Adams as a symbol for Caribbean colonials and subjects in the protectorates of Africa and Asia as well.

The League informed its constituency of developments in the Caribbean. They reported on the 1947 Montego Bay Conference on the prospect of West Indian federation. They lauded delegates for recommending "the setting up of a standing committee to deal with Closer Association of the British West Indian Colonies."[66] The activities of West Indians in London also elicited the League's attention. With leadership from Africa and its diaspora, the League considered issues affecting West Indians to be central to its mission. Upon the arrival of the *Windrush*, League officials "had talks with Trade Union officials and are following up all possible avenues of work for the men."[67] The League criticized the popular media coverage of the incoming West Indians. The *Evening Standard* described the arrival of the *Windrush* as "return to the Motherland" for the colonials though the League indicated that ex-servicemen would struggle to find accommodation because of the prevalence of the color bar in Britain. The League prepared for continued migration of West Indians because "widespread unemployment in the colonies, particularly in Jamaica, and the growing numbers of ex-servicemen with newly acquired skill qualifying them for industrial work which, in present conditions the colonial territories are unable to provide"[68] drew many to the opportunities life and work in Britain provided.

EDWARD SCOBIE AND *CHECKERS*

As Moody and the League of Coloured Peoples pursued integration and interracial friendship as mechanisms for the amelioration of race prejudice in Britain, Dominican-born Edward Scobie also advocated for collaboration between blacks and whites to facilitate the assimilation of the colored colonials. Born in 1918, Scobie joined the Royal Air Force and served as a pilot in Bomber Command in Germany during World War II. He was a British correspondent for the *Chicago Defender* and later wrote *Black Britannia: The History of Blacks in Britain*. Scobie also founded the periodical, *Checkers* first published in July 1948, a month after the arrival of the *SS Windrush*.

Scobie regarded *Checkers* as Britain's "premier Negro magazine," the magazine's title reflected the editors' wish to "to conjure up a checker-board with its black and white squares" suggesting interracial cooperation.[69] Scobie and his cohorts imagined blacks and whites in harmony, focusing on commonalities and collaboration. He lamented "the certain section of the British Public," who know "surprisingly little about the Colonies." Scobie bemoaned the Britons who "who think that a West Indian's someone who comes from the Western part of India."[70] He mentioned the "others who imagine that every coloured person they meet should be completely uncivilised, and capable of the vilest form of vice."[71] Yet, Scobie also categorized ignorant Britons as "luckily . . . in the minority" who could be "given authentic articles to read and true pictures to see, to that they can at last realise that a coloured person is in every way just as good as the other fellow."[72] Scobie countered the problem of racial ignorance through regarding racial biases as reflective of minority opinion in Britain. He instead praised those, "who are anxious to learn more about the Negro" and insisted it was "our duty to see that they are given the facts plainly and truthfully."[73] He believed that uninformed Britons, "must really be convinced that a coloured person is fit to take his place in decent society."[74] Scobie revealed his moderate conciliatory approach to earning acceptance from the majority British population.

Scobie's integrationist drive was notable because of the realities of racial discrimination in housing, jobs, and school. *Checkers* pledged to "carry a special page devoted to help those . . . to apply for Living accommodation."[75] In 1948 black people experienced everyday housing and employment discrimination in Britain. *Checkers* enlisted contributors who professed their loyalty to Britain and a commitment to pursuing an idealized version of British citizenship. R. Donaldson, a "Jamaican in London," explained that if any Jamaican were "lucky enough to possess sufficient funds," they "quickly embark for other parts of the world to start life anew."[76] Donaldson recognized barriers to assimilation and explained a typical Jamaican:

> applies to the Labour Exchange in London for work . . . asked his capabilities. Maybe he is a competent builder; he is asked if he has any tools . . . he is told that he cannot get work without the tools . . . Day after day he tried to get work . . . he hears the radio crying out for workers . . . he begins to think: they want workers here and there, I see Poles and even Germans getting jobs, what's wrong with me?[77]

Race functioned as the central component of British identity and a determining factor in employment and social acceptance. Nevertheless, Donaldson argued that "in no part of the British Empire are there more loyal subjects to the British Crown than in Jamaica. These people worship the Mother Country."[78] Donaldson portrayed Jamaican migrants as sycophants, eager and uncompromisingly willing to acquiesce to Britain. The obsequiousness of *Checkers* writers and editors highlighted perspectives of deferential colored colonial subjects in pursuit of acceptance from Britons. Preoccupied with managing and promoting integrationist ethics, Scobie and *Checkers* resisted sentiments of interracial strife, despite racialism repressing black West Indians. Scobie explained that *Checkers* "at all costs . . . want to avoid a senseless tug-of-war between races . . . this magazine . . . cast[s] such barriers aside with a firm hand."[79] The paper continued to argue for racial inclusivity and asserted it must be practiced by both whites and blacks.

In 1948, mayor of Kingston, Alexander Bustamante arrived in London to give a lecture at Caxton Hall in which he decried "the word 'Colonial' . . . that . . . tends to create inferiority in us [West Indians], and superiority in others."[80] Furthermore, because the mixed-race Bustamante noted "many of us . . . have Negro blood in our arteries" he urged Caribbean people to, "discontinue thinking that you are white, half white, and what not."[81] *Checkers* interviewed Bustamante who further explained, "I do not think of races, I think of people of the world . . . I do not want to be separated from the British Commonwealth, but I do not want to be called a 'British Subject,' I am a British Citizen."[82] Bustamante argued for British nationality even as a Jamaican. This moderate approach reflected many of the ideals of Scobie and other contributors to *Checkers*.

Along with Bustamante, his cousin Norman Manley was a leading figure in Jamaican nationalist circles and Manley returned to Jamaica to head the Peoples' National Party after his Rhodes Scholarship at Jesus College, Oxford. Scobie regarded Manley's example as the ideal trajectory of Caribbean students in Britain. When reflecting on the lack of guaranteed housing for colonial students, Scobie remarked, "students came over to this country to study under Colonial Development and Welfare schemes . . . they received definite guarantees from Colonial Office that they would be accommodated during their stay in Britain . . . quite a number of these students are ex-servicemen . . . poor substitutes are not good enough for men who will, in the near future, have a say in the affairs of the Colonies."[83] Scobie intonated that time spent in the United Kingdom prepared colonial citizens to return home and administer their home territories, just as had been the case for Manley. While students struggled to find housing, Scobie implored the British to be mindful that if racial animus were not eliminated, "the future of Great Britain as the Mother Country and host to her colonial people will be jeopardised."[84] Scobie urged officials to recognize that "the eyes of every dark citizen, not only of Britain's vast empire, but all over the world are focused on the Colonial Office," urging them to stay true to his view that "Great Britain stands for Justice, Fairness and Decency."[85] Scobie's pleas teemed with colonial loyalty. The greatness of Britain for Scobie could be questioned if the nation did not adequately respond to the needs of its citizens—especially those who served and the educational elite. Scobie pointed to a history of "over half a century, men from the Colonies . . . arriving in Britain to further their knowledge. There must be some leaders among these men. They are prepared to lead their people."[86]

He offered a premonition about the African and diasporic leaders who would return from the metropole equipped to manage home territories with firsthand knowledge of the state and imperial apparatus.

Migrant students retained a significant place in West Indian and British imaginations. *Checkers* readers thought of students as "ambassadors from their respective countries," who deserved fair treatment so that "when they return home they have . . . a good word to say for Britain."[87] Scobie combatted the common misconceptions of nonwhites ranging from "whether the black man has a tail coiled beneath his trousers" to when "a passport official says, 'Oh, yes, Trinidad. That's a town in Jamaica, isn't it?'"[88] These examples of the colorful language of bias, discrimination, and racialization in the British imagination highlight metropolitan ignorance regarding the colonies and their citizens.

In September 1948, a Conference of African Chiefs was held at Lancaster House, London. Deputy Prime Minister Herbert Morrison hosted sixty-seven delegates from eleven territories and identified "the need for the growth of responsible local government, improved social conditions, better equipped schools, and the economic development of Africa."[89] *Checkers* lauded the British for bringing "traditional enemies like the Hausas and Yorubas . . . side by side discussing vital issues in an atmosphere of cordiality and friendship."[90] The Colonial Office convened African representatives to work within the confines of colonial structures in order to make claims on democratization.

The assimilationist perspective of *Checkers* privileged Britain to an extreme degree, also denigrating African cultural and social formations. The Conference, they argued, would allow "the African . . . to forget old customs, superstitions and tribal prejudices, which have always been a bar in his social and economic advancement."[91] Conceding to the primary of Britain, *Checkers* invited "the African" to recognize that "only by close co-operation with the white man that he can ever hope to improve himself and build a great continent," including "forget[ing] the word 'exploitation.'"[92] Morrison himself remarked, "We must wipe out the word 'exploitation'—put it among the antiques with 'piracy' and 'slaver.' . . . let us keep always in our minds that contributions to the economic and social development and the benefits therefrom can be shared."[93]

Checkers supported the continued relationship between Britain and colonies in Africa and the Caribbean. Contributors regarded British intervention as collaboration, praising government promises of "£120,000,000 together with another £180,000,000 from the Colonies on Colonial development and Welfare Programmes—road building, agricultural improvements, communications, irrigation, conservation of land, medical supplies, etc."[94] The paper lauded Morrison for his approval of the "Colonial Development Corporation, with a capital of £100,000,000 mainly for encouraging public and private enterprises in the African Colonies."[95] Morrison had outlined the major tenets and methods of neocolonialism and *Checkers* received these overtures positively, justifying the role of Britain in African affairs. Desperate for acceptance, *Checkers* emphasized that, "every one . . . reassured Mr. Morrison of the loyalty of the West African peoples, who were always prepared to stand by Britain."[96] *Checkers* reproduced stereotypes and caricatures of black Africans to support claims for acceptance and interracial harmony.

Scobie wished to impart a well-informed position for black people in Britain and *Checkers* responded directly to reader queries while also promoting an agenda of uplift and education. In a recurring section entitled, "Books You Should Read," the *Checkers* editors demonstrated interest in issues affecting black people in Britain and abroad. The December 1948 issue suggested books such as *Colour, Race and Empire* by A. G. Russell, *Cry, the Beloved Country* by Alan Paton, Wright's *Black Boy* and *Native Son*, *Negroes in Britain* by K. L. Little, and *Inside Black America* by Roi Ottley.[97] Some of these works highlighted British sensibilities regarding race and were placed alongside works which considered racial formation across different contexts.

It is evident that the influx of West Indians in Britain marked a period of tension in the capital, as questions of citizenship and race became central to the public and intellectual discourse of postwar British society. West Indians carried with them sophisticated understandings of racial formation, specific to their island homes which did not necessarily align with the predominant racial attitudes of the colonial mother country. The relationships between West Indians which in the next decades would be essential to facilitating, growing, and promoting a distinctly West Indian political consciousness were fomenting. The work of scholars, activists, trade unionists, and artists laid the foundation for the development of specific patterns of consciousness of the West Indian migrant population particular to their experiences as racialized, colonial subjects in London.

Beyond academic and political mobilization and consciousness building in the early twentieth century among Africans and West Indians in London, artists and entertainers also played a role in developing radical perspectives. Paul Robeson, the legendary African American singer whose passport was revoked due to his affiliation with the Communist Party of the United States, maintained correspondences with the British Communist Party and expressed solidarity with blacks in England and throughout the African diaspora. Robeson explained that he "first entered the Labour movement in England"[98] and credited his connections there with his ongoing commitment to economic and racial justice. The Stepney Communist Party publicized Robeson's 1951 concert at the Royal Albert Hall in London.[99] Robeson supported the anticolonial insurrection led by the Kenya Land and Freedom Army against British rule. He believed all colonial people should have freedom and respected their aspirations in "choosing new ways of life."[100] From the United States, Robeson expressed solidarity with revolutionary Kenyans through the periodical organ of the Communist Party in the United Kingdom. The breadth of the worldview of diasporic Africans in Britain was remarkable as members of this vanguard had arrived from disparate locations in the Commonwealth and worked against the particular injustices and patterns of exploitation in various contexts. Robeson articulated a sense of belonging to a transnational community of radicals by supporting anticolonial movements through the radical print in the very metropole those movements fought against.

NOTES

1. C. L. R. James, "Abyssinia and the Imperialists," *The Keys*, Vol. 3, No. 5. (January-March 1936) from *The C. L. R. James Reader*, edited by Anna Grimshaw, (Oxford ; Cambridge, Mass: Blackwell, 1992), 63–66.
2. David A. Vaughn, *Negro Victory: The Life Story of Dr. Harold Moody* (London: Independent Press, 1050).
3. Harold Moody, *Freedom for All Men* (London: Livingstone Press, 1943).
4. Harold A. Moody, *The Colour Bar*, St. Luke's College Extension Lectures, No. 1 (London: New Mildmay Press, 1945); British Library Shelfmark: P/T 3119, 1.
5. Ibid., 5.
6. Ibid.
7. Ibid., 7–8.
8. Ibid., 8.
9. Ibid., 21, 26.
10. Ibid., 26–27.
11. Ibid., 28.
12. Vaughn, *Negro Victory*.
13. Among the British-based groups organizing or attending were West African Students' Union, League of Coloured Peoples, International African Service Bureau, Coloured Peoples' Association. Hakim Adi, *The 1945 Manchester Pan-African Congress Revisited* (London: New Beacon Books, 1995); Marika Sherwood, "Pan-African Conferences, 1900–1953: What Did 'Pan-Africanism' Mean?" *Journal of Pan-African Studies* Vol. 4, No. 10 (January 2012), 106–126.
14. See: Laura Tabili, ""Keeping the Natives under Control": Race Segregation and the Domestic Dimensions of Empire, 1920–1939," *International and Working Class Labour History* 44 (1993): 64–78.
15. Adi, *The 1945 Manchester Pan-African Congress Revisited*, 78.
16. Ibid., 67.
17. Ibid., 69.
18. George Padmore, *Africa: Britain's Third Empire* (London: Dennis Dobson, 1949).

19. Eric Williams, *Capitalism and Slavery* (London: Andre Deutsch, c1944); Eric Williams, *British Historians and the West Indies* (London: Deutsch, 1966).

20. Cedric Robinson offers a comprehensive and detailed narrative of the importance of John Jacob Thomas in the evolution of the Trinidadian intellectual classes in *Black Marxism*.

21. Eric Williams, *Inward Hunger: The Education of a Prime Minister* (Chicago: University of Chicago Press, 1971, c1969).

22. Eric Williams, *My Relations with the Caribbean Commission, 1943–1955* (Port-of-Spain, Trinidad, self-published, 1955), 1; Eric Williams, *The Negro in the Caribbean* (Manchester, England: Panaf Service, 1945).

23. See Jacqueline Jenkinson, *Black 1919: Riots, Racism, and Resistance in Imperial Britain* (Liverpool: Liverpool University Press, 2019).

24. See Hakim Adi, *West Africans in Britain 1900–1960: Nationalism, Pan-Africanism and Communism* (London: Lawrence & Wishart, 1998).

25. Williams, *My Relations with the Caribbean Commission, 1943–55*, 32.

26. Philips interview with Oswald Denniston, in Peter Fryer, *The Politics of Windrush* (London: Index Books, 199), 12.

27. Ibid.

28. Williams, *The Negro in the Caribbean*, 75.

29. Ibid., 76.

30. Ibid.

31. Ibid., 79.

32. C. L. R. James, *The Black Jacobins: Toussaint L'Ouverture and the San Domingo Revolution* (New York: Dial Press, 1938).

33. See C. L. R. James, *Beyond a Boundary* (New York: Pantheon Books, 1963).

34. C. L. R. James, "The Case for West Indian Self-Government," in *The C.L.R. James Reader*, eds. C. L. R. James and Anna Grimshaw (Oxford; Cambridge, MA: Blackwell, 1992), 51.

35. Ibid.

36. Ibid.

37. James was particularly fond of Thackeray's *Vanity Fair* as an insight into the intricacies of British Victorian culture. See *Beyond a Boundary*.

38. C. L. R. James, "The Case for West Indian Self-Government," 61.

39. Ibid.

40. See Paget Henry, *Caliban's Reason: Introducing Afro-Caribbean Philosophy* (New York: Routledge, 2000).

41. George Padmore, "Hands Off Liberia," "Under the Banner of the Red Aid," *Negro World*, October–November 1931, 5–13, 31–37.

42. See: Minkah Makalani. "Internationalizing the Third International: The African Blood Brotherhood, Asian Radicals, and Race, 1919–1922," *The Journal of African American History* 96, no. 2 (2011): 151–78.

43. C. L. R. James, Anna Grimshaw, eds., "Notes on the Life of George Padmore," in *C.L.R. James Reader* (Oxford; Cambridge, MA: Blackwell, 1992), 290.

44. See Minkah Makalani, *In the Cause of Freedom: Radical Black Internationalism from Harlem to London, 1917–1939* (Chapel Hill: University of North Carolina Press, 2011).

45. *The Colonial Worker*, Stepney Communist Party, c1950. Black Cultural Archives: Banton1/4.

46. Ibid.

47. Gramsci, Quintin Hoare, and Geoffrey Nowell Smith, *Selections from the Prison Notebooks of Antonio Gramsci* (New York, NY: International Publishers, 2010), 12–13.

48. George Padmore, *Life and Struggles of Negro Toilers* (London: Red International of Labour Union Magazine for the International Trade Union Committee of Negro Workers, 1931), 7.

49. Ibid., 122.

50. Ibid., 112.

51. Harold Moody, "President's Message," *League of Coloured Peoples' Newsletter* XII, no. 67 (April 1945), 2.

52. "News Notes," *League of Coloured Peoples' Review, Newsletter* XI, no. 64 (January 1945). British Library Shelfmark: P.P.1122.na.

53. "Message from the Founder and President Dr. Harold Moody," *League of Coloured Peoples' Review, Newsletter* XI, no. 64 (January 1945), 66. British Library Shelfmark: P.P.1122.na.

54. Ibid., 67.

55. Ibid.

56. Anglo-Negro Fellowship, League of Coloured Peoples' Review, *Newsletter* XI, no. 65 (February 1945).

57. "President's Message," League of Coloured Peoples' Review, *Newsletter* XI, no. 66 (March 1945), 106.

58. "President's Address Delivered at the Fourteenth Annual General Meeting of the League of Coloured Peoples Held at the Memorial Hall, Farringdon St., Friday March 16th, 1945," *Newsletter* XII, no. 67 (April 1945), 4.

59. Ibid.

60. Ibid.

61. President's Letter, *League of Coloured Peoples' Review. Newsletter*, XII, no. 68 (May 1945), 23.

62. *League of Coloured Peoples' Review*, January–March 1948, 2.

63. Ibid., October–December 1948, 107–108.

64. "No Mandate for Empire Peoples," *League of Coloured Peoples Review*, October–December 1948. British Library Shelfmark: P.P.1122.na.

65. Ibid.

66. "Steps Toward West Indian Unity," *League of Coloured Peoples Review*, April 1948, 39.

67. "Editorial," *League of Coloured Peoples Review*, October–December 1948, 107–108.

68. Ibid.

69. "From the Editors," *Checkers: A Monthly Journal in Black and White* 1, no. 5 (January 1949), 2. British Library Shelfmark: P.P.5939.bfb.
70. From the Editor, *Checkers Magazine* 1, no. 1 (July 1948), 5. British Library Shelfmark: P.P.5939.bfb.
71. Ibid.
72. Ibid.
73. Ibid.
74. Ibid.
75. Ibid.
76. R. Donaldson, "A Jamaican in London," *Checkers Magazine* 1, no. 1 (July 1948), 23.
77. Ibid.
78. Ibid.
79. Edward Scobie, "Editorial," *Checkers: Britain' Premier Negro Magazine* 1, no. 2 (October 1948), 2.
80. "Bustamante Busts into London," *Checkers: Britain' Premier Negro Magazine* 1, no. 2 (October 1948), 11.
81. Ibid.
82. Ibid.
83. Edward Scobie, "Nutford House Story," *Checkers: Britain' Premier Negro Magazine* 1, no. 2 (October 1948), 12.
84. Ibid.
85. Ibid.
86. Scobie, "Editorial" (November 1948), 3.
87. Ruth Davis, "Letters to the Editor," *Checkers: Britain' Premier Negro Magazine* 1, no. 3 (November 1948), 2.
88. Scobie, "Editorial" (November 1948), 2.
89. "Conference of African Chiefs," *Checkers: A Monthly Journal in Black and White* 1, no. 3 (November 1948), 23.
90. Ibid.
91. Ibid.
92. Ibid.
93. Ibid.
94. Ibid.
95. Ibid.
96. Ibid.
97. "Books You Should Read," *Checkers: A Monthly Journal in Black and White* 1, no. 5 (January 1949).
98. Derek Kartun, "The Man They Can't Gag: A Talk with Paul Robeson," *Daily Worker* (November 26, 1952).
99. *Colonial Worker*, Banton1/4.
100. Ibid.

Chapter 3

After 1948: Existentialists in Exile

Intellectual Responses to Racialized Realities

[At Oxford] Paradoxically, the more integrated I became, the more aware I was of not belonging. Possibly because the more integrated I became the more people expected me to share not just their small loyalties but their bigger loyalties and their unpalatable assumptions . . . as a West Indian I was very familiar with English and British culture, had in fact been nursed on it, it became more and more necessary to establish in spite of this I was different . . . There was a need . . . to speak out and assert my differentness. And if I was to assert my differentness, why not my identity? And what was my identity?[1]

The prevalence of British ideals in Caribbean colonies allowed migrants an intimate familiarity with a particular notion of British society—one in which they could enjoy equal treatment and the prospect of social and economic ascendance. Jamaican William Natley, who joined the Royal Air Force in 1943 and moved to Wandsworth, southwest London after his service, expressed allegiance to Britain despite his growing up an ocean away. He explained, "Jamaicans were always singing songs like 'Land of Hope and Glory and mother of the free' . . . we felt we were a part of Britain . . . we want to defend Britain in certain respects."[2] Another Jamaican *Windrush* passenger, Vince Reid, who was thirteen on arrival, later joined the RAF and subsequently studied at Sussex University, expressed a similar sentiment. Reid knew "more about England than . . . Jamaica . . . absolutely nothing about Jamaica . . . didn't feel particularly Jamaican because you had no sense of what Jamaica was."[3] The pervasiveness of discrimination against migrants, however, was a surprise to them as it contradicted the very essence of their ideological conceptualization of Britain as the "mother country."

Most migrants had never traveled to Britain before settling there and needed to learn the ways of life, climate, and attitudes in the metropole.

Settlement problems extended to migrants from all walks of life arriving at different sites across Britain. Often with no friends or family to welcome them and inadequate knowledge of the social services available, migrants appealed to their home governments for assistance. One S. M. Green, a Jamaican ex-serviceman, appealed to the Jamaica Governor for guidance and financial support to aid his stay in Britain. The governor appealed directly to Oliver Lyttleton, secretary of state for the colonies, for a resettlement grant for Green.[4]

While migrants forged personal bonds with one another, organizations and governments in the Caribbean vested interest in protecting their citizens and preparing them for life in the metropole. In late 1955, Dr. Clarence Senior published *A Report on Jamaican Migration to Great Britain* for prospective migrants to the United Kingdom informing them of the social and political environment of the so-called mother country. The *Report* was based on a series of interviews conducted in the summer of 1955 with representatives from organizations in Britain.[5] Senior characterized the experiences of West Indians in Britain as directly tied to predominating British attitudes regarding foreigners. Senior explained that in Britain, "the West Indian or African migrant is a coloured person . . . thus liable to race-associated prejudices . . . the colonial migrant is considered a foreigner . . . since some Britons associate coloured people with extremely low social status, he may be subject to class discrimination."[6] As a warning regarding the dominant attitudes of the day, Senior emphasized the notion that native Britons viewed West Indians as being outside of the British national community. He noted that in addition to being marked as foreigners, color prejudice in Britain also constructed West Indians as socially inferior, leading to class-based discrimination. Pervasive attitudes on race, Senior suggested, trumped the claims to national or imperial belonging West Indian migrants could make. He explained, "Even when nationality or class is the primary factor, the migrant's race makes him highly visible and focuses upon him an attention disproportionate to the comparatively small numbers of the coloured population."[7] Despite the appeals West Indians made to belonging to the British Empire, Senior cautioned that native Britons were unsympathetic to claims on Britishness made by foreigners and that race played a major factor in their estrangement from the majority of British residents. Drawing on the contemporaneous work of sociologist A. H. Richmond who classified the racial attitudes of Britons,[8] Senior suggested "while the British exaggerate the 'backwardness' of coloured people, the coloured colonial tends to exaggerate the alleged superiority of British culture—a situation likely to lead to the irritation and disillusionment of all concerned."[9] This observation complements migrant claims that British culture was superior to West Indian cultural formation and worthy of their admiration and deference.

Senior's pamphlet highlighted notions of difference in Britain and emphasized the social reality that native Britons would likely mark Jamaicans as racially and culturally inferior. He reported on the numerous problems facing Jamaicans in Britain including, "those faced already by large numbers of the British working class; those encountered by any 'stranger' who enters an area where he does not know how to cope with everyday problems of life as well as the local citizen does and those arising from his colour."[10] The prejudices against Jamaicans in Britain were therefore threefold: along lines of race, nationality, and class background. Senior's *Report* was designed to inform Jamaicans of the potentially pernicious situation awaiting them in Britain.

The British Caribbean Welfare Service (BCWS) was established in 1956 on the recommendations of Senior and Norman Manley.[11] BCWS was incorporated into the Commission in the United Kingdom for the West Indies, British Guiana, and British Honduras as the Migrant Services Division. The Welfare and Reception Section interviewed individual West Indians to determine effective methods for assimilation. Furthermore, the Welfare and Reception Section was forewarned by the Governments of the West Indian unit territories of the arrival of migrants. The Section obtained arrival information including ship or aircraft arrival times in order to coordinate with the London City Council or Church Army to arrange pickups. The Community Development Section addressed issues regarding the entire community of migrants, including problems of color prejudice, housing discrimination, complaints against the police, and racial disturbances. The Community Section persuaded influential citizens to sponsor West Indians in organizations, liaised between English and West Indian organizations, and arranged tours for distinguished visitors in Britain.[12] The BCWS sought to ameliorate race relations through both encouraging and developing leaders among the migrants and fostering cooperation between white and colored groups.

STUDENT PERSPECTIVES

While Moody and Scobie argued for the practical pursuit of assimilation, migrant students were faced with a different conceptualization regarding their status in the mother country. The promise of belonging to an idealized British state encouraged many to defer to British notions of acceptability and civility. Students, however, were still developing important components of their political outlooks and strove to articulate their changing perspectives and unique sensibilities while studying in the mother country. They offered insights into their position as some struggled to articulate their identifications in flux—as students, migrants, persons of color, and British citizens.

Stuart Hall arrived in London from Jamaica in August 1951, two months before his first Oxford term began. After disembarking at Avonmouth, Hall traveled by train toward London observing the English countryside which "provoked a deep psychic recognition," despite Hall having never seen the English wilderness. Although viewing cows feeding on English fields for the first time, Hall nevertheless assumed "this was how it *should* look."[13] His youth in Jamaica had been so informed by British iconography and Britishness that Hall could upon arrival, experience a certain "illusory after-effect" while traveling to an altogether new place. Like other student migrants in the 1950s, Hall's initial observations on Britain largely reaffirmed what he believed to already have known—that he was of this society.

Accompanied by his mother in London, Hall encountered future luminaries during a stay at Methodist International House, a residence for overseas students in the Bayswater area. He met A. N. R. Robinson, later president and prime minister of Trinidad and Tobago, who was studying law at the Inns of Court, as well as Doris Wellcome, from British Guiana, who would later marry Barbadian poet Edward Brathwaite. Because the House was full of African, Asian, and Caribbean students, Hall's earliest times in Britain were not, in his words, "impenetrably English."[14] The scene in London was revelatory for Hall, where he witnessed a variety of black, brown, and white persons from around empire and across social strata converging in the metropolis. His arrival in Oxford would jolt Hall to a different space—the laboratory of British cultural hegemony.

Hall arrived in Oxford, "the very cultural heartland of England,"[15] in October 1951 beginning his many decades long encounter with "a bewildering farrago of reality and fantasy."[16] His early memories in Britain suggest a rupture between what Hall had been conditioned to expect and the realities that collided with and turned these ideals upon their own heads. He enrolled in Merton College, founded in the fourteenth century, and for Hall, "a place of medieval seriousness, solidity, and gloom."[17] Merton was "a plunge into the icy depths and arcane complexities of Englishness," despite Hall's self-regard as "someone who thought they knew England well."[18] Along with other colonial students, Hall arrived in Britain confident in his understanding of British culture and society. Many created and refashioned institutions that reflected their particular consciousnesses.

The West Indian Students' Union (WISU) committed to "stimulate interest in, and represent the cultural . . . [political] and economic development of the West Indies."[19] WISU was founded to represent the Caribbean colonies in the metropole and to enhance the reputation and publicize developments in the region. Migrant students in Britain sought to publicize developments in the Caribbean and to interact and engage with fellow students from the United Kingdom and the Commonwealth. WISU's orientation provided the foundation for globalized perspectives of subsequent generations of West Indian activists and organizers in London and abroad. Their pledge to "establish contacts with similar organizations in other parts of the world"[20] suggested WISU aspirations were borne of a transnational perspective and sensitive to the needs of people of color globally. Despite the color bar preventing many students from renting rooms in various areas of the city, WISU maintained an inclusive membership, open to "Non-West Indian students and graduates ... actively interested in the aims and objects of the Union."[21]

Anglophone Caribbean islands offered no independently-operated institutions beyond secondary school and this dynamic persisted in the consciousnesses of university attendees after arriving in Britain. The International Union of Students explained in 1954, "in colonial and dependent countries, vast numbers of young people are denied access to education ... the vehicle of education is not the mother tongue, but the language of the metropolitan country ... the entire national history of the colonial country is falsified or ... suppressed to foster a feeling of servility and inferiority among the people instead of self-respect and pride in the national heritage."[22] The hegemonic nature of colonial education alienated West Indian students in numerous ways. They were taught to look to Britain as the mother country for their own history. Limited resources forced students to travel abroad for post-secondary education.

Within the educational system of the British Caribbean, migrants remembered the influence of British ideals in their everyday learning. On the history of slavery and abolition in the West Indies, Jamaican Vince Reid was taught, "the person who freed the slaves was a white man called Wilberforce ... [I] was always encouraged to believe that one must be beholden to white people ... whatever you became, it was due to the benevolence and goodwill of white people ... the whole imperialistic thing was drilled into you."[23] Euton Christian, another Jamaican who joined the Royal Air Force during World War II and arrived in Britain aboard the *Windrush*, corroborated Reid's recollections. Christian explained, "growing up in school, we always regarded England as the mother country ... we knew that Jamaica was ... ruled by England and we accepted that."[24] Grenadian Ros Howells arrived in Britain in 1951, settled in London and worked as a counselor there. She explained that in Grenada "all the educators ... came down from England ... 'There'll always be an England and England shall be free' used to be one of our school songs."[25] Schooling in the Caribbean colonies treated the West Indies as an extension of the metropole with little regard for the particularities of life in the islands. This dissonance contributed to the fundamental question of the character of West Indian identity among the *Windrush* generation students.

Cultural traditions and social formations present among West Indians were the products of the colonial encounter with the British in the Caribbean.

British subjugation of West Indians as well as the campaign of psychological transformation that prioritized and valorized British identity worked persistently to arouse West Indian migratory efforts. Britain figured heavily in West Indian consciousness, as from a young age, West Indians were exposed to the history of Great Britain. Reid remembered his indoctrination well, "I was taught in school that the black people in Jamaica were somehow better off than black people in South Africa."[26] The transatlantic flow of ideas between the Caribbean and Great Britain worked in both directions. Transplanting racial hierarchy in the West Indies conditioned black West Indians to recognize the preeminence of whites in the colonial setting. Current scholarship has drawn on the notion of British citizenship and the construction of a colonial identity as primary factors in West Indian migration. Since race was a central factor in determining social relations among citizens of London in the postwar era, the demographic makeup of the West Indian contingent complicated that assertion. In addition to arriving in Britain from a variety of locales in the Caribbean, the migrants were descendants of African, Asian, and mixed-race peoples.

Recounting his childhood impressions of England before his arrival Reid remembered, "I knew far more about England than I did about Jamaica . . . I didn't even realise that you had slavery . . . in Jamaica. I knew very little about the history of Jamaica."[27] Schools in Jamaica in the early twentieth century often neglected references to or investigations of the central historical forces of the island or its neighbors. Reid also remembered the strict racial divisions in Caribbean society and his expectations for life in Britain as marked by the same characteristics. He explained,

> I didn't mix with white people when I was growing up. The only white people I saw were in downtown Kingston who were in business . . . and you didn't associate with them particularly if you were a child . . . there was a colour bar and black people knew their place in the scheme of things . . . you had gradations of colour so the lightest skinned was seen to be better than the darker skinned . . . that stratified society based on colour . . . coming to England I more or less expected the same kind of hierarchy to exist . . . and it did.[28]

Despite an overwhelmingly black population, Reid and other Jamaicans were aware of the whites who wielded considerable power in the island. Prior to migrating, many Jamaicans already associated whites with power and prestige due to their unparalleled privileges in the Caribbean. Before his arrival in London, Reid presumed that British society would be structured in similar ways to Jamaican racial hierarchy. He remembered the clear racial demarcations, referring to his estrangement from white businesspersons as a colour bar.

Sam King, also from Jamaica, reflected on the shortcomings of education in the British Caribbean. When prompted to reveal what he was taught about the history and geography of other places, King replied, "we learned very little about the West Indies . . . we knew nothing about Citizen Toussaint . . . I came to England I had the privilege of meeting a family in Bulwell . . . I could speak to them about Prince John and the Magna Carta . . . because I was taught that. I wasn't taught about my local things."[29] King remembered that he knew, "about Prince John and the Magna Carta [and knew] more than they, the local people."[30] In Britain, King observed Britons to be less informed of their history than he was, even with his admittedly rudimentary education in the islands. In Jamaica, King received an education that emphasized the achievements of the British while dismissing the accomplishments and history of the people of the Caribbean. He arrived in Britain with an incomplete rendering of British and colonial history and thusly was unprepared for the realities of life in the metropole. There is no doubt that imbuing West Indian children with valorized notions of British culture and history contributed to the patterns of deference and subordination between racial groups in Britain.

King, admitted in school he "knew nothing about Jamaica history . . . they said Paul Bogel [sic] . . . a Jamaican hero, was a bandit and all that . . . I decide[ed] not to learn the local history."[31] Curricula in the colonies were oriented around the metropole and were insufficient regarding the histories, cultures, and societies of the region. Particularly striking for King was Bogle's legacy as a bandit rather than as the leader of the Morant Bay Rebellion. King's sense of history, though limited by his formal schooling, was nonetheless countered by what he learned of Bogle and L'Ouverture through the "grapevine."[32] Jamaicans were invested in maintaining their histories and perpetuating epistemologies that were absent from the dominant educational institutions in colonial schools. Despite his insufficient schooling, King knew "Haiti is about a hundred and twenty miles off Jamaica and the story goes that during Toussaint times the Maroons did help a little bit."[33] Through Caribbean oral tradition, King learned historical facts that were not part of his official schooling.

The condemnation of West Indian students by their English peers made for an experience of alienation and they were treated as outsiders in most of these daily interactions. Tryphena Anderson, who arrived in Liverpool from Jamaica in 1952, remembered seeing a black man on the street while riding the bus and imagined she "would get off it and just run and hug him . . . because you feel lost."[34] Anderson felt the latent hostility of Britons on an everyday basis. In school she remembered teachers treating her as though she "was supposed to be stupid . . . they didn't give me the complete . . . *David Copperfield* or *Great Expectations*, just a chapter."[35] Even for West Indians who arrived as children, teachers and classmates subjected them to blatant patterns of discrimination and fundamentally questioned their capabilities.

WISU established itself as a resource for students and concerned migrants interested in the political and social life of the Caribbean and metropole. WISU secretary John A. Holness issued an invitation to interested parties for a talk by Norman Manley in January 1951 at the London School of Economics. Holness championed Manley, leader of the PNP in Jamaica, as "the most brilliant advocate practising at the West Indian bar [with] . . . a personal reputation and following compared to that of Mr. Nehru in India."[36] WISU engaged migrants in London, invoking the successful independence movement in India led in part by Nehru and supporting Manley's status as leader of the opposition in Jamaica. Even in Britain, political developments in the Caribbean remained central to students' politics and WISU organizing continued engagement with the events in their homelands.

In March 1952, a WISU committee met with under-secretary of state for the colonies, Lord Munster, who considered their proposal to have a club and center in London for meetings and public events. Munster proposed "to write to the West Indian Governments about [support]."[37] Beyond his initial support of the Union and its center, Munster reported on attempts to procure a hostel for students, one at a former all-girls' lodging which became the Collingham Gardens site of the eventual West Indian Students' Centre. The students however, argued for, "placing a hostel not in the expensive districts of the West End but in areas such as Camden Town and Highbury where the hostel could be obtained more cheaply and possibly run more economically."[38] The committee was aware of Kensington's expensive rentals and the difficulties migrants of color faced in obtaining accommodation there due in part to the racial prejudice in letting practices.

Throughout the 1950s WISU also worked closely with students to facilitate their assimilation to British society. Mary E. Wright, a Committee Member of WISU Executive Council, wrote to Colonial Office agent G. E. Mills explaining interest in "getting in touch with young West Indians who have come up to England . . . in the hope of finding employment or obtaining further education."[39] Wright surmised that "by keeping in touch . . . with them much harm may be avoided."[40] Wright's appeal highlighted the efforts of WISU in aiding the settlement of young West Indians as well as a subtle acknowledgement of potential dangers to the migrant students. WISU would be most effective in protecting students from harm if they could account for their arrival. WISU also organized student groups for extra-curricular activities. In April 1950, WISU organized a cricket side "composed mainly of students reading at various universities, strengthened by other West Indians, some of whom graduated from London University"[41] to play a team visiting London during their tour of England.

Although WISC was a resource for students and politically engaged migrants in London, its presence concerned some white Britons who resented the influx of colored migrants in the capital. In 1957, neighbors complained of noise from the Centre to Sir Patrick Spens, Member of Parliament for Kensington South. Ms. D. Dent wrote first to the WISC Warden, complaining of "the intolerable noise which emanates from the Club when your piano and radiogram blares . . . to the disturbance of the whole neighbourhood . . . there is never any noise at all of any description from any other house."[42] Warden W. K. Hynam ensured Dent that music would be played only during organized functions. Dent continued to complain of the piano music, claiming it ruined summer evenings she and other residents had always enjoyed.[43]

Despite the Centre's compliance, Dent continued sending argumentative letters. Spens wrote to A. R. Thomas of the WISC to inform them of Dent's protest of their "using that terrible jungle drum on their band . . . disturbing their neighbours . . . such an instrument should . . . not be allowed in a resident neighbourhood."[44] Spens sympathized with Dent and requested the Centre lower their music. Dent's outrage persisted whether or not the music was exceedingly loud and her complaints to the WISC and Spens persisted for three years. Dent's derision for the "jungle drum" illustrated the perception many Londoners had of the migrants as uncivilized, bush dwellers who brought their insufferable barbaric sounds into the quiet, civil confines of metropolitan Britain.

Spens continued the campaign against the Centre, complaining of the parties at the WISC to J. D. Profumo, the Parliamentary under-secretary of the Colonial Office. Spens argued that the Centre was inconsiderate in hosting meetings and parties. Profumo relayed his communications with the Centre to Spens and explained that the warden ensured him that "dances . . . [were] held on the average once a week . . . at no time do those dances continue after 11 p.m." and that "Mrs. Dent has only spoken with him on two occasions during the last twelve months . . . he was under the impression that she was reasonably satisfied with the efforts being made at the centre to avoid causing a nuisance to its neighbours."[45] The warden reported "two letters of complaint of the noise made by . . . piano and radiogram . . . received from Mrs. Dent . . . care is being taken to see that members keep the playing of instruments as quiet as possible at all times . . . apologies have been sent to Mrs. Dent for any disturbance."[46] WISC was aware of neighbor complaints and made efforts to rectify the situation. Nevertheless, the South Kensington residents remained bitter toward colonial students.

Jamaican Mervyn Morris, who arrived at Oxford in 1958, noted that skin color had the greatest influence on his interactions with other students and native Britons outside of university. Morris arrived as Rhodes Scholar after reading English, French, and History at the University College of the West Indies. He also played tennis for Jamaica and debated for the college. His achievements, however, did not preclude Morris from experiencing the active and passive aggression of native Britons in Oxford. He explained, "Throughout England ... even in Oxford, I was told 'You speak English very well ... the questions they asked were usually fundamental and innocent ... they wanted to touch my hair.'"[47] As a black Jamaican, Morris faced constant harassment from his peers, whether their insults or questioning were based on phenotypical difference or judgments reflecting their naiveté regarding West Indian intellectual capability and social mores. Queries and physical harassment, such as reaching for and grabbing a young West Indian's hair were commonplace and done with little regard for differently coiffed students. That most English students had not seen or gone to school with black children growing up was typical; the same was true of the reverse: most West Indians had scant intimate, personal contact with whites before they continued their education in metropolitan Britain.

Most disconcerting for Morris were the attitudes of colleagues and classmates who harried him as it if was their right. Eager to gain acceptance from white students and fearful of retribution in the event that they were viewed as unfriendly to native Britons, Morris and his West Indian peers were left anxious and uneasy. Although new to Britain, Morris did not treat fellow students as curiosities and expected reciprocity. The lack of infrastructural support for West Indians in Oxford, such as a center in which they could live or plan events, made their experience more difficult because there were little options for congregating or organizing with other nonwhite students. Furthermore, that some of Morris's peers were baffled by his competence with English points to critical misperceptions harbored by some Britons at midcentury. There was perhaps a willful ignorance of the state and composition of the declining empire among many Britons. If education on the history of Britain and its empire did not make references to the peoples in Africa, Asia, and the Americas, English was nevertheless the lingua franca throughout the empire. And, while social customs and manners that predominated in Britain would never excuse unsolicited touching of another white person's hair, pinching of their skin, or other forms of physical contact, West Indians could and did experience such intrusions.

Morris conveyed an astute understanding of typical attitudes regarding race in England noting, "the English are notorious for xenophobia ... even when ... there is no deep-seated objection to a particular foreigner, there remains I think the tendency to dismiss all foreigners."[48] Native Britons expressed hypersensitivity and awareness of those different from them, with racial difference among the most significant and resilient markers. Morris's commentary reflected the durability of British notions of national origin as a central component of the British imperial and national imagination.

Morris remembered three separate incidents that shaped his understanding of the role racialization played in English society. On holiday from university, while traveling in London, Morris recounted an incident in which a group of Teddy boys[49] approached him on a London Underground platform in the West End. He explained, "I looked at them, I have no idea whether my glance was contemptuous . . . [one] attempted to move in my direction muttering . . . 'Black bastard' . . . a larger . . . lad restrained him, commenting, 'He's the same colour as Louis Armstrong man.'"[50] Morris continued his recollection, noting "the significance of the fact that the peacemaker should have chosen to make peace in this way, through the interracial symbol of a jazz hero."[51] Morris' suggestion that Armstrong was an "interracial jazz figure" is illustrative because he described the black music icon as transgressing his blackness, to the degree that despite his Black American background he could be viewed as an interracial musician. Morris noted the widespread interracial acceptance and adoration of black American jazz music, but ultimately his characterization of Armstrong as "interracial" represents a transgression of his blackness. For the Teddy boys, Armstrong's success whitened him, made him more acceptable, and in turn protected Morris from further aggression.

Morris remembered another episode witnessing and experiencing racial prejudice firsthand, while in the presence of other students. On a trip to the Folkstone Hockey Festival with coresidents of St. Edmund's Hall, Morris went to a party at a jazz club and approached a young woman with her back to him to ask for a dance. After extending his hand, Morris remembered that the woman "turned with her arms in the ready position for dancing and then saw I was black. Her confusion was lamentable. She muttered something that must have been an apology and fled."[52] Morris was confused by this rejection, assuming he approached the partygoer in a respectful manner. The fact of Morris's blackness overwhelmed the young woman's initial response and made clear the pervasive role race played in British social settings. Morris was left alone, despite his position as an Oxford student and being in the company of his classmates and fellow college residents.

Upon further reflection, Morris cited an incident related to university athletics. He aspired to qualify for a combined Oxford and Cambridge tennis team that would tour the United States to play a team of students from Harvard and Yale. When trying out for the team Morris was told, "the Lawn Tennis Association (L.T.A.) had decided that only Englishmen should be considered for the combined team, as the tour was in the interest of English tennis and Anglo-American relations."[53] Morris explained, "I accepted the decision easily . . . the L.T.A. reversed their decision. In the end [an] Indian went and I did not . . . What is most interesting . . . is the early obtuseness of the L.T.A . . . imagining that anybody intelligent enough to get into Oxford or Cambridge could swallow so ridiculous a reason . . . no doubt they said they were not prejudiced themselves but that their neighbours the Americans might not like to entertain coloured players."[54] Morris's exclusion from the team, based on his race rather than skill or some other relevant factor, exacerbated his unwelcome status at university. Despite his commitment to athletics and academics, color alone excluded him from representing Oxford in an international sporting (and ostensibly diplomatic) event. The L.T.A.'s insistence that their American counterparts were against the inclusion of nonwhite players drew on prevalent notions that racial prejudice and discrimination were particular to the United States and did not reflect British social realities.

Despite his credentials, classmates and administrators often rebuked Morris solely on account of his race. Indo-Trinidadian Kenneth Ramchand had similar experiences at university and recalled the collective alienation of Caribbean migrants of all ethnicities and colors. Ramchand explained, "Coming to Britain [was] like entering a land where the natives suffer from a curious kind of colour blindness . . . an insensitivity to racial discrimination and variant shades within the category 'black' . . . in the rarefied atmosphere of the mother county . . . all West Indians are black."[55] The black-white dichotomy in England obscured the complex ethnic composition of the West Indian migrant community living there. The simplistic understanding of race relations among many in Britain was insufficient to accurately discuss and address the multiplicity of experiences endured by the migrant population.

Ramchand remembered white youths ominously twirling and spinning bicycle chains, as they watched the comings and goings of West Indians around the university. After a few weeks, his fear of the bicycle chain subsided, concomitant with his joining of the local West Indian Association. Ramchand explained, "I stuck firmly to the group. For a year I had lunch with West Indians, coffee . . . dates . . . and attended purely West Indian parties."[56] Ramchand noted that many interracial personal relationships, specifically between white women and black men, were scandalized. He also noted, "The deep malaise in the man-woman relationship involving coloured men and white women is paralleled by a total absence of relationships between white men and coloured women."[57] Sexual relationships between migrants and native Britons were widely reported in the cities and university towns. In particular, white British women who engaged in relationships with black, Indian, or mixed-race men of foreign birth were typically viewed as victims of primitive, unbridled sexual desire and abasement. Colored sexuality was characterized as uncivilized, unmanageable, and a visceral threat to individual white women's safety as well as a threat to the fabric of British national culture and society.

Ramchand noted that white women were scrutinized for dating or socializing with nonwhite men, to a greater extent than any other group, whether they were dating other students or workers who had come to England for employment in the industries. He explained, "the attitude of the British male undergraduates . . . carries a strong load of sexual fear and jealousy: it expresses itself in a strict slating of female offenders against an unspoken masculine code. The university woman who forms a possible love relationship with a coloured man is quietly ostracized. The male of the species considers her contaminated by a phallic performer, the West Indian."[58] Despite this perception, Ramchand continued, "in the days of the plantation, white men satisfied organic needs on slave women . . . the prevailing attitude that white men only associate with black women for possible exotic sexual thrills . . . the relationship between white men and black men at the university seems to be, strangely, a kind of passing acquaintance."[59] Ramchand observed that the sexual activities of white women were more closely monitored than that of their male counterparts. He explained that "women at the university are reluctant to form relationships with coloured students . . . however . . . there existed a tribe of nurses, au pair girls, typists, shop assistants, one or two divorcees, a few erring wives, a nymphomaniac and various rejected university girl who satisfied the emotional needs of coloured students."[60] While excluded on account of his racial background, Ramchand expressed quintessentially chauvinist attitudes toward women. Those women who pursued relationships with him were "nymphomaniacs," depressingly lonely, or desperate. Furthermore, Ramchand understood that among these women most likely to enter relationships with men of color, "the degree of promiscuity varies . . . many are intelligent . . . unloved . . . [though] the overall impression . . . is that a hasty sexual connexion has taken place of a settled human relationship between black men and white women."[61] Ramchand suggested that white British women who sought the company of foreign-born men were regarded as morally corrupt and the nature of their relations with these men was characterized as fleeting and purely sexual.

Ramchand understood that Britons viewed him according to racialized mythology and prevalent stereotypes. He explained, in terms of academic achievement, "a successful West Indian becomes a phenomenon . . .' How *can* you be so *clever*? . . . intelligence, by a mental flick of the wrist, becomes cleverness, a gimmick and success has nothing to do with effort . . . the successful West Indian is either clever . . . or a performer in his own special field or at least 'an uncharacteristic West Indian,' that non-defining definition."[62] Ramchand noted his perceived exceptionalism and recognized that because of his race other students found his academic success peculiar. Ramchand further explained, "The symptoms of racial prejudice at the university are hard to discern. One finds oneself looking not for scars on one's own body but for an attitude determining the behaviour of one's fellow students . . . self-confidence is being destroyed. The constant necessity to ask oneself, 'Is it because

I am black or is it because I am, in fact, inferior and objectionable?' leads to a sapping of vital creative energy and a withdrawal into introspection."[63] Ramchand drew on notions of self-consciousness particular to the experience of racialized colonial subjecthood. Despite his achievements, Ramchand struggled against the imposition of prejudiced attitudes regarding his ability, resulting in self-condemnation. The psychological violence of colonial racism perpetually came to bear throughout Ramchand's university experience.

While Ramchand maintained that his difficulties were a product of racialism, his internalization of racist ideology affected his studies in Britain. Harboring a negative self-image exacerbated by interrogations from his university peers and other Britons forced Ramchand to reconceptualize his identification with Britain. He articulated a complex relationship with Britain as the colonial mother country as well as Trinidad. Ramchand often referred to himself as "black" despite his Indo-Trinidadian heritage, likely in response to the analogous racialized treatment both Indians and blacks faced in England. Such cross-racial solidarity was a product of the pervasiveness of anti-nonwhite racial discrimination in metropolitan Britain.

Trinidadian Patricia Madoo arrived in Oxford in 1960 and corroborated Ramchand's sentiments. The blight of negative self-consciousness among Africans, West Indians, and Asians was so pervasive that some students characterized other colonial citizens as inferior. Madoo explained that "the light-coloured West Indian student, on arrival in Britain . . . seems to share the colour prejudice of the white people among whom he has come to live . . . he regards himself as more white than black, more like the English than like the black man from his own or any other country."[64] The desire to fit in as an Englishman while maintaining Caribbean identity was difficult for migrants to negotiate. Madoo emphasized that West Indians with class-based racial superiority complexes regarded "the Indian [as] a strange, rather frightening creature, associated unconsciously with the 'coolies' who work on the plantations at home. The African is alien and exotic, very much nearer the primitive than he is. The black West Indian he links automatically with the rough lower classes of his own country."[65] Madoo's critique of the educated classes of colored migrants tied directly with the notion that race and national origin were significant markers of status in Britain and throughout empire. Some educated black and Indian migrants held themselves in higher esteem and looked down upon their fellow colonial citizens, despite sharing racial, ethnic, and national backgrounds; education in the empire was viewed as a tool for social uplift and as an indicator of white superiority.

Although nonwhite students were unfairly characterized as incompetent, educational opportunities in Britain were nevertheless plentiful. The notion that within the colonies "young people [were] . . . denied access to education . . . the very vehicle of education is not the native tongue, but the language of the metropolitan country . . . the entire national cultural history of the colonial country is falsified or even totally suppressed to foster a feeling of servility and inferiority among the people, instead of self-respect and pride in the national heritage"[66] pervaded among colonial students at home or studying abroad. The lacunae in opportunities in the Caribbean, as well as in the consciousness of white and nonwhite students regarding complex ways that colony and metropole informed identities on both sides of the Atlantic cannot be understated. The hegemonic presence of Britain stagnated the political imaginaries of some West Indians so that modes and methods of social, economic, and political progress were routed and cast both metaphysically and geographically *through* the metropole.

Lionization of Britain persisted through Caribbean colonies and A. T. Carey's *Colonial Students: A Study of the Social Adaptation of Colonial Students in London* explored how students of color conceived of their relationship to Britain after arriving for study. Initially submitted as his dissertation in anthropology at the University of Edinburgh, Carey was an assistant adviser on Aborigines in the Federation of Malaya by 1957. Through guided interviews and questionnaires with one hundred colonial students of color, informal interviews and casual conversations with another 150 students of color, and interviews with fifty British landladies and officials, Carey emphasized the discrepancies between student expectations and the reality of their experiences in Britain. One of Carey's informants' reflections upon his arrival with respect to treatment from native Britons demonstrated the dissolution of the positive associations he brought to Britain. After one week in London, the informant "asked a woman in the street to change sixpence for me . . . she looked at me and burst out: 'Get away from me, for God's sake . . . get away from me' . . . Perhaps I had behaved in an uncivilised way? It was only later that it struck me: the woman, and not I, had been uncivilized."[67] Every notion of etiquette the student held was undermined by the stranger's response. Rather than engaging him, the woman's defensive reaction illustrated the deep-seated disgust for nonwhite peoples held by some Britons. Her derision was, like the specter of discriminatory attitudes of native Britons toward blacks and Asians, a ubiquitous presence in the everyday lives of migrants.

The instantaneous refusal to engage the student reflected the desperation of the woman on the London street. The student's testimonial affirmed notions that migrants were more willing to accommodate the attitudes of native Britons than the reverse. He explained, "West Indians wish to adapt to the life of this country . . . because they regard it as their own . . . West Africans . . . want to accommodate to British ways insofar as this serves their desire for independence . . . the systems of expectations . . . have little counterpart in the attitudes of British people who regard these students as Coloureds and as foreigners, rather than as the representatives of any particular country."[68]

While West Indian and West African migrants held different views on their relationship to Britain, native Britons seemed to hold general opinions of non-native, nonwhite populations. Their understanding of the constitution of the empire was often shallow and ignorant of the diversity and scope of Britain's colonial citizens and subjects. White British resentment toward the colonial migrants was simplistic—offering little conceptualization of the varied peoples and cultures the empire dominated. The fact that Casey's informant noted that Britons were unable to recognize the numerous places migrants traveled from starkly contrasted to the imperial consciousness of the migrants of color who were more cognizant of the extent of the empire. This testimonial also revealed the disparate opinions and attitudes among migrants from Africa and the Caribbean.[69] The informant explained that while West Indians preferred accommodating British attitudes in order to assimilate, West Africans instead engaged British ideals so long as they also could be utilized for their independence movements. African migrants, in this student's estimation, had clearer notions of differentiated national identities than did West Indians and life in the metropole seemed to exacerbate these epistemological differences.

Though students often lived in close proximity to others, problems of acclimation nonetheless persisted. African students were especially prone to alienation while living in London. In 1956, three African students committed suicide in the span of one month. Despite 1,000 of the 17,000 foreign students in the United Kingdom residing in the Bayswater area of London, black migrants struggled to find decent accommodations, welcoming community, and adequate mental health services.[70] Students in Paddington complained about the difficulty of acquiring sufficient housing at reasonable rates. Some even suggested they found "five yards into an English home longer than 5,000 miles to England."[71]

Remembering his arrival in England, Hall had "no West Indian consciousness to speak of."[72] Not having traveled through the Caribbean, Hall effectively became "West Indian in the metropole."[73] Along with others, who "read Lamming's *In the Castle of My Skin* and Sam Selvon's *The Lonely Londoners*," Hall embraced Caribbean arrivals as part of a communal "us."[74] He invoked Lamming's prescient observation from *The Pleasures of Exile*, noting "most West Indians of my generation were born in England."[75] West Indian students realized their West Indian-ness not in their home islands but rather through a process of reasoning and acclimating to British society while studying abroad—in the metropole.

Hall approached the central problem of identity from a position of racialized cultural existentialism. For West Indians, Hall suggested that black Caribbean identities were "framed by two . . . vectors . . . the vector of similarity and continuity; and the vector of difference and rupture."[76] In much the same way that Caribbean students expressed dismay and disappointment with regard to the cold reception they encountered upon their arrival in London, Hall suggested that the specific quandary of Caribbean migrants hinged on the battle between these opposing and simultaneous directions. Migrant students reckoned with the in-between space of belonging and unbelonging predicated on the lacunae between the shared experience of histories of forced enslavement and displacement from Africa on one side and the conceptual promise of belonging to the British imperium on the other. As Caribbean students from various islands began to look upon one another as members of a common Caribbean community in London, Hall noted the phenomenon of "diaspora identities . . . constantly producing and reproducing themselves anew, through transformation and difference."[77]

Hall and West Indian students considered themselves interlocutors of multiple positions within the world of British imperial identity. They often were privileged in their home societies and were shocked by antagonistic receptions they faced in Britain. Their newly subjugated position enabled these students to critique the contextual purchase of race, gender, and national origin because their academic credentials went unnoticed or were rejected. Hall's insistence that students had double consciousness invokes their capacity to exist both in the world of the colonies and of the metropole at all times and in multiple locales. The persistence and reckoning of the youthful intellectuals of Hall's university years provided the basis for the transformation of British society during the final years of formal empire. It would be the ingenuity, theorizing, and alternative racially oriented, activist existentialist self-conceptualizations of Caribbean, African, and Asian migrants that would undermine British characterizations from within the center of empire, only to contribute to a new multicultural rendering of British national identity and the acceleration of anticolonial resistance and the development of decolonized identities.

Much has been made of the way in which newly arrived West Indians viewed themselves—as members of the British national community, the empire at large, or marginalized outsiders negotiating a supposedly familiar space. Negotiating public space, both as individuals and as a group was a daunting exercise because of circumstances of racialization and displacement. The decision to migrate from the Anglophone Caribbean was often as influential in shaping perspectives of the migrants as their experiences in the metropole. The notion that "black skin is undoubtedly the most significant status marker for Jamaican migrants in English society"[78] placed phenotype as the determinant factor in social relations in London. Furthermore, it suggests that for blacks, race took on a greater meaning in the metropole, with its predominantly white population, than it had in Jamaica, where although subject to the hand of the imperial government, black Jamaicans could establish themselves socially and economically. Understanding themselves as citizens in their homeland left Jamaicans and others unprepared for the reality of racial discrimination and inequality in Britain. The social and cultural capital of whiteness was prevalent both in predominantly Afro-descended Jamaica and Great Britain. Although black Jamaicans were imperial citizens, an internalized color complex marred their inclusion in the imperial body politic. Fernando Henriques characterized colorism in Jamaica as ubiquitous because among the island population "black is associated with the backward, primitive and undesirable qualities in man; and white is associated with everything that is desirable."[79] Furthermore, Henriques recognized "white bias" as a fundamental component of Caribbean life. He noted the "barrier to complete assimilation of European cultural values is contained in 'colour' itself. The physical fact of colour symbolizes to the individual that there can never be complete identification with the superior culture . . . Government at the highest level, orthodox religion, education, are all associated with white superiority."[80] Particularly with regard to prestige, education, and the national discourse, lighter skin was viewed as positive and a marker for increased opportunity. Violence in Notting Hill only further upset notions of belonging to the British national community for West Indians.[81] Local antagonisms soon morphed into corporeal harm in the streets of London. Caribbean responses reflected a novel and developing racialized resistance.

NOTES

1. Mervyn Morris, *Disappointed Guests. Essays by African, Asian, and West Indian Students*, ed. John L. M. Dawson (London; New York: Oxford University Press, 1965), 13. Morris became a poet and professor at the University of the West Indies.

2. Philips, Interview with William Natley, *Windrush*, 14.

3. Philips, Interview with Vince Reid, *Windrush*, 13–14.

4. Letter from the Governor of Jamaica to the secretary of state for the colonies January 1, 1952. British NA: CO 137/885/7.

5. Clarence Senior and Douglas Manley, *A Report on Jamaican Migration to Great Britain* (Kingston, Jamaica: Government Printer, 1955). See the *Report's* Appendix I for the list of interviews conducted. University professors, Colonial Office officials, Local Government agents, trade unionists, and local social, cultural representatives from London are among the interviewees.

6. Ibid., 23.

7. Ibid.

8. Richmond's rendering of British racial attitudes was "one-third is tolerant of coloured people, one-third is mildly prejudiced and one-third is extremely prejudiced." *A Report on Jamaican Migration to Great Britain*, 23.

9. Ibid., 25.

10. Ibid., 27.

11. Clarence Senior and Norman Manley, *A Report on Jamaican Migration to Great Britain*.

12. "The Commission in the United Kingdom for the West Indies, British Guiana and British Honduras," May 1, 1959. Migrant Services Division. British NA: CO 1031/2545.
13. Stuart Hall, *Familiar Stranger: A Life Between Two Islands* (Durham: Duke University Press, 2017), 152.
14. Ibid.
15. Ibid., 149.
16. Ibid.
17. Ibid., 155.
18. Ibid.
19. "West Indian Students' Union Constitution," 1959.
20. Ibid.
21. Ibid.
22. International Union of Students, "Colonial Education," British Library Shelfmark: 8356.t.11. 1954.
23. Mike and Trevor Phillips, Interview with Vince Reid. *Windrush*, 13.
24. Phillips, Interview with Euton Christian, *Windrush*, 12.
25. Phillips, Interview with Ros Howells, *Windrush*, 13.
26. Philips, Interview with Vincent Reid, *Windrush*, 13.
27. Alan Dein, Interview with Vincent Reid April 1998. "London Voices," Museum of London.
28. Ibid.
29. Rory O'Connell, Interview with Sam King, February 1, 1993; "London Voices," Museum of London.
30. Ibid.
31. Ibid.
32. Ibid.
33. Ibid.
34. Phillips, Interview with Tryphena Anderson, *Windrush*, 97.
35. Ibid., 391.
36. "Invitation from John A. Holness," 1951. CO. British NA: CO 876/156.
37. "Minutes of a Meeting Between Lord Munster and a Deputation from the West Indian Students' Union," 1952. British NA: CO 876/156.
38. Ibid.
39. "Letter from Mary Wright to G.E. Mills," April 20, 1951. British NA: CO 876/155.
40. Ibid.
41. "Letter from G.E. Mills to Mr. Howson," April 20, 1950. British NA: CO 876/155.
42. "Letter from D. Dent to the Warden." June 17, 1957. British NA: CO 1028/68.
43. Ibid.
44. "Letter from Sir Patrick Spens to A.R. Thomas," 1955. Colonial Office. National Archives of the United Kingdom.
45. "Letter from John Profumo to Patrick Spens," 1957. Colonial Office. British NA: CO 1028/68.

46. "Warden's Report for the Month Ending 30th June 1957," British NA: CO 1028/68.
47. Morris, *Disappointed Guests*, 7.
48. Ibid., 13.
49. Dick Hebdige, *Subculture: The Meaning of Style* (Hoboken: Taylor and Francis, 1979 [2012]).
50. Morris, *Disappointed Guests*, 18.
51. Ibid., 19.
52. Ibid.
53. Ibid., 20.
54. Ibid., 21.
55. Kenneth Ramchand, in *Disappointed Guests: Essays by African, Asian, and West Indian Students;* Henri Tajfel and John L. Dawson, editors (New York: Oxford University Press, under the auspices of the Institute of Race Relations, 1965), 28.
56. Ibid., 31.
57. Ibid., 33.
58. Ibid., 34.
59. Ibid., 33.
60. Ibid., 32.
61. Ibid., 33.
62. Ibid., 35.
63. Ibid., 36–37.
64. Patricia Madoo, in *Disappointed Guests: Essays by African, Asian, and West Indian Students*, 55.
65. Ibid.
66. International Union of Students, "Colonial Education," 8356.t.11, 1954.
67. A. T. Carey, *Colonial Students* (London: Secker & Warburg, 1955), 39.
68. Ibid., 42–43.
69. See Brent Hayes Edwards, *The Practice of Diaspora: Literature, Translation, and the Rise of Black Internationalism* (Cambridge, Mass: Harvard University Press, 2003).
70. "Prejudice Begins at Home," *The Times Supplement* (November 8, 1957).
71. Ibid.
72. Hall, *Familiar Stranger*, 165.
73. Ibid., 164.
74. Ibid., 166.
75. Ibid., 167.
76. Stuart Hall, "Cultural Identity and Diaspora," in *Identity: Community, Culture, Difference* (London: Lawrence and Wishart), 226.
77. Ibid.
78. Nancy Foner, *Jamaica Farwell: Jamaican Migrants in London* (Berkeley: University of California Press, 1972), 23.
79. Henriques, *Family and Colour in Jamaica* (London: Eyre & Spottiswoode, 1953), 62.
80. Ibid., 169.
81. Ibid.

Chapter 4

"We're Here, and We're Here in a Big Way"

West Indians Respond to the Notting Hill Race Riots

It all started one Saturday night, 23 August 1958, when a group of nine white youths . . . set out on a pleasure tour of west London which was to end with three black men in hospital for several weeks and . . . nine youths locked up in prison for four years . . . They set out in the early hours . . . the car full of home-made weapons . . . Spotting the first solitary West Indian in a deserted street they pulled over, chased after the man and smashed him over the head with an iron bar . . . Between three and five o'clock in the morning they made three further attacks—the third in Notting Hill—seriously injuring five West Indians.[1]

The Notting Hill Riots were racially charged violent outbursts over two weeks in late summer 1958. Initially instigated by white Teddy boys, who harassed West Indian passersby throughout West London, the riots engulfed multiple areas in the city. White and black young men wielded broken glass bottles, bicycle chains, and bats against each other in the streets. Teddy boys destroyed business displays while chasing and attacking any West Indians they encountered. Participant memories of the riots provide insight into the tense atmosphere of mid-century London. Mainstream English newspapers were slow to cast the violence as riots, opting instead to label them "disturbances" and initially avoiding the racial component altogether. *The Manchester Guardian* contended, "by no stretch of the imagination could the hooliganism that took place be called racial riots."[2] *The Guardian* described the fear of many "dark faces" rushing home from work but resisted characterizing the riots as fundamentally racialized. While British social scientists begin to research and investigate the changing nature of race relations in the United Kingdom in the 1950s, the popular press obfuscated the increasingly tense atmosphere in areas such as Notting Hill and Paddington as youthful disturbances. "Hooliganism" became a placeholder for racial aggression in the British public press. It was a catchall term that avoided racial identity, at once indicting and excusing black and white rioters.

GIVING RISE TO THE RIOTS

The mainstream press cited disillusionment among white British youth as the primary cause of the disturbances but also depicted West Indians as unwelcome intruders in the metropole. The notion that colonial citizens were traveling to the United Kingdom and taking jobs from the unemployed white working classes was widespread, propagated by the British Union of Fascists led by Oswald Mosley. Declining rates of employment coupled with Mosley's public denouncement of non-native workers contributed to growing anti-immigrant sentiment, especially among struggling youth. Mosley's politics were framed around the Union Movement's radical nationalism, which was virulently anti-immigrant in nature.

The Times reported on racial antagonisms but also provided in-depth analysis that minimized the racialized nature of the conflicts. White residents, according to the *Times*, "have nothing against coloured people" though bands of youths from around London arrived in Notting Hill armed with chains, pipes, and the slogan of "Keep Britain White." Furthermore, white residents resented colored migrants for three reasons: "they are alleged to do no work and to collect a rich sum from the Assistance Board . . . are . . . able to find housing when white residents cannot . . . they are charged with all kinds of misbehaviour, especially sexual."[3] While acknowledging that these were exaggerated characterizations, the *Times* nevertheless attributed the dangerous, seemingly lawless environment of Notting Hill to *both* white and black residents. *The Times* also acknowledged reasons given by Teddy boys as racially oriented. When faced by a mob outside of his home "one teenage coloured boy sauntered out . . . walked up to a crowd of white youths, drew a flick knife and walked off."[4] The man continued undisturbed but soon the same, "white gang chased a young coloured student who had blundered into the area unawares, kicked him and made him take refuge."[5] Despite black residents of Notting Hill protecting and arming themselves against aggression, the *Times* considered both whites and blacks to be responsible for the continued violence in the area. White youths on "pleasure tours" of violence and destruction were dismissed as insignificant, according to the *Times* because Notting Hill was "a rough area, suspicious of strangers and used to settling its differences with fists and knives anyway."[6] Reports of the riots in Notting Hill highlighted commonly held notions of place, as much of the earlier coverage of the migrants also contended. Black migrants living in the neighborhood were accused of invading an already undesirable environ and exacerbating their status as aliens in the capital. Rather than providing an insight into the pervasiveness of racialism among the white working classes, the *Times* attributed the racial violence to the extant view of Notting Hill as an undesirable neighborhood. Furthermore, West Indians who were bold enough to protect themselves were singled out as instigating the masses of white youth from the area, and throughout London who waited outside Tube stations and apartment blocks, hoping to attack the area's black residents.

The riots were a watershed moment in the articulation of West Indian patterns of identification and resistance in the United Kingdom. These patterns emerged from the threat of everyday violence, quotidian discrimination, and the disruptions in Notting Hill rather than from an inherent, essentialized shared past among Caribbean migrants. Mutual identification of migrants from the Caribbean in the wake of the Notting Hill Riots marked a historical moment that defined newly oriented association of these collectivities in Britain.

Edward Pilkington's seminal history of the events of 1958 is the most comprehensive study of the racial antagonism against black West Indians that led to the violent outbursts.[7] Pilkington connects the alienation experienced by many West Indian migrants with the decision to actively defend themselves and other migrants from attacking native Britons. Baron Baker, a black resident of Notting Dale, was shocked by the aggression of white neighbors whom he remembered shouting in the streets "Let's lynch the niggers! Let's burn their homes!"[8] Baker and other black residents resorted to walking in groups and eventually "stayed indoors, in the hope that . . . the crowds would fade away."[9]

Although Notting Hill residents and workers remembered young working-class white men from the area as instigators, by September 1, men from other neighborhoods began to descend on the area. Peter Taylor, who worked across the street from the Latimer Road Tube station, explained the earliest outbursts were "purely a local thing—all whites got down on to the street and everybody got stuck in."[10] John Garrett, a white rioter, explained the shared feeling of enmity toward black people united white aggressors from Notting Dale and neighboring Paddington, Shepherds Bush, and Hammersmith. Garrett explained many Teddy boys had been rivals but "during the riots . . . all got together and became allies."[11] Teddy boys assembled en masse in Notting Hill forming "a crowd of 150 . . . [then] blocked the tow-path along the canal . . . black people were chased and attacked."[12] Hundreds more soon arrived on the numbers 28 and 31 buses set on "coming to see the nigger run."[13] Metropolitan Line trains were packed with "sightseers pouring into Notting Hill . . . as though they were going to a funfare . . . carrying weapons with very little interference from the police."[14] Whites from across London converged on Notting Hill to agitate and spectate. The police initially did not attempt to impede the unrest.

Black residents sought refuge from white rioters' aggression. West Indians were forced "to run the gauntlet between rows of white people lining the roads . . . armed with broken bottles, knives, sticks, chair and table legs, petrol bombs, chains, iron bars and whips."[15] Teddy boys circled neighborhood thoroughfares on motorbikes or piled into cars searching for West Indians to attack. Alfred "King Dick" Harvey, a Jamaican area resident, was struck with a bike chain and witnessed "a group of white men attacking a black woman . . . they . . . kicked over the pram she was pushing, throwing her baby onto the pavement."[16] Teddy boys were ruthless throughout the area, resorting to brutally violent tactics over the course of the riots.

After leaving Oxford, Stuart Hall taught in a secondary school in London during the 1958 riots in Notting Hill.[17] Hall's interactions with young Londoners provide particular insights into the existentialist nature of the Caribbean migrant condition. Several of his white students admitted to participating in the conflict. Hall later explained that they "believed . . . West Indians were savages flooding the country taking jobs, filling up classrooms, stealing women; that they were a lower order of society altogether and should be encouraged to 'go home.'"[18] He noted that despite these critiques and resentment toward migrants, the students, "had the friendliest attitude toward . . . [Hall] a teacher who, after all had stolen a job in their school and their own West Indian classmates."[19] His students showed an affinity for Hall despite his Jamaican background. Their closeness to Hall assuaged the same fears and resentment they expressed toward migrants they did not know.

Notting Hill agitators targeted those they considered different regarding migrants as intruders. Hall regarded their hostilities as "compounded by the alienness . . . 'otherness' of the coloured strangers, accentuated by differences of background, religious beliefs, family relationships, cultural and dietary habits."[20] Hall identified disparities in lifestyles and perspectives the native Britons and Caribbean migrants held—so plentiful and fundamentally different he determined there was little room for understanding nor sympathy between the groups. Nevertheless, white youths from around London initiated violence in Notting Hill. Despite the extant poor conditions in areas where West Indians settled, Hall recognized "the coloured immigrant and his family have become the personification of the troubles of the twilight zones—troubles which existed long before he arrived."[21] West Indians became the symbols of ills that plagued British society despite these problems proliferating before their arrival. Even as white Britons perpetrated violence against the West Indians, migrants were blamed for the disturbances.

Hall sympathized with immigrant teenagers, comparing their experiences to that of "the traveler whose routes in and out of the home take him . . . across deep and dangerous chasms . . . the . . . immigrant is trying to span the gap between Britain and home; trying to make some sense of the striking contrasts in climate, environment, tempo of life, and social position."[22] He explained differences were exacerbated because, "there is the identity which belongs to the part of him that is West Indian, or Pakistani or Indian and is certainly affirmed in the home and reaffirmed in his relation with his family, in the language he speaks with them."[23] For Hall, migration was not a wholly transformative experience. Although migrants traveled to Britain, they did not immediately relinquish ties to their homelands nor did they suddenly lose their Caribbean identities. Hall noted continued relations with West Indians or South Asians were the very mechanism by which migrants could hold on to their ethnic and alternate national identities. Utilizing networks of communication, relying on extant connections for housing and jobs, keeping up with news in the Caribbean, all were part of the affirmation of identity for the migrants in London.

Hall invoked notions of double consciousness to describe the young immigrant or child of Caribbean immigrants in Britain. Migrant teenagers needed to be aware of both their parents' knowledge and cultural lore *and* extremely conscious of the dominant cultural and social forms of everyday British life. Hall suggested young people of immigrant parents passed "every day between the two . . . camps . . . highly conscious of themselves as a group . . . which is constantly being watched and tested and which is aware that what they do as individuals is accredited to the group as a whole."[24] Their distinctiveness in Britain made them "the conscience of their race . . . [carrying] their social identities around with them like packs on their backs."[25] After the attacks on migrants in the riots, Caribbean residents were burdened with their classification as unwelcome trespassers, reinforcing nativist sentiment that they were interfering with British national culture that was exclusive to native Britons. These restrictions notwithstanding, Hall noted their youthful pride, attributing their resolve to their capacity to survive and determination to respect and honor themselves and their families. Hall suggested integration was farther away after the violence in Notting Hill arguing that the colored youth's disillusionment, bitterness, and resentment would only grow.

CARIBBEAN RESPONSES

Trinidad-born Michael de Freitas[26] organized a group of West Indians to defend themselves in response to the rioting. De Freitas met with Frances Ezzrecco, Baron Baker, Frank Crichlow, and others in the Calypso Club in central Notting Hill. De Freitas shirked at Caribbean defense through relying on "committees and representatives" opting instead, "to get a few pieces of iron . . . so that tonight when they come in here we can defend ourselves."[27] De Freitas and his cohorts gathered sticks, knives, meat cleavers, and iron bars from a local steel smith. In the afternoon, the men congregated in Totobag's Café and the women in another building down the road. Over 300 West Indians waited for whites to begin the expected attacks. As night fell, white crowds milled around Totobag's, because it was a West Indian business. When the crowds began shouting "Let's burn the niggers out," West Indians responded by throwing Molotov cocktails from the third floor of the buildings. They soon emerged onto the street brandishing knives and other weapons chasing the whites from the block.[28]

West Indians were emboldened by de Freitas and those assembled in Totobag's and joined in fighting back. Jamaican Ivan Weekes remembered fellow Jamaicans who "came over from Brixton, night by night, to help their brothers in Notting Hill . . . if they didn't have friends in the area, they had relatives . . . Jamaicans bore the brunt of the fight . . . they fought back fiercely."[29] West Indians took to the streets on one another's behalves, exhibiting a commitment to racial solidarity in the face of Teddy boy aggression.

The aftermath of the riots, especially the circumstances surrounding the death of the Antiguan carpenter Kelso Cochrane in May of 1959 also merit discussion. Although the riots and Cochrane's murder were separated by eight months, the events are often conflated in the memories of West Indians. I offer a unique scholarly treatment of extant ethnography. The interviews from Mike and Trevor Phillips' *Windrush* expose a correlation in the recollection of the events of the riot and Cochrane's murder. These interviews provide the voice of the migrant community and articulate the experiences of West Indians in London. The conflation of Cochrane's murder and the riots is significant because it demonstrates lingering fear of white British aggression. Rather than treating the riots and Cochrane's murder as isolated events, they are remembered as part of a continuum of racial violence. The memories of victims and eyewitnesses of the riots who connected Cochrane's murder to the violence of the previous year demonstrate that the interval between the events was insufficient for dissociation. A closer investigation into the conflation of these events would lead to establishing concrete rationale as to why the connection was made even as time passed.

The vivid accounts of the riots, provided by both witnesses and participants, provide insight into the historical memory of members of London's West Indian community. More recent interviews, however, are structured around lines of questioning which typically prioritize notions of identity and group belonging, suggesting that these categories have figured prominently in the historical memory of the riot participants. Furthermore, contemporaneous responses and popular media coverage serve to highlight the most prominent issues in British public discourse at the time.[30]

Migrants' aspirations to belong to the British imperial body politic are central to understanding West Indians' own notions of identity, citizenship, and community formation. This analysis draws from Ann Stoler who argues, "British colonial officials . . . constituted populations into ethnically specific, gendered subjects, marked peoples as different and ruled them according to those differences. They utilized categories and classifications that legitimated inequalities of power."[31] Further complicating Stoler's dissolution of demarcations between "metropolitan and the colonial—here/there, then/now, home/away . . . [as] a fiction that was at the very heart of the taken-for-granted view of Britain as an imperial power . . . by showing how . . . the British metropole was an *imperial* 'home.'"[32] The durability of Britain as the mother country for West Indians remained reliable. Fomenting specifically West Indian patterns of identification in the United Kingdom was a response to the threat of violence in Britain, the estrangement of Caribbean migrants from British society, and was exacerbated the 1958 riots.

This chapter moves toward an analysis of processes of identification rather than conceptualizing identity as a staid category. The complicated notion of "identity" among West Indian migrants was neither uniform nor static. Students and workers often differed in their experiences in the Caribbean and in their expectations for life in the metropole. Students belonging to the West Indian Students' Union (WISU) and the West African Students' Union (WASU), therefore, encountered discriminatory patterns distinct to the universities but overall akin to the prejudices endured by workers in the myriad English industries. The summer fortnight marred by violence in Notting Hill further solidified the notion of racial inequality and racialism in London, radicalizing some members of the migrant community.

West Indians articulated a keen awareness of how to protect themselves in Britain. Migrants were not necessarily aware of the prevalent anti-black biases among the white British working class prior to arrival, but often quickly adjusted their behavior to cope and protect themselves once in London. Their coping mechanisms were widespread—rather than expressing feelings of insufficiency—West Indians instead demonstrated behaviors which would endear them to and prevent violent and antagonistic responses from native Britons.

Rudy Braithwaite, a Barbadian osteopath who arrived in Britain in 1957, needed constant self-awareness in the mother country. He explained, "You would find incidents on buses, and on tubes . . . you felt surrounded all the time . . . you felt that you were an intruder, and truly, you were a foreigner . . . an outsider. You did not belong, but you had to bear it."[33] Before the

Notting Hill disturbances, Braithwaite recognized the prospect and specter of violence in the capital. He expressed a sense of exclusion from British society, referring to the threat of violence he witnessed or was aware of, such as incidents on buses and trains.

Herman Ouseley, a Guyanese migrant and community organizer, remembered his isolation and the constant threat of violence in Britain, strategizing his commute on a daily basis. Ouseley remembered, "the biggest problem that I faced was knowing very quickly where to go and where not to go; where you weren't welcome . . . where hostility could be violence . . . I felt very often instinctively that there were places where you had to avoid . . . that was proved to be right by people who would get their heads beaten in and had very difficult experiences."[34] His trepidation while traveling through certain London areas developed because of the prospect of violence rather than an inferiority complex. British buses and trains were the vessels representing the tenuous and precarious nature of migration for West Indians. Despite many making their living working on the rails and bus lines, migrants rode public transportation always with a sense of exclusion and the need to protect themselves. Ouseley's movement through London was determined by considerations for his own personal safety. Even before the riots, many West Indians were fearful in London, careful not to tread into areas where they believed they were unwelcome.

The cultural capital of Britishness and of whiteness deeply affected many migrant West Indians, instilling in them a racialized self-consciousness. Ken, an Indo-Trinidadian migrant, explained to the community activist Donald Hinds[35] that he "was a white supremacist with a dark skin, a champion of white people against the injustices of the blacks. How unspeakably offensive that you should address a white man with hands in your pockets!"[36] Racialized attitudes informed interactions in Britain between migrants and native Britons, with both groups expecting deference toward white British residents. Ken's objection to his perception of a lack of respect toward a white man was palpable because of racialized notions of right and wrong. Migrant testimonials exhibit a near ubiquitous deference toward white Britons. Ken disciplined himself and other migrants for fear of upsetting the racial status quo in Britain. Despite threats of violence from Teds and their role in initiating and perpetrating the riots, Ken nevertheless charged the migrant community with upholding a certain dignity and admonished his compatriots for any perceived shortcomings.

ARTICULATING IDENTIFICATION

The violence in Notting Hill shocked many of West Indians in London and highlighted the changes in British society during the *Windrush* era. Blacks made up a considerable portion of the medical and public service sector in Britain and were working in hospitals across the city during the riots. A cartoon from the *Sunday Express* in September 1958 depicted four white bandaged Britons exiting a hospital where a black doctor and nurse bid them farewell from the doorway. Graffiti covering the hospital's outside wall read, "go home blacks."[37] Britons relied on the labor provided by colored migrants, and many received treatment from black doctors and nurses during the crisis in Notting Hill. Another cartoon from the *Daily Mail* depicted a Teddy boy standing near broken glass bottles cleaning his bloodied hands with the Union Jack.[38] For Britons, ideals of egalitarianism and justice were thrown into disarray by the disorder. British principles seemed to be disintegrating through the actions of the Teds. Even for the British masses, Teds represented a marginalized, extreme element tarnishing the principles of the British nation.

The premise that Britons harbored racial antipathy and discriminated against colored migrants represented a shift in British national identity as well. Many Britons characterized American segregation and apartheid South Africa as obviously racist regimes. A *Daily Express* cartoon from 1963 depicted three long lines of American Ku Klux Klansmen arriving in Shannon Airport, fully hooded and wielding spades.[39] The cartoon's caption read: "Another party of American tourists for a trip round the English countryside."[40] Britons did not consider themselves racialists; they instead charged the radical far-right elements in the nation to be influenced by American Southern racists. Many understood the radical racialism as an offshoot of Nazism, again not British in origin. Most characterizations of the violent racism of the riots were attributed to foreign influence and ergo inherently non-British.

During the riots, on September 2, The *Daily Mirror* published a cartoon portraying a Teddy boy brandishing an ice pick with "Our Own Racialist Thugs" smeared across his chest. "Racial persecution, intolerance, prejudice" was etched into the brick wall behind him and to his left Hitler stood, whispering into the young man's ear. Cartoonist Victor Weisz captioned "On September 3, 1939, Adolf Hitler started the Second World War." His rendition of Hitler encouraged the Ted, "Go on boy! I may have lost that war, but my ideas seem to be winning."[41] The actions and sentiments of Mosley, the Union Movement, and Teds were attributed to residues of Nazism from World War II. Many Britons viewed the white British riot perpetrators as marginal outsiders within British society. The notion that the particularity of the violence in Notting Hill was homegrown did not enter into the public discourse. Rather than analyzing the British roots of British racialism, the riots were instead deigned to be the product of other imported racialisms—whether American, South African, or German.

Testimonials of West Indian participants and witnesses to the riots illustrate the menace of racial violence in Britain and highlight methods of black political resistance. Jamaican Ainsley Grant remembered the uncertainty under which he and his friends lived due to racial prejudice. He explained, "I am inclined to trust no white man . . . I think the Fascists only cashed in on the hatred that was going around. There was a lot of jealousy between the white boys and the coloured boys over the white girls."[42] Grant noted that Teddy boy racism coincided with Nazism but nevertheless developed distinctly in Britain. He recognized that tensions developed between young black and white men over the attention of English women. He insisted, "1958 was the height of the rock'n'roll craze and those young white girls used to be really crazy about a fellow with a radiogram and the latest records . . . all the coloured boys had radiograms . . . a coloured boy throwing around a lot of money . . . was all that the girls wanted to see."[43] Whether or not the riots began mainly due to liaisons between black West Indian men and white English women, Grant understood race as the essential marker of difference and source of the violence. He articulated the reservations many West Indians had in engaging with native Britons. Migrants were desperate for acceptance and needed to find accommodation and companionship but concomitantly were hyperaware of British perceptions of their every move.

Alfred Harvey, a stowaway who arrived in London in 1954, recalled his position during the riots. He claimed defense against the Teds and others inspired by Oswald Mosley's Union of Fascists.[44] Harvey explained, "We had to prepare ourselves because, otherwise with Mosley and his black jacket, they worrying us . . . we had a hardware shop along Portobello Road . . . anything that could cut, we'd buy it . . . we did arm ourselves, just like they did."[45] Harvey argued that he defended himself against racism, carrying weapons only to stand against Teddy boy intimidation. Teddy boys, who were viewed by the West Indian community as a threatening element of virulent nativist antagonism, were themselves seen as intruders on spaces on which the migrants had made claims. Harvey noted that the racist platform of Mosley and the Union Movement served as a reminder that many Britons viewed the migrants as undesirable invaders. In Harvey's view, the Teds were realizing the threat of the English right-wing agitators. The precarious nature of life in London for colored migrants was manifest in the racial violence over the course of the Notting Hill Riots.

In Ladbroke Grove on September 1 "a well-dressed coloured man was kicked in the back as he was leaving the Underground station," before a group of nearly 100 youths rushed from the streets "where they had been marching, shouting, and throwing stones." The attackers were called to action by "the occupants of large cars . . . cruising round the area." Teddy boys mobilized rioters through word of mouth and intimidated and attacked random West Indians throughout the area. After descending on the lone man leaving the Underground, the crowd then set upon another man and woman chasing them down Lancaster Road, throwing bottles and shouting, "let's gets the blacks."[46]

Vincent Reid offered a narrative of the riots that charged white youngsters in Notting Hill as the aggressors. He explained the disturbances began when,

> some black guy was accused of being a pimp for some white woman. Whether it's true or not . . . it spread from Notting Hill Dale right up into the . . . whole large area. You had white men with clubs and knuckledusters and all kinds of things, you know you couldn't walk in the street by yourself . . . you had to walk in gangs . . . once you were in a gang this made you a target for the police who would then stop search you.[47]

Reid recognized the influence of Mosley and suggested white rioters ". . . were politically organized . . . they weren't even living here. They came from outside you know."[48] Although Teddy boys and the Union Movement were adamant about the intrusive nature of colonial migration, Reid suggested that white youth with whom he battled in the streets of Notting Hill were outsiders to that community. Reid, like other West Indians, lived in Notting Hill because it was one of the few London districts where nonwhites could reliably find housing. The Teds, themselves area visitors, considered white Britons to be the rightful residents and protectors of that same community. Reid dispelled the notion that Teddy boys were rebellious youth, characterizing them as patrolling crowds of mostly grown men. Rather than dismissing the Teddy boys as antisocial children, Reid instead charged them with actualizing the promises of violent backlash against West Indians. Migrants understood the actions of the Teddy boys as an organized backlash against their presence, not an aberration of wayward juvenile troublemakers.

Reid remembered the ominous presence of bands of armed white youth in the streets and confessed the impulse to defend himself. He continued, "I was living in Ledbury Road . . . near the heart of the riot and . . . you knew that they were coming and you would show solidarity by . . . using whatever weapon you could in defence of your . . . shebeen . . . that's the only cultural place you had . . . so you had to defend it."[49] Shebeens—unlicensed drinking houses—were the center of social life for much of Notting Hill's West Indian community and were used to organize against the continued threat of violence during the riots. Banned from pubs and clubs across the city, West Indians established shebeens and used their friend and kin networks to protect themselves from the aggression of their white neighbors.

CARIBBEAN DIASPORIC SOLIDARITIES

Jamaican chief minister Norman Manley traveled to London to investigate the riots and found racial bias to be prevalent among both civilians and the police. Metropolitan Police stopped Manley while he was speaking with four of his countrymen in Paddington only a week after the fracases subsided. Manley was told that he was not allowed to hold a public meeting in the street despite the fact that thirty or forty whites were congregated down the road at the very same time.[50] Although discouraged by such hostility, Manley insisted that limits on migration to Britain were wrong and impracticable. More than 1,000 people, mostly West Indians, attended Manley's address at Friends House on September 8, 1958. Manley explained he arrived on behalf of all West Indians in London and came "to give . . . [them] courage and strength . . . advice, and . . . to challenge decent British public opinion."[51] He insisted, "it would be tragic . . . if the British Government departed from the policy of an open door to immigration for citizens from the Commonwealth because of the violence of a minority."[52] He praised the Commonwealth and advocated for the continued open relationship between the West Indies and the metropole. Manley commended the Commonwealth for "millions of people in the world . . . believe . . . [it] is one of the most hopeful and greatest institutions of modern civilization."[53] West Indians had been pilloried by native Britons for their perceived unwillingness to assimilate into the British way of life and the Jamaican Premier, on the cusp of independence in the British Caribbean nevertheless offered his praise and adoration for the Commonwealth, the strongest tie to British colonial dominance.

Manley was especially convinced of the potential power and influence of a unified migrant community. During his visit he urged West Indians to "build up solidarity between you"[54] as a call for collective action. Manley's encouragement galvanized West Indians throughout the city. Trinidadian Frank Crichlow who, along with Michael de Freitas and hundreds of others, battled Teddy boys in the street, noticed the impact Manley's pleas for solidarity had on his political perspective. Crichlow explained the concerted effort undertaken to "meet in blues dances . . . socialising, getting to know folks from the different Caribbean islands." He remembered parties where "people dropped their guards because although we were a hundred people in a dance hall all from different parts of the Caribbean we were still West Indians in London we had all suffered the riots, and we had a lot in common to talk about."[55]

Dr. Nnamdi Azikiwe, prime minister of Eastern Nigeria, corroborated Manley's sentiments. He did not "support any idea of [immigration] control solely on the basis of race."[56] Azikiwe also praised the Commonwealth regarding it as an institution which "had always set an example of liberalism on racial issues" crediting liberal ideals as "responsible more than anything else for the survival of the Commonwealth."[57] Manley and Azikiwe both championed the legacy of racial inclusiveness as central to the Commonwealth ethos and as a major impetus for citizens from their constituencies to travel to Britain. Like the images and iconography of empire that spurred many thousands of colonial citizens to the metropole, both leaders reaffirmed the notion that Britain was an accepting place where Jamaicans and Nigerians should be able to enjoy full privileges of citizenship, even after Notting Hill. The promises of greater opportunity in Britain for Commonwealth citizens forced colonial leaders to investigate the plight of migrants and to ensure their protections once in the mother country.

Over more than two weeks, white youths throughout London travelled to Notting Hill and attacked West Indian residents. Twelve people who were apprehended after rioting in Shepherd's Bush appeared before the magistrate at West London Court; they were sentenced and fined for their role in perpetuating the disorder. Michael Smith, a display artist from Tottenham, North London, was fined £12 for possession of a jack-knife and claimed that he ventured to Notting Hill "out of curiosity." Smith explained that he carried the knife as defense "against black people."[58] Robert Cooper, a 23-year-old driver from Middlesex, traveled to Lancaster Road brandishing a kitchen knife for which he was sentenced to three months in prison. Cooper traveled more than an hour on public transport in order to participate in the chaos in West London.[59] While many West Indians involved in the riots lived in Notting Hill, whites arrived from around London and suburbs in order to fight local residents. Many rioters of color were also arrested and charged with inciting violence and possession of dangerous weapons.

The swift mobilization of West Indians from across London to Notting Hill represented a revolutionary moment in the expression of patterns of solidarity among the migrants. Although many West Indian residents of Notting Hill initially sought refuge in their homes or congregated among themselves to avoid conflict with the Teds, people of color from around the capital came to their defense. The defiant rebuttal from other black and brown people from Brixton, Stepney, and Paddington was a response to white aggression and also codified the connections among disparate local populations. Jamaicans, Barbadians, Indians, Nigerians, and others residing in districts around the city mobilized to protect the safety of their fellow people of color. Teddy boys and the Union Movement, had unified against all people of color and in a moment of chaos and violent outbursts, these very populations united in mutual defense. The fragmented nature of intra-migrant relations paused during the outbreak of violence and in the subsequent years, morphed into a wide-ranging political movement.

On September 15, nine of the initial agitators of the riots each received four-year prison terms for their role in beginning the violence. Justice

Salmon scolded the boys: "Your quarry was any man . . . whose skin happened to be a different colour from your own . . . you savagely attacked five peaceful and law-abiding citizens without any shadow of an excuse . . . as far as the law is concerned you are entitled to think what you like, however vile your thoughts . . . but once you translate your dark thoughts and brutal feelings into savage acts such as these, the law will be swift to punish you and protect your victims."[60] Despite the popular coverage of the riots, Salmon's decision identified the fundamentally racialized quality of the violence. The assailants were convicted on the basis of attacking innocent citizens solely on account of their own racial prejudices. Because none of the assailants, who ranged in age from seventeen to twenty, had prior convictions, Salmon decided on sentences of four years, despite his condemnations.

Relationships between West Indians grew out of a shared sense of migrant experiences, built on exclusion from British society and common colonial pasts in the Caribbean. These connections intensified after Notting Hill and in areas across Britain. Born in 1958 in Dudley, West Midlands, Lenny Henry, remembered from early age communal associations and networks of communication among West Indians in his town. He recalled,

> The main thing I remember of my parents in Dudley was walking around and nodding to other black people who I didn't know. "Who was that?" "Oh, I don't know. It's just somebody, you've got to show your respect. Just to say Hello, it's good to just incline your head." . . . It was a nod of recognition of who we were . . . there was at first, a loneliness, and as people got to know each other, a network of people grew via the church, via bingo, via dominoes, via the pub, people in the same situation grew close. You grew your circle of friends, and I think that's what happened, eventually.[61]

Henry expressed a sense of belonging that he found difficult to fully articulate while describing his youth in Dudley. He acknowledged his interactions with strangers while walking down the street based on their outward appearance. Henry's reasoning that nodding was "recognition of who we were" articulated an identification that developed out of individual and shared consciousness. Black men in Dudley gestured to each another not necessarily because they knew each other's names, hometowns, or families, yet Henry recognized this moment as a demonstration of mutual recognition between strangers. The close link between ostensible strangers suggests an unspoken familiarity among West Indians in Great Britain. The initial cause for Henry's father to implore him to nod toward fellow West Indians likely developed from the need for belonging and recognition in the community. Though Henry was born in England, his Jamaican parents were not and their daily recognition of particular people suggests that they sought an unspoken bond. These bonds would strengthen and expand in the years after Notting Hill.

Henry's identification derived not only from his self-consciousness but also from his awareness of others. Ethnic self-identification was not an innate characteristic of West Indian migrants in Britain but reflected as process developed through relationships and systems of communication. West Indians socializing in pubs or at sporting events, or gathering in church were part of larger processes of community formation. As Henry suggested, the role of family in imparting particular social awareness was integral to his understanding of his place in society. From a young age, he paid respect to others based on their appearance, allying himself with other black West Indians. Henry, like many other interviewees, referenced the fact that his parents were Jamaican, noting an important distinction between his upbringing and theirs. These experiences highlight the blackening of British culture through claims-making efforts in public places in drinking establishments even in places like Dudley.

The significance of Henry's everyday interactions lies in their profoundly racialized nature. Henry was undeterred by the presence of white Britons in Dudley though he remained hyperaware of fellow black residents. Henry's lack of animosity toward whites, or non-black citizens suggest his identification was based on likeness with other West Indians and blacks rather than as oppositional with respect to the overwhelming white majority in Dudley. For Henry, black self-identification was learned from his family before he recognized its significance and became more pronounced in social settings beyond passing by strangers on the street. His last reflection that eventually he and other black youths grew closer suggests a sort of organic community formation with little reference to the racialized politics and social context of the time. Henry grew to appreciate the camaraderie of other West Indians because of the lessons his family gave him, but not solely from an individual racial identification. The initial exposure to other West Indians was stimulated by his father's motivations but Henry acknowledged social settings and a common racial and regional home as major influences on his consciousness. Much like sentiments expressed by West Indian eyewitnesses and participants in Notting Hill, Henry's associations with other West Indians were borne out of his estrangement from the majority of native Britons and the commonalities of experience with Caribbean migrants.

RESPONSES TO THE RIOTS

Baron Baker, a riot participant and ally of de Freitas, organized the United Africa-Asia League after Notting Hill. The League held open-air meetings on Thursday nights outside the Fortress (where they maintained a defense base during the riots). Amy Ashwood Garvey formed the Association for the Advancement of Coloured People and ran a hostel and Afro-centre in Notting Hill. Frances Ezzrecco began an organization, the Coloured People's Progressive Association in Notting Hill. By the end of 1958, CPPA had 500 members and de Freitas was vice president. During the inauguration of the CPPA Ezzrecco declared their plan "to bind the coloured people together and to make our people speak up for themselves."[62] Ezzrecco organized delegations to the Notting Hill police station to protest harassment, to Kensington Council to demand improvements in housing, and to the Trades Union Congress to agitate against the colour bar in employment. Sociologist Colin Prescod (chair of the Institute of Race Relations) was thirteen during the riots and watched from his Notting Hill home, his mother the Tobago-born actress Pearl Prescod at the front of anti-racist struggles with Trinidad-born Claudia Jones. Prescod was a classically trained opera singer who failed to find work in London because "opera was not integrated yet." Prescod remembered Jones and his mother's efforts after the riots to lift, "from victimhood to resistance . . . a community [that] became more militant and said 'We're here and we're here in a big way."[63]

The threat of violence persisted after the riots subsided. On May 17, 1959, Kelso Cochrane, an Antiguan carpenter, was stabbed by a gang of white teens on a London street corner. Cochrane walked down Golborne Road in North Kensington, when five or six white youths came up behind him and struck. At the intersection of Golborne and Southam Street a woman witnessed youths approach Cochrane and a fight last all of two minutes.[64] Cochrane fell to the ground as the boys ran away before two black men picked him up and ushered him into a taxi. He died in the hospital from stab wounds to his chest.[65] Kenneth Augustus Steel witnessed the scuffle and ran toward Cochrane after the white youths fled. As Cochrane lay in the street he said to Steel, "those blokes asked me for money . . . I didn't have any, and they started fighting."[66] Cochrane's murder, like the riots of the prior year, spurred the public denouncement of racial violence and became a tragedy for people of color in London around which to rally. Alan Bashorun, chairman of the Committee of African Organizations, explained "coloured peoples feel they have confidence in the ability of the police to keep law and order."[67] Bashorun released this statement after meeting leaders of more than twenty colored people's organizations in the days after Cochrane's murder.

More than 1,200 people lined Ladbroke Grove for Cochrane's funeral procession. Near his grave the crowd "was crushed together . . . under the trees in Kensal Green cemetery . . . balancing on tombstones or clinging to the branches of trees."[68] The Interracial Friendship Co-ordinating Council planned the funeral, which wound a mile through the streets of

Notting Hill from St. Michael and All Angels' Church in Ladbroke Grove to Kensal Green. One West African boy in white robes and turban ambled through the crowd handing out leaflets that read "It could be you."[69] The brutality of Cochrane's murder was significant for migrants and the notion that the staunchly anti-black agitators would attack again engulfed the day. Cochrane's death brought many local residents as well as luminaries from the West Indies including Grantley Adams, prime minister of the Federation of the West Indies and Garnett Gordon, the Federation's Commissioner in London.

Cochrane's murder spurred the migrant community to action immediately. Less than a week after his killing, on May 22, a "defence committee for the immediate protection of African and West Indian people and property in Britain . . . [had] been set up by an association of African, West Indian, and British organizations."[70] Migrants were intimidated by both the police and Teddy boys so deigned to protect themselves and their community through their own vigilante force. Bashorun, chairman of the Committee of African Organizations in Britain, petitioned Home Secretary R.A. Butler to "allow able-bodied Africans and West Indians to join a special constabulary to add to the force in troubled areas such as Notting Hill."[71] Despite the disjointed organization of rioters on both sides, migrants sought firstly to align themselves with the police in order to retain stability in the affected areas. Bashorun explained that failing approval to be absorbed into the police force, West Indians would organize their own defense and "make every household aware of what is happening in the next house, so that any little thing that happens we shall know about in a few minutes."[72] Intimate relationships were essential for the migrant population as they sought to ensure one another's safety and recognized that they could not rely on either the "good nature" of their British neighbors or the protection of the police. Bashorun noted that the local migrants did not have confidence in police authorities and complained that the local councils "had failed to speak out against the violence in the Notting Hill area."[73] Dissatisfied by the protections offered to them, Bashorun spoke out for colored migrants who insisted that they take control of their residences and protect one another.

Bashorun led a delegation comprising representatives from forty African, West Indian, British, and Asian organizations (Interracial Friendship Co-ordinating Council) in a meeting with the Home Office soon after he announced plans for a West Indian defense group. The representatives charged the police with "continued tolerance . . . of race hate propaganda . . . [which] resulted in Cochrane's murder."[74] In their meeting with Home Secretary Butler, the Council suggested "an appeal for a cessation of racial propaganda should be made to the nation from the highest level."[75] The deputation also noted that racist incitement increased since the murder of

Cochrane. They cited increased activity of, "League of Empire Loyalists, White Defence League, National Labour Party, Ku Klux Klan, and the Union Movement . . . openly propagating race hatred . . . which has resulted in a situation in which ordinary citizens of all races cannot walk the streets without fear of being involved in the disturbances."[76] West Indians felt vulnerable during the riots and the weak governmental and police response in the months after only exacerbated these feelings. While they were mobilizing in new organizations, colored migrants also noticed the accelerated racist mobilization of a plethora of far-right, anti-immigrant organizations.

While West Indians were aware of the influence of the Union Movement on the Teddy boys, the *Times* absolved Unionists as the cause of the riots. Despite Unionists distributing their newspaper *Action* throughout Notting Hill as well as pamphlets encouraging followers to "Back Mosley in the Fight," the *Times* argued, "there is no evidence that the party are the cause of them [riots]."[77] The Unionists held meetings to quiet the Teddy boys and affirmed that their propaganda was "directed towards diverting racial hatred to anti-Government feeling rather than inciting violence."[78] Mosley preferred to frame his racist platform as a critique of the British government and argued that he offered alternative immigration and employment policies. G. Hamm, a Union Movement spokesperson, blamed "the Government which has thrown open the floodgates to a stream of coloured immigrants driven here by unemployment at home."[79] Mosley and his followers maintained that they were exploiting the riots to their advantage rather than inciting them through any official party policy. In addition to *Action*, Mosley published a monthly magazine, *European*, which contained his periodical political commentary. The *Times*, like much of the popular press, regarded the activity of Union Movement members to be largely out of line with Mosley's official policy. They recognized the anti-immigrant and anti-Communist foundation of the Movement while ignoring the possibility that these tendencies also contributed to violence in the streets of Notting Hill.

A. K. Chesterton, chairman of the Policy Committee of the League of Empire Loyalists, affirmed accusations that the League engaged in inciting racial hatred. He admitted he did not know "what is meant by the term 'racist'" but nevertheless "if it be used to indicate a Briton who is proud of being British we accept the label."[80] He framed his racist politics as a British nationalist platform. Chesterton charged migrants with inciting the racial problems which exploded in the riots in Notting Hill and claimed the League was "opposed to the creation of colour problems . . . where none have hitherto existed . . . West Indians should be given an economic square deal in their own lands so that they are not driven abroad by economic pressures."[81] Chesterton's racialized perspectives were couched in the discourse of providing nonwhite, non-native Britons with opportunities in their homelands as a means to keep them out of the metropole. Chesterton asserted that the League did not promote hatred against the migrants, only advocating that they not venture to Britain.

Chesterton's views of nonwhites in Britain was reflected in the views of other native Britons and represented in the popular press. Some white Britons stereotyped West Indian migrants as prone to all manner of criminality from prostitution to bodily harm. In 1959, a year after the riots, "118 out of the 156 cases of serious assault reported to the police had involved white people only . . . 16 . . . involved white and coloured persons."[82] Despite colored migrants bearing the brunt of culpability for the riots just a year prior, police records showed that whites were responsible for the overwhelming majority of violent crime in the area.

The White Defence League established offices in Notting Hill after the riots and mobilized against integration of colored peoples. The League maintained that racial troubles in Notting Hill were attributable to West Indian residents and that opening their office there was a dutiful response to the existent problems. One representative argued the most important issue raised by the West Indian presence was "mass interbreeding . . . that must lead ultimately to a mulatto Britain."[83] He insisted that the League felt, "if we have a mulatto population in the future that must mean the downfall of the civilization and culture of our nation which we hold so dearly."[84] This representative maintained that, "preventing the evils which must result from mass colored immigration by removing the problem completely . . . by stopping all further colored immigration into our country . . . and repatriating with every humane consideration colored immigrants who are already here."[85] After the violence in the area, the League intensified their racist, anti-immigrant campaigns, promoting their opposition to the ideals of Commonwealth from the center of the conflict.

At the end of May 1959, more than 600 people, mostly Asians, Africans, and West Indians, attended a meeting at St. Pancras Town Hall in memory of Cochrane. Agents from the Interracial Friendship Co-ordinating Council, the West Indian Federation, and the British Caribbean Association spoke on race relations in Britain, paying tribute to Cochrane and discussing methods of restoring confidence in the residents of Notting Hill.[86] Unlike some of the agitators during the riots, no one was tried or convicted for Cochrane's murder.

Many West Indians hoped to codify their place in British society to ensure their protection was absolutely necessary. West Indians began to offer sharp, consistent, and widely publicized critiques of British race relations along with recommendations for amelioration. Friends and family in the Caribbean were aware of the happenings in Britain and expressed concern and solidarity with migrants. On September 2, 1958, the West Indies Federal Government announced, "deputy Prime Minister, Dr. Carl Lacorbiniere would fly to

London immediately to confer with members of the British Government."[87] The Council of State held an emergency meeting where they expressed "growing alarm" at the racial disturbances in London and dispatched the deputy prime minister as soon as possible.

Lacorbiniere arrived in London with a mandate urging the British government to take immediate action to "stamp out racial hostility in Britain."[88] He chastised the government's response and insisted that they eliminate racial acrimony "in the same way, and just as ruthlessly, as the Mau Mau were stamped out in Kenya."[89] Lacorbiniere exposed the prolific and repressive nature of British colonial governance that kidnapped and tortured members of the Kenya Land and Freedom Army. The official response to the riots was viewed as lukewarm by migrants and colonial citizens in Africa and the Caribbean. Lecorbiniere indicted the British government for their vindictive response to the anti-colonial uprisings in Kenya and their comparatively passive response to racial disturbances in the metropole. The next year, he affirmed that throughout the West Indies "we are deeply disturbed . . . you will find it almost impossible to convince any West Indian that this was not a racial murder."[90] For Lecorbiniere and other West Indians, acknowledging the racial aspect of Cochrane's murder was crucial to their cause. Coroner Gavin Thurston retorted, "this must be regarded as a particularly wanton, somewhat aimless and very cowardly crime . . . there does not appear . . . to suggest that it necessarily has any racial connotation at all."[91]

Officials hesitated in recognizing the role race played in the murder of Cochrane. Popular coverage of his murder argued that "Cochrane was not murdered because he was coloured, but for money."[92] The whites who attacked Cochrane and Teds generally were regarded as being of "low mentality . . . professional criminals" and making up only a tiny percentage of the white population in Notting Hill. Despite most West Indian residents in Notting Hill having been relegated to that district purely on the basis of the unwillingness of landlords in other London areas to rent to them highlighting the prevalence of the housing color bar throughout the city, the violence of the riots was attributed solely to racist outliers like the Teddy boys. Whereas revolutionary anticolonialists in Kenya were targeted, Lecorbiniere declared, "Teddy boys . . . should be stamped out just as ruthlessly."[93] He lauded West Indians for their pride in "the way their multiracial society worked" and suggested the British government send "40 or 50 of these Teddy boys to the West Indies, so they could see how decent people live there."[94] Inverting the commonly held belief among Britons that they were more sophisticated and civilized than the incoming colonials, Lecorbiniere suggested young Britons travel to the colonies to experience civil society.

Dr. Hugh Cummins, Premier of Barbados, arrived in London on September 7, 1958, to support West Indian migrants and charged Teddy boys with instigating the disorders. Cummins explained Caribbean people "were worried about the possibility of a Ku Klux Klan organization being responsible for racial disturbances."[95] He noted that the troubles were result of Teddy boy aggression and the influence of fascism on young people in Britain. Cummins speculated that "the average Englishman doesn't explode into intense racial feeling . . . there is something deeper behind this."[96] The violence stirred what Cummins described as "harm to the Commonwealth." The Colonial Office long extolled the West Indian colonies as integral imperial holdings and the events in Notting Hill complicated the question of who was welcome in the metropole. Cummins was acutely aware of the perceived opportunities of migration to Britain and knew that violence would dissuade many of his constituents and countrymen from traveling to the capital for work or school. Furthermore, Barbados enjoyed an employment recruitment scheme to Britain and Barbadians in turn were especially used to friends or family heading to the metropole.[97] Although Lacorbiniere and Cummings ventured to London from the Caribbean to visit their countrymen and women in the aftermath of the riots, not one senior British politician traveled from Westminster to West London to do the same.

Migrant frustrations with police protection were exacerbated by the government's opinion that "police . . . [took] all the necessary action that lies in their power to preserve law and order."[98] As far-right groups were openly propagating anti-immigrant sentiment and intimidating migrants throughout the city, the government considered the police response adequate. The government also argued that "the suggestion that Africans and West Indians . . . be allowed to join a special constabulary . . . is not likely to be accepted . . . neither . . . that the African and West Indian organizations . . . be permitted to organize [their] . . . own defence."[99] West Indian and African appeals to the government were rejected even after the continued prospect of violence from white Britons persisted.

Disillusionment and frustration among migrants intensified following the riots although they responded in novel, politically radical ways. Migrants began unprecedented levels of civic engagement and social justice activism. Soon after the riots, migrants began publishing their own periodicals and organizing conferences to address the issues of racial inequality and prejudice in the United Kingdom and abroad.

POST-RIOT PRESS REACTIONS

Local newspapers such as the *South Kensington News* wrote on the simmering anxieties in West London but, some tabloids preferred to cover a wider variety of issues regarding black migrants. Racial animosity contributed to violence in Notting Hill and efforts to dispel these prejudices, campaigns advocating acceptance emerged in London. To mitigate noxious feelings between the races, the *Daily Mirror* offered a series of articles introducing the migrants of color to their readership. In presenting the "boys from Jamaica," the paper insisted to its audience that "people are human beings even though they come in different colours."[100] The paper presented data on the West Indies of the most basic and elementary level. Despite the historical relationship between Britain and the Caribbean, in September 1958 the *Daily Mirror* found it worthwhile to describe the West Indies as "a sunny chain of islands in the Caribbean, between North and South America."[101] To disabuse their readership of their limited knowledge of the constitution of empire, the paper reminded Britons that "Jamaica makes the sunshine things . . . sugar, banana, coffee, cocoa, rum, tobacco." In recognition of the poverty rife in the island, readers were alerted to the difficult economic conditions of "few jobs . . . [that] pay poor."[102]

Basic conditions of empire were largely unknown to metropolitan Britons. The *Daily Mirror* wrote of the imperial war effort when "10,000 Jamaicans [who] came voluntarily to this country to fight for Britain."[103] Contesting popular notions of migrants arriving to "live on the dole" a series of "Facts" were offered including the inability of criminals to be admitted to Britain, the largely Christian religious background of the migrants, and the poor conditions and difficulty in finding employment for the migrants.

On September 9, 1958, The *Daily Mirror* published an article on West Africans in London. Commending African migrants for arriving "to learn" the *Daily Mirror* hoped to mitigate the "ignorance of how people live . . . their aims and their ambitions" which was "behind the race riots." Journalist Keith Waterhouse offered the "facts about the coloured people who come to Britain."[104]

When Waterhouse introduced the "West Africans" to the *Mirror*'s readership, he firstly asserted that they "were not savages." Mainly arriving from Ghana and Nigeria, Waterhouse informed readers that these decolonizing states "produce 90 per cent of Britain's cocoa . . . [as well as] gold, tin, bananas, cotton, rubber, [and] groundnuts."[105] Because West African "earth is rich" but "people are poor" Waterhouse explained that the prevalence of diseases such as "malaria, smallpox, [and] blindness" in the region contributed to poor public health and high rates of childhood death.

Waterhouse explained that West Africans arrived to "learn about medicine, law, engineering . . . [to] take technical apprenticeships . . . learn about port and harbor duties, transport, tailoring, accountancy, banking, flying."[106] To depict the West Africans as deserving of Commonwealth membership, Waterhouse reminded Britons that "Ghana Parliament is based on our Parliament . . . their system of justice is based on our system . . . their Civil

Service is based on ours."[107] Similar to other perspectives on integration and acceptance from native Britons, Waterhouse characterized African migrants as acceptable because they were coming from societies whose political structures were modeled after British ones. Britons who argued for the integration of nonwhite peoples couched their descriptions of colored colonials in language recalling British ideals. Waterhouse lauded the Africans for paying Britain a "compliment . . . they look to us as the model for their future."[108]

An alternative to limiting colonial migration was advocacy for the development of a friendly Commonwealth. Although the backlash following Notting Hill villainized black and brown participants, not all British media coverage was unequivocal in placing blame. The *News Chronicle* in September 1958 argued for the importance of maintaining Britain's place in the Commonwealth by keeping the border open to migrants. George Tansey and George Holt, writing for the *Chronicle*, argued that migrants benefited from "our universities . . . continuously conveying culture, tradition and technology to the coloured mind."[109]

Tansey and Holt engaged spokesmen from Britain's communities of color who each argued that the imposition of an immigration ban would have significant ramifications across empire and particularly in the Commonwealth nations. West Indian Reverend Ronald Campbell insisted legal restrictions on migration "would be bowing to colour discrimination." The West African "spokesman" Bankole Timothy suggested "repercussions would be titanic in a predominantly coloured Commonwealth."[110] Jamaican student Herbert Lloyd George, frustrated by social relations in the United Kingdom, explained migrants of color "did not want or expect sympathy for the white man . . . no racial discrimination, anywhere, must be taught."[111]

Tansey and Holt argued for the "adoption and pursuit of more vigorous social legislation on vice and overcrowding, and in the creation of a greater sense of social responsibility."[112] Rather than legislating West Indians and Africans out of Britain, the investigators pursued policy reforms that would ameliorate the social ills that contextualized the violence in West London.

The *Daily Express* reported that "the majority of people in Britain think that the immigration of coloured people in this country should be controlled." Citing their own poll conducted over the first week of September 1958 the paper noted "79% want influx of colored people to be controlled."[113] Additionally, "81 percent of the poll's respondents in London favored immigration restrictions."[114] West Indians were charged with responsibility for the riots in Notting Hill by the British public; many Britons wished to prevent future outbreaks through the control of migrants from Africa and the Caribbean. Less critique was levied upon Teddy boys yet, West Indians further devised and implemented innovative responses in the wake of the riots.

NOTES

1. Edward Pilkington, *Beyond the Mother Country: West Indians and the Notting Hill White Riots* (London: Tauris, 1988), 106–107.
2. "Children March Through Streets," *Manchester Guardian*, September 2, 1958, 1.
3. "London Racial Outburst due to Many Factors," From Our Special Correspondent. *The Times*, Wednesday, September 3, 1958, 7.
4. Ibid.
5. Ibid.
6. Ibid.
7. Pilkington, *Beyond the Mother Country*. Pilkington is thorough in retelling the violence of the riots, and accounts for the tenuous atmosphere of Notting Hill during these two weeks. More than other studies, Pilkington's accounts of the actual violence present the clearest perspective into the type of environ Notting Hill was the time. Pilkington's specificity in addressing the housing crunch and discrimination in employment and services is critical. He pays special attention to precursor events that were linked to the riots. The added social contextualization in London works to fully communicate the riot's development.
8. Pilkington, conversation with Baron Baker, September 19, 1983, *Beyond the Mother Country*, 114.
9. *Daily Mail*, September 1, 1958, 1.
10. *Kensington News*, September 5, 1958, 1.
11. Pilkington conversation with John Garrett, January 20, 1988, *Beyond the Mother Country*, 119.
12. *Daily Mail*, September 2, 1958, 7.
13. Pilkington conversation with Chris Lemaitre, September 20, 1983, *Beyond the Mother Country*, 119.
14. Letter from Donald Chesworth to Edward Pilkington, January 10, 1985, *Beyond the Mother Country*, 119.
15. *Manchester Guardian*, September 4, 1958, 2.
16. Pilkington interview with King Dick, *Beyond the Mother Country*, March 21, 1988, 120.
17. Pilkington, *Beyond the Mother Country*.
18. Hall, *The Young Englanders Pamphlet*. Miscellaneous Pamphlets, National Committee for Commonwealth Immigrants, 3–5. British Library Shelfmark: X.0802/117.
19. Ibid.
20. Ibid., 9.
21. Ibid.
22. Ibid., 10.
23. Ibid.
24. Ibid.
25. Ibid.
26. De Freitas changed his name to Michael X in the mid-1960s as he became one of Britain's most prominent Black Power advocates.

27. Michael Abdul Malik, *From Michael de Freitas to Michael X* (London: Andre Deutsch, 1968), 76–79.
28. *Daily Mail*, September 2, 1958, 1.
29. Pilkington interview with Ivan Weekes, December 13, 1983, *Beyond the Mother Country*, 122.
30. *Windrush* was created for a popular audience and was a response to late twentieth-century notions of the multiracial makeup of Britain.
31. Catherine Hall and Sonya Rose, *At Home with the Empire: Metropolitan Culture and the Imperial World* (Cambridge: Cambridge University Press, 2006), 20.
32. Ibid.
33. Phillips, Interview with Rudy Braithwaite, *Windrush*, 164.
34. Phillips, Interview with Herman Ouseley, *Windrush*, 143.
35. Hinds wrote a memoir, *Journey to an Illusion*, which included interviews and accounts from other migrants he encountered throughout the city.
36. Donald Hinds, *Journey to An Illusion: The West Indian in Britain* (London: Heinemann, 1966), 11.
37. Ronald Carl Giles, "Now There's an Embarrassment for Yer, Tosh," *Sunday Express*, September 7, 1958, n.p.
38. John Musgrave-Wood, *Daily Mail*, September 3, 1958, n.p.
39. Ronald Carl Giles, *Daily Express*, August 9, 1962, n.p.
40. Ibid.
41. Victor Weisz, *Daily Mirror*, September 2, 1958, n.p.
42. Hinds, *Journey to an Illusion*, 134.
43. Ibid. Also see Dick Hebdige, *Subculture: The Meaning of Style* (New York: Routledge, 1979).
44. Mosley initially formed the British Union of Fascists and changed the name to the Union Movement in 1940. Richard Thurlow, *Fascism in Britain: A History, 1918–1998* (London: I.B. Tauris, 1998), 214.
45. Mike and Trevor Phillips, Interview with Vincent Reid, *Windrush*, 178.
46. "Renewed Racial Disturbances in London," *The Times*, Tuesday, September 2, 1958, 10.
47. Alan Dein, Interview with Vincent Reid, April 1998, "*London Voices*, Museum of London, April 1998.
48. Ibid.
49. Ibid. There were a number of important black-owned pubs and restaurants including the Mangrove, Totobag's Café, the store I Was Lord Kitchener's Valet and the earlier meeting space operated by Amy Ashwood Garvey, the Florence Mills Social Club.
50. *The Evening Standard*, September 8, 1958, n.p.
51. "West Indians Give Mr. Manley Enthusiastic Reception," *Times*, September 8, 1958, 6.
52. Ibid.
53. Ibid.
54. *Manchester Guardian*, September 8, 1958, 1.
55. Pilkington, Interview with Crichlow, January 20, 1988.

56. Our Correspondent, "Nigerian Leader on Racial Problem," *Times*, September 9, 1958, 6.
57. Ibid.
58. "55 Charged After Racial Street Disturbances," *The Times*, Thursday, September 4, 1958, 7.
59. Ibid.
60. "You Filled the Nation with Indignation," *Daily Mail*, September 16, 1958, n.p.
61. Phillips, Interview with Lenny Henry, *Windrush*, 143. Henry was from the Midlands—away from the violence in London—his memories of racial animosity reflected realities throughout Britain. A racial riot in St. Ann's, Nottingham also erupted in August 1958.
62. *Kensington News*, September 19, 1958, 1.
63. "White Riot: The Week Notting Hill Exploded," *The Independent*, August 29, 2008.
64. "Coloured Man Stabbed to Death," *The Times*, Monday, May 18, 1959, 6.
65. "Jim Crow Shout Near Notting Hill," *Daily Herald*, May 18, 1959, n.p.
66. "Murder Verdict on West Indian," *Times*, August 6, 1959, 6.
67. "We Have Lost Confidence in London Police," *Daily Herald*, May 20, 1959, n.p.
68. "Big Crowd at West Indian's Burial," *Times*, June 8, 1959, 6.
69. Ibid.
70. Defence Group for Coloured People. *The Times*, Friday, May 22, 1959, 7.
71. Ibid.
72. Ibid.
73. Ibid.
74. "Talks on Race Tension," *Times*, May 25, 1959, 10.
75. "Coloured Plea to Mr. Butler," *Times*, May 28, 1959, 12.
76. Ibid.
77. Our Special Correspondent. "Union Movement Not Cause Of Racial Clashes," *Times*, September 8, 1958, 6.
78. Ibid.
79. Ibid.
80. A. K. Chesterton, "Inter-Racial Conflict," *Times*, June 4, 1959, 13.
81. Ibid.
82. A Special Correspondent. "Immigrants Put Out New Roots," *Times*, June 3, 1960, 7.
83. "Racial Troubles in Notting Hill," (1959) British Pathé https://www.youtube.com/watch?v=aGi_wIWRYys.
84. Ibid.
85. Ibid.
86. "Murdered Man Mourned," *The Manchester Guardian*, May 29, 1959.
87. "Reports Made to Mr. Butler," *The Times*, Wednesday, September 3, 1958, 10.
88. "West Indies Call for Ruthless Suppression of Race Hostility," *The Times*, Monday, May 25, 1959, 6.

89. Ibid.
90. Ibid.
91. "Murder Verdict on West Indian," 6.
92. Our Special Correspondent. "Superficial Quiet of North Kensington," *Times*, May 20, 1959, 4.
93. "Murder Verdict on West Indian, 6.
94. Ibid.
95. "Barbados Premier Arrives," *The Times*, September 8, 1958, 8.
96. Ibid.
97. See the Barbados London Transport Hiring Scheme of mid-1950s.
98. "Africans at Home Office to-Day," *Times*, May 27, 1959, 10.
99. Ibid.
100. "Introducing You to the Boys from Jamaica," *Daily Mirror*, September 8, 1958.
101. Ibid.
102. Ibid.
103. Ibid.
104. "The Men Who Come Here from West Africa to Learn," *Daily Mirror*, September 9, 1958.
105. Ibid.
106. Ibid.
107. Ibid.
108. Ibid.
109. "Keep Britain's Door Wide Open," *New Chronicle*, September 11, 1958.
110. Ibid.
111. Ibid.
112. Ibid.
113. "It's an Emphatic Yes! 79% Want Influx of Coloured People to be Controlled," *Daily Express*, September 6, 1958.
114. Ibid.

Chapter 5

Diasporic Artist-Activists and Imperial Reckoning

Academic and Grassroots Responses to Notting Hill

After 1958, Caribbean and African activists radicalized their political attitudes and the mechanisms of their engagement. Rather than addressing the common problems of lack of access to electoral privileges or civil rights, after Notting Hill radicals developed resistance predicated on novel racial and class-based identifications in Britain and extending to networks around the world. The emergence of a politically perspicacious black press in London initiated a reframed perspective on the problems of racialization—black people would now control the narratives constructed around their presence in the metropole.

THE BLACK PRESS AND POLITICAL PRESSURE

Link debuted in autumn 1958, claiming (inaccurately) its place as "The First British Negro Magazine." In an article titled "Does the Negro Hate the White Man?" J. Egyptien Compton argued that blacks' "regard for the white man is more one of resentment at his injustice rather than actual hatred." Compton made this claim in the immediate aftermath of the riots.[1] He affirmed the notion that black people were especially capable of sophisticated rational thought. Blacks did not hate whites because they were unaware of the extent of the damage of slavery, colonialism, and racialization. Rather, they resented whites for failing to meet their own standards of justice and equality. Compton offered suggestions for the British government in dealing with the status of black Britons after Notting Hill. He explained the government needed to ensure blacks were "not refused employment; charged higher rentals; persecuted on unjustified charges of immorality."² Compton contested that the government was responsible for unfair treatment of its citizens.

Link prioritized Black History as critical to the promotion of solidarity among the black migrant class. The magazine celebrated the first anniversary of the Black Star Line, a Ghanaian shipping line operating voyages on the *SS Volta River* between Ghana and Europe. *Link* praised Marcus Garvey for sowing "the spiritual seeds of self-respect . . . in the Negro . . . Negroes . . . began the slow, tortuous, upward, return journey to self-respect and worldwide recognition as human beings."³ *Link* educated black people of their histories to raise awareness and the self-respect and dignity of the race. In November 1958, the *SS Volta River* completed its fifth trip between Ghana and Europe and the Black Star Line planned to add two more ships to its fleet. Despite no actual ties between Garvey's planned line and this Ghanaian Merchant Navy operation, the shared name was enough for *Link* to highlight and celebrate the two, as a direct correlation between black peoples in Africa and the diaspora in Jamaica and Europe.⁴

Beyond historical references, *Link* also appealed to its readership to take an active role in British politics. *Link* urged readers to strive to become Britain's first black Members of Parliament. Readers were reminded that there were "several cities in England where there is a concentration of Negroes . . . at least enough to . . . give Negro voters their first opportunity to genuinely exercise their vote . . . give other . . . Negroes courage to follow his example and strive for political honours in Whitehall and . . . by the proper conduct of his campaigning establish such a pattern of behaviour as to prevent the future possibility of 'vote baiting' on the basis of colour."⁵ Blacks throughout Britain were encouraged to politically mobilize and to utilize their citizenship rights, including holding elected office. Despite the quotidian discrimination they faced, Caribbean colonials had full rights of Citizens of the United Kingdom and Colonies. *Link* lamented, "if they are Negro, British, and over 21 there is little reason why they cannot hope to become Britain's first Negro M.P."⁶ This suggestion illustrated how *Link* understood the potential of framing British politics despite coming from the colonial territories.

Link broadened its coverage of multiple facets of black migrant life through updates on the sporting triumphs of black boxers who were in a glorious heyday during the late 1950s. Since "negroes do not think much of themselves because they do not know enough about themselves," *Link* announced, "the heavy, light-heavy, middle, welter, light, and featherweight champions of the world today are Negroes."⁷ *Link* hoped to bolster the self-confidence, race pride, and dignity of black peoples by celebrating these leading athletes.

Organizations such as the Clapham Interracial Club, founded in the spring of 1959, intended to become an avenue for interracial cooperation and community building. Jamaican Vince Reid credited the riots with the "formation of the Black Political . . . social cum political groups like the Association of Jamaicans . . . people like Claudia Jones . . . publishing her paper, her journal, so you started to get politicisation of black people around that time . . . it was after the riots that they came into existence."[8] For Reid, the riots were the impetus for the radicalization of a black political consciousness in Britain.

CLAUDIA JONES

Among the most influential activist-organizers was Trinidad-born Claudia Jones. Jones arrived in London in 1955 after being deported from the United States for violating the McCarran Act due to her membership in the U.S. Communist Party.[9] Her work advancing racial issues within the British Communist Party led to further marginalization and estrangement from the Party, but also provided the stimulus for Jones to reorient her work to racial uplift rather than solely class-based politics. Her work in establishing the *West Indian Gazette* in Brixton allowed Caribbean writers to express themselves in a widely circulated periodical intended for a specific local audience. Although the Caribbean community was composed of migrants from various island origins, their histories in the West Indies united them into a collectivity within Britain. The sense that West Indians were constantly striving for a place in British society must be questioned when contrasted with recollections of Jones' efforts to advance a particular community formation. Rather than focusing only on a British ideal or migrant identity in flux, Jones pursued an explicitly West Indian consciousness. Although unbound by national boundaries, the West Indian community Jones envisioned was reflective of a group tied by ancestral linkages and origins in the Caribbean.[10] For Jones, the riots figured as the "extreme manifestation of the racialism which underlies the present status of West Indians in Britain."[11] Despite the exposure of the undercurrents of racialism, Jones championed the solidarity between West Indian, African, and Asian migrants in the face of white antagonism. She identified the latent racial political consciousness among the migrants of color in the capital.

As founder and editor of the *Gazette*, Jones was integral in the radicalization of the London West Indian community and her efforts in drawing connections between migrants from an array of colonies remains influential. Jamaican Sam King campaigned with Jones to build a network of West Indians in London. He explained, "just before the Notting Hill Riot . . . I was allotted Camberwell, Claudia was allotted Brixton . . . the new people coming in they had to be documented . . . get other people to take them to the labour exchange . . . you were a caretaker."[12] King, Jones, and others welcomed West Indians to Britain and assisted them in obtaining jobs. King remembered media coverage of events in the West Indian community and the wide-ranging networks of communication among migrants throughout Great Britain. He explained, "the established newspaper always say what was happening but it was very negative in England. The *Jamaica Gleaner* started having a weekly series here . . . we have the *West Indian Gazette* and *Afro-Asian Opinion* . . . we also have a system . . . a large amount of us are in the hospitals or the railway or the Post Office. Whatever happen in Manchester if it was urgent I would know in London within two hours."[13]

Donald Hinds, contributor to the *West Indian Gazette* and author of *Journey to An Illusion: The West Indian in Britain*, a narrative account of his life in Britain, articulated the notion of West Indian identification in the United Kingdom. Hinds observed,

> Outside the world of cricket the West Indies is not a nation and does not act as one. Yet the migrant in Britain speaks of himself as a West Indian . . . he clings to his "West Indian" status . . . he probably shared the first floor of a house for two months with some Barbadians before it was discovered that he was not from "Little England." He is probably teamed up with a Guianese driver at the bus garage . . . the prototype Barbadian is no longer Clyde Walcott, nor is the Trinidadian Dr. Eric Williams. The Barbadian is the girl he goes to evening school with and the Trinidadian the Indian who cuts his hair at the barber-shop![14]

The intimacy of the migrant experience—boarding, working, and traveling together throughout England—brought West Indians together in unprecedented ways. Hinds noted that the archetypal Trinidadian in England was not Prime Minister Williams but more likely another migrant working in the community. For Hinds, West Indian networks operated outside of nation-states and national identity, the shared experiences in the metropole facilitated a heightened political consciousness.

The *West Indian Gazette* advanced a radical political platform, advocating for the equal treatment of people of color in Britain while engaged with anticolonial movements and newly independent state formation throughout the Caribbean, Africa, and Asia. In the months after the riots, the *Gazette* reported on the consistent harassment of West Indians by London Metropolitan Police and white youths. Racial epithets were scrawled across street signs and buildings on a weekly basis, a reminder of the wave of violence from earlier in 1958.

The paper campaigned for civil rights for citizens of the colonies, often invoking the notion of Britain as the "mother country." In late 1959, the *Gazette* reported on the introduction of anti-discrimination legislation in Parliament, urging "Notting Hill and Nottingham are bad polities for any party and are not easily forgotten. Official condemnation of outbreaks of racial violence is something on which all major political parties can agree."[15] In 1961, the *Gazette* explained the ramifications of the Commonwealth Immigrants Act in detail, highlighting the restrictions on migration in the bill. Clause 2 of the bill stated Commonwealth citizens would not be denied entry, "(c) if the person wishes to enter for the purposes of employment and holds a current voucher issued by the Ministry of Labour (UK) [or] (d) if he is in a position to support himself and his dependents without taking up employment in the United Kingdom."[16] Legal immigration to Britain would be restricted along lines of employment, preventing those without prearranged jobs from entry. The *Gazette* valued its role as a vehicle for the dissemination of information as well as the vanguard of political awareness and activism in the West Indian community. Jones and the *Gazette* staff considered the periodical to be a crucial element for political mobilization and representative of the radical and racialized perspectives of London's migrant community.

In the 1960s, the *Gazette* reported on other incidents of racially motivated violence throughout London. In January 1960, the *Gazette* offices were under threat of violence from British Nazis, seeking to avenge the imprisonment of abusive white officers who had been reprimanded. An anonymous caller threatened the *Gazette* warning that their offices would be attacked. This message prompted Jones to issue a statement denouncing the menace of Nazism and championing the anti-racist politics of the newsletter. Serving as the political mouthpiece of its leadership, the *Gazette* frequently read like a manifesto, projecting anti-racist and anticolonial politics in its editorials and including sections that highlighted contributions West Indians made in British society. After the Nazi threats, the editorial board appealed for a unified West Indian political engagement. They insisted, "West Indian unity, whether a product of necessity or not, is real . . . we need not look to the years of common experience of a colonial administration, the common racial stock of our people or even the common phenomena of slavery and the subordination of our wills. We need only look to our present common poverty and the need for joint economic planning, the common defamation and humiliation we encounter in some places abroad."[17] By formulating a politics based on shared history as well as the common experience of discrimination and violent aggression in London, the *Gazette* developed a racial political consciousness that was historically aware and oriented around the particular experience of migrants in Britain.

A recurring column in the *Gazette*, "Know Your History," retold major events in the Caribbean to inform migrants of the Caribbean past while abroad. Donald Hinds also wrote a column, "About People," chronicling the efforts of people of color in obtaining work in London, retaining connections to the Caribbean, and negotiating British social relations. A Jamaican born London Transport worker offered an opinion encapsulating the sentiments of many migrants. When asked how he legitimated his claim to employment and residence in Britain he told Hinds, "this is our Mother Country, and as such we have a right to be here."[18] Many migrants made similar claims, emphasizing their understanding of close connections between the Caribbean and Britain. Despite growing native resentment to the migrant presence, West Indians retained a sense of their right to belonging in Britain.

CULTURE AND POLITICS

The *West Indian Gazette* went beyond printing and circulating ideology; they reported on the establishment of cultural and political institutions in London. In 1960, the *Gazette* reported on the founding of the New Caribbean Committee, the growth of the largely West Indian congregation of Roscoe Methodist Church in Leeds, and celebrated a successful Caribbean Carnival. First held at St. Pancras Town Hall in 1959, and modeled after the Trinidad Carnival, the event recreated that specific Caribbean tradition in the United Kingdom.[19] Jones's keynote speech at the Carnival, "A People's Art is the Genesis of Their Freedom," espoused the cultivation of a West Indian social space within the British context. Jones lauded the work of the Carnival organizers:

> Rarely have the creative energies of a people indigenous to another homeland been so quickly and spontaneously generated to such purpose as witness the work of the Caribbean Carnival Committee . . . it is as if the vividness of our national life was itself the spark urging translation to new surroundings, to convey, to transplant our folk origins to British soil. There is a comfort in this effort . . . for all West Indians, who strain to feel and hear and reflect their idiom even as they strain to feel the warmth of their sun-drenched islands and its immemorable beauty of landscape and terrain.[20]

Transplanting folk origins to the British metropole enabled the carving out of a distinctly West Indian public space within London. Jones emphasized the common distinction of Caribbean homelands in order to promote a consciousness that accounted for disparate groups who were living in Britain.

Carnival provided Jones with the opportunity to endorse pride in West Indian identity. She characterized West Indians as unique peoples who had contributed both to their new home in Britain and the world. Jones proclaimed, "A pride in being West Indian is undoubtedly at the root of the unity: a pride that has its origin in the drama of nascent nationhood, and that pride encompasses not only the creativeness, uniqueness and originality of West

Indian mime, song, and dance – but is the genesis of the nation itself. It is true to say that [this] pride extends not only to what the West Indians have proudly established in the culture of the Caribbean but to the treasury of world culture."[21] Jones insinuated that West Indians had more to offer metropolitan Britain than could be recognized by its native white citizens. Carnival was a manifestation of a developing West Indian community outlook in London. Jones's characterizations bonded West Indians from disparate locations into a burgeoning collectivity.

Carnival was a novel expression of West Indian claims over public space in London. Although initially held indoors, Carnival moved to an outdoor street festival in Notting Hill in 1966. The struggle for representation in public spaces continued in the aftermath of the riots, with many West Indians resorting to meeting in shebeens when refused service at pubs or restaurants. Soon after the founding of the New Caribbean Committee, D. L. Fitzpatricio, the *Gazette's* West Indies journalist, reported that the lack of safe public space concerned migrants. He explained, "We have almost no facilities for recreation; no halls of our own, no club premises where games may be played. The fight for integration is often too gradual . . . For tomorrow is born today and if social integration is to become a reality then it rests with our people and with these types of genuine white colleagues who desire with us first class citizenship for all."[22] Outside of Carnival, West Indians struggled to freely associate without the threat of violence from fascists or police harassment.

The violence in Notting Hill shocked West Indians living in London and their friends and families back in the Caribbean, but also represented metaphysical assault on notions of belonging to the empire and Commonwealth. Reflecting on the impetus for migration earlier in 1958, Jamaican poet John Figueroa explained that "causes of the migration are . . . not only economic . . . West Indians . . . are looking for . . . more money . . . also going to the place where they actually make the razor blades one has been using for years . . . where the 'Reading Book' used during the few years of schooling was printed, where the great game of cricket comes from."[23] After Notting Hill, migrants' salutary notions of the mother country had been critically impinged, many West Indians were existentially displaced before leaving their home islands. Figueroa explained the prestige assigned to West Indians able to travel and live in the "mother country." He recalled that West Indians strove to earn "diplomas and certificates which will ensure . . . not only a good job but certain status and prestige when one returns to the West Indies."[24] The unprovoked violence of the Teddy boys and Unionists in summer 1958 undermined positive impressions of the metropole for West Indians across the city and empire. Britain functioned as the material, epistemological, and cultural center of the colonial worldview. Rather than seeking jobs in the severely limited political economies of the Caribbean, migrants understood their right to enter and work in Britain and also vaunted the accomplishments and experiences of their kin and friends who had success in the metropole. The Notting Hill Riots irrevocably mutated the notion of Britain as the mother country for some migrants throughout the Caribbean as well as some who had settled in Britain.

Caribbean networks of communication helped migrants to organize in the 1960s. Newspapers were tools for politically radical West Indians to spread their messages and to broaden their support base. The *Gazette* focused on issues of race and racialism throughout Britain, the United States, the Caribbean, and Africa. The paper's wide-ranging political perspective, including advocating the amelioration of racial prejudice and striving toward anticolonialism, was influential for migrants in Britain who remained tied to the Caribbean and who maintained connections outside of Britain. Over 500 people who came to St. Pancras Hall in September 1960 to hear Paul Robeson sing to commemorate the second anniversary of the *Gazette* exemplified what its founders sought to establish through mobilizing black political consciousness in Britain. Because the Caribbean figured largely in the political imaginations of migrants, the *Gazette* offered a vital link for West Indians to the political and cultural affairs of Caribbean and African homelands. The paper's transnational perspective framed its radical politics, emphasizing linkages between people of color in Britain and throughout the world and promoting an anticolonial, anti-racist agenda.

Beyond reporting on racial prejudice in Britain and chronicling the political transformations throughout the world, the *Gazette* also aimed to make a lasting epistemological contribution for West Indians. "Know Your History" columns provided readers with information about historical events in the Caribbean which offered a connection to West Indian history for the migrant community and located the origins of West Indian culture and society in events in the Caribbean, acknowledging the critical role of West Indian agency. Rather than reverting to histories which valorized the role the British played in the development of the Caribbean, such as the lionization of William Wilberforce's abolitionism, informing West Indians of the activities of Paul Bogle during the Morant Bay rebellion fundamentally reoriented Caribbean history to highlight the contributions of blacks. Tributes to contemporaneous figures such as Eric Williams, citing his intellectual and political contributions to the modern Caribbean deepened connections between West Indians at home and abroad.

Regarding itself as a beacon of the West Indies, the *Gazette* "played an important part in the lives of West Indians four thousand miles from home . . . [it] has identified itself with the aims and aspirations of many West Indians in this country as well as it has helped to keep them in touch with the tremendous efforts and progress in the West Indies."[25] Conceptualizing itself as representative, the *Gazette* articulated a West Indianess in Britain based on shared pasts, and similar political orientation. The riots were a milestone in the politicization of West Indians but the *Gazette*'s coverage of the near quotidian expression of anti-immigrant sentiment in Britain demonstrates that the specter of racial violence continued to figure significantly in migrants' lives and impacted their interactions with one another and with native Britons.

Government response to the riots was mixed—some perpetrators were arrested, arraigned, convicted, and sentenced for their role in the riots;many of the problems which contributed to the strained race relations in Notting Hill were nonetheless attributed to the colored migrants. West Indians and Africans were charged with congregating "in limited areas . . . where the housing is of a low standard . . . many coloured persons . . . are very ignorant of public health and housing standards in this country and . . . are more likely to accept without question lower standards and amenities."[26] The presence of West Indians in Notting Hill, according to the Health Office, disrupted social relations in the area. West Indians were deemed responsible for overcrowding, despite being kept out of housing accommodations throughout most of the city. Patterns of racialized exclusion were attributed to the West Indians and colored migrants rather than the prejudiced landlords and employers.

R. J. Youard, Minister of Housing and Local Government in Kensington, complained of colored immigrants' "inability" to live in a metropolitan area. She cited reports from Public Health Inspectors that referred to "the dirt and incontinence of coloured people . . . men urinating on the floors of their rooms."[27] Health Inspector records show little proof of human waste in the West Indian residential units though the notion that the migrants were unkempt in their homes persisted. Youard attributed West Indian behaviors to foreignness claiming, "what is permissible in back gardens in the Islands is not acceptable indoors in London."[28] Rumors of decrepit conditions in West Indian residences in Notting Hill abounded and were emphasized to codify the differences between native Britons and incoming migrants. Youard suggested that the tensions arose because of "the extreme sensitiveness of coloured people which made it difficult, if not impossible, to explain why some request of theirs could not be agreed to without their saying, 'It is just because I am coloured.'"[29] Youard charged West Indians with expressing poor attitudes toward assimilation and accused migrants of assuming social problems were due to racial inequalities in Britain. Despite these specious claims, Youard acknowledged that during the riots "the hooligans were locals . . . the damage was organised by the Union Movement . . . the attacks were made on houses . . . occupied by coloured men."[30] Even from the perspective of local community leaders, who charged the colored immigrants with poor hygiene and mismanagement of their accommodations, they nonetheless recognized the agitators and instigators of the riots had ties to the Union Movement.

It is evident that the violence in Notting Hill was a part of a longer history of anti-immigrant, racist aggression in Britain. Notting Hill, however, spurred politicization along lines of race and national origin to such a degree that numerous organizations emerged as a direct result of the riots. Memories and testimonies of riot participants point to two major trends: claims of self-defense in the face of violence from native Britons, and the framing of their action as part of West Indian articulations of identification. The rapid development of racial cooperation committees reflected the need for West Indians to address problems of their particular condition but also their struggle for belonging with greater British society. Even the *West Indian Gazette*, with its radical platform, emphasized inclusion into the British body politic rather than Caribbean separatism. West Indians retained their aspirations for inclusion in British society and their political outlook in the aftermath of the riots continued to reflect the pursuit of belonging to the British national community. The expansion of mutual identification among West Indian migrants in London and between radical members of the migrant community and the Caribbean was developed out of a radicalized politics in the aftermath of Notting Hill.[31]

The media coverage of the riots, though biased in favor of the white agitators, was nevertheless widespread, reaching the Caribbean on a regular basis. Eric and Jessica Huntley, born in 1920s British Guiana but living in London since 1954, opened Bogle-L'Ouverture Books in west London and maintained substantive connections to friends, family, and colleagues in Guiana for decades. Bogle-L'Ouverture was a crucial organizational space for Caribbean, Indian, and African intellectuals and activists. A month after the riots, in October 1958, Cheddi Jagan, who had been the chief minister of British Guiana from May 1953 until the British government suspended the constitution later that year and dissolved the position, wrote to the Huntleys to express his support for the migrants and to update them on the political developments in British Guiana. A leader in the People's Progressive Party (PPP), Jagan explained that "our party had to take every due care not to give the impression that we are catering only for the Indian community . . . [we must] play-down racial communalism in this country."[32] The son of Indian sugar plantation workers, Jagan paid close attention to the simmering racial tensions between Afro- and Indo-descended Guyanese working toward fomenting national consciousness during the final stages of formal British dominance. He was concerned about the prospect of federation with other British Caribbean territories. Jagan admitted, "We are not . . . aware of the reception in the West Indies on this debate . . . [though] I am keeping in touch with some of the West Indian leaders . . . we are also looking forward to an early Election in Britain and a change in the Government . . . with the Labour Party's victory it may be possible for us to have early constitutional change."[33] Remaining connected to the political happenings in Guiana was essential for the Huntleys. Jagan expressed concern for his compatriots as he noted with "the present unemployment situation in England and the Fascists stirring up trouble, things may get a bit tighter."[34] He explained that British news was regularly disseminated in Guiana via the local press. He wrote, "In Wednesday's paper . . . the Tory Party is to consider the question of restrictions on immigration. I hope that they will ultimately decide not to take any action to restrict people coming from these parts."[35] Communication between the Huntleys and Jagan persisted despite the transatlantic distance. This connectedness was a critical influence in the radicalization of Caribbean peoples in the West Indies and abroad. Both the Huntleys and Jagan were aware of the problems of independence and state formation in Guiana, the British Caribbean, and Africa while simultaneously critiquing the racial violence of Notting Hill and the injustice of racialized citizenship and quotidian discrimination in Britain. Processes of political radicalization were transatlantic, concomitant, and premised on burgeoning contemporaneous diasporic racial and political consciousness.

Collective political action of Caribbean migrants following the riots pointed toward a particularized novel social formation as a result of the development of a shared consciousness among the migrants. The banding together of young men to fight antagonistic Teddy boys and later the efforts of women and men to organize and mobilize politically—beginning periodical broadsheets and offering support to the American civil rights movement, anti-apartheid groups in South Africa, and anticolonial movements throughout the global South, was the manifestation of radical migrant consciousness rather than specifically British-centered activism.

ORGANIZING IN THE AFTERMATH

The *West Indian Gazette* conceptualized Caribbean migrants as a distinctive group with similar concerns that extended beyond the individual islands or territories they came from, hence the regional distinction in the paper's title.[36] During the riots, disparate groups of migrants and children of migrants reached out to one another for support and security. The British Caribbean Welfare Service (BCWS) prohibited their staff from entering Notting Hill Gate after dark by the second week of the riots.[37] The government's reaction to problems facing West Indians did not lead to immediate policy reform but there were efforts to initiate conversations among local city leaders and migrants. After the riots, the Conference on West Indians in London, organized by the London Council of Social Service, was held at County Hall in South Bank in October 1958. One hundred and forty representatives of seventy-nine different governmental and independent voluntary associations attended the one-day conference.

The conference represented the mobilization of various groups in London, inspired by the violence that immediately preceded it. Though the first conference organized by the London Council of Social Service was held in 1956, the post-riot gathering was more radical in its composition and more inclusive of a wide variety of activists and concerned parties. The riots hinted at the overwhelming specter of violence cast over London in late 1958. Special reference was made to the riots in Notting Hill as having, "the good effect of drawing public attention to the existence of both colour bars and colour prejudice in this country and dispelling the previously felt smug satisfaction about this."[38] Because West Indians were easily distinguishable from white Britons, their visibility made them targets for disillusioned white aggressors. C. H. Charlesworth of the Aggrey Housing Society of Leeds explained that the white instigators were responsible for the riots and that their perspectives on Commonwealth migration differed substantially from migrant views. Whereas Caribbean residents who "had served in the war learnt about . . . racial tolerance and love of their neighbour in the Army . . . the Education Authorities in this country had entirely failed to put over to the young hooligans involved in the disturbances,"[39] Sheila Patterson, a social anthropologist, attributed the problems Caribbean residents in London faced to difficulties in both adaptation and acceptance. Patterson characterized British society as xenophobic, though she also noted, attitudes and personal prejudices rather than rigid legal barriers defined racialization in British society. Patterson explained that West Indies were classed at the lowest level by the local British population, contributing to the lower class by association of anyone interacting with them and further stymying Caribbean migrant assimilation.

Patterson warned against white Britons directing social justice organizations that emerged in the aftermath of the riots. She explained that interracial collaboration would be ineffectual if white British partners did not leave the organizational and administrative control to the Caribbean members who often were responsible for the formation and day-to-day management of these groups while also bearing the brunt of racial antagonism. Many migrants felt that they relied too heavily and for too long on the benevolence of their British neighbors, with little results.

Another topic at the conference was the ongoing problem of employment for migrants. With many arrivals struggling to obtain consistent employment, various theses on their exclusion were submitted, as well as different strategies for amelioration. Harkening back to efforts by the Colonial Office to aid in migrant acclimation, C. C. Conn, an executive of the London Transport

Recruitment Office suggested, "more could be done when the migrant had become accustomed to live in England by giving instructions about Trade Unions and social life." He encouraged West Indians to "play an active part in trade union activities."[40] The difficulty migrants had in gaining the respect of potential employers was mainly due to extant British prejudices—specifically racialized notions of diligence, workmanship, and capability. Suggestions for West Indians to engage more closely with their British counterparts aimed to ease tensions among the groups by making the dominant white British population more familiar with and less antagonistic toward the Caribbean migrant workers. Despite admitting the prevalence of British racial prejudice, Conn nevertheless concluded that "the solution lay with the West Indian himself. He must 'sell' himself by being hardworking, industrious and punctual."[41] British ignorance of the colonies and the scope of their empire was only further emphasized by J. Fraser of the BCWS who urged "Education Authorities . . . to ensure that teaching about the Commonwealth is brought up to date . . . schools should give further consideration to anything that might give children a greater understanding of communities other than their own."[42]

Disagreements over responsibility for racial tensions continued at the conference. Some attendees charged migrants for presenting themselves negatively as intruders, others argued that native Britons were hostile to the sheer presence of colonial students and workers. The latter faction insisted that British landlords, employers, and labor leaders created hostile environments in which migrants found integration nearly impossible; they further claimed that racial bias in British society often masked the pernicious, damaging effect of these prejudices on the migrants because the dominant white population was largely personally unaffected. The problem of education and consciousness was therefore a central issue in the aftermath of Notting Hill. Whereas colonial subjects were more aware of the constitution of the empire than their metropolitan counterparts, there was a palpable discrepancy in the fundamental understanding of colonial and metropolitan political consciousness.

Further tensions arose over the question of how to lessen the effect of racial discrimination on the migrants. In particular, the goals of social justice were primarily contested between those advocating legislative change and others who argued educational reform would be sufficient. Though an agreement was never reached, each side conceded that cross-racial cooperation was an essential component of social justice work, both in matters of education and official public policy.

This post-riot conference further solidified the place of race relations, immigration, and the state of the empire in British national political discourse. Intra-imperial consciousness accelerated among local London activists as the notion that the colonial émigrés were only temporary visitors waned. The presence of Caribbean workers agitated the disaffected native white British youth and contributed to gendered, sexist notions of their prospective preying on innocent British girls. The problems of interracial socialization developed from biases held by white Britons who remained reluctant to accept colonial citizens into the British social body. Unknown to the mainstream British press and most English laypeople, a vibrant and articulate counter-narrative of anticolonialism and the experience of racialization was developing among Caribbean, South Asian, and African migrants in the capital.[43]

Caribbean radicalism in Britain did not begin only after the Notting Hill violence. A lesser-known movement of activists began in earnest in the mid-1950s. Though migrants, including Claudia Jones, were disillusioned by the race politics of the British Communist Party, the West Indies Commission of the Party printed and distributed a corresponding *West Indies Newsletter* in the years preceding the riots. Although some migrants resented the Party's emphasis on class preceding race in its political philosophy and corresponding activism, the *Newsletter* suggested the opportunity for racially conscious Party members to voice their concerns. The *Newsletter* served as the mouthpiece for activists who considered themselves to be oppressed on multiple levels and needed an outlet to publicize their struggles as well as their aspirations for equality. The *Newsletter* criticized the Caribbean Commission as a "study in imperialist trickery" in an issue from 1951, suggesting that any concession the imperial administration made was a nominal pacification measure—including the West Indian delegation of the Commission.[44] The *Newsletter* characterized the Commission as lackeys of the exploitative, imperialist-minded powers (United States, United Kingdom, Netherlands, France) that organized it, rather than a body working toward regional economic and political unity and freedom.

Despite the disparate settlement of many migrants, various groups established mutual aid organizations throughout London. The Stepney Coloured Peoples Association (SCPA), founded in 1951, began in London's East End to protect and defend the rights of people of color in the area. The Association's constitution affirmed the importance of acclimation and community building for the migrants. In its earliest iteration, the constitution called for the establishment of a housing bureau, "to seek out accommodation for coloured people . . . and to recommend responsible prospective tenants to the landlords or landladies concerned."[45] SCPA pledged to "consider steps to obtain legal representation for any members involved in disputes caused by or arising from racial discrimination[and] . . . to publicize the needs of the coloured community and attempt to correct some of the false impressions which are current."[46] From an early point in the mass migration of Caribbean peoples to London, there was a need to organize and the SCPA's formation exemplified initial efforts toward amelioration.

SCPA was active in grassroots efforts within Stepney, advocating on behalf of the migrants who were discriminated against in Britain and arrived from the colonies where they often toiled in a number of occupations to survive while American, British, and multinational corporations reaped extensive benefits. Their *Colonial Worker* pamphlet was distributed throughout the area beginning in the early 1950s.

Conferences on the acclimatization of Caribbean people became the major conduit for activists and migrants to convene and exchange ideas and strategies in London. The preponderance of conferences organized around issues of assuaging race relations or advocating anticolonial activism were rooted in political sensibilities originating outside of metropolitan Britain and in the colonies of British East and West Africa, South Asia, and the Caribbean. Leaving their homelands, where they were often members of the majority, despite the influence of British imperial culture and notions of equality and jurisprudence, allowed these activists, artists, and intellectuals to fundamentally challenge the white supremacist status quo of British society and its various manifestations ranging from riots to the color bar in pubs and nightclubs and employment discrimination in the major industries. The conferences after the riots combined practical methods and a progressive theoretical basis in their conception and duration. The inclusion of academic professionals emphasized the notion that the contemporaneous developments in Britain were significant issues for study as well as apropos with respect to the everyday lives of London residents.

Organizations across London worked against the rising tide of anti-immigrant sentiment and protested the continued discussions of immigration restrictions. The Afro-Asian Caribbean Conference organized a meeting at the House of Commons in February 1962 calling West Indians in various professions to meet for a vigil outside the Home Office. By the 1960s, the political activity of West Indians had been established through the founding and operation of a number of institutions. The Afro-Asian Caribbean Conference cited no less than seven organizations[47] and a number of individual supporters.

At the "Colour and Culture" Conference held at Pendley Manor, in Tring, thirty miles northwest of London in May 1960, Dr. Kenneth Little led a program session entitled "The Racial Factor in Society." Little's scholarship on contemporaneous race relations and theories of racialization in Britain were vital to students and community organizers during this period. Because many activists had arrived for university education, their embracing of sophisticated academic theories and approaches to race relations was suitable. Little's lecture appealed to both students and the working classes, as he combined detailed analysis with thoughts on race in its broadest social aspects. He provided extensive historical context for his presentation, identifying the transatlantic slave trade as the originary point of modern race relations in Britain and throughout empire. He emphasized the role racialization played in the development of colonial enterprises for the material benefit of European nations. Little's commentary on racialization correlated with many of the firsthand accounts of colonial students of color who were dismayed by unfair treatment and pervasive stereotyping on the part of white students.

In the first half of 1959 the Community Development Section of BCWS engaged organizations in London including the London Council of Social Service, Paddington Council of Social Service, Citizens Advice Bureaux in Wandsworth, Kensington, and Paddington, the Hornsey YMCA, and Information Bureaux in Hornsey and Wood Green.[48] The Community Section also visited five police stations in areas with large West Indian populations and recent histories of heightened racial tensions.[49] Because the riots were months earlier, Notting Hill remained an area of concern for the Migrant Services Division. The Coloured People's Progressive Association and the UK Interracial Brotherhood met to discuss the relations between West Indians and the police in a special forum organized by the Division. The groups agreed that removing Moseley and his fascist followers would be a major step in solving the problems of relations with police.[50] The Division also worked to become more influential as members of various affiliated organizations attended meetings.[51]

The substantial number of organizations involved in the meetings of the Migrant Services Division suggested migrants were especially sensitive to the problems of racialization and proactive in contributing to assuaging social tensions. Beyond Parliament and its special committee, white Britons were neither thoroughly nor actively engaged in social justice restoration to any appreciable degree compared to West Indian, African, and Asian migrants. Jamaican Garnet Gordon maintained important relationships with native Britons and engaged colleagues and friends in the Caribbean. In June 1955 he hosted a party of visitors from the Caribbean including Dr. Michael Beaubrun, a prominent psychiatrist at the University of the West Indies and Sir Donald Jackson, the chief justice of the Windward and Leeward Islands.[52]

The Colonial Office was under intense scrutiny from West Indians who expected adequate protections from the British government, especially after Notting Hill. In a May 1959 meeting, Colonial Office administrators determined it would be best "for . . . West Indians to move away from [Notting Hill] . . . and . . . out of London altogether."[53] The Colonial Office attributed the difficulties in obtaining work to the nature and character of West Indians, rather than understanding the role racial prejudice played. West Indian women were thought to "not . . . [take] easily to mass production work . . . to attain the standards of speed called for in factory mass production of clothing." Furthermore, migrants were charged with being unwilling or "reluctant to take up domestic work." Migrant women were viewed as either incompetent or unwilling to work available jobs, even as the British far-right made clear their disgust and opposition to the hiring of colored labor. The Colonial Office did not create alternatives for West Indians after Notting Hill beyond imploring them to leave the district and accept any job they might be offered.

The BCWS offered some perspective that countered the Colonial Office's notion that many West Indians were unfit or unwilling to take on available jobs. In their study, *Some Aspects of West Indian Migration*, BCWS argued "the West Indian is prepared, in the main, to undertake any form of employment if he feels he can do it."[54] Furthermore, rejecting the prevailing narrative of the paucity of West Indian skilled labor, the BCWS *Report* confirmed "the majority of West Indians . . . bring with them some degree of education and a variety of skills . . . the most difficult problem . . . is that of being accepted by the community . . . he remains a coloured man, a man of another race, a stranger."[55] Although the Colonial Office did not adequately acknowledge the pervasiveness of racialization and its impact on migrant social and employment chances, the BCWS conversely attributed migrant alienation in some degree to the racial attitudes and behaviors of native Britons. According to the BCWS white Britons needed to accept the colonials, as their prejudices were "the final hurdle to the full enjoyment of living in England."[56]

Social justice mobilization in Britain demonstrated that West Indians were unwilling to submit to racialism by leaving for the Caribbean nor by passively accepting the violence of Teddy boys and unresponsiveness of British agencies and officials. Jamaican Ivan Weekes emphasized that "people were determined that they were here to stay and no amount of fighting would get them out . . . we were militant . . . and claimed our right to be here."[57] Emboldened by the solidarity of West Indians during the riots, Weekes proclaimed "we made it quite clear that if anyone tried those race riots again they would have much more bloodshed to reckon with."[58] Weekes and others were not intimidated by the violence in Notting Hill; they were heartened by collective resistance and steadfast in their desire to live in the metropole. West Indians developed patterns of identification deriving from their shared background *and* their political responses to discrimination and violence in metropolitan Britain. Despite their alienation, activist West Indians would embark on revolutionary transformative politics and unprecedented mobilization in London in the next decade.

In the years after the riots, Notting Hill retained its reputation as a dangerous, hostile environment. J. Waring Sainsbury, Town Clerk of the Royal Borough of Kensington, explained that the problems in the district stemmed from "the ever-increasing number of people flooding into an already overcrowded area . . . [and] the total absence in Kensington of vacant land upon which to build."[59] Sainsbury, however, neglected to mention the strained racial relations in the area as a cause for trouble, reflecting the widespread view in Britain that Britons were tolerant and held no biases against people of color. Furthermore, he suggested that the government was unable to curtail problems in the district and continued to charge neighborhood residents with improving and maintaining social relations in Notting Hill. Sainsbury acknowledged that authorities were aware of problems in the area but explained they could not solve "the many human problems presented by North Kensington."[60] He charged local residents—both West Indian and white Britons—with instigating and spreading violence in Notting Hill and charged individuals with changing the racial relations in the district. Sainsbury insisted the government was blameless despite not providing protections for colonial citizens and understood West Indians as culpable in the affrays in Notting Hill.

CARIBBEAN RADICAL RESPONSES

The violence of Notting Hill accelerated the political activity of West Indian migrants in Britain—they mobilized around issues of racialization in the metropole and anti-racist, anticolonial efforts throughout the declining British empire. The twinned discriminatory patterns derived from racialized notions of capability in the universities and skilled industries would not waver, even as the Caribbean migrant population increased annually through the early 1960s. The prospect of independence in the Caribbean, however, provided the impetus for a more radicalized vision among migrants living in Britain. Possibilities for self-determination altered the expectations colonial citizens had in the metropole. For migrants of color, their experiences of discrimination and inequality in Britain corroborated notions of class and race-based inequality throughout the empire. Events in Notting Hill magnified the latent racial problems in Britain and provided an analogue to more internationally well-known systems of racial discrimination such as Jim Crow segregation in the southern United States and apartheid in South Africa. Claudia Jones was aware of events in the United States due both to her experience as a Communist activist in New York and her continued correspondences with American civil rights leaders like Paul Robeson. After her deportation to Britain in December 1955, Jones and Robeson kept one another abreast of the struggle for civil rights in Britain and the United States, respectively.[61]

Whereas migrants arrived in the immediate postwar years with notions of their own British identities (however specious these claims seemed to be to white, Britons), activists in the aftermath of Notting Hill sought to emphasize their racial connections across national and imperial boundaries.

Along these lines, social justice activists in Britain viewed racial justice struggles in both South Africa and the American South with which to ally themselves.

In 1963, the Committee of Afro-Asian and Caribbean Organizations planned a march in solidarity with Americans fighting racial discrimination. The march on the American Embassy in London was planned to raise international voices against the practice of racialism in the United States. By 1963, the American civil rights movement had gained traction internationally. Black West Indians in Britain were aware of the discriminatory practices of Jim Crow segregation in the United States and allied themselves alongside black Americans to "help smash bigotry."[62] Noting the impending March on Washington scheduled on August 28, the Committee planned a march on August 31 "as an act of solidarity with those who demonstrate against racial discrimination in the United States."[63] The Committee invoked the historical legacy of "workers of Liverpool, who [in their opposition to slavery during the American Civil War refused to spin American cotton raised by slave labour and . . . weakened the Southern Plantocracy."[64]

The Committee likened the condition of black Americans to "racial discrimination in jobs, housing and civil liberties deeply affect[ing] British Commonwealth citizens of the West Indies, Africa, and Pakistan . . . a second-class citizenship status for these . . . peoples."[65] They viewed black Americans as struggling against analogous forms of racial discrimination. Black and brown residents of London saw themselves as similarly disempowered and subjugated as black Americans. International solidarity was a core principle of black activism even through the passage of immigration restrictions.

The Huntleys, despite having migrated to London in the mid-1950s, remained closely linked to Guiana's PPP along with other leftist groups in the Caribbean through the period of decolonization. Like many migrants, they maintained ties to their homeland after their arrival in London; in the case of the politically-minded Huntleys, their involvement and engagement with politics in the Caribbean intensified from abroad. The PPP was initially ethnically and racially diverse in with leadership including Afro-Guyanese Eric Gilbert from Central Georgetown and Indo-Guyanese Balram Singh Rai of Central Demerara. During the general election in August 1957, PPP encouraged citizens to cast their vote and provided some details on the party's political platform. PPP supported the proposed West Indian Federation with the specific caveat of dominion status for the Federation and internal, self-government for each constituent territory. Caribbean independence and citizenship would soon become a reality and progressive thinkers opted to radicalize further away from statist modalities, whether British or tied to newly configured sovereignties in the West Indies.

NOTES

1. J. Egyptien Compton, "Does the Negro Hate the White Man?" *Link* 1, no. 2 (December 1958), 3. Black Cultural Archives: Periodicals/127.
2. Ibid.
3. "Black Star's 1st Anniversary," *Link* 1, no. 2, 6–7. Black Cultural Archives: Periodicals/127.
4. "Black Star" has significance in Ghana to this day—the Ghana National Football team, for instance, is nicknamed the Black Stars.
5. "Wanted—A Black Man in Parliament," *Link* 1, no. 2, 11. Black Cultural Archives: Periodicals/127.
6. Ibid.
7. "Negroes Rule the Boxing Ring," *Link* 1, no. 2, 12. Black Cultural Archives: Periodicals/127. The boxing champions in the same order were Floyd Patterson, Archie Moore, Sugar Ray Robinson, Virgil Atkins, Joe Brown, and "the only British Negro," Hogan Kid Bassey.
8. Alan Dein, Interview with Vincent Reid, April 1998. "London Voices," Museum of London.
9. The McCarran Act required Communist organizations to register with the U.S. attorney general and prohibited noncitizen ("alien") members from becoming U.S. citizens and severely limited their entry and exit into the nation.
10. For a comprehensive work on Jones see Carole Boyce Davies's *Left of Karl Marx*.
11. Jones, "The Caribbean in Britain," *Freedomways*, Third Quarter, Summer 1964, 343.
12. Rory O'Connell, Interview with Sam King, February 1, 1993.
13. Ibid.
14. Hinds, *Journey to an Illusion: the West Indian in Britain* (London: Heinemann, 1966), 208–209.
15. "Anti-Racial Legislation: A Key Need," *West Indian Gazette*, December 1959, 5.
16. *West Indian Gazette*, December 1961, 9.
17. "Unity—A Necessary," *West Indian Gazette*, June 1960, 4.
18. "About People," *West Indian Gazette*, January 1960, 4.
19. For more on Carnival see Joshua Guild, *You Can't Go Home Again: Migration, Citizenship, and Black Community in Postwar New York and London* (PhD Diss., Yale University, 2007). Beginning in 1966, Carnival moved outdoors permanently through efforts of original organizers in tandem with the formation of the Carnival Board including Trinidadian Ansel Wong.
20. Marika Sherwood, *Claudia Jones: A Life in Exile* (London: Lawrence & Wishart, 1999), 156–157.
21. Ibid.
22. "Our Race Relations Are Reasonably Harmonious," *West Indian Gazette*, November 1960, 4.

23. John Figueroa, "British West Indian Immigration to Great Britain," *Caribbean Quarterly* 5, no. 2 (February 1958), 117.
24. Ibid.
25. "Gazette Fills a Great Need in Lives of West Indians," *West Indian Gazette*, September 1960, 3.
26. "Housing and Overcrowding Problems in Connection with Coloured Immigrants," "Race Relations in London in the Years After the Notting Hill Riots; Includes Official Correspondence, Letters from the Public, Pamphlets, Newspaper Clippings" c 1958. NA: HLG 117/122.
27. Minutes of Meeting Between Mrs. R. J. Youard, Ministry of Housing and Local Government, and officers of Kensington Borough Council, September 17, 1958. HLG 117/122.
28. Ibid.
29. Ibid.
30. Ibid.
31. For more on public violence in Britain see Panikos Panayi, *Racial Violence in Britain in the Nineteenth and Twentieth Centuries* (London; New York: Leicester University Press, 1996).
32. "Letter from Cheddi Jagan to Eric Huntley," October 10, 1958. London Metropolitan Archives LMA/4463/B/10/0/001.
33. Ibid.
34. Ibid.
35. Ibid.
36. The full title of the periodical was the *West Indian Gazette and Afro-Asian Opinion*.
37. "Letter from General Secretary to A. Bullock, Warden North Kensington Community Association; 4th September 1958," from West Indian Advisory Committee 1958, LMA ACC/1888/036.
38. C. H. Charlesworth, Aggrey Housing Society Ltd. Leeds, "West Indian Migration to the United Kingdom 1945/58," in "London Council of Social Service Conference on West Indians in London," UK NA: HLG 117/139.
39. Ibid.
40. "Reports from the Leaders of Discussion Groups," 1959. HLG 117/139.
41. Ibid.
42. "Family Welfare," leader J. Fraser, presented by Mr. D. Chesworth, c1959. London City Council. HLG 117/139.
43. Jordanna Balkin's *The Afterlife of Empire* is illustrative in its treatment of the lived experiences of decolonization in metropolitan Britain. Lisa Lowe's *The Intimacies of Four Continents* draws important connections between longer imperial historico-geographies, diasporic formations, and the interconnectedness of disparate peoples under and within transoceanic European modalities.
44. *West Indies Newsletter*, West Indies Committee of CP UK, January 1951, Michael Banton Pamphlets, Black Cultural Archives, Banton 1/4.
45. "The Stepney Coloured People's Association Proposed Constitution," Black Cultural Archives, Banton1/2/2.

46. Ibid.

47. These organizations were the *West Indian Gazette*, the West Indian Student's Union, People's National Movement (London Branch), UK Coloured Citizens' Association, British Guiana Freedom Association, Indian Workers' Association, Committee of African Organizations, and Farme Park International Fellowship. Afro-Asian Caribbean Conference Calls You to a Commonwealth Lobby, February 13, 1962; Institute of Race Relations Reference Code: 01/04/04/01/04/02/09.

48. "Review of Work of Community Development Section January to 1st September 1959," British National Archives: CO 1031/2545.

49. The Section reported visiting police stations in Brixton, Hornsey, Wood Green, Notting Hill, and St. Marylebone and the maintenance of a close liaison directly with Scotland Yard.

50. "Review of Work of Community Development Section," CO 1031/2545.

51. These attendees represented the following organizations: London Council of Social Service, International Voluntary Service, Workers Education Association, and International Friendship League. CO 1031/2545.

52. "Visits to the United Kingdom of Jamaican Minister," June 10, 1955. British National Archives: CO 1031/1603.

53. Extract from West Indian Immigrants Record of Meeting Held in the Colonial Office at 3 p.m. on Thursday, May 21, 1959. WIS 1188/462/08.

54. Excerpts from *Some Aspects of West Indian Migration* (A paper prepared by the British Caribbean Welfare Service) October 7, 1958. London Metropolitan Archives Reference No.: ACC/1888/109.

55. Ibid.

56. Ibid.

57. Pilkington interview with Ivan Weekes, December 13, 1983, *Beyond the Mother Country*, 143.

58. Ibid.

59. Pearl Jephcott, *A Troubled Area: Notting Hill* (London: Faber and Faber, 1964), 145. British Library Shelfmark: X.808/795.

60. Ibid.

61. Jones and Robeson correspondence can be found in the Claudia Jones Memorial Collection at the Schomburg Center for Research in Black Culture.

62. "Join in Solidarity Against Racial Discrimination," Leaflet, 1963. Institute of Race Relations Reference Code: 01/04/04/01/04/02/12.

63. Ibid.
64. Ibid.
65. Ibid.

Chapter 6

British Caribbean Independence and the 1962 Commonwealth Immigrants Act

Meanings of British Nationality

Eric Huntley left British Guiana in December 1956, arriving in Britain in January 1957. Huntley was fired from his previous job as a postman for his political activism and traveled to Britain because he had few employment prospects in British Guiana. After 130 days in power, the British government suspended the constitution and removed the PPP from office. The two major employers in Guiana were the British Government and Booker Group Sugar Holdings. Huntley had no desire to work for the Booker Group and the PPP were expelled from political power.

PPP was founded in 1949, holding its first Congress 1950. The Huntleys then lived in Buxton, one of the oldest black villages in the Demerara region. Before entering the Party, they were deeply engaged in the civic life of Buxton. They organized a study circle, ran a drama group, school, and youth festival. Interpersonal relations were critical to their later political roles. Eric Huntley explained that they engaged a political base prior to joining the PPP and were aware a community of like-minded people in Buxton at the time of their joining. Jessica was a trade union member and Eric was secretary of the postal workers union before joining the Party. Jessica had organized a strike among women garment workers years prior to becoming a Party member. She was a member of a cultural group called the Sunshine Workers Association and remembered playing dominoes while socializing. Just as in London, where West Indians sought respite and leisure in the city, in Guiana the Huntleys made connections and strengthened community ties through social activities and organization. Eric compared Georgetown to the other major cities of the world. He claimed in cities "you've got to have clubs and links and old school ties"[1] to nurture community. Many migrants in London recognized the need for networks once they arrived in the metropole. Eric commented on how "school boy"² ties paid great dividends during his time in London, as he was able to find other Queen's College alumni throughout the city. Jessica Huntley founded the Women's Progressive Organization within the PPP in 1953. She also was Organizing Secretary of the PPP after Eric left for London. Although the British Government suspended the Constitution, the PPP nevertheless had won eighteen of twenty-four seats in the legislature and thus were elected to office but out of power.

The Huntleys considered themselves more radical within the Party and hewed closely to the radical wing of the organization. Eric Huntley explained that prior to 1953, PPP supported West Indian Federation, advocating for an independent federation constituting autonomous Caribbean constituent territories. Neither the territories nor the federation would remain under Crown Colony status. The Huntleys noted a split in the Party exacerbated by racial differences in British Guiana at large. The Huntleys claimed PPP leader Cheddi Jagan warned them about their radicalism and too often sided with ethnically chauvinist Indo-Guianese members of the Party. Both Afro- and Indo-Guianese within the Party had united over the desire to end the British regime in the territory and clashed over the meaning and implementation of independence and sovereignty. The ethnic divisions within PPP would eventually lead to the formation of another party, the People's National Congress by Afro-Guianese activist and former PPP member Forbes Burnham, in 1958.³

In London, the Huntleys' Caribbean connections persevered because they maintained regular correspondence with friends and family in British Guiana. They worked closely with Londoners, aiming to improve the situation for all migrants. In 1967, Eric Huntley wrote to Professor Asa Briggs, Vice Chancellor of Sussex University, for permission to interview university personnel and students about the emerging Caribbean Studies program there. Jill Sheppard, the Warden of the Barbados Centre for Multi-Racial Studies, was delighted in welcoming Huntley "at the University . . . about the Barbados Centre."⁴ The Huntleys remained involved in social and academic communities among migrants and were original members of the Black Parents Association in North London. They engaged with both Stokely Carmichael and Malcolm X during their visits to the United Kingdom, and frequented events and activities sponsored by WISU and WASU who hosted luminaries from across the African diaspora. The Huntleys engaged the Black Panther Movement in London, including Trinidadian Althea Jones-LeCointe. Eric Huntley explained that visits by dignitaries sparked the West Indians students' and activists' imaginations and contributed to an accelerated political mobilization in the universities and throughout the city.⁵

According to the Huntleys, the most radical activists and organizers—Malcolm X, Carmichael, Eldridge Cleaver—were the most influential among the mobilized students and intellectuals in London. Some black radicals in Britain regarded Martin Luther King Jr. as being "soft" and Jessica remembered the notion that "black people said they were not turning the other cheek."[6] Many of the radical black activists in Britain were frustrated by what they read as King's mildness, especially in comparison to later Black Panthers and other Black Power activists. Trinidadian-born revolutionary Michael de Freitas helped to invite Malcom X to London and housed him in his "Black House" Black Power commune on Holloway Road in North London.

Carmichael's visit to London in 1968 was profound for the Huntleys as well as Jamaican-born sociologist Harry Goulbourne, who was a university student at the time. Jessica Huntley remembered hundreds of people gathering to hear Carmichael speak at the Roundhouse in Chalk Farm, northwest London, and his request that blacks alone sit and stand in the front of the audience. Huntley pushed others out of the way to take her seat near the stage.[7] Carmichael affirmed the awareness of events in the United States, by explaining, "America was on fire."[8] Along with other black radicals in London, the Huntleys were eager to hear Carmichael ignite a fire for racial justice in the United Kingdom. Students expelled a number of sympathetic white women (some of whom had black partners) from proceedings at the West Indian Student Centre after Carmichael's visit. They emphasized the role of race and racialization in British society by excluding white participants and allies.[9] The more radicalized iteration of WISC also singled out middle-class sympathizers from whom they felt estranged.

FEDERATION AND ITS DISCONTENTS

Caribbean political leaders debated Federation since the 1930s, with many of the constituent territories of the British Caribbean conflicted over who would shoulder the burden of providing jobs and stabilizing the regional political economy and who would benefit most from the new, independent and consolidated political formation. PPP argued strongly against the domination of politics in Guiana by Colonial Office administrators. They explained, "If a multiplicity of parties and independents are returned [in the election] without any single party having an overall majority, the Governor and the Colonial Office will still be bossing the show."[10] The Party charged the Colonial Government with operating a disguised dictatorship in the region and urged voters to collude and elect only PPP candidates in order to push through a unified anticolonial agenda for Guiana. The Party's *Manifesto* credited Eric Williams' ascendancy in Trinidad to a united electoral front and heralded his ability to demand for greater control in the appointment of representatives there.

Decolonization, enfranchisement, independence, and political sovereignty were the core of PPP philosophy. Like their allies in other Caribbean colonies and Britain, PPP advocated for workers' rights and contested the economic domination of the majority by wealthy landowners, corporate executives, and government representatives. PPP aligned itself closely with Williams' People's National Movement in Trinidad and other leftist parties in the region including Norman Manley's People's National Party in Jamaica and Sir Grantley Adams's Barbados Labour Party under the umbrella of the regional West Indies Federal Labour Party. PPP emphasized "the need for unification in the trade union movement . . . trade unions . . . which have the confidence of the majority of workers in an industry . . . should be recognised to bargain for, and on behalf of these workers."[11] PPP also echoed attitudes of the Caribbean diaspora in Britain with regard to culture, the arts, and sports, promising a Cultural Centre in Georgetown and expanded library facilities and sport programs in the outlying areas of British Guiana. Just as many found themselves drawn to particular forms of community development in the metropole through various groups—such as West Indian cricket clubs or student groups, PPP advocated for similar cultural-based organizing in Guiana concomitantly.

Claudia Jones's black radical activism developed through articulations of particularly West Indian identification among the migrants in London. In 1964, Jones penned "The Caribbean Community in Britain" for the leading African-American political and cultural journal *Freedomways*. *Freedomways*, first published in 1961, was founded by W. E. B. DuBois, Shirley Graham DuBois, Edward Strong, Louis Burnham, and edited by Esther Cooper Jackson. DuBois, who had been instrumental in earlier pan-Africanist mobilizations and conferences in Britain and elsewhere and in his late life, continued to engage with developments and activists in Britain. *Freedomways* was pan-Africanist in orientation and published literary writings from Pablo Neruda, Derek Walcott, and James Baldwin as well as political contributions from Kwame Nkrumah, C. L. R. James, and Julius Nyerere. Reflective of the African-American activist establishment *Freedomways* also showcased visual artists including African-Americans Romare Bearden, Jacob Lawrence, and Elizabeth Catlett.

Jones summarized West Indian migration to the metropole, characterizing the growth of the Caribbean community as "a stop-gap measure to ease the growing economic frustrations in a largely impoverished agricultural economy."[12] She bemoaned the exploitative nature of Caribbean economies wherein "the wealth of these islands is dominated by the few, with the vast majority of the people living under unbearable conditions."[13]

Jones's radical politics expanded beyond the borders of metropolitan Britain. She charged the ruling Conservative Government with capitulating as "junior partner . . . [of] the United States imperialist NATO nuclear strategy."[14] For Jones, Britain's "subservience to U.S. imperialism . . . [was] demonstrated in the case of its denial of long over-due independence to British Guiana."[15] An ally of the Huntleys, Jones criticized the attempts of the British colonial government to exploit one of its last remaining colonial possessions. She decried the institution of Proportional Representation in British Guiana that deposed the democratically elected government of PPP leader Cheddi Jagan.

Similar to insightful critiques leveled against Britain's role as the world's leading democracy by C. L. R. James and Eric Huntley, Jones condemned the British colonial project and manifestations of racialism at the end of empire. Jones asserted "the roots of racialism in Britain are deep and were laid in the eighteenth and nineteenth centuries through British conquests of India, Africa . . . as well as the British Caribbean." She noted that "all the resources of official propaganda and education, the superstructure of British imperialism, were permeated with projecting the oppressed colonial peoples as 'lesser breeds,' as 'inferior colored peoples,' 'natives,' 'savages.'"[16]

METROPOLITAN BRITISH ANTAGONISMS

In May 1960, Garnet H. Gordon, chairman of the Board of Governors of the West Indian Students' Centre, issued a circular to all West Indian students that reemphasized the role of the Centre as a cultural club for students from the Caribbean studying across the United Kingdom and the Republic of Ireland. Gordon explained that the idea for a center in London for Caribbean students predated World War II and the eventual purchase of a building at 1 Collingham Gardens in Earls Court in West Central London, to house the center in January 1954.

WISU and WISC were not rival organizations but sometimes attracted different students. WISU consisted of chapters across the United Kingdom, while WISC focused efforts on issues affecting students in London. Furthermore, each organization required membership dues, preventing students with financial constraints from joining both. The Centre waived fees for Union members who gained admission to the Centre and a room at Collingham Gardens was designated for the Union's sole use in commemoration of the Union's role in the establishment of WISC. Gordon explained that tensions arose due to the expectations of maintaining the Centre falling largely on the Union despite the Centre's constitution calling for "the day-to-day management . . . of a full-time resident Warden or Secretary who will work under the general direction of the Board of Governors."[17] The friction between the bodies, Gordon explained, was the impetus for his letter as he wished to inform students of the organizations' histories and to clear the air on behalf of protecting the rights of students and continuing to be resources for the growing populations of arrivants. WISC issued a new constitution in the same year with the approval of the government of the newly formed West Indies Federation. The Constitution called for a Board of Governors consisting of

> a chairman selected by the Board; five members nominated by the governments of Barbados, Jamaica, Trinidad and Tobago, the Windward Islands, and the Leeward Islands, respectively; one member each from British Guiana, British Honduras, and the Bahamas so long as those governments contribute to the Centre's financing; one member nominated by the Federal Government; three students—one each nominated by the Federation of West Indian Students' Union of Great Britain and Ireland, the WISU London, and the House Committee of the Centre; and the Secretary for Student Affairs.[18]

Throughout the early 1960s, the Centre held events attracting students from London and universities around the United Kingdom. In April 1961, the Centre's table tennis and cricket clubs participated in matches against local London clubs and the Centre hosted talks with Donald Chapman, MP, on economic development and migration in Jamaica and the Centre Delegation to Africa, which examined the connection between the Rastafari movement and the Caribbean.[19] The Centre's activities were responses to a range of issues facing the students on the local, national, and international level. Members of the Centre programmed around racial, geographic, and political identities, engaging with white Britons, and Caribbean and African migrants in the capital. Each month the Centre hosted at least one MP who addressed questions related to the West Indian experience both in the metropole and in the newly semi-independent Caribbean nations of the Federation.

In London, WISC and WISU supported young migrants and maintained relationships with local businesses and employers. The WISC Cricket Club arranged matches against a number of clubs in London including the Fulham Power Station C.C., the Chelsea Police, and the Staines C.C. WISC numbered 598 members in May 1961, with 167 of the membership residing outside of London. The group gained ninety-seven members from the previous year despite increased antagonism from Teddy boys and the British press arguing against multiculturalism in Britain and the continued migration of colored people from the colonies to the metropole.

In addition to metropolitan organizations in London, possibilities of Caribbean cooperation and Federation shaped political discourse in the West Indies. Jamaican poet and social anthropologist M. G. Smith considered the question of West Indian regional culture during the short period of Federation in 1961. Smith asserted, "West Indians . . . recognise the cultural diversity within their own and neighbouring territories, without being clear how these differences fit into the larger schemes of national or cultural unity and distinctiveness."[20] Smith emphasized the premise that neither British Honduras nor British Guiana were part of the Federation but nevertheless integral Caribbean territories. He claimed the French Caribbean islands of Guadeloupe and Martinique, as part of the "West Indies." Smith argued that "the West Indies Federation in its present form does not correspond with the West Indian area whose common culture is . . . [his] concern."[21] Smith stressed that linguistic and historical differences distinguished the region further, to wit "the British Caribbean . . . is one form of Creole culture; the French or Dutch West Indian cultures are other forms."[22] Smith later corroborated anthropological thought of the time in reinforcing the fundamental differences between socialization and community relations in the Caribbean and European metropoles. He affirmed that Caribbean creole cultures contained "many elements of African and slave derivation which are absent from metropolitan models."[23] The cultural formations and modes of socialization present in the Caribbean were therefore foreign to and distinct from corresponding European patterns. The West Indians who lived communally in Notting Hill or Paddington and hosted large parties in residential settings thusly transported their cultural traditions to the "mother country."

After more than a decade of accelerated migration from the West Indies, Smith addressed the African background as an essential component of West Indian identity and culture, both in the Caribbean and in Britain. He invoked Melville Herskovits's notion that "'rarely . . . do . . . African traits [persist] . . . in a pure form . . . they are overlaid by Creole influences and situations . . . or they are associated with elements of European origin.'"[24] Central epistemological and cultural problems for migrants were the British refutation of the historicity of Africa in their culture and the subsequent valorization of European narratives and methods in its place. Migrants often struggled to acclimate to British society because there were not cultural formations or institutions that corresponded to those already familiar to them. For instance, Smith criticized the identification of "Shango . . . with Christian saints"[25] rather than recognition of the African origin of the orishas and their prevalence among creolized Caribbean spiritual formations. Smith further bemoaned the notion that "the Creole culture which West Indians share is the basis of their division."[26]

Beginning in 1959, the Institute of Race Relations published the journal *Race* to investigate the role of racialization in British society. The debut issue identified links between race relations in the Caribbean and the United Kingdom. Social anthropologist Michael Banton explained that "in the West Indies there is a fairly clear association between colour and social position . . . the highest classes have the fairest complexion, the lowest have the darkest."[27] Even if a dark-skinned man has economic success he will marry a woman from the class he attained rather than from which he came. "Marrying light" came to be regarded as socially desirable for many throughout the region. In the United Kingdom, these distinctions were exacerbated due to both the paucity of Caribbean people and the dominance of whiteness in the national culture.[28] *Race* offered criticism and analysis from the perspective of socially conscious native Britons and Caribbean migrants. Contributors to *Race* provided analyses of race in Britain by also considering the social conditions in the colonies. Banton's observations regarding colorism in the West Indies were particularly useful because his work extended the association between color and social position to the United Kingdom and cited British responses to the migrants as tantamount to that effect. Just as in the Caribbean, lighter-skinned peoples enjoyed greater social privileges in the United Kingdom, whereas darker-skinned people were regarded as lower class.

Banton critiqued British attitudes and actions in strained race relations in his 1959 study *White and Coloured*. He charged native Britons with cultivating and reproducing national and racially chauvinistic views. Banton argued that Britons practiced self-segregation in the midst of migration from the West Indies and Africa. He claimed that Britons were "more impressed by the African in a colorful and native robe than in morning dress . . . [and] respect the African who professes Islam more than one who says he is a Christian."[29] Even when nonwhites behaved in patterns analogous to that of the typical distinguished Englishmen and Englishwomen, the Britons resented the African, Asian, or West Indian for their behavior or appearance.

Philip Mason, founding director of IRR, remarked on the persistence of racial tensions in the aftermath of Notting Hill. In the foreword to an IRR pamphlet, *Coloured Immigrants in Britain*, Mason explained that, despite the Commonwealth's claim "to be multi-racial . . . the affair was damaging [and] more serious was the danger that it might prove only the first of a series."[30] The prospect that public violence in West London could forecast more underscored the notion that people of color lived under a quotidian specter of racial violence through the early 1960s. IRR research indicted Britons for undermining notions of peace and civility by instigating the violence. Mason suggested that nativist resentment was directed primarily at nonwhite people and that the riots were an aberration within the scope of nationwide British resentment against Caribbean people. Donald Wood, deputy director of the IRR, emphasized feelings of exclusion migrant students endured due to racial prejudice. Wood noted that while students who withstood prejudice would "go home with the prestige of having studied in Europe . . . workers . . . faced . . . the intricate and often unspoken conventions of industrial life which cannot be learnt in a day and to which they seldom have any introduction."[31] He bemoaned the plight of students while reorienting focus on the working class who also arrived in substantial numbers. Thousands of Caribbean citizens served during world wars and their desire to live and work in Britain was met with unanticipated contempt from native Britons. Workers faced hostility from the beginning of the period of large-scale migration. In 1955, the first colored employee was recruited by the West Bromwich Transport Department in the West Midlands and the white traffic staff went on strike for two separate Saturdays in protest.[32] Years before public racial violence, white workers expressed resentment and antipathy toward the colored workers in numerous industries.

Upon the allocation of £70,000 to the IRR (from the Nuffield Foundation) in 1963 to fund investigations of race and racial hatred in Britain, Mason explained that while multiculturalism had come to Britain in the 1950s, questions of racialized prejudice were important on a global scale because of the preponderance of racial inequalities across national boundaries.[33] The Nuffield Foundation also supported studies on the lives of Indians in Britain and charted their assimilation and patterns of association and communication with the subcontinent.[34]

Despite prejudices in the industries, Caribbean migrants were employed in transport corporations of cities across Britain.[35] Because many migrants brought expertise with them to Britain, they could find employment more quickly than unskilled native Britons. Wood's analysis was prescient as he explained that prior to the end of World War II, "the British West Indies . . . [had] . . . been a region of emigration since the first attempt to dig the Panama Canal in the 1880s . . . It was natural that West Indians, faced with unemployment and under-employment at home, should turn to Great Britain, the mother-country of the Commonwealth."[36] Intra-regional migration in the Caribbean predated the large-scale migration to the metropole. Consequently, migrant workers left their homes to work on British and American projects in Panama and within the British industries after World War II.

In addition to the organizations that were oriented around international and transnational campaigns and anticolonial solidarity, groups with specifically local perspectives also emerged. The West Indian Mother's Club, founded in July 1960, exemplified the localized support groups established in the wake of the violence of Notting Hill. The Mother's Club was made up of West Indian immigrant mothers and grandmothers who organized events and social functions for their children in order to introduce them to other West Indians.

SOCIAL SCIENTIFIC INVESTIGATIONS

In 1963, Sheila Patterson compiled an extensive study of immigrants throughout London to address the changing nature of social relations as evinced by the riots in Notting Hill.[37] Enlisting more than a dozen community leaders to participate, Patterson presented data on Notting Hill, Brixton, Willesden, Hackney, and Paddington.[38] In addition to demographics, Patterson offered recommendations for action in *Immigrants in London*. She suggested a three-pronged program for integrative action: "Encouragement of newcomers to adapt themselves to local mores; encouragement to join local groupings such as trade unions, religious congregations, recreational associations, political parties; and liaison, mediation, and conciliation work between the newcomers and population."[39] The Willesden International Friendship Council began conciliatory work Patterson advocated by dispersing teams of one white and one nonwhite member to visit the homes and flats of nonwhite tenants who had quarrels with their white landlords. The Council's activity was hyper-local in its implementation but illuminated larger issues affecting British society. Patterson suggested approaches for improving race relations including legislating against discriminatory behavior. She insisted, "Anti-discriminatory legislation and action would not only help to establish egalitarian patterns of behavior . . . but could help to create a favourable climate of opinion for more long-term action."[40] Without formal legislation protecting migrants from discrimination, prejudices would continue to pervade British society, preventing migrants from gaining stability in Britain. The study group also suggested special action for younger and second-generation migrants including recreational spaces or homework centers in areas like Brixton, English classes for those in need, and special flat-lets for young, unmarried mothers.[41]

Grenada-born Labour Party politician, doctor, and activist David Pitt offered critical analysis of race relations by focusing largely on West Indian political activity in London. A member of the London City Council, Pitt noted that Camberwell and Hammersmith were the only constituencies represented by West Indian councilors. He identified a general apathy among the migrants with regard to metropolitan politics. Pitt explained that migrants "fear[ed] victimisation if they find themselves identified with the wrong political party and prefer to be strictly neutral."[42] Problems of acclimation were often so severe that migrants found no time to invest in political engagement—they were constantly on the hunt for employment, housing, and social services benefits. Pitt noted migrants felt "spied upon . . . the attempts to get them on the electoral roll are merely a way of trying to be sure of their whereabouts."[43] Many Caribbean people were threatened by surveillance in the capital and wished for protections from police harassment and Teddy boys. Voter registration was but another way to be officially monitored.

Race functioned as more than a news source—its political bent meant it was mouthpiece for leftist, antiracist activism in London and throughout Britain. Maurice Freedman, Reader in Anthropology at the London School of Economics, offered a scathing critique of G. C .L. Bertram's 1958 study

West Indian Immigration, which offered shallow analyses of the link between race and cognitive ability, social prestige, and intelligence. Bertram's pamphlet, published by the Eugenics Society, was a paranoid tract on the threat of "miscegenation" in Britain because of the possibility of intermarriage and interracial sexual relations between colored migrants and native whites. Bertram indicted migrants for social problems in the regions where they settled. He suggested that "slum conditions, excessive charging for what little is provided, a degree of fraud, frustration . . . soon build up into a situation which is thoroughly undesirable in the eyes of any local authority in the United Kingdom."[44] Rather than recognizing the role slum landlords, Teds, and hostile neighbors played in the declining areas where migrants lived, Bertram concluded that the migrants alone were culpable for the numerous problems in these areas. Despite disgruntled white youth perpetrating the riots, Caribbean migrants were held accountable for the disintegrating social relations in British cities. Bertram's work exhibited an extreme resistance to West Indian migration and an ominous stance on the tensions white Britons helped to perpetuate.

Freedman noted that Bertram's insistence on "the genetic differences between West Indians ('chiefly Africans at second remove') and white inhabitants . . . [rested] on eugenicist assumptions."[45] In arguing against the rising anti-Caribbean sentiment in Britain, Freedman ridiculed Bertram's notion of the inherent inequality between the races and further criticized his pamphlet's lack of tangible evidence. Freedman instead argued that Britain's "moral and political problems in regard to coloured immigrants are difficult enough to analyse and solve with the distracting irrelevancies of Dr. Bertram's 'opuscule.'"[46] He sought to elevate the theorizing and analysis of race relations beyond eugenics and find solutions in action rather than dichotomized renderings of the social Darwinist tradition.

Freedman participated in a working group organized by the Board for Social Responsibility of the Church of England and contributed to a handbook on British race relations. Published in 1960, *Together in Britain* was the church's effort to offer a theological understanding of race and strategies for righteous Christian action in Britain. The Anglican Church long credited itself for a progressive stance on abolitionism and considered its theology to be more empathetic to nonwhites. The church discarded the attitude to race relations that was engendered by the primitive view of African culture on one hand and by the growth of the idea of imperial vocation on the other.[47] The church stated, "Anti-colour feeling in Britain has behind it a long history of colonialism . . . the disintegration of the colonial empire has left some people . . . disgruntled and resentful."[48] Furthermore, they maintained that racial prejudice in Britain was responsible for divisions between West Indians and native Britons. Migrants "expect[ed] to arrive in ordinary society . . . they speak English and are Christians ... they are rebuffed in their attempts to be ordinary people ... the outward-looking dispositions with which they arrive will be turned into inward-looking ones."[49] Caribbean migrants, while possessing what the Church deemed "good initial qualifications" for membership in British society as English-speaking Christians, were nonetheless excluded. They looked toward other migrants for support. Attempts by West Indians and Africans to form a common front in the face of the hostile environment were a response to British racial antagonism.

Racial problems were not limited to political matters and pervaded civil society. The explosion of literature by West Indian migrants addressing inequality and racialization was a critical response by artists and intellectuals to their contemporary social station. In addition to providing detailed accounts of the prejudices and struggles they encountered, these authors emphasized the connections they developed with other migrants with whom they shared experiences of alienation and discrimination. The shared experiences of second-class citizenship encouraged migrants to organize and mobilize on behalf of all migrants of color. The status of the West Indians as colonial migrants in the metropole was so different than what they expected that they created a new consciousness in order to survive in Britain. Literature was one of many cultural expressions that figured into this new consciousness. Music, sports, and popular representations also were significant in the burgeoning immigrant imaginary in post-riot London.[50]

CULTURAL INGENUITY

Trinidad-born Samuel Selvon's *The Lonely Londoners* described problems of acclimation West Indians faced upon entry to Britain. First published in 1956, Selvon's novel exposed much of the realities of life of poor and working-class black citizens in postwar London. Moses Aloetta, the protagonist, conveys a perpetual sense of alienation and a distinct unbelonging as a black resident in the capital. The shock of life in London presented in literary form deepened the memorialization of the migrant experience.

Color consciousness became a major theme in the postwar literary production of Caribbean writers. Harold Pollins, writing for *Race* in 1960, characterized the migrants in two distinct groups: the smaller composed of students coming for a limited period of study and the larger, more permanent group comprised of workers. In A. G. Bennett's *Because They Know Not*,[51] the hero is a clerk who objects to mixing with "uncultured" ordinary migrants on the ship to England. Bennett emphasized class differences in his novel by having the "ordinary" migrants speak in Jamaican accents while the protagonist's voice has only traces of his ancestral lilt. Pollins suggested that class differences were familiar to West Indians as they were the dominant social code in the Caribbean. Their appearance in Caribbean-British literature was a result of the migrants carrying these codes with them. Pollins also cited G. R. Fazakerley's 1959 work, *A Stranger Here*, whose protagonist was a fair-skinned, white-collar worker. Pollins argued that the class and color distinctions, while common in West Indian literature, were utilized largely to illustrate the problems of treatment the migrants encountered in Britain. He explained that "the problem in . . . [these] novels centre on prejudice and discrimination . . . the hero arrives in England . . . comes up against two major problems; housing and employment."[52] Pollins recognized the central role of migration in West Indian literature in Britain that illustrated the predominance of questions of belonging, opportunity, and exclusion for the Caribbean community. Fazakerley's work emphasized the essential instability of life in Britain for the migrants.[53]

While people of color engaged one another as activists and organizers, Caribbean writers in Britain also made solidarity an important theme for central characters.[54] Pollins identified the coherence of the West Indian group as the most important thematic in this wave of literature. He explained that from novel to novel "the hero . . . has to live in a house with other West Indians because he cannot get accommodation elsewhere . . . his leisure time is spent with West Indians because English people are not easy to get on with."[55] Prejudice in Britain was a central component of migrants' art that reflected the everyday experience in their lived realities. West Indians relied on one another largely due to the circumstances of racialized exclusion. Pollins's reviews provided insight into migrant perspectives on social standing and included criticisms of the racial status quo in Britain.

Pollins also reviewed *The Pleasures of Exile* by Barbadian George Lamming. Published in 1960, this series of interrelated essays on cultural politics incorporated Lamming's memories of his life as writer in England and travels through the Caribbean, West Africa, and the United States. Lamming ruminated on his position as a self-exiled writer resident in Britain. He explained that, for the West Indian, "the exile is a universal figure . . . we are often without the right kind of information to make argument effective . . . we have to feel our way through problems for which we have no adequate reference of traditional conduct as a guide . . . chaos is . . . therefore, the result of our thinking and our doing."[56] Lamming rationalized the difficulties of being a West Indian immigrant in England by deconstructing the prevalent notions of Caribbeanness and by emphasizing the colonial condition of the writer-migrant class. He considered the Caribbean marginal within the Commonwealth and the declining empire; West Indians were, moreover, seen as inadequate in British society. Lamming offered, "When the exile is a man of colonial orientation . . . his chosen residence is the country which colonised his own history . . . he has to win the approval of Headquarters . . . England."⁵⁷ Lamming further characterized West Indians in England as having brought with them the "habitual weight of a colonial relation."⁵⁸ If a number of migrant accounts bemoaned the material insufficiency of luggage transported on ships from the Caribbean—many migrants arrived with little winter clothes and without rain boots—Lamming suggested that the psychological baggage of colonial conditioning was the most substantial parcel any migrant could have carried with them.

Lamming's work also addressed issues affecting migrant students in British universities. He explained students' "whole development as . . . person[s] is thwarted by the memory, the accumulated stuff of a childhood and adolescence . . . maintained and fertilised by England's historic ties with the West Indies."⁵⁹ Lamming suggested the colonial relationship between England and the Caribbean overwhelmed the potential for healthy academic and personal growth for students. Some students, as shown in chapter three, were inundated by the notions of insufficiency due to the enduring predominance of British racial attitudes.

Lamming was part of a growing community of West Indian artists and writers living in Britain and drew on the legacy of earlier seminal figures. *The Pleasures of Exile* was dedicated in part to C. L. R. James, and Lamming paid tribute to *The Black Jacobins* throughout his work. Lamming explained that James's work "should be Bible-reading for every boy who would be acquainted with the period in question . . . James shows us . . . a slave who was a great soldier in battle, an incomparable administrator in public affairs . . . a humane leader of men."⁶⁰ He lauded James's depiction of Toussaint L'Ouverture and regarded his history of the Haitian Revolution as vital, especially for West Indians interested in understanding their own historical achievements. Lamming praised *The Black Jacobins* as the "epic of Toussaint's glory . . . rendered by C.L.R. James . . . a neighbor of Toussaint's island . . . within the tradition of Toussaint himself . . . that came to life in the rich and humble soil of a British colony in the Caribbean."⁶¹ Lamming made a case for Caribbean solidarity and paid tribute to the contributions of his forbears who he regarded as continuing the legacy of West Indian radicalism, dating back to the revolution in Haiti.

Reflecting on his journey to England, Lamming remembered the immediate shock of arrival. He argued, "No Barbadian, no Trinidadian, no St Lucian . . . sees himself as a West Indian until he encounters another islanders in foreign territory."⁶² Like migrants who ran to one another's defense during the riots in Notting Hill regardless of whether they shared an island home with those under attack, Lamming argued, "to be a bad West Indian means to give priority of interest and ambition to the particular island where you were born."⁶³ He championed, "Barbadians, Trinidadians and Jamaicans who go to great trouble in order to establish that they are first of all a West Indian . . . [and] say . . . I am from the Caribbean, hoping the picture of French and Spanish West Indies will be taken for granted."[64] Lamming's identification expanded on what he called the "British colonial limitation" of the term West Indian and included peoples from throughout the archipelago whether Anglophone, Francophone, or Hispanophone. Many migrants in post–Notting Hill Britain also related to their countrymen and other Caribbean islanders in similar ways.

Beyond association with other West Indians, Lamming lamented the double consciousness of migrant students, who he claimed wrongly viewed England as a place where everybody had "'an equal chance.' 'Their relative comfort in Oxford or Cambridge,' Lamming mused, 'will [only] help to reinforce the illusion.'"[65] Furthermore, he sympathized with the conflicting images and behaviors students experienced, referring to their plight as "an experiment in double-think."[66] The contemporaneous reality of racialization in Britain forced West Indian students to question their status as citizens because of the seeming mutual exclusivity of their university privileges and discriminatory treatment in their everyday lives.

In addition to *Race*, the Institute of Race Relations also commissioned independent studies to investigate and publicize the realities of migration and the changing economics in the metropole and the West Indies. R. B. Davison's study, *West Indian Migrants*, was financed by the Institute of Social and Economic Research of the University College of the West Indies to investigate changing demographics and political economies in the Caribbean. The opportunities in Britain encouraged West Indians to migrate and created a population drain in the Caribbean. Davison argued for "an overhaul of the social services . . . West Indians are providing sorely needed labour in Britain. They ought not be left unaided to solve the severe problems that have arisen."[67] IRR promoted activism and scholarship that was not limited in scope to problems affecting Britain. Davison's study reflected a wider-ranging political viewpoint—one that considered problems in the Caribbean as important to migrants as those impacting them directly every day in Britain.

IRR recorded the frequency of meetings and conferences addressing race relations in the early 1960s. Among the most prominent were the All-African People's Conference in May 1960, All-African Students' Conference in November 1960, and the Conference on Overseas Students in November 1962.[68] The increasing regularity and rising attendance of these conferences reflected the growing importance race relations had in the British national discourse in the mid-century.

The Committee of the London Conference on Overseas Students warned West Indians who considered traveling to Britain for university in a series of handbooks issued after Notting Hill. In February 1959, the Committee explained "general relations between coloured students and the British people are on the whole good . . . colour prejudice still arises and . . . many coloured students . . . come . . . prepared for some prejudice . . . to the extent of imagining that the insignificant rebuffs . . . arise from colour prejudice."[69] Migrant students had been alerted to the racialized nature of British society and arrived prepared for unjust treatment on the basis on their racial background. In the same way that West Indians found work or housing through interpersonal relationships with those already living in the capital, students arrived with the knowledge from friends or family that they would not be welcomed warmly in Britain. The pamphlet, prepared by white Britons, sought to convince students of color of the fundamentally different culture in Britain. West Indians were urged to understand that Britons, "are apt to leave the students alone and not interfere with them . . . they will realize that they are perfectly free to join in our activities if they wish to do so . . . students mistake this attitude for indifference or unfriendliness."[70] The cold attitudes of British students, the Council maintained, reflected typical British behaviors, not a particular response to students of color. Nevertheless, in the 1960 edition of *Overseas Students in Britain*, the Council acknowledged, "it is easy to understand why coloured students who . . . encounter it [prejudice] become embittered."[71] Native British manners were an obstacle for West Indian assimilation. Students and workers were not resistant or resentful of native Britons but were reacting to the unsympathetic and antagonistic reception they received.

DIVERSE OPINIONS AND BLACK IDENTITIES

Dr. Edward Scobie, born in Roseau, Dominica, in 1918, edited *Flamingo*, a monthly published in London for African peoples in Britain, the Caribbean, and Africa, from 1961 to 1963. *Flamingo* was wide-ranging, disseminating politics and popular culture. Though *Flamingo*'s subject matter varied, a number of letters were published that addressed intra-racial tensions between West Indians and Africans. Gbola Akinsanya of London criticized Scobie for detailed coverage of Caribbean issues and the relative paucity of attention paid to African news and opinions. Akinsanya argued that "West Indians . . . are a nuisance in Britain . . . *Flamingo* is gradually becoming West Indian. Everything Syd Burke. Everything the Writers of the Caribbean."[72] This critique emerged in the wake of a feud between Nigerian Akinsiki and Norman Gayle of the West Indies over the role West Indians played in Nigerian independence. Akinsanya asked Scobie a pointed question: "As a true African, would the Editor be frank and admit that the West Indians contributed anything to the Nigerian Independence?"[73]

Londoner Sam M. Spence praised *Flamingo* as, "an instrument for the welding together of the social, political, intellectual and sporting talents of the black peoples universally."[74] Spence appealed for solidarity, hoping that "in the future there will be no literary battles between Nigerians and Jamaicans . . . in spite of the wide differences created between each faction through the perfidious slave trading of the last two or three centuries all black people are basically one blood and race."[75] Spence called on black people in London to put their differences aside for the sake of the race's prosperity. He implored his fellow blacks, "we must all unite in love and honesty for the future glory of Mother Africa and all her people at home and abroad."[76] Spence's proclamations of diasporic unity were especially profound because of the bitter squabbles between Africans and West Indians locally.

J. N. Philip, of Luton, Bedfordshire addressed tensions between West Indians and Africans in local industries. After commending *Flamingo* for a visit "to the Vauxhall Plant . . . on behalf of West Indians working there," Philip claimed that "there [have] been no racial troubles during my services with the company . . . myself and son Ivan A. Philip are very proud to be members."[77] He urged solidarity between Africans and West Indians, proclaiming, "I am very proud of my African ancestors . . . let both West Indians and Africans . . . stop this feud of whom among the Negro race is superior . . . and think of the whole Negro race as one family and work towards this end."[78] As one of many black migrants who allied themselves with other migrants from across the diaspora while residing in London, Philip advocated solidarity among all black peoples in Britain.

Differences within black communities were pressing during the 1960s for West Indians and Africans in Britain as well as at home. N. A. J. Chew, a Jamaican living in Wiltshire, southeast England, pled *"Flamingo* . . . why not stick to the job of helping to educate both the West Indians and Africans in loving each other . . . how can we . . . enjoy freedom and independence without unity?"[79] Jerry M. Nwankwo from Port Harcourt, Nigeria, urged *Flamingo* to provide reports on the struggles and successes of black people everywhere. He encouraged the editors to include coverage that would "arouse that fighting spirit in us by getting home to us news of our brothers' plight in the strife-torn under-developed and segregational countries . . . we are on the march to total freedom."[80] Black readers in London and throughout diaspora were eager to remain informed of the revolutionary events happening throughout the world. Their political consciousnesses were based centrally on racial solidarity.

Lamming further reflected on the relationships between Africans and West Indians in London while recollecting his travels to Ghana in 1958. He suggested the West Indian's "relation to . . . [Africa] is more personal and more problematic . . . the conditions of his life today . . . are a clear indication of the reasons which led to the departure of his ancestors from that continent . . . that migration was not a freely chosen act."[81] Black West Indians were forcibly removed from Africa through transatlantic slavery and Lamming insisted due to imperial hegemony, West Indians had not been introduced to Africa through history and "education did not provide . . . any reading to rummage through as a guide to the lost kingdoms and names and places."[82] British Caribbean colonials were physically estranged from Africa and colonial education withheld their historical connections with the continent.

Colorism remained an unresolved problem after West Indian colonies became independent. *Flamingo* reader Joanne Pinto, pled for West Indians to "stop discriminating against ourselves." "If we hope to stamp out discrimination," Pinto urged, "we must start it at home, and stop thinking that simply because we are a shade lighter in the colour of skin we are better than the next man. How ridiculous."[83] Like others who invoked the exploitative history of the Caribbean, Pinto maintained that "from the days of slavery [lighter skinned people] . . . have claimed superiority to the ordinary black and . . . a substantial majority of them still do."[84] Black migrants appealed for solidarity and the ultimate breakdown of long-held biases and prejudices that divided colonial peoples for centuries. These radical pleas were revolutionary in their conception and present throughout sites of diaspora at a transformative moment in late-imperial history.

M. R. Edwards, writing from Southall, Middlesex, asked *Flamingo* to "influence its readers to form an organization to which all West Indians can contribute to give the necessary care and protection to their cause and interest."[85] Edwards observed that colonial migrants related to one another because of similar national origins, class status, and race but nonetheless identified as separate groups—Jamaican, Grenadian, Barbadian, Trinidadian.[86] The reality of West Indians having "come into the U.K. from different islands and . . . looking at each other with some difference . . . justice is handed out to them in a most unfair manner . . . being assaulted and cheated and no adequate protection is received."[87] Caribbean migrants were targeted similarly and their disputes in the metropole, according to Edwards, prevented a sense of solidarity and compassion between different islanders. The recent scars of Notting Hill highlighted the need for collective attitudes and action from all migrants of color.

The West Indian Students' Centre, despite its place as a resource for migrant students, was not exempt from controversies regarding chauvinism or bias toward West Indians, or charges regarding racialism toward Asian and African students. For example, Indo-Trinidadian student Ramon Vernon wrote a scathing critique of the Centre for the *Trinidad Chronicle*.

Vernon claimed the Centre "excluded many East Indians . . . the warden carries on a gambling game in his flat . . . [and] prostitutes are allowed the run of the place."[88] After the article's publication, Vernon wrote directly to Garnet Gordon, the WISU Commissioner, threatening the release of "a more elaborate [story] . . . for the English press."[89] Gordon defended the Centre and reiterated its purpose and utility for the migrant student community. He insisted that "there is no discrimination against West Indians who qualify for membership of the Centre whether those West Indians be East Indians or otherwise . . . as a non-member you were not on the premises in accordance with the rules."[90] Gordon confirmed, "the Centre . . . provide[s] amenities for West Indian students . . . it is difficult to understand why you [Vernon] who have long since ceased to be a student and belong to a different age group and are married and settled in this community should persist in wishing to go to the Centre without conforming to the rules."[91] The Centre Executive Committee ensured that the space would be the hub of West Indian student culture in the United Kingdom. They hosted visitors including C. L. R. James and Cheddi Jagan in 1957 and 1958.[92]

Similar to "Know Your History" columns in the *West Indian Gazette*, Scobie penned a "History" section for *Flamingo*. He commemorated black American Matthew Henson as the "first mortal to stand on top of the world"[93] as part of the first successful mission to the North Pole. As part of Commander Robert Peary's expedition, Henson never received the same accolades for reaching the pole first, that honor was reserved for the white expedition leader. Scobie urged black people to take pride in Henson's achievement and to "let the whites keep their Captain Scotts."[94] Robert Falcon Scott was the British Royal Navy officer who led two expeditions to the Antarctic in the early twentieth century, dying on his return from the second and being forever immortalized as a British national hero. Scobie implored black people to take interest and pride in their history, citing Henson as the man "who placed the Stars and Stripes at the top of the world while the leader [Peary] sat exhausted on a sledge and feebly waved his hand."[95]

Racialized hierarchies in Britain defined the social structure and *Flamingo* sometimes reflected the predominance of white supremacy. In a profile of a Jamaican postal worker, *Flamingo* referred to the mail carrier as "Sammy" and his superior (an Englishman) as "Mr. A. Field." For *Flamingo* this particular convention was two-fold. First, in order to connect the readership with Sammy, they refer to him in the most familiar way and his supervisor is addressed with typical British respect. Secondly, *Flamingo* could not avoid the very real inequalities in the relationship between black worker and white leader.

Along with the *West Indian Gazette* and *Caribbean Times*, the magnitude and frequency of immigrant issues with discrimination and policing necessitated continued organizing and conferencing to develop strategies to counter British patterns of racialization. The Family Welfare Association developed a "Project for the Welfare of Coloured Peoples" as a response to the disturbances in Notting Hill. In 1959, FWA indicted the white British community for their denial of immigrant civil rights and denying them "opportunity of housing and employment equal to any other citizen's."[96]

FWA was part of the Kensington Citizen's Advice Bureau and reported on many of the conferences on immigrants in Britain. FWA noted that because "the newcomers have been denied opportunity of housing and employment ... they tend to view with suspicion any agency which claims to be concerned with this problem."[97] Migrants were skeptical because of the poor conditions and reprehensible treatment they received from native British antagonists. FWA determined the greatest success of the race relations conferences was the "knowledge and understanding of the immigrants and their cultural background" but noted that their shortcomings included allowing some "to express their prejudices in public without ... any time ... for educational purposes."[98] Problems of racialization were new to many Britons and they did not thoroughly strategize how to deal with these issues. Conference organizers were unaware of how to discuss racial strife in public in a manner that advocated against discrimination and often provided another setting for antagonists to air their grievances. FWA offered that "conferences should concentrate on the question of prejudice, its source and removal, and on understanding the significance of race and cultural difference and a on finding ways and means of developing techniques which could help to modify attitudes."[99]

GOVERNMENT RESPONSES

The British-Caribbean Association, formed by volunteers including members of Parliament, promoted understanding and friendship between people from the Commonwealth Caribbean and native-born Britons. In 1960, a B-CA convoy traveled to the Caribbean to build relationships with the newly formed independent governments. Nigel Fisher, MP and future Under-Secretary of State for the Colonies, visited British Guiana, Trinidad, and Jamaica. Parliamentarians Sir Roland Robinson, Sir John Vaughn Morgan, George Thomson, and Freddie Bennett visited Trinidad for the annual meeting of the Commonwealth Parliamentary Association. Leaders in the Caribbean also engaged in metropolitan politics and affairs as Sir Grantley Adams visited London for the wedding of Princess Margaret.[100]

B-CA chronicled activities of various agencies working to improve race relations in London. The Clapham Inter-Racial Club met "every Wednesday evening and held a dance [in 1960] attended by 400 people at the Wandsworth

Town Hall . . . a programme from the Hall was recorded by the B.B.C. and transmitted the same evening to the West Indies."[101] B-CA members also attended a Special Council Meeting in the House of Commons on legislation against racial discrimination. Chairman Charles Royle suggested that the Council advocate for "legislation . . . to ensure . . . no discrimination on grounds of colour in public places in this country."[102] Another member, Mrs. Thirlwell mentioned, "many West Indians were worried and had no sense of security under the present legislation."[103] After Notting Hill, activists charged the government with preventing similar events and establishing protections for citizens of color.

B-CA also publicly appealed to Parliament. B-CA chairman Nigel Fisher suggested "it would help towards good relations with coloured immigrants if a pamphlet could be published . . . to publicise the work of the various officials and voluntary bodies operating in this field."[104] Previously, the Association proposed a Government-issued annual pamphlet with the proposed title of "Getting to Know Your Neighbour," to include the names of these resources in the United Kingdom and throughout the Commonwealth along with organizations concerned with exchange schemes and vocational training programs. B-CA suggested distributing the pamphlet to libraries, Citizens' Advice Bureaux, Chambers of Commerce, Rotary Clubs, and local educational departments.[105] The problems for migrants, however, frustrated MPs who complained that West Indians were "not the responsibility of any single U.K. Department."[106] The Colonial Office vested interest in Caribbean migrants but local problems such as police brutality and housing discrimination were assigned to other agencies. B-CA acknowledged that the presence of West Indians in London had ramifications beyond typical immigration issues; they were changing the fabric of British society.

Although B-CA sought to ameliorate the problems West Indians encountered, members nevertheless charged migrants for many problems they endured. In 1960, J. M. Ross of the Home Office found it "hard to believe that there are West Indians in this country who do not know where to seek help . . . the Migrant Services Division . . . exists exclusively to help them . . . an officer of that Division invariably meets all parties on arrival here."[107] Conversely, migrants explained that officials from the Migrant Services Division neither greeted them upon arrival nor were they informed about the existence of the Division or available resources. Ross's criticism of West Indians who were unaware of extant social services was repeated in popular media and many Britons considered migrants to be difficult guests, resistant to assimilation in Britain. For more than a decade, West Indians reported that they had been duped by untrustworthy persons waiting at the docks for ships of newly arrived—and presumably gullible migrants to exploit. Ross's counterargument suggests that a fundamental fissure existed between the British government's attempts at welcoming colonials and the difficult realities that migrants faced. The violence of Notting Hill, the aggression of the Teddy boys, and the murder of Kelso Cochrane did little to change the perceptions Britons had of the migrants; they continued to view colonials as responsible for the problems that abounded in Britain by the 1960s.

Relations between the police and migrants of color worsened after Notting Hill despite the central role of Teddy boy antagonism. Nadine S. Peppard, Secretary of the Immigrants' Advisory Committee of the London Council of Social Service, wrote to the Police Commissioner petitioning for a statement on relations between the police force and migrants. The Commissioner's Office replied that "arrangements have been made by the Home Office for a representative of the High Commissioner for Jamaica to give lectures at the National Police College about the many problems which arise in a multi-racial population."[108] The Metropolitan Police acknowledged the problems between attendant officers and neighborhood residents and suggested that "these talks will . . . apply equally to problems of other coloured immigrants including Indians and Pakistanis."[109] In a meeting at the Home Office in May 1963, Sir Laurence Lindo, High Commissioner for Jamaica, relayed, "over the last 5 months he had become conscious of a deterioration relations between the police and the Jamaican community in London."[110] A constable on the beat actually approached Lindo's legal advisor when he visited Berkeley Square in the West End, "due to the fact that he was a coloured man."[111] Lindo also received reports of Jamaicans being driven away by police while waiting outside of Labour Exchanges to collect benefits.

Lindo met with Jamaican residents in London in June 1963. Many migrants of color lived under perpetual surveillance and were targeted for police stops. He explained that due to "the likelihood of coloured persons being about in the streets at later hours than the rest of the community,"[112] they were seen as suspicious and therefore subject to more searches. Lindo also acknowledged that "many Jamaicans in this country come from parts of Jamaica where Police were inclined to handle them rather roughly and where there was a certain element of anti-Police feeling . . . resentment expressed about Police . . . was a legacy of their previous environment."[113] Lindo, the first native Jamaican to serve as High Commissioner, attributed poor treatment of migrants to their own behavioral patterns, whether it was traveling the streets at night or congregating for recreation. The Commission suggested West Indians were familiar with discriminatory and punitive treatment from the authorities. Black Caribbean functionaries, who occupied Commonwealth-oriented positions like Lindo, overestimated the familiarity with excessive police tactics they believed West Indians had.

Many Afro-Caribbean migrants understood themselves to be a part of a global community of color. Indians and West Indians enjoyed cricket and football, as well as American jazz, Brazilian samba, and other diaspora music forms. Paul Robeson, the black American musician, singer, and actor who could not leave the United States for eight years due to his leftist leanings and support mobilizing the US Communist Party, returned to Britain in 1958 to perform. He received a massive welcome in London that July, met by "200 admirers . . . among them . . . an M.P. and a minister of a British colony—Dr. Cheddi Jagan of British Guiana."[114] Across Britain and empire, people of color connected to Robeson who they recognized as a proponent of black solidarity. Robeson professed camaraderie with Britons and advocated for colonial freedom. In reference to the uprisings in 1950s British East Africa, especially the Kenya Land and Freedom Army, Robeson explained "African people in Kenya have the same aspirations as the British people themselves . . . the struggle for African independence must reach the high levels of unity between the oppressed peoples."[115] He recognized the need for unity and cooperation among the disenfranchised across the colonies, a perspective that would soon grow and explode with the accelerated mobilization of people of color in the next decade.

DEBATES ON MIGRATION AND RACE

Race relations in Britain were increasingly strained during the 1960s and migrants of color were concerned with their chances of staying in Britain or having family join them. The absence of antidiscrimination legislation permitted employers and landlords to continue to ignore or willfully discriminate against Caribbean migrants. In 1963, *The Evening Standard* ran a cartoon that depicted two white Britons in Bristol reading the following note: "congratulations on your stand for white supremacy—Minister of Interior, South Africa."[116] If racist discrimination in Britain was analogous to apartheid in South Africa, the extent of discrimination and prejudice seemed all-encompassing for colored migrants in England.

Race relations in 1960s were part of transnational discourse, extending beyond the confines of metropolitan Britain and contesting with the notions of sovereignty and equality in newly independent Caribbean nations. Eric Huntley penned a series of articles from 1966 to 1967, "Cold Comfort for Coloured Strangers," which highlighted ongoing problems of assimilation for colonial migrants in the metropole. Not only did Huntley attribute the persistence of racial discrimination in Britain to "the British people," he contended that racialism was "deeply rooted in the history and culture of [these] people."[117] He indicted Britain as "the nation which has been the foremost slave trader and colonialist . . . [incubator] of the ideas which have helped rationalise the barbarous system of slavery and to act as a reassuring balm to the consciences of the more susceptible."[118] Furthermore, Huntley noted that Britons continued to perpetuate these ideas and simultaneously disregarded the histories of their former colonial holdings. He cited Professor Trevor Roper, who delivered a Reith Lecture[119] in 1963 which "discourage[d] . . . young scholars for the curiosity they showed in learning the history of Africa by stating that the continent had no history only darkness."[120] Huntley viewed the prevailing racist perspectives of influential Britons as a product of a long history of domination of others and its corresponding ignorance of native citizens.

The racial antagonism during the riots was unofficially sanctioned by the "Keep Britain White" campaign, which was promoted by fascists in the 1950s. Huntley charged Sir Cyril Osborne, MP for Louth, Lincolnshire, with supporting the campaign. Along with Osborne, the mass media lent support to Keep Britain White. Huntley recounted television networks that were "present at the places of disembarkation . . . the *Times* [drew] . . . attention to the fact that by 1970, the number would reach one million."[121] Anti-immigrant sentiment became so strong that Huntley noted Britons were leaving for Australia or South Africa because of attitudes that "Britain was 'finished' . . . coloured people would certainly ruin the country."[122] A number of white Britons hoped to leave their homes to live in other places where white supremacy operated in more public, severe, and dominant ways.[123]

Restrictions on Commonwealth migration became central in British public discourse after the violence in Notting Hill. In a December 1961 cartoon from *The Guardian*, white Britons are shown holding signs reading "Keep Britain White" and "Commonwealths Go Home" at a disembarkation point where arriving West Indians were queued. Cartoonist David Low captioned the scene: "O.K.! So we keep 'em all out—and we close down the underground and the buses and let the country go dirty again."[124] Low acknowledged a critical reality of life in postwar Britain—colored migrants supplied the labor for the public services and were indispensable in national recovery efforts. Scores of migrants operated the London Underground, drove buses in the Transport for London scheme, and worked as cleaners, janitors, and carpenters throughout Britain. Low highlighted the irony of native Britons viewing colored migrants as unwelcome nuisances despite the fact that migrants played a major role in essential jobs that stabilized Britain after World War II.

Low's cartoon reflected both ongoing antipathy of native Britons toward colored migrants and official debates about immigration policy. In the early 1960s, the Colonial Office wrestled with the question of continued immigration from the Caribbean. Colonial Office officials determined reduced immigration could be achieved only by "the U.K. Government imposing restrictions on entry or . . . by the West Indian Governments restricting the issue of passports."[125] The Government recognized that West Indians remained eager and willing to travel to Britain and only through official governmental action, by either West Indian governments or the metropolitan government, could migration rates be slowed. Furthermore, the Colonial Office assumed West Indian Governments would be unprepared and unwilling to enact any restrictions, placing the burden on the metropolitan government.

Initially, the British Government aimed to convince West Indian Governments of the need to decrease migration from their territories. CO officer Norman Pannell revealed that he received "assurance . . . that the West Indian Governments would co-operate in this matter."[126] Pannell noted that from January through October 1960 there were 43,450 immigrants from the West Indies compared with 16,400 for the entirety of 1959.[127] Despite difficult conditions that West Indians faced once they arrived in Britain, migration rates from the Caribbean increased during this period. The Colonial Office pressed the need for West Indian Governments to publicize for migrants "the difficulties which they are likely to find in the U.K., particularly with regard to housing and employment."[128]

Claudia Jones decried the 1962 Commonwealth Immigrants Act as "ostensibly restrict[ing] Commonwealth immigration as a whole, but in fact, [it] discriminates heavily against colored Commonwealth citizens."[129] Jones argued that the newer restrictions specifically targeted migrants of color and "established a second class citizenship status for West Indians and other Afro-Asian peoples in Britain."[130] Additionally, she cited Sheila Patterson's Institute of Race Relations and Nuffield Foundation sponsored study *Dark Strangers*, highlighting the role activist social scientists played in the mobilization for civil rights and equality. Patterson explained that Commonwealth migrants justifiably showed "an inclination to judge Britain's good faith in international relations by her ability to put her own house in order."[131] For West Indians, South Asians, and Africans from newly independent nations and their diasporas to take seriously the claims of a fair Commonwealth, they needed to live the proof of a non-racialist metropolitan Britain.

Migrants acknowledged a range of social and political difficulties they encountered. In light of 'Keep Britain White' campaigns, organizations by, of, and for migrants became especially important sources of support and mobilization—particularly for activist-minded migrants such as the Huntleys. For example, Eric Huntley recalled that upon arriving in Britain in the 1950s he could not find any space within the establishment or in political or social organizations in which to function.[132] The Huntleys sought out the British Communist Party and attended only one meeting of the West Indian Committee of the Party. Including the Huntleys, only five West Indians constituted the Committee and this lack of representation contributed to their never officially joining the Party. Eric Huntley remembered the British Communists lending uncritical consensus support for Cheddi Jagan without sufficient knowledge of the situation in Guiana. During the lone Party meeting the Huntleys attended in Farringdon, the City of London, they were shocked when the convener abruptly ended at 9:00 p.m. Both Eric and Jessica recounted how in the Caribbean there were no strict time limits on meetings; they were aghast when "some grey-hair white man" tersely ended proceedings.[133] They expressed confusion over the differences in social and political meetings in England. Huntley recognized the British Communist Party's influential role in the student movement and in anticolonial politics, especially in Ghana, India, Malaysia, and Singapore. Furthermore, the Labour Party never established a stronghold in Guiana as it had in other West Indian territories. Members of the Manley family in Jamaica were influenced by the British Labour Party and the Fabian Society and carried elements of their politics and platform to their home island. Without the same Labour presence in Guiana, the PPP allied itself most closely to the stance of Communists in Europe and throughout the decolonizing world.

At the behest of Trinidadian John La Rose, the Huntleys organized a secret West Indian Communist Party in London. They worked with Guianese Walter Rodney through this organization during the early 1960s. Stuart Hall also joined with the West Indian Communists. Without the Communist Party's support or knowledge, Eric Huntley organized a symposium on British Guiana in 1965 held at La Rose's home in Hornsey. The British Guiana Freedom Association predated the formation of the West Indian Communist Party and was instrumental in the conference. BGFA was a predominantly black organization that included small numbers of Indo-Guyanese members. The Huntleys long envisioned their radical politics as wide-ranging, from discussions on Federation in the West Indies to independence for British Guiana, anti-apartheid in South Africa, and their support for the anticolonial insurgency in Kenya. The Huntleys' political orientation was unbound by strict nationalist perspectives. They were concerned for Guiana and its future prospects of decolonization, but were also aware of similar situations throughout the West Indies and issues further abroad, such as the war in Vietnam. Jessica Huntley cited developments in India, Kenya, and China as central to their overall thought, as Communists and as activists. Diasporic political orientation spurred the Huntleys to be cognizant of developments in their homeland. They were acutely aware of the typical trajectory for West Indian migrants—many of whom would travel abroad as students and work tirelessly in radical mobilization projects—and then return home to government jobs in the Caribbean. The notion of "radicals abroad and conservatives at home"[134] reflected a common colonial attitude toward living in the metropole. Some migrants were assailed by the racialized status quo in Britain and worked to improve their condition while abroad; they also remained motivated by opportunities to train in the capital so that they could move back to the islands and live comfortably once resettled.

The Huntleys engaged a number of influential activists and intellectuals who arrived in Britain as students, and further strengthened the bonds of West Indian identification with like-minded people. They worked with Jamaicans Trevor Munroe, Norman Girvan, and Richard Small who were students in London during the early 1960s. Munroe, Girvan, and Small were frequently at the West Indian Students' Centre located near Africa House where the Huntleys regularly visited. All three men would become influential members of the West Indian intelligentsia and remained active in the social and political upheavals in Jamaica following independence. Munroe was a Rhodes Scholar and earned his DPhil in political science for his landmark study on the process of independence in Jamaica, *The Politics of Constitutional Decolonization*, published in 1972.[135] The Huntleys also worked with future Grenada Prime Minister Maurice Bishop while he studied law and worked as a barrister in London. They also spent time organizing with Winston Bernard Coard, who initially worked as a postcolonial leader in Grenada alongside Bishop.[136]

The Huntleys developed an especially close relationship with Walter Rodney while he lived in London. They were friends with Rodney's paternal grandmother who lived in North London and were able to see him whenever he visited. Jessica aided Rodney in typing his doctoral dissertation while he was at the School of Oriental and African Studies.[137] Moreover, Rodney was closely involved with the activities of the West Indian Students' Union and the Huntleys often went to social gatherings with him, a reflection of their personal closeness and shared political consciousness.

Despite growing resentment from white British nationalists, the Huntleys praised the efforts of an increasing number of migrants organizing throughout the 1960s. David Pitt chaired the Campaign against Racial Discrimination (CARD), an umbrella body of migrant organizations.[138] Pitt helped to found the West Indian National Party in Trinidad and after returning to Britain, lost a parliamentary election to Conservative Henry Brooke. Alongside CARD, the Huntleys cited the West Indian Conference and the Indian Workers Association as representative of burgeoning radical Caribbean consciousness in London.[139] Huntley also confirmed that while resident in Britain "much concern . . . is the role which could be played by many migrants . . . in giving support to the movements in favour of genuine independence in their respective countries."[140] Life in Britain did not signal the end of the relationships between migrants and their friends and families in their home countries. Eric Huntley recommended that migrants send financial support home and protest the domination of the Caribbean by foreign-owned corporations. He explained, "many . . . capitalists e.g. Bookers of Guyana, Fayeths of Jamaica

... have their head quarters in London ... [thus] migrants could carry the struggle before the door step of the enemy."[141] The Booker sugar operation and Fayeth banana traders continued to exploit the labor of the families and friends of the Caribbean migrant classes.

In the 1960s, acquiring and maintaining employment remained a problem for colored migrants as the previous discriminatory policies and practices continued. A CARD memorandum presented to the Royal Commission on Trade Unions in 1966 observed, "even the children of coloured people with at least ten years of schooling in Britain find it difficult if not impossible to obtain jobs ... especially ... those seeking apprenticeship training."[142] Labor exchanges perpetuated the informal color bar by agreeing not to send colored workers if employers so requested. Public institutions designed to aid migrants were themselves guilty of the exact biases private sector enterprises practiced. Because 1950s labor shortages required additional workers from the Caribbean, industries were willing to relax their discriminatory cultures but once the economy stabilized, foreign workers of color were the first to be made redundant and struggled to find further work.[143]

While West Indian colonials could freely travel into and out of the metropole, the lack of legal protections for them upon arrival continued to be an issue through the 1960s. The color bar prevented many West Indians from obtaining work or securing housing in large swaths of London and throughout Britain. Claudia Jones advocated for the passage of the Bill to Outlaw Racial Discrimination, initially proposed by Fenner Brockway, Labour MP from Slough, Berkshire. Jones noted the Conservatives blocked the Bill nine times by 1964.[144] The bill outlawed "discrimination in public places, lodgings, inns, dance halls, and other leases; and ... put penalties on incitement to racialism."[145] Jones cited the exploitation and domination of all peoples in Britain (both white working classes and the incoming migrants of color) by the British bourgeoisie as the root of continued racial animosity. She suggested "the small top section of the working class, bribed and corrupted ... have been imbued with this racialist 'white superiority' poison."[146] Rather than unite against capitalist domination, Jones argued that the logics of white supremacy benefitted white working classes and pitted them against colored workers from the same class background.

The Huntleys' urging of financial support did not go unheard. Migrants sent money home for as long as they lived and worked in Britain. In 1965, the *Guardian* reported that "since 1955 Jamaicans in England have sent home £40 millions, more than five times the total British aid to Jamaica since the war."[147] Despite British colonial rule, Jamaican migrant-citizen remittances totaled more than governmental aid during the *Windrush* era. This financial support, however, coincided with the loss of skilled workers in the West Indies. For instance, Jamaica could have a maximum of 1275 people admitted to Britain (15% per country of the Commonwealth total of 8,500 per year) though the majority would be skilled workers and professionals already employed in Jamaica.[148] Furthermore, one of the most important Jamaican industries, bauxite, was controlled by one Canadian and three American companies. The most profitable industry in the islands remained under the purview of foreign ownership, never trickling down to the Jamaican working classes.

Debates over the tenability of the Commonwealth Immigrants Act reflected the pernicious nature of Britain compromising its cultural position as mother country in the face of continued social unrest brought on by increased racialized antagonism in the metropole. Norman Pannell, MP for Liverpool Kirkdale, pressed Secretary of State for the Colonies Iain Macleod to restrict West Indian migration with the aid of the West Indian governments. According to Macleod, "West Indian Governments . . . show[ed] . . . an understanding of the problems involved in migration to this country and a readiness to co-operate with H.M.G. in the United Kingdom in dealing with them."[149] Macleod insisted that he "impressed upon all West Indian Governments that the ability of the United Kingdom to absorb unskilled immigrant labour . . . [was] not unlimited."[150]

"BELONGERS" AND "NON-BELONGERS": COMMONWEALTH IMMIGRANTS ACT AND RACE RELATIONS BILL

The Commonwealth Immigrants Act came into effect on July 1, 1962. Immigration was theretofore significantly restricted from former Caribbean colonies; within British political circles the discursive parameters of the debate changed as well. R. F. Wood, assistant secretary in charge of the Commonwealth Immigrants Division of the Home Office, explained that there was no option but to pass all the "non-belongers" from within and outside the Commonwealth through immigration control. By the 1960s, the British government demarcated its metropolitan population and the constitution of its former empire into "belongers" and "non-belongers." The problems of assimilation and acceptance for migrants of color was reaffirmed and legally sanctioned and corroborated by British immigration policy at the end of empire.[151] Much of the debate was skewed to the point of ubiquitous criminalization of the migrants. Upon receiving the Royal Assent in the House of Lords, the Act was lauded for providing the Courts the "power to recommend deportation . . . [to] clear out Commonwealth immigrants who have come to Britain with no intention of doing any real work and have run brothels or lived on the immoral earnings of women."[152] Administrators and politicians acknowledged the racial tensions across Britain and credited the passage of the Act as a measure that would lessen racial acrimony. The Act was publicly praised for "making . . . possible for the first time . . . [keeping] out misfits who have in the past contributed disproportionately to friction."[153] Britons were convinced that West Indians were the aggressors and instigators of racial tensions despite clear evidence of the predatory role played by Teddy boys in the riots and exploitative lending practices of landlords in poorer urban districts. West Indians and other migrants of color were regarded as ungracious visitors and temporary interlocutors who resisted assimilation and worsened social conditions in the capital. While numerous industrial trade unions actively excluded colored laborers from their ranks, West Indians nonetheless were charged with "indifferent . . . hostile attitudes" toward union membership.[154]

On the first day after enactment, 14 of 599 Commonwealth arrivants at London airport were refused entry to Britain. One man from British Guiana was in Britain for only two hours before boarding a plane back to South America. A man from Aden begged on his knees in front of an interpreter before being sent away. Six others from Aden were interrogated for nearly an hour before immigration officers refused them entry. Groups of Pakistani and Indian men were also detained and sent back to their home countries over the course of the day. The migrants were the first arrivants encountering the more restrictive immigration regulations of the new Act.[155]

A sweeping component of the Act was the ability for magistrates to recommend Commonwealth citizens for deportation. In July 1962, a month after the Act's passage, one hundred twenty-five residents were recommended for deportation. No formal guidelines were distributed to magistrates detailing the requirements for advocating deportation. G. Graham Don, the West Ham Magistrate, suggested that "the power to recommend deportation be restricted to H.M. Judges . . . [and] the deportation provisions be repealed as harmful to the Commonwealth family of nations."[156] Numerous calls for deportation were made from various parties and from judges of varying rank with little legal basis or rationale. In its first month, the Act quickly became a powerful tool identifying and expelling migrants of color from Britain.

Despite the ominous precedent that the Commonwealth Immigrants Act set for migrants throughout empire, in its first month, the West Indies, Cyprus, and Canada were the only territories which maintained an increase of arrivals over departures. Even as the policy made clear resentment toward migrants of color, West Indians nonetheless continued to venture to the metropole.[157] The promise of employment secured by a voucher issued by the Ministry of Labour was often enough to convince West Indians to travel to the United Kingdom. Through summer 1962, the Ministry of Labour received 7,901 applications for vouchers and issued 6,221 (79%) of that total. Among West

Indian applicants, 78 percent of applications were approved. Within the Caribbean, applicants from Barbados received more vouchers than any other territory, perhaps as a legacy of a government sponsored recruiting agency operation.[158]

Many white Britons expressed disdain and antagonism toward the non-whites in their midst, even after the passage of the Act and decreased numbers of arriving immigrants. The playwright Monja Danischewsky, writing from Highgate in May 1963, countered with scathing sarcasm:

> The number of coloured people in the world is immense . . . the number of white people who are intolerant of coloured people is comparatively small . . . and it is hoped, decreases yearly as education spreads . . . would it not be a logical solution . . . if reservations could be established in remote and unpopulated places where this minority could be protected and allowed to live in peace, unmolested by Negro children . . . or so-called progressive reformers?[159]

Danischewsky at once criticized the conservative views of anti-black Britons *and* imagined the founding of anti-black safe havens for white British agitators akin to Afrikaner villages in apartheid South Africa. Though Danischewsky provided a tongue-in-cheek critique, the progressive voices in Britain were nonetheless dwarfed by the reactionary right-wing activities of the Mosleyites and Teddy boys.

The Race Relations Bill, passed on April 7, 1965, was an antidiscrimination measure to quell the disruptive resentment and outward prejudices plaguing Britain due to the influx of coloured migrants. The Bill intended to "prohibit discrimination on racial grounds in places of public resort; prevent the enforcement or imposition on racial grounds of restrictions on the transfer of tenants and penalize incitement to racial hatred."[160]

TRANSATLANTIC RADICAL POLITICAL ARTICULATIONS

After dissolution of the West Indies Federation and independence, migrants in Britain remained engaged with political developments in the Caribbean. On October 15, 1968, the Jamaican government banned Walter Rodney from reentering the country. Guyanese Rodney, lecturer in African history at the University of the West Indies, Mona, was returning from a Black Writers' Conference in Montreal. Prime Minister, Hugh Shearer of the Jamaica Labour Party, banned Rodney on the grounds of his socialist ties, visits to Cuba and the Soviet Union, and his radical black nationalism. In response, UWI students and workers in Kingston demonstrated in protest against the government and were met with brutal military and police suppression including battery and gassing.[161]

After Rodney was barred from Jamaica, West Indians in Britain responded to what they viewed was an illegal and unjust criminalization of the historian. British black power collective the Black Eagles castigated Shearer and "his henchmen" for detaining Rodney and celebrated Jamaican "Brothers and Sisters [who] are organising themselves."[162] The Eagles rejected Shearer's characterization of Rodney as "an evil and wicked young man" and instead celebrated Rodney's refusal to "remain on the posh university campus" after taking his appointment as a lecturer in Mona. Rodney had reached out to a wider cross section of Jamaican society upon his appointment, traveling to garrisons in Kingston and engaging directly with Rastafarians in the hills beyond the city.

According to the Eagles, Rodney's immersion into multiple levels of Jamaican society disturbed some of the postcolonial establishment. Jamaicans who protested the government's action against Rodney resisted the bourgeois postcolonial elite and its restrictive policies. The Eagles saluted the "masses of Jamaican people . . . [who] knew . . . that the Government were concerned only with the interests of the rich white racists, who were living off the hungry, the poor and the Black." They articulated solidarity between "Black people in England" who were "with them all the way" and imagined the "day . . . not far off when the riches of Jamaica will be shared by all Jamaicans; the BLACK and the PROUD."[163]

The Huntleys advocated on behalf of Rodney from London. Jessica was involved with the Caribbean Education and Community Workers Association (CECWA) who picketed the Jamaican High Commission and organized a march (along with student groups) in Rodney's defense. Numerous activists were arrested during the protest, including Selma James and Richard Small, Chair of the West Indian Students' Union. Rodney arrived in Britain and met with this contingent of activists. He brought with him papers and transcripts of talks he had given in Jamaica. Rodney and the Huntleys wished to publish scholarship and writings to be distributed in the United Kingdom as well as across the Caribbean diaspora. They received financial donations from friends and colleagues to fund the printing (about £300) of Rodney's *The Groundings with My Brothers*.[164] Initially, the Huntleys and Rodney considered a number of prospective titles for this work including *Walter Rodney Speaks*, which would pay tribute to the audiences in Jamaica who witnessed his testimonials and talks while he was at Mona.

Within four days of Rodney's detention, three people were killed by police violence in Jamaica and a flyer pleading for an end to the brutality circulated throughout Britain. Circulars urged West Indians in Britain to "phone and complain to the High Commissioner for Jamaica in London . . . write letters of condemnation . . . demonstrate in mass rallies."¹⁶⁵ The protests continued along with increased correspondence between migrants and their friends and governments in the Caribbean. Jessica Huntley, Richard Small, and the Jamaican novelist and poet Andrew Salkey collectively wrote a letter to Eric Williams, Prime Minister Trinidad and Tobago, calling on him to act against the banning of Rodney in Jamaica. They contended that "the ban has been a blow against the efforts towards unification of the territories in the area . . . a blow against the autonomy of the University . . . restricting academic freedom and a blow against traffic of ideas between Mother Africa and Ourselves."¹⁶⁶ In making such claims, Huntley, Small, and Salkey wrote on behalf of attendees of a meeting held in London including West Indian writers, playwrights, novelists, poets, lawyers, students, journalists, architects, and workers.¹⁶⁷ Many were dismayed by the Jamaican government's interference in university matters and the fact that Rodney was a Guyanese banned from Jamaica. The unity that formally existed with the West Indies Federation and had recently broken down was further compromised due to Rodney's status as a foreign national in Jamaica. UWI was a regional institution maintained by personnel and financial backing of the entire West Indies.¹⁶⁸ A critical mass of West Indians in London saw themselves as brethren and sistren and they sought to revitalize feelings of unity among the people in their homelands.

A formal petition was delivered to the Jamaican High Commissioner on August 15, 1968, protesting the Jamaican Government's banning of black power writings of Stokely Carmichael, Malcolm X, and Elijah Muhammad. A coalition¹⁶⁹ issued the petition, indicting the Jamaica Government for censorship. They charged Jamaica with "joining hands with white racist America . . . Jamaica associates herself with the American policy of enslaving black people who oppose oppression . . . to silence the voice of freedom and dignity which means as much to black people in Jamaica as it does to our brothers in the United States and the rest of the third world."¹⁷⁰ The coalition's denunciation was coupled with a declaration of solidarity throughout the global South and a critique of the historical plight of black peoples in the United States. The petition linked many people—tied by race and homeland. It reminded the High Commissioner that "Stokely is a son of Trinidad; Malcolm's mother is a daughter of Grenada; Malcolm's father was a Garveyite; Malcolm tells how much he owes to Marcus Garvey . . . Stokely says how much he owes to Malcolm."¹⁷¹ The signatories called on the government to lift the order against "Garvey . . . our National hero [whose] . . . writings, philosophies and . . . opinions are now deeply a part of how we think and act . . . we appeal to the people of Jamaica to rededicate themselves to the 'thoughts of Marcus Garvey.'"¹⁷² The petitioners traced a direct lineage from their hero Garvey to two of the most well-known radical proponents of black power, Malcolm X and Carmichael, whose familial, philosophical, and geographic roots originated in the West Indies.

GLOBAL GROUNDINGS

Rodney's influence persisted after his banishment from Jamaica. His connection to the Huntleys allowed Rodney to continue to spread ideas about capitalist exploitation and the necessity for an innovative socialism in newly independent Caribbean nations. Bogle-L'Ouverture Publications issued Rodney's *The Groundings with My Brothers* in 1969.[173] Rodney articulated his logics of black power and urged black people to educate themselves on black history and use knowledge to mobilize and revolutionize postcolonial futures. In the manifesto, Rodney historically framed the Caribbean region— "West Indian society is a veritable laboratory of racialism . . . We virtually invented racialism."[174] He suggested that "the fantastic gap between master and slave was translated into a feeling on the part of the white slavemaster that he had inherently to be superior to that black man who was slaving out in the fields . . . it was in that part of the world that modern racialism was engendered."[175] Rodney's work reflected the radical turn of West Indians in the United Kingdom but also of those in the West Indies agitating against the neocolonial regimes propping up newly independent nation-states.[176]

The Groundings opens with Rodney's critique of the contemporaneous political situation in newly independent Jamaica. Rodney noted that since independence, "the Black police force of Jamaica have demonstrated that they can be as savage in their approach to black brothers as the white police of New York."[177] Comparison between Jamaica and the United States reflected a diasporic perspective that permeated Rodney's thought and work. He contextualized similar patterns of discrimination and repression against Africans across nation-states. Rodney cited the emergence of the Rastafari movement in Jamaica as actualizing a black revolutionary politics and worldview. He recognized that Rastafari "have been joined . . . by large numbers of other black people . . . influenced by the struggle and example of black brothers in the U.S.A."[178] The Rastafari exhibited *post-national* awareness of black liberation and black power movements that separated them from mainstream Jamaican society. Rodney lauded the Rastafari who, upon the arrival of Haile Selassie I in Jamaica in 1966, forced police to "stand back while the population thrust forward enthusiastically to pay homage to the Ethiopian Monarch."[179] If Jamaicans increasingly expressed a far-reaching revolutionary politics by the close of the 1960s, Rastafari embodied the frustrations Jamaicans had with the current regime as well as alternative ways of thinking and being.

Rodney outlined the precepts of the emerging Black Power movement in *Groundings*. Like members of the Caribbean Artists Movement, he traveled extensively, lived in a number of countries, and expressed awareness of the happenings in various sites of the African diaspora. "[I]n the U.S.A. if one is not white . . . one is black," Rodney elucidated, "in Britain, if one is not white then one is coloured . . . [and] in South Africa, one can be white, coloured or black."[180] Through his experiences and correspondence with peers and other activists, Rodney thoroughly understood racialized oppression across the world. He knew well the depth of racialization in British society. Rodney explained that "when a Pakistani goes to the Midlands he is as coloured as a Nigerian . . . the Indonesian is the same as a Surinamer in Holland."[181] Rodney argued that racial consciousness in Europe conflated nonwhites as outsiders; ergo West Indians, and Asians constituted the same disenfranchised group in multiethnic European societies. He understood black people as "the hundreds of millions of people whose homelands are in Asia and Africa, with another few millions in the Americas."[182] Rodney appealed to people of color globally to mobilize the potential of *political blackness* against the forces of white supremacy at work on all continents.

Rodney's emphasis on the revolutionary potential of Black Power was distinct, even as former colonies had thrown off the yoke of imperialism in the preceding decade. Rodney located his understanding of Black Power as rooted in the legacy of Garvey and recognized that although, "Black power as a slogan . . . [was] new . . . it is . . . an ideology and a movement of historical depth."[183] Like other West Indian luminaries who traveled to England and many other places, Rodney firmly placed his politics within the Caribbean radical tradition.

CONFLICTS AMONG BLACK PUBLICS IN THE METROPOLE

Jamaica's policy on Rodney was critiqued and commentators also linked the island's postcolonial realities to policy and doctrine of the United States. Writing in the West Indian Students' Union *Newsletter*, Earl Greenwood contended that "Jamaica . . . [was] an American protectorate . . . the northern coastline . . . is owned exclusively by Americans and Canadians . . . you fall from Hilton Hotel you are bound to end up in Alcan . . . a great portion of Southern Jamaica is owned by Tate and Lyle."[184] In making such claims, Greenwood underscored that much of Jamaica's political economy was dominated by foreign capital, a phenomenon reflecting foreign-control that the island endured during British colonial rule. Greenwood urged black people to accept black power as a refutation of the colonial and neocolonial powers and an embracing of novel ways of thinking and prospects for governance. Greenwood decried the condition of black migrants in Britain. Schoolchildren were deliberately neglected and, in his experience, Greenwood saw children "in Brixton . . . being literally driven out of the schools . . . drifting along . . . not being aware of the importance of the basic qualifications to help them along in this vicious white society."[185] The schools that young people of color attended were poor and had inadequate facilities and administrations. An anonymous black mother lamented that these educational problems existed but also stressed that "teenagers are the products of the BRITISH GHETTOES . . . black people did not create these areas, they are the victims of the exodus of the white middle class . . . the social and economic deprivation of these areas all work against our black teenagers."[186] This mother expressed a crucial element in the discourse on race relations in Britain. She insisted that the problems affecting West Indian teenagers in Britain were specific to them because they arose in Britain and were a product of the racial biases and prejudices in the metropole. Race and racialization in Britain therefore operated in particularly distinct patterns for which Britons were responsible. Problems of racialization and unfair treatment did not subside in Britain even decades after major migration and the passage of civil rights legislation.

Difficulties for West Indian students in London began in childhood and continued into university years. By the late 1960s, West Indian families moved together to Britain or began families after migrating earlier. Katrin Fitzherbert, an Anglo-German social worker, highlighted the differences in West Indian family life and British society that made acclimation and assimilation difficult for migrant children in her 1967 study, *West Indian Children in London*. "[T]he life of an English child centres completely on its home," Fitzherbert wrote, "the nuclear family is the first and only important social unit it knows . . . when it breaks up, it faces the collapse of its whole universe."[187] For West Indians in England, however, Fitzherbert claimed that "the nuclear family is weakly structured, but, to compensate . . . other associations in the community are much more binding than their English equivalents and enter much more into everyday life."[188] While English children relied heavily on the nuclear family and home life West Indians were used to an "extended family and wide circle of kin play[ing] a more active role."[189] Furthermore, Fitzherbert recognized the different social geographies of family life in Britain and the West Indies. She noted the importance of the West Indian "yard,"

> a group of huts clustered round an open space . . . on the same piece of land, sharing an entrance . . . houses often face one another . . . and the 'yard' is the community within which people borrow, gossip, co-operate, quarrel and children play together . . . related households may be found in the yard . . . associations are based on kinship, neighbourliness and common interest.[190]

Fitzherbert's observations reflected the fact that, since 1948, Britons had complained about an ostensible West Indian propensity for noisemaking and boisterous gatherings. Fitzherbert rightly described the social tradition of communal living migrants brought with them from the Caribbean and utilized to associate with one another while abroad. Furthermore, migrants acquired housing accommodations through personal relations and often shared residential units with friends, coworkers, or family. The notion of an English traditional nuclear family was foreign (and *unnecessary*) to the incoming West Indians.

Fitzherbert highlighted another component of West Indian socialization—movement and displacement. Because families were often mixed and children had "little chance to become totally dependent on a single mother and father figure," Fitzherbert concluded that "there is invariably a connection . . . through the complex interrelations between different branches of the family group."[191] West Indian youth were used to moving from one family member's home to another and to sharing space with close relatives and friends. They relied much less on nuclear family structure and were able to acclimate to various settings from an early period. Despite their capacity to adapt, British society brought a new set of challenges for young West Indians.

The lack of adequate housing and social settings for migrants in London highlighted the depth of racialization in Britain. Without the privilege or ability to establish "yards" or communal living situations, West Indians developed a "semi-organised stag-life which centres round clubs and bars, betting ships and West Indian barbers."[192] Because housing was difficult to acquire and maintain, West Indians resorted to non-domestic modes of socialization. In Stepney, Notting Hill, and Brixton, for instance, West Indians bought and operated pubs and drinking establishments turning these businesses into important social institutions for other migrants. Pubs, barber shops, and bakeries in these areas acted as meeting places and enabled West to avoid condemnation from white Britons in their recreational time after work.[193]

British-Caribbean Association engaged activists and government officials to address the issues of colonial immigration policy and the recently passed Commonwealth Immigrants Act. BC-A chair Donald Chapman regretted that "there was no Minister with overall responsibility for immigration . . . [and] that the present system had worked to the disadvantage of the West Indies."[194] The Commonwealth Immigrants Advisory Council only included West Indians in limited roles. Mr. Ryner, the chief welfare officer for Coventry, who was born in Yorkshire and of West Indian origin, was selected "because of his experience as a welfare officer . . . [not] because of his colour . . . he could hardly be said to represent the coloured population."[195] Another member, Lady Coussey, was described as "half-caste" and non-representative of the colored population. The presence of colored migrants or citizens was deemed problematic for the workings of the Council. Nonwhites were not sought out to serve on the Council because it would "not make for ease of working relationships . . . to have members who are regarded as representatives."[196]

Problems associated with police treatment of the Commonwealth migrants continued even after the lectures given by the High Commission for Jamaica at the Police College during autumn 1963. In response a "Chief Superintendent . . . [was] made responsible for liaison with the coloured communities in London and maintain[ed] close contact with the Jamaican High Commission in particular."[197]

Herbert Hill, Labour Secretary of the National Association for the Advancement of Colored People in the United States, expressed anxiety over the racial tension in Notting Hill after visiting the area in the year after the riots. Hill explained that "the American Negro community has numbers, resources and leadership . . . [but] the coloured groups in Britain are poor . . . leaderless, and geographically dispersed . . . [they are] dependent on allies for assistance."[198] He noted that in the United States, the longer history of a diverse population contributed to an established class of politicized black radicals supported by various institutions whereas in Britain, the early stages of migration left many West Indians to fend for themselves in an unfamiliar setting. For Hill, coalition building was a method through which blacks in Britain could improve the overall situation for migrants of color.

The accelerated radicalization of West Indians in London was buoyed by artistic, literary, and intellectual traditions and grew to incorporate a wider, transnational political orientation during the end of empire. Black Londoners were concerned with the rights of their counterparts in various diaspora sites and those struggling against imperialism in Africa. Black peoples historically found allies in disparate locations—in schools in colonial capitals that drew students from across many regions or in European metropoles. Metropolitan arrival was commonplace for radicals and activists in the diaspora. The critical mass of artists and intellectuals from the West Indies in late imperial London was a distinct grouping of mobile, displaced activists. The transformation from colonial subjects to national citizens of independent states occurred concomitantly with the conservative racist backlash of native Britons preoccupied with the transformative power the presence of people of color would have on Britain and notions of its national identity.

West Indian migration to Britain transformed the politics and social culture of the "mother country" despite the biased reception most migrants endured and continued to contest across generations. The quotidian experiences of discrimination and prejudice, however, did not dissuade West Indians from journeying to London nor did it slow their revolutionary fervor. By the late

1960s, many West Indians were further radicalized and mobilized around issues of race and class in their political campaigns.

THE BIRTH OF BLACK POWER IN BRITAIN

Black social justice activism and articulations for greater representation and recourse for West Indians was spearheaded by a diverse range of organizations motivated by the pursuit of liberation. The Universal Coloured People's Association (UCPA) emerged in the early 1960s advocating for an intersectional radical politics. They argued, "The colour line has coincided with the class line."[199] UCPA laid out their critique of the fabric of racial ideology and white supremacy by arguing.

> It is men who make slaves of other men. It is therefore absurd to talk about making people free. You can only talk about stopping oppression. There is no such thing as the abolition of Slavehood. You can only talk about the destruction of masterhood. There is no such thing as the Negro problem. What we are talking about is the White problem . . . a race of people who, because of an illusion about the colour of their skin, are determined by words and deeds to reduce the rest of humanity to a level of animality from which they can never rise again.[200]

UCPA offered rhetoric that decried the foundations of English society as embedded in the oppressive nature of white supremacy. Rather than suggesting solutions for "race trouble" or advocating for "goodwill," UCPA instead identified the "white problem" of racialized sub- and super-ordination intrinsic in colonial and metropolitan British societies.

UCPA went beyond previous iterations of interracial collaborations and efforts to mitigate the problem of race in Britain through direct articulations and denouncement of the unequal dynamics that empowered whites and disenfranchised blacks. UCPA identified the ubiquity and multiplicity of white supremacy in various contexts. They noted "Black peoples of Britain think that it is only the White men of Britain who oppress Black people . . . the racial organisations of Britain think that the Black man's problem would be over once Brixton, Paddington and Perry Barr are integrated,"[201] just as the "African in Nigeria once thought that political independence for Nigeria meant real freedom for the Black man . . . the Indian worker in Bombay once thought that the Black man in the Caribbean has a different problem from his."[202] UCPA recognized the intertwined iterations of white supremacist oppression in contexts around the former British colonies and in the cities and enclaves where West Indians, Africans, and South Asians lived in Britain.

UCPA extended their critique beyond Britain and Commonwealth as they criticized the phenomenon of "millions of Africans in Southern Africa sincerely believe that it is only a handful of White settlers who are keeping them down and actually expect the White men of Britain to come to their aid"[203] as well as the pernicious reality in the United States were "the Afro-American of Detroit, thought, until recently, that his White oppressor was a different man from the White oppressor of the Vietnamese people."[204]

UCPA mobilized a transnational race-based political movement. Through articulating a race-first political identity, UCPA regarded "the Negro of Harlem . . . [having] much more in common with the African in Angola than he has with the man in a White neighbourhood of Manhattan."[205] The diasporic relationship, predicated on racial identification, was the factor of unification UCPA intended to maximize and marshal. In assessing the various regimes that repressed black people around the world UCPA criticized Southern Rhodesian prime minister Ian Smith and British prime minister Harold Wilson for both believing "that the African is an inferior being incapable of administrating his own community"[206] and for applying only "only a difference in tactics"[207] to subjugate black people in their respective domains. For UCPA, "the quarrel between Smith and Wilson is not a quarrel between fascism and anti-fascism, but a quarrel between frankness and hypocrisy within a fascist framework."[208] UCPA critiqued neoliberalism, neocolonialism, settler politics, and the expression of white supremacist thought in Britain with respect to Africa and Africans.

Problems of race outside of Britain were central to the UCPA platform. UCPA considered the forms of white supremacy and alienation and British Commonwealth as specifically Anglo-Saxon in orientation. On Smith and Wilson, UCPA noted, "both . . . are merely reflecting the Anglo-Saxon global attitude . . . in America, Black people are being lynched by Anglo-Saxon fascists . . . in Canada, Anglo-Saxon fascism has crystallized into European Preferential Migration and the Anti-Asiatic Act . . . in Australia, the Anglo-Saxon civilisation has . . . enshrined itself as the White Australia Policy . . . in South Africa, it has escalated to the dizzy heights of Apartheid . . . in Rhodesia, the Anglo-Saxon fascism is rearing its head as U.D.I. and the White world . . . are applauding the 'rebels.'"[209] Smith implemented the Unilateral Declaration of Independence in Rhodesia in 1965, initiating Rhodesia as a rogue independent state sanctioned by the Commonwealth because of its policy of white minority rule. Furthermore, UCPA pinpointed the reality that, "the areas of the world's most despicable racisms today . . . coincide with the locus of Anglo-Saxon dispersion . . . what we are facing . . . is NOT . . . isolated pockets of White oppression, but INTERNATIONAL WHITE POWER. And the only force that can quell it is INTERNATIONAL BLACK POWER."[210] "Anglo-Saxonism" contributed to the development and spread of international white power which could only be countered by an international black power. UCPA rejected the prominence of Anglo-Saxonism which undergirded the logic of "belongers" and "non-belongers" in British metropolitan policymaking.

Black Power in the UCPA lexicon represented "a NEW STAGE IN THE REVOLUTIONARY CONSCIOUSNESS OF THE BLACK MAN."[211] UCPA argued for the black power as a morally sound ideology and refuted other existent conceptualizations of the term and its possibilities. They argued that black power was *not* "the slogan of dissident Blacks . . . is not Black fascism . . . does not mean the demand of every White head on a platter . . . BLACK POWER does not even mean Black domination of the world."[212] Rejecting a politics of replacing white supremacy for its black version, UCPA offered a revolutionary program rooted in alternative conceptualizations toward social justice. The revolutionary consciousness of black peoples for UCPA would emerge from the pursuit and acquisition of veritable knowledge of Africa and black peoples. Contrary to the white-dominated epistemology upon which anti-black racism and subordination was scaffolded, UCPA insisted that the quest for the black past culminated in black people understanding that, "Africa was never a cultural vacuum . . . Suddenly, the Negro was no longer the Black American ashamed of any identification with Africa . . . [black] cultural nationalism was born, and with it the Negro's rediscovery of Africa and Asia."[213] UCPA credited the recuperation of history as a central component of empowering black people. They defined black power as "the totality of the economic, cultural, political, and if necessary, military power which the Black peoples of the world must acquire in order to get the White oppressor off their backs."[214] UCPA articulated a radical perspective of total revolution and racial empowerment of black peoples worldwide.

Publications were critical mechanisms of radicalization among migrants during this period. For example, the Black Unity and Freedom Party issued *Black Voice,* which advocated their revolutionary political platform. BUFP's platform extended beyond Britain or its former colonies but nonetheless maintained a local perspective as well. BUFP gleaned a great deal of its revolutionary politics from movements from across the global South. Looking toward the Marxist liberation theology in Latin America, BUFP suggested that "the time has come for us to respect the religious beliefs of Black people . . . Latin America has . . . shown us that there is no reason why Christian and Marxist [cannot] fight side by side against the oppressor."[215] In making such an argument, the Party cited "Camilo Torres, the Colombian catholic priest who . . . understood that once we . . . have liberated ourselves then we can decide the religious orientation of the state."[216] BUFP mobilized black peoples across all identities—national origin, class background, religious beliefs—in order to eliminate the divide in rights and representation in Britain drawn across racial lines. They organized "around the complete unity of

Black people" because, "anything less . . . will allow the racist government to . . . divide and rule, whilst the sinking Black community . . . lashes out at various diversions, and the main enemy, Capitalism/Imperialism, flows on."[217]

Black Voice reflected the internationalist perspective of BUFP by reporting on news from abroad. In any given issue one could read of the FBI raiding a New York bar where H. Rap Brown was meeting with other black radical leaders later to be dragged to jail. BUFP insisted, "we have a duty as Black people to organize in support of brother Rap . . . this is an inherent part of our general struggle against imperialism, which is worldwide and not confined to the United States or Britain."[218] The Party espoused a commitment to anti-racism and anti-imperialism, finding allies across the African diaspora.

Black Voice covered the recurring issues of lack of police protection and complimentary problem of police brutality. BUFP indicted British authorities for their nonchalance and considered them enemies of black freedoms. In addition to Teds and racist landlords who were prevalent in disparate London districts, BUFP proclaimed, "there is a racialist element . . . in this country . . . the establishment . . . the pig police, and the majority of the white population."[219] Racialism in Britain had so pervaded the society that BUFP indicted British laypeople and the government for perpetuating racial inequalities. Further, the Party explained "Black people cannot gain political power . . . because we are a small minority . . . not protected by our High Commission . . . they are only bootlickers of the imperialist."[220] BUFP professed its ultimate aims to "organize to combat racism and fascism . . . and build a socialist state in our country."[221]

RIVERS OF BLOOD

While Black Power expanded among activists and intellectuals in London, the English far-right mounted challenges to the presence of nonwhites in the metropole. Popular coverage of the Notting Hill Riots held Teddy boys and West Indian youths responsible for the violence and the heightened restrictions on Commonwealth immigration reaffirmed the notion that Caribbean citizens were unwelcome in the United Kingdom. Enoch Powell, Conservative Member of Parliament for Wolverhampton South West, frequently decried the ills of British society as attributable solely to the presence of the West Indians and other nonwhite citizens. In 1968, the Labour Government proposed a Race Relations Bill which prohibited "discrimination on grounds of colour, race, ethnic or national origins . . . in the provision of goods, facilities and services, in employment, by trade unions, employers' and professional organisations, in housing and business premises, in advertisements and notices."[222] This Bill was a response to racial discriminatory patterns that prevailed across Britain since the close of World War II. Powell vehemently opposed the Bill and, at a meeting of the Conservative Political Center in Birmingham, articulated his disgust in a speech known as the "Rivers of Blood."

In the speech, Powell recounted a conversation with one of his constituents who worked in a nationalized industry and was prepared to leave Britain. Powell explained that this "decent, ordinary fellow Englishman" was quite certain that "in this country in 15 or 20 years' time the black man will have the whip hand over the white man."[223] Powell sympathized with the man, whom he considered unable to bear the thought of his children having to live in this "new England." Powell argued that incoming migrants were responsible for the "total transformation" of British society, an unprecedented change in the course of English history.

Powell's polemic condemned the West Indian and colored migrant effect on British social services. He criticized the migrants and their children as "50,000 dependents, who are . . . the material of the future growth of the immigrant-descended population."[224] Powell argued that colored migrants drained the welfare system in Britain and their demographic growth would further deprive native Britons of these resources. He maintained that "the Commonwealth immigrant came to Britain as a full citizen, to a country which knew no discrimination between one citizen and another, and he entered instantly into the possession of the rights of every citizen, from the vote to free treatment under the National Health Service."[225] Powell dismissed the notion that Britons expressed discriminatory preferences and attributed any prejudices as emerging, "not from the law or from public policy or from administration, but from those personal circumstances and accidents which cause, and always will cause, the fortunes and experience of one man to be different from another's."[226] Powell supported the ideal of a just British society and considered any evidence of racial bias as aberration rather than the status quo.

Powell's coupled dismissal of the concerns of nonwhites in Britain with a prodigious empathy for native white Britons. He sympathized with the native population which "for reasons . . . they could not comprehend . . . found themselves made strangers in their own country."[227] Powell reaffirmed predominant arguments against colored migration from the early *Windrush* period. He understood that white Britons were suspicious of and cold toward colored migrants primarily because of the potential social, cultural, and political impact they would have on metropolitan society. Powell assumed that native Britons would become strangers at home, at once acknowledging the transformative power of the migrant classes and charging migrants with alienating the existing British national community. The most common racialized characterizations of West Indians—laziness, incompetence, salaciousness, greed—were, in Powell's rendering, destroying the British way of life. He bemoaned the supposed problems of native Britons, "unable to obtain hospital beds in childbirth, their children unable to obtain school places . . . homes and neighbourhoods changed beyond recognition . . . employers hesitated to apply to the immigrant worker the standards of discipline and competence required of the native-born worker."[228] Powell viewed British society as bifurcated; on one side, colored migrants were responsible for the decline of Britain and drained the social services; on the other, native Britons struggled to cope with the colored invasion and enjoyed none of their birthright privileges. Powell concluded his speech with a foreboding reference to the *Aeneid*, he claimed, "to see the River Tiber foaming with blood . . . only resolute and urgent action will aver it even now."[229]

Public reaction to Powell's speech was palpable. *The Times* declared it "evil," and Powell was relieved of his post as Shadow Defence Secretary by Conservative leader Edward Heath the next day. In the *Times*, the speech was described as "the first time that a serious British politician has appealed to racial hatred in this direct way in our postwar history."[230] Ten days after Powell's speech, a family of color was attacked in a slashing incident in Wolverhampton by "14 white youths chanting 'Powell' and 'Why don't you go back to your own country' at patrons of a West Indian christening party . . . one of the West Indians who was cut . . . had to have eight stitches over his left eye."[231] White aggressors in Wolverhampton invoked Powell's name as if paying tribute to his incendiary ideas while attacking and assaulting colored citizens. A Gallup Poll taken at the end of April 1968 found that 74 percent agreed with Powell's speech, 15 percent disagreed, 69 percent felt Heath was wrong to sack Powell, and 20 percent believed Heath was right.[232] "Rivers of Blood" seemingly reflected the attitudes of some Conservative white Britons twenty years on from the arrival of the *Windrush*. The same poll revealed that 24 percent of respondents favored Powell to replace Heath as Conservative leader and 83 percent felt immigration should be restricted.[233] Despite his removal from the Shadow Cabinet, Powell gained wider respect from swaths of British society. West Indian migrants viewed Powell's political rise as a referendum on the racialized experiences they had endured for the preceding two decades. Coverage of Powell's sentiments emphasized the degree to which his racist provocations reflected the views of many Britons. In a *Punch* cartoon published weeks after "Rivers of Blood," Powell was depicted rising from the ground holding a plate adorned with a Roman soldier wielding a Union Jack shield, revealing a tangle of snakes underneath. Cartoonist Norman Mansbridge captioned, "the Snake Pit Support for Enoch Powell's speech has revealed the alarming extent of racial intolerance in wide sections of the British public."[234] Powell gave voice and a face to the racialist attitudes of substantial portions of British society and his continued notoriety after being sacked only accentuated the notion that many Britons were intensely opposed to racial justice in their country.

Michael Cummings, a cartoonist for the *Sunday Express*, portrayed migrants taking advantage of British government and employers under the guise of racial equality. A day after "Rivers of Blood," Cummings published a cartoon depicting a man of color in tropical shirt and sandals carrying a "Race Relations Act Pains and Penalties!" card in his oversized hat and arriving at a business advertising a managing vacancy. The subject's companion explained to the prospective employers, "My friend's qualifications are as follows: he landed illegally, doesn't speak English, can't read or write, has a siesta from 2 o'clock until 6 o'clock and if you don't give him the job he'll have you arrested for racial prejudice!"[235] The *Sunday/Daily Express* had been a voice of the Conservative Party since the World Wars and supported the most right-leaning members of the Party.

BLACK ATLANTIC SOLIDARITIES

A WISU Special *Newsletter* provided extensive tribute to Rodney and explored the myriad problems affecting West Indians in London and their friends and families in the Caribbean. Migrants experienced discrimination every day and were encouraged to return to the West Indies. Such reverse migration was not without its problems, however. Betty Davison, a lecturer at the University of the West Indies and wife of a Jamaican government adviser, explained that returning Jamaicans find "there is no work for them in Jamaica . . . housing is in short supply and . . . expensive . . . cost of living has risen alarmingly and their compatriots view them with jealousy and reserve."[236] Frantz Fanon had prophesized the quagmire of the educated returnee West Indian, finding themselves back "home" in a country unrecognizable to them and in turn unfamiliar to their compatriots.[237] Despite decolonization and independence, Jamaica and other former colonies had developing economies, high unemployment rates, and expensive costs of living. Davison noted resentment among Jamaicans who had never lived in the metropole toward returning countrymen. Returning Jamaicans were in the unique position of having traveled to Britain for greater opportunity and then returned to the Caribbean after enduring discrimination in the metropole, only to be resented by their compatriots because they were able to go to Britain. Returning migrants were viewed as having "made good" abroad and thus received another sort of cold, indifferent welcome to their home island.[238]

By the close of the 1960s, racial animosity between the British far-right and people of color had intensified. The threat of a multicultural Britain inspired reactionary politics of Mosleyites and Powellites despite the concerted efforts of West Indians, Africans, and Asians to acclimate and contribute to

British society. West Indian activists and intellectuals would nonetheless be undeterred by rising racial antagonism and in turn mobilized further against racialization in Britain and abroad.

Although independence had arrived in former British territories in Africa and the Caribbean, black residents in Britain continued to stake significant claims over public space in the metropole. In addition to the Calypso Club, which had been in operation during the Notting Hill Riots, by the late 1960s Trinidad-born community activist and civil rights campaigner Frank Crichlow owned and operated the Mangrove Restaurant in Notting Hill. Along with the increase in West Indian controlled spaces in Britain, a rise in the production and distribution of radical Caribbean visions marked a critical turn toward new imaginaries. Perhaps the West Indian community found its greatest capacity for epistemological reconceptualization in the establishment and operation of knowledge-making and disseminating institutions—bookstores, arts organizations, and publishers.

NOTES

1. Harry Goulbourne, Interview with Eric and Jessica Huntley, Tape No. 2. LMA 4463.
2. Ibid.
3. See Kate Quinn, "Colonial Legacies and Post-colonial Conflicts in Guyana," in *Post-Colonial Trajectories in the Caribbean: The Three Guianas*, eds. Rosemarijn Hoefte, Matthew L. Bishop, and Peter Clegg (London: Routledge, 2016).
4. Jill M. Sheppard, "Letter to Mr. Huntley," March 30, 1967. LMA/4463/A/02/01/001.
5. Goulbourne, Interview with Eric and Jessica Huntley, Tape No. 5.
6. Ibid.
7. Ibid.
8. Ibid.
9. Ibid.
10. "People's Progressive Party Manifesto Programme," n.d. LMA 4463/B/10/01/001.
11. Ibid.
12. Claudia Jones, "The Caribbean in Britain," *Freedomways*, Third Quarter, Summer 1964, 342.
13. Ibid.
14. Ibid., 345.
15. Ibid.
16. Ibid., 347.
17. "Circular Letter from the Chairman of the Board of Governors of the West Indian Students' Center to All West Indian Students," May 1960. British NA: CO 1028/95.

18. "West Indian Students' Centre Constitution," August 1960. CO 1028/95.
19. "West Indian Students Centre Warden's Report for April, 1961," May 9, 1961. CO 1028/95.
20. M. G. Smith, "West Indian Culture," *Caribbean Quarterly* 7, no. 3 (December 1961), 113.
21. Ibid., 114.
22. Ibid., 115.
23. Ibid., 116.
24. Ibid.
25. Ibid.
26. Ibid., 119.
27. Michael Banton, "Sociology and Race Relations," *Race* 1, no. 1 (November 1959), 13. British Library Shelfmark: Ac.6236.a.
28. Ibid.
29. Michael Banton, *White and Coloured: The Behaviour of British People towards Coloured Immigrants* (London: Alden Press, 1959), 77–78. British Library Shelfmark: 8298.b.8.
30. Philip Mason, "Foreword," in *Coloured Immigrants in Britain*, ed. J. A. G. Griffith, Judith Henderson, Margaret Usbrone, and Donald Wood (London: Oxford University Press, 1960), vii.
31. Donald Wood, "The Immigration," in J. A. G. Griffith, Judith Henderson, Margaret Usborne, *Coloured Immigrants in Britain*, (London: Oxford University Press, 1960), 8.
32. Ibid., 28.
33. The Nuffield Foundation is an independent charitable trust founded in 1943 by William Morris, Lord Nuffield to fund research to inform social policy in education, welfare, and justice.
34. Philip Mason, "Long Look at the Colour Question," *The Times*, September 27, 1963, 13.
35. At the time of publication, *Coloured Immigrants in Britain* listed the following cities as employing colored workers: Bedford, Birmingham, Bradford, Derby, Doncaster, Glasgow, Ipswich, Leeds, Leicester, Liverpool, London, Manchester, Newcastle-on-Tyne, Nottingham, Oldham, Oxford, Rugby, Southampton, Sheffield, West Bromwich, and Wolverhampton. *Coloured Immigrants in Britain*, 28.
36. Wood, "The Immigration," 9.
37. There is also a substantial historiography on the problems of settlement and ensuing social strife in the 1950s, much of it initiated by Michael Banton. See index or bibliography.
38. The study group members were Hamza A. Alavi; D. Case, Racial Brotherhood Association, Brixton; Pauline Crabbe, National Council for the Unmarried Mother and her Child; G. A. Evans, Hackney Council for the Welfare of Coloured Citizens; J. E. Fraser, formerly Migrant Services Division, West Indies Commission; Ms. I. Harrison; Abdul Hye, High Commission for Pakistan; V. Jackson, Kensington Citizens' Advice Bureau; P. Jeffrey, Kensington Citizens' Advice Bureau; W. M. Klingender, International Social Service; Rev. David Mason, Notting Hill Social

Council; O. U. Murray, Willesden International Friendship Council; Dr. David Pitt, London City Council member; Leslie Smith, Secretary, Friends Race Relations Committee; D. P. Thirlwell, Paddington Overseas Students and Workers Committee; N. S. Peppard, London Council of Social Service, Secretary. Sheila Patterson was the group leader and Kenneth Little of the Department of Social Anthropology at the University of Edinburgh was the Consultant. Sheila Patterson, *Immigrants in London: Report of a Study Group set up by the London Council of Social Service* (London: London Council of Social Service, 1963), British Library Shelfmark: W49/1980.

39. Patterson, *Immigrants in London*, 47.
40. Ibid., 49–50.
41. Ibid., 51.
42. Ibid., 60.
43. Ibid., 61.
44. G. C. L. Bertram, *West Indian Immigration* (London: Eugenics Society, 1958), 14–15. British Library Shelfmark: Ac.3820.id/7.
45. Maurice Freedman, "West Indian Immigration, by G.C.L. Bertram," *Race* 1, no. 1 (November 1959), 79–80. British Library Shelfmark: Ac.6236.a.
46. Ibid., 80.
47. Church Assembly Board for Social Responsibility, *Together in Britain* (London: Church Information Office, 1960), 26, British Library Shelfmark: 3044.aa.6.
48. Ibid., 27.
49. Ibid., 29.
50. See Sandhu, *London Calling: How Black and Asian Writers Imagined a City* (Italy: Harper Perennial, 2004); J. Dillon Brown, *Migrant Modernism: Postwar London and the West Indian Novel* (Charlottesville, University of Virginia Press, 2013).
51. A. G. Bennett, *Because They Know Not* (London: Phoenix Press, 1959).
52. Harold Pollins, "Coloured People in Post-War English Literature," *Race* 1, no. 2 (May 1960), 9.
53. G. R. Fazakerley, *A Stranger Here* (London: Macdonald & Co. Ltd., 1959).
54. Also see J. Dillon Brown, *Migrant Modernism: Postwar London and the West Indian Novel* (Charlottesville: University of Virginia Press, 2013).
55. Pollins, "Coloured People in Post-War English Literature," 10.
56. George Lamming, *The Pleasures of Exile* (Ann Arbor: University of Michigan Press, c1992), 24.
57. Ibid.
58. Ibid., 25.
59. Ibid.
60. Ibid., 119.
61. Ibid., 150.
62. Ibid., 214.
63. Ibid.
64. Ibid., 214–15.
65. Ibid., 218.
66. Ibid.

67. R. B. Davison, *West Indian Migrants: Social and Economic Facts of Migration from the West Indies* (London: Oxford University Press, 1962), 87. British Library Shelfmark: 8298.f.47.

68. Institute of Race Relations, *Newsletter*, May 1962, British Library Shelfmark: P.P.7612.zt.

69. "Race Relations and Colour Prejudice," Overseas Students in London: *A Handbook for All Who are Interested in the Welfare of Overseas Students*. Issued by the Committee of the Conference of Voluntary Societies on the Welfare of Overseas Students in London c/o The British Council, 3 Hanover Street, London, W.1. October 1958, Reprinted with Revisions, February 1959. British Library Shelfmark: 8313.i.43.

70. Ibid.

71. Overseas Students in Britain: *A Handbook for All Who Are Interested in the Welfare of Overseas Students*. Issued by the Standing Committee of the London Conference on Overseas Students. c/o The British Council, 3 Hanover Street, London, W.1. Revised Edition, October, 1960. British Library Shelfmark: 8314.n.29.

72. Gbola Akinsanya, "Akinsiki-Gayle Feud," *Flamingo* 3, no. 3 (November 1963), 2–3. Black Cultural Archives: Periodicals/36.

73. Ibid.

74. Sam M. Spence, "Literary Battles," *Flamingo* 3, no. 3 (November 1963), 3. Black Cultural Archives Periodicals/36.

75. Ibid.

76. Ibid.

77. J. N. Philip, "Vauxhall's West Indians," *Flamingo* 3, no. 3 (November 1963), 1. BCA: Periodicals/36.

78. Ibid., 2.

79. N. A. J. Chew, "West Indians and Africans," *Flamingo* 3, no. 4 (January 1964), 1. Black Cultural Archives. Periodicals/36.

80. Jerry M. Nwankwo, "Wider Coverage," *Flamingo* 3, no. 4 (January 1964), BCA: Periodicals/36.

81. Lamming, *The Pleasures of Exile*, 160.

82. Ibid.

83. Joanne Pinto, "Discrimination Among Ourselves," *Flamingo* 3, no. 4 (January 1964), 1–2. BCA: Periodicals/36.

84. Ibid.

85. M. R. Edwards, "Division Between the Islands," *Flamingo* 3, no. 4, 2. BCA: Periodicals/36.

86. Ibid.

87. Ibid.

88. Letter for Ramon Vernon to Garnet Gordon, February 1, 1959. British NA: CO 1028/69.

89. Ibid.

90. Letter from Garnet H. Gordon to Ramon Vernon, February 24, 1959. British NA: CO 1028/69.

91. Ibid.

92. Fourth Annual Report by the Board of Governors and in respect of the period of October 1, 1957 to September 30, 1958. British NA: CO 1028/69.
93. Scobie, "History: Arctic Explorer," *Flamingo* 3, no. 3 (November 1963), 28. BCA Periodicals/36.
94. Ibid.
95. Ibid.
96. "Project for the Welfare of Coloured People," Family Welfare Association, Kensington Citizens' Advice Bureau, 1959. LMA/4462/P/01/031.
97. Ibid.
98. Ibid.
99. Ibid.
100. British-Caribbean Association, *Newsletter*, no. 3, August 12, 1960. LMA: ACC/1888/116.
101. Ibid.
102. "British-Caribbean Association, Report of a Special Council Meeting to discuss legislation against Racial Discrimination," held in the House of Commons on November 20, 1959. LMA: ACC/1888/116.
103. Ibid.
104. "Letter from M. Z. Terry to Mr. Kennedy," August 26, 1959. British NA: CO 1031/2420.
105. "Memorandum for the attention of the Home Secretary on the subject of publicity material on race relations," British NA: CO 1031/2420.
106. "Letter from M.Z. Terry to Mr. Kennedy," August 26, 1959. British NA: CO 1031/2420.
107. J. M. Ross and P. Rogers, February 9, 1960, Proposals by the British Caribbean Association to promote improved race relations, 1960. CO 1031/3453.
108. Draft Letter, Commissioner's Office to Nadine S. Peppard, Secretary, Immigrants' Advisory Committee, London Council of Social Service 11/59/185, November 1963, British NA: MEPO2/9854.
109. Ibid.
110. "Note of a Meeting held in Lord Jellicoe's Room at the Home Office," Thursday, May 16. British NA: MEPO2/9854.
111. Ibid.
112. Notes of a Meeting held at the Office of the High Commissioner for Jamaica, 6–10 Bruton St., W.1. Wednesday, June 19, 1963. British NA: MEPO2/9854.
113. Ibid.
114. "Paul Robeson Gets Big London Welcome," *Bristol Evening Post*, July 11, 1958, n.p. LMA/4232/B/02/002.
115. Derek Kartun, "The Man They Can't Bag: A Talk with Paul Robeson," *Daily Worker*, November 26, 1952, n.p. LMA: LMA/4232/B/02/002.
116. George Smith, *Evening Standard*, May 8, 1963, n.p.
117. Eric Huntley, "Cold Comfort for Coloured Strangers," (1967–1967). LMA: LMA/4463/F/02/01/002.
118. Ibid.

119. Reith Lectures are annual talks given by leading figures of the day and broadcast on BBC Radio 4 and the BBC World Service. Bertrand Russell delivered the inaugural lecture in 1948.

120. Huntley, "Cold Comfort for Coloured Strangers."

121. Ibid.

122. Ibid.

123. In South Africa the National Party came to power in 1948 and formalized the rules of apartheid through a series of extensive legislative measures. The white Australia Policy prohibiting nonwhite immigration to Australia was not dismantled until the Racial Discrimination Act passed there in 1975.

124. David Low, "Family Entrance," *The Guardian*, December 6, 1961, n.p.

125. "Future Prospects of Employment for West Indian Immigrants in the United Kingdom," British NA: CO 1031/3938.

126. Extract from Official Report of December 1, 1960. CO 1031/3938.

127. Ibid.

128. Notes for Supplementaries. CO 1031/3938.

129. Jones, "The Caribbean in Britain," 345.

130. Ibid.

131. Ibid., 344. Sheila Patterson, *Dark Strangers: A Sociological Study of a Recent West Indian Migrant Group in Brixton, South London* (Bloomington, IN: Indiana University Press, 1963).

132. Goulbourne, Interview with Eric and Jessica Huntley, Tape No. 3.

133. Ibid.

134. Ibid.

135. Trevor Munroe, *The Politics of Constitutional Decolonization, Jamaica, 1944–62* (Mona, Jamaica: University of the West Indies, 1983).

136. For more on the Grenada Revolution see Laurie Lambert, *Sister Comrade*.

137. Goulbourne, Interview with Eric and Jessica Huntley, Tape No. 4.

138. Perry's *London Is the Place for Me* is especially thorough in narrating CARD's relevance.

139. Goulbourne, Interview with Eric and Jessica Huntley, Tape No. 4.

140. Ibid.

141. Ibid.

142. Ibid.

143. Ibid.

144. Jones, "The Caribbean in Britain," 347.

145. Ibid.

146. Ibid.

147. Norman Girvan, "Jamaica's Woes Will Rebound on Britain," *The Guardian*, August 20, 1965. LMA: ACC/1888/121.

148. Ibid.

149. Reply for Thursday, December 1, 1960. "Future Prospects of Employment for West Indian Immigrants in the United Kingdom," British NA: CO 1031/3938.

150. Reply for Thursday, December 15, 1960. British NA: CO 1031/3939.

151. "Assurance on Immigrants," *The Times*, June 15, 1962, 9.
152. "Royal Assent for Immigrants Act," *The Times*, April 19, 1962, 12.
153. "Not a Closed Door," *The Times*, June 15, 1962, 13.
154. Ibid.
155. "14 Refused Entry into Britain," *The Times*, Monday, July 2, 1962, 12.
156. "Deportation of Immigrants," *The Times*, August 15, 1962, 11.
157. "More Migrants Go Than Arrive," *The Times*, August 27, 1962, 5.
158. "How Immigrants ACT Is Working," *The Times*, October 24, 1962, 15.
159. Monja Danischewsky, "Colour Problem in Britain," *The Times*, May 9, 1963, 13.
160. Ibid. See also Perry, *London is the Place for Me*.
161. "Protest Oppression by the Jamaican Government," pamphlet. (1968) LMA4462/C/01/04. Also see Horace Campbell, *Rasta and Resistance*.
162. *Black Dimension*, 1968 Institute of Race Relations Reference Code: 01/04/04/01/04/01/03.
163. Ibid.
164. Goulbourne, Interview with Jessica and Eric Huntley, Tape No. 4.
165. Ibid.
166. Huntley, Salkey, Small, "Letter to Eric Williams," October 23, 1968. LMA: LMA4462/C/01/04.
167. Ibid.
168. Ibid.
169. The signatory organization on the petition were West Indian Standing Conference, Caribbean Arts Movement, Campaign Against Racial Discrimination, Racial Adjustment Action Society, Movement for Colonial Freedom, African Descendants Advancement Movement, and Black Power Movement. "Petition Handed to the Jamaica High Commissioner on Thursday 15th August 1968," LMA: LMA4462/C/01/04.
170. Ibid.
171. Ibid.
172. Ibid.
173. John La Rose also owned and operated New Beacon Books—a publisher and bookseller in Finsbury Park, north London.
174. Walter Rodney, *Groundings with My Brothers* (London: Bogle-L'Ouverture, 1969), 59.
175. Ibid., 59–60.
176. See Adom Getachew, *Worldmaking After Empire: the Rise and Fall of Self-Determination* (Princeton: Princeton University Press, 2019).
177. Rodney, *Groundings with My Brothers*, 13.
178. Ibid., 14
179. Ibid., 13.
180. Ibid., 16.
181. Ibid.
182. Ibid.
183. Ibid., 21.

184. Earl Greenwood, "The Farcicality of Jamaica's Independence," WISU *Newsletter*, August 1969. LMA/2262/C/01/110. Note: Alcan (Rio Tinto Alcan Canada, Ltd.) is a Canada-owned business and one of the world's largest aluminum manufacturers. Tate and Lyle is a British multinational agribusiness.

185. Greenwood, "Editorial-The Plight of Our Black Kind in the British Classroom," WISU *Newsletter*, August 1969, 1. LMA/2262/C/01/110.

186. "A Black Mother: Our Black Teenagers," WISU *Newsletter*, August 1969, n.p. LMA/2262/C/01/110.

187. Kathrin Fitzherbert, *West Indian Children in London*, Occasional Papers on Social Administration No. 19 (London: G. Bell & Sons Ltd.1967), 27. British Library Shelfmark: 8299.i.7/19.

188. Ibid.

189. Ibid., 27–28.

190. Ibid.

191. Ibid., 28.

192. Ibid., 38. Also establishments such as I was Lord Kitchener's Valet, the Calypso Club, and Mangrove Restaurant.

193. There is a useful multimedia Black British Geographies Map.

194. Note of the minister of state's Meeting with a Deputation from the British-Caribbean Association held at the Commonwealth Relations Office January 5, 1965. British NA: HO 344/291.

195. Note on Matters Raised at Mr. George Thomas's Meeting with the British Caribbean Association on December 21, 1964, signed 3.3.65. HO 344/291.

196. Ibid.

197. Ibid.

198. Herbert Hill, "A Negro in Notting Hill," from Committee on West Indian Immigrants in the UK 1959. British NA: CO1031/2946.

199. *Black Power in Britain: A Special Statement*, Universal Coloured People's Association (1967) British Library Shelfmark: YD.2009.a.3412

200. Ibid., 3.

201. Ibid.

202. Ibid.

203. Ibid.

204. Ibid.

205. Ibid.

206. Ibid., 4.

207. Ibid.

208. Ibid.

209. Ibid.

210. Ibid.

211. Ibid., 5.

212. Ibid.

213. Ibid., 6.

214. Ibid., 8.

215. "Religion and Revolution," *Black Voice* 3, no. 1 (1972), 3.

216. Ibid.
217. Ibid.
218. "International News," *Black Voice* 3, no. 1 (1972), 9.
219. "Letters: Racism," *Black Voice* 3, no. 1 (1972), 12.
220. Ibid.
221. Ibid. This is also related to Brathwaite's notion of "nation-language" more fully developed in *History of the Voice: The Development of Nation Language in Anglophone Caribbean Poetry* (London: New Beacon Books, 1984).
222. Race Relations Act, 1968, 71 Eliz. II.
223. Enoch Powell's "Rivers of Blood" http://www.telegraph.co.uk/comment/3643823/Enoch-Powells-Rivers-of-Blood-speech.html.
224. Ibid.
225. Ibid.
226. Ibid.
227. Ibid.
228. Ibid.
229. Ibid.
230. "An Evil Speech," *The Times*, April 22, 1968, 11.
231. "Coloured Family Attacked," *The Times*, May 1, 1968, 1.
232. Simon Heffer, *Like the Roman: The Life of Enoch Powell* (London: Orion, 1999), 467.
233. Ibid.
234. Norman Mansbridge, "The Snake Pit," *Punch*, May 1, 1968, n.p.
235. Michael Cummings, "Vacancy for Managing Director," *Sunday Express*, April 21, 1968, n.p.
236. Brian McConnell, "Immigrants are Outcasts at Home," *The Daily Mirror*, July 15, 1969, n.p.
237. See Fanon, *Black Skin, White Masks* especially "The Negro and Language."
238. McConnell, "Immigrants Are Outcasts at Home."

Chapter 7

Black Publishers and Revolutionary Epistemologies
Radical Knowledges and Black Post-Nationalism

According to Barbadian Edward Brathwaite, the Caribbean Artists Movement began in December 1966 in his Bloomsbury basement flat. Brathwaite recently arrived in Britain and sought out African artists and writers. He had not seen "any West Indian writers, painters, and only a very few actors . . . [in stereotyped parts] on British Television"[1] and committed himself to discovering and fostering community among Caribbean artists. Brathwaite reached out to Trinidadian John La Rose who began a publishing house designed to make out-of-print West Indian literature available as cheaply as possible. Brathwaite and La Rose recruited popular Jamaican writer Andrew Salkey, as well as Jamaican Orlando Patterson, a lecturer in Sociology at the London School of Economics. From its inception CAM engaged with visual and plastic arts, social sciences, and literature. Brathwaite also invited, "Evan Jones, the Jamaican-born television and screen writer; Dr. Louis Jones . . . who had . . . arrived back in Britain to take up . . . appointment at the University of Kent; and Aubrey Williams, an internationally recognized Guyanese painter."[2] By the first CAM public meeting, membership numbered fifty with over one hundred audience members in attendance.

Early CAM correspondences illustrate founding visions and articulations of the organization's purpose in London, Britain, and abroad. Brathwaite wrote to Bryan King, a St. Kitts-born Fellow of Law whom Brathwaite met while both were studying at Pembroke College, Cambridge. Brathwaite raised the possibility of forming CAM to King in autumn 1966. He wished to establish, "some sort of WI artists and writers' group concerned with . . . WI art and literature . . . [that] would take the form of critical symposia."[3] Brathwaite sought out, "students and others who feel they have something to say."[4] He also considered a wider perspective on the meaning of "Caribbean," writing to King of his desire to, "meet and discuss the work of French and Spanish-speaking West Indians."[5] Despite the awkward and uncomfortable welcome extended or withheld from Anglophone West Indians in Britain, Brathwaite nevertheless conceived of a broader and more inclusive "Caribbean" identity across linguistic and political boundaries.

King corroborated Brathwaite's desire to forge a broad identity for CAM and its activities. He mentioned that adjacent to the West Indian Students Centre, African students utilized the Unity House which would allow CAM to "bring in the Africans."[6] King connected Brathwaite and CAM with Edward Lucie-Smith, Salkey, and John Press of the British Council. Brathwaite campaigned among friends and colleagues, seeking a platform to explore the variety of intellectual and literary achievement of Caribbean and other diasporic creators. He wrote to Lucie-Smith of his desire to "see French and Spanish West Indians . . . as well as African writers . . . Ngũgĩ wa Thiong'o (earlier known as James Ngugi), for instance."[7] Brathwaite networked beyond his personal connections imagining, "University Departments like SOAS, Sussex American Studies, the Kent and Leeds Commonwealth Literature sections [all] contributing something." He envisioned CAM's immediate impact and sought to highlight the group's contributions through building up "some sort of archive material and . . . even . . . a magazine."[8] From its inception CAM relied on the input and suggestions of members and potential collaborators.

Lucie-Smith suggested that the nascent CAM utilize British resources for their programming and organization, including applying to "the Arts Council's Literature Panel for a grant."[9] Similar to experiences throughout imperium and during the period of decolonization that many migrants had with the British Council in their home territories, Lucie-Smith recognized the potential financial support that British-helmed institutions could offer. Brathwaite hoped to harness the potential La Rose's New Beacon Books would have on burgeoning Caribbean literary culture in Britain. New Beacon published history, social sciences, and fiction. According to Brathwaite, by 1967, they produced a "study on Marcus Garvey and a set of literary essays on Wilson Harris . . . already . . . taken up by the University of the West Indies."[10] For La Rose, the establishment of a press served not only to publicize fiction and literature but also contributed to the expanding academic bibliography of the nascent UWI. Initially, CAM meetings rotated among the residences of the original members and Brathwaite hosted La Rose, Salkey, Evan Jones, Tony Haynes, Patterson, and Louis James at the first convening in December 1966.

CAM was founded primarily as an artists' cooperative and workshop for material relevant to West Indian societies. CAM members were "concerned with meeting . . . readers, viewers and listeners, and setting up a dialogue with them."[11] Their public meetings encouraged attendees to engage West

Indian experts. Brathwaite and CAM also sought artists and intellectuals from outside the Caribbean. Louis Jones brought colleagues from the University of Kent. Donald Wood and Gerald Moore of the University of Sussex also joined in gatherings. Brathwaite lauded the presence of "Arthur Ravenscroft, an editor of the *Journal of Commonwealth Literature* and Rosey Pool, editor of the anthology of Negro American poetry, *Beyond the Blues*."[12] CAM pursued artists and intellectuals from throughout the African diaspora and the Commonwealth of Nations including the Australian novelist and poet Randolph Stow, Ghanaian poet Kwabena Amoaka, and Kenyan novelist Ngũgĩ wa Thiong'o.[13] CAM programs represented peoples from throughout the West Indies and the Commonwealth with an emphasis on their cosmopolitan perspectives.

Inspired by the relative high concentration of West Indian "writers and . . . painters, having made their homes here [England]" Brathwaite appealed to Trinidadian Kenneth Ramchand in soliciting support from his entire network of artists and writers.[14] Ramchand had earlier reflected on his position as a student at the University of Edinburgh.[15] He resented the failure of West Indies Federation and ensured his involvement with CAM would contribute in some way to "check the political and cultural separatism of the islands."[16] Ramchand argued for interdisciplinarity when framing and investigating West Indian art and aesthetics. The essence of Caribbean art and society was unbound by the confines of one particular intellectual discipline or pursuit.[17] Ramchand's feeling of exclusion because of his position in Edinburgh made him feel "like a raving fanatic"[18] a suggestion that after traveling across the ocean to Britain, Caribbean writers remained estranged from one another as cultural and intellectual elites spread throughout the metropole.

In January 1967, Salkey interviewed Dr. Rudranath Capildeo for the BBC, who was head of the Democratic Labour Party, the opposition in Trinidad and Tobago. Capildeo was also an uncle of writer V. S. Naipaul. Salkey remembered Capildeo as "one of the most richly rewarding . . . West Indian intellectuals."[19] From its inception CAM connected with artists, intellectuals, and political actors on each side of the Atlantic. CAM was concerned not only with the notion of exile from the region while living in Britain but also a nuanced and continued relationship with the West Indies, following developments there and reciprocating by broadcasting their London-based activities back "home."

Brathwaite's ingenuity in the formation of CAM was reflected in his commitment to fostering and facilitating the development of younger intellectuals and aspiring artists. He solicited Guianese Gordon Rohlehr to participate in meetings despite Rohlehr only having been "on a WUI post-graduate award . . . at Birmingham University."[20] Rohlehr was new to Britain and not established beyond his doctoral program; he needed to lodge in Brathwaite's home during his visit to London. Brathwaite also hoped to grow the influence of his CAM cohorts as well as other West Indians in Britain. He offered Trinidadian Frank Collymore a promise to circulate Collymore's periodical *BIM*.[21]

By summer 1967 the original CAM members forged relations with contacts and organizations in the West Indies. Sociologist Orlando Patterson at Mona and Dermont Hussey of Radio Jamaica were point-persons based in Kingston.[22] Meanwhile, Brathwaite planned the first Conference on Caribbean Arts in Britain. He avoided any mention of the Pan-African Congress to cast CAM Symposia as distinct propositions. The conferences were forged around the question and expression of art and arts production rather than as "political" movement-based organizing.[23] The history of pan-African organizing in Britain can formally be traced to the 1900 London Conference organized by Trinidadian Henry Sylvester Williams, and Brathwaite offered a cultural production framework for CAM.

CAM reached outside Caribbean artistic circles in Britain. Just as Patterson and Hussey established a chapter in Jamaica, in Dominica, local newspaper *The Star* carried CAM advertisements. *The Star* explained, "Only £1 a year will keep young West Indian intellectuals informed on trends among the brilliant exiles as well as giving them fresh thoughts from the homelands."[24] CAM conceived of the position of Britain-based artists as an exile, their creativity facilitated through reckoning with their status in the former colonial center. Additionally, the *Star* advertisement mentioned the work produced by CAM affiliates from around the West Indies. The Caribbean and its diaspora remained linked through CAM on each side of the Atlantic. Chalmer St. Hill, from the Public Library in Barbados commended Brathwaite for CAM's successes and asked for "any newsletters, lectures and conference papers and proceedings related to the Movement."[25] St. Hill expanded the Library's West Indiana Collections, soliciting forthcoming and back issues of CAM publications.

In London, Locksley Comrie, Discussion Officer of the Union of West Indian Students in Great Britain and Ireland, hoped to organize a meeting at the West Indian Students' Centre on black power, which due to reservations from "big brothers in high places" was amended to "Human Rights and the Black Man."[26] Beyond Britain and the Caribbean, Comrie and his cohorts in WISC hosted "Sammy Davis . . . and . . . a prominent Black Nationalist leader."[27] Black Americans also figured into the rapidly radicalized political activities of CAM and their collaborators and colleagues in London. Oliver Clarke wrote to Brathwaite from Jamaica where he successfully solicited funds for the Conference brochure highlighting the ways West Indians were contributing directly to CAM-initiated efforts across multiple geographies.[28]

FIRST CONFERENCE ON CARIBBEAN ARTS

Attendees from universities throughout Britain (and UWI): Cambridge, Oxford, London, Birmingham, and Kent, joined CAM's first Conference on Caribbean Arts at the University of Kent from September 15 to 17, 1967. Editors from academic and popular British presses such as Longmans, Heinemann, and Macmillan also attended. Honorary Member of CAM C. L. R. James joined others including George Lamming, Horace James, Ramchand, and Aubrey Williams. Brathwaite articulated hopefulness for the movement, citing the need for "contact and correspondence between West Indian artists here in exile and the society that still awaits them back in the Caribbean."[29] His concluding lament encapsulated the essence of CAM as a body that engaged peoples from throughout the Commonwealth and produced revolutionary art and scholarship reflecting the experiences of West Indians in various locales.

Brathwaite characterized West Indians abroad as living "in exile," an important political and epistemological distinction. The University of the West Indies' *Caribbean Quarterly* issued a "Survey of the Arts," special edition in Spring 1968, "devoted to...arts . . . from practicing artists who regard the West Indies as their home, whether they function at the moment in the Islands or abroad in exile."[30] The year 1968 also saw the opening of the Creative Arts Centre at the University of the West Indies and students and activists in both London and Jamaica were conscious of and engaged with the respective institutions in each site. "Exile" status affirmed West Indians who considered themselves firstly Caribbean and retained their West Indian heritages despite having traveled to London or elsewhere for school or work. West Indians exhibited a sophisticated notion of consciousness whether they remained in the Caribbean or lived abroad. These connections were strengthened through the deliberate work of a vanguard of scholars and artists. After the racist aggression and violence of the Notting Hill Riots coupled with subsequent immigration restrictions, London ceased being the metropole for West Indians, and those who ventured to the capital understood themselves as "living abroad."

After the *Daily Telegraph* reported on the CAM meeting in September 1967, Brathwaite wrote to the paper's editor to correct errors and admonish the staff for misreporting and misrepresenting the Conference. Brathwaite wrote that contrary to the *Telegraph*'s report, "C. L. R. James did not . . . defend his cultural dependence on Europe . . . James . . . acknowledged . . . debt to European culture, [but] also in the radical political and cultural movements in Africa and the Caribbean, also disrupted this dependence."[31] Brathwaite reminded the newspaper that "the conference . . . was . . . attended by delegates from Australia, Ghana, Nigeria, Canada, British publishers and university academics . . . [and] West Indians from all walks of life."[32] CAM rejected popular notions of their meetings and directly confronted a press corps that they believed delegitimized their efforts.

After the first CAM conference, Brathwaite was encouraged by literary and intellectual figures across Britain. Francis Pike of Faber and Faber wrote to Brathwaite impressed by the conference and remembering, "It was exciting simply to rub shoulders with such illustrious figures as C. L. R. James and George Lamming but on top of that the real intellectual meat in the various sessions . . . I hope you will accept, from the firm, the enclosed contribution to the funds of C.A.M. with our best wishes. I would be very glad to have copies of your [newsletter] to pass round here as they come out."[33] CAM piqued the interest of various figures in the literary and cultural world of London.

Brathwaite's conceptualization of the exiled status West Indians faced in the Caribbean and in Britain was encapsulated, by his own admission, through reading Frantz Fanon's *Black Skin, White Masks*. Borrowing from Fanon, Brathwaite insisted "I am not a potentiality of something, I am wholly what I am. I do not have to look for the universal . . . My Negro consciousness does not hold itself out as a lack."[34] CAM did not exist merely to "color" British literary culture but was fully realized in its own articulation with or without the approval of Britons. Furthermore, CAM sustained contact between West Indians in the metropole and those in the Caribbean. CAM reflected a transatlantic network of thinkers and activists through communicating with people in UWI like Don Wilson of the Department of Education.[35]

CARIBBEAN ARTISTS MOVEMENT CONFERENCE AUGUST 1968

Andrew Salkey opened the 1968 CAM conference at the University of Kent by welcoming Stuart Hall, Deputy Director of the Centre for Contemporary Cultural Studies at the University of Birmingham. Hall delivered a talk entitled "West Indians in Britain" in which he suggested that rather than arriving for study, most migrants "have come to work . . . driven . . . by deep and long-standing economic necessity."[36] Diverging from his own experience of arriving in Britain as a student, Hall argued that the working-class and less formally educated background of the migrants of the 1950s and 1960s was rooted in "a kind of historical idealism . . . a part of the history of migration out of the West Indies."[37] Stymied by the lack of economic and educational opportunities in their home region, Hall argued that the historical experience of financial and political disenfranchisement drove the masses of West Indians to Britain after World War II.

A veteran of elite schooling and having experienced the rarified atmosphere of Oxford, Hall underestimated the perspectives of some West Indians and consequently, privileged English perceptions and attitudes. He suggested that not until "coloured immigration . . . has . . . the final demystification of some areas of darkness in the English consciousness [begun]."[38] For Hall, only through the phenomenon of "direct physical face to face . . . [that] attitudes in the English experience have at least been brought to light." Hall surmised that with the Atlantic separating Britain from Caribbean colonies, Britons were not obviously articulating their racial prejudices.

Hall's Englishness complicated his presence at the Conference and may be read as a refutation of some of the linkages between Africa and its diaspora. Hall argued that "the central experience in the formation of the West Indian personality . . . is not and cannot be Africa."[39] He claimed that "between Africa and now, Slavery and the deep insertion of a people into the depths of a plantation civilisation and colonialism have intervened . . . things that defined us in some crucial historical way is an experience which we share with other Caribbean islands, with the southern plantation . . . of North America . . . Latin America . . . South America."[40] Hall's formulation necessitates close reading in the context of the Conference. Firstly, he postulated "Africa and now" as if the continent and its history were ahistorical remnants of an unknowable past. Hall's distancing the West Indian and African experiences conflicted with some of the work done by CAM thinkers and activists, most centrally Brathwaite who had sojourned in Ghana for nine years before arriving in London.

Hall recognized that the geographic spread of British Empire allowed for metropolitan citizens to remain ambivalent about the mechanisms of empire. He noted that "the whole imperial and colonial period was . . . far away from the actual shores of this country [England] . . . by having such a big empire out there, you could maintain a much nicer kind of atmosphere in here."[41] Hall attributed articulations of racial prejudice in Britain to "the intrusion of that group [colonials] into the society . . . [that] cuts the distance between Westminster and Governor House."[42] The spatial proximity of colony and metropole abutting one another for Hall fundamentally transformed the relationship of the mother country in particular to its colonial subjects and citizens.

Other conference attendees were more frustrated by the harsh treatment they encountered in Britain. Jamaican-born Edward Lucie-Smith commented on Britons' hesitance when faced with the reality of West Indian migration when he remembered a poetry tour he and Brathwaite arranged across the West Midlands. After concluding their tour in Birmingham, Lucie-Smith recalled that "the presence of a highly intelligent black intellectual threw mostly middle-class audiences into a state of violent social confusion . . . it was that voice, the Brathwaite voice, coming out of that body, to put it bluntly."[43] Despite the audiences full of "people of good will" Lucie-Smith and Brathwaite were received by crowds questioning or discomfited by their presence. The West Indian intellectual, even in the privileged space of a poetry performance, was met with British indignation. Brathwaite recognized that through these experiences he was "upsetting the status quo."[44]

John La Rose noted the diversity of black radical ideals in the late 1960s. Black power politics figured directly in the configurations of CAM activists and intellectuals. La Rose remarked that after his visit in August 1967, "the effect of Stokely Carmichael . . . was a catalyst in a way nothing before . . . had been."[45] Small concurred with La Rose, and noted the politics of black people in Britain began to reflect a consciousness "of themselves, not as immigrants in England, not as minorities, not as organisations . . . but in terms of the slogans of the Third World and Black Power."[46] Not content with struggling for a predetermined set of civil and social rights and sense of national belonging in Britain, Small argued for the radicalization of the black political in Britain that conceptualized itself as broader, more ambitious, and globally conscious within the framework of race. Small insisted that in considering the potential role of the artist in the black communities in Britain, he would encourage artists to "talk in terms of where we are . . . to lay the foundations for the international overthrow of racism."[47] He recognized the specific realities of race prejudice in Britain as part of a more ambitious struggle for global racial justice.

While the problems of race in Britain initially mobilized CAM, its leadership remained concerned with broader racialized visions for the organization. CAM circulated its *Newsletter* from London and in March 1968 one newsletter for CAM's Jamaica chapter was published. Concomitant with domestic unrest in response to Rodney's banishment in 1968, CAM's Jamaica affiliate struggled to establish a permanent presence in the island. Nevertheless, CAM Jamaica offered a revolutionary perspective on the possibilities of artistic and political collaboration. In association with the New World Group in Jamaica, CAM hosted a talk by Marina Maxwell (Acting Secretary of CAM in early 1968) entitled "Towards a Revolution in the Arts."[48] Maxwell argued that the "upheavals, revolutions, new attitudes and thought in the Third World . . . [caused] serious reverberations in the West Indies." She applauded, "writers, musicians, poets . . . [for] 'coming home' not only literally but psychologically."[49] Maxwell, reflecting CAM perspectives in Britain and abroad, sought to reconcile their current status through reclaiming "shattered history" of black African peoples. Maxwell evoked both Brathwaite and Elsa Goveia's previous addresses that located the revolutionary potential of CAM in the foregrounded articulation of racial identity.

Maxwell broke with traditional Eurocentric epistemologies that characterized much political thought in the Caribbean. She targeted "sick Europe . . . that rejects me with every migrant Bill . . . American materialism that has no place for people of colour but as role-playing Samboes as Stepand Fetchits and as cheap labour" and instead sought to foster a class of artist-intellectual-activists that would serve as "translator of my people's voices . . . part of the throbbing explosion of the pan-sawing masses . . . the wailing tender guitar . . . the power of the drum."[50] Maxwell evoked Brathwaite's earlier claims for the place of creative artists at the vanguard of revolutionary struggle. She recalled his proclamation that "the alternative tradition is belly-centered; in the beat, the drum . . . this region . . . of the 'head' is the center of Sparrow's art, the source of Louise Bennett's vitality . . . the bloodbeat of ska and jazz . . . and behind the whole revolt . . . there lies the deep rhythmical and formal influence of Africa."[51] The link to Africa for Maxwell was essential as an origin-space for resistance and the potential root of new revolutionary thought.

Maxwell acknowledged that the slogan, "Black is Beautiful" encouraged, "a beginning of identification" but also contended that "these . . . superficial but virally important marks of identification take root and grow to understanding and conscious action and choice . . . we witness the birth here."[52] Merely looking around the Caribbean "on the streets, in the Sound System yard, in the calypso tents, in the tremendously significant rejection statement of the Rastafari" allowed Maxwell to "know that we are in the presence of our own gods."[53] She advocated reoriented perspectives on Caribbean identification, knowledge, and culture. Rather than looking toward Europe or the United States, Maxwell insisted that the foundation for revolutionary thought was present in the Afrocentric and Caribbean-based artistic and spiritual innovations of the region. Maxwell explained the early postcolonial era was an exciting time reflecting a "surrealist point where we [West Indians] can experiment wildly, madly, freely with our own rich elements."[54]

Like Claudia Jones's advocacy that a "people's art is the genesis of their freedom" during the first Caribbean Carnival in London, Maxwell emphasized the unique revolutionary potential of Carnival. She suggested Carnival linked "the frail tendrils in some places with the central cord of masquerade . . . from New Orleans, through Mexico across the whole Caribbean, through Haiti, Puerto Rico, Jamaica . . . Trinidad . . . Guyana to Brazil."[55] As Jones regarded the expressive articulation of Caribbean identity through Carnival practices, Maxwell understood its "surrealist explosion . . . as one of the main sources for the creation of our own conventions . . . the central seedbed of West Indian theatre where we can create our own."[56]

Maxwell celebrated Jamaican novelist Lindsay Barrett's *Song for Mumu* which followed the example Brathwaite and others established rooted in "anger at the black man's condition in the USA, the Caribbean, in exile in Europe. . . meet[ing] his gods. . . his African identification. . . to point to his real future. . . following the drum-sound to home."[57] While initially lauded for reflecting the "African phase" of Caribbean writing, Maxwell instead championed Barrett for the essential place of Africa in the novel which was "not... any phase... [but] very central to and here to stay."[58] Fellow Jamaican Vic Reid was heralded for his work *The Leopard*. Maxwell regarded it as "the most utterly beautiful pieces... written yet in the West Indies."[59] She agreed with Jamaican Edward Baugh's assessment of Reid suggesting his mastery over moving between worlds of magic and madness "is doing something not dissimilar to what... Wilson Harris and Alejo Carpentier have done."[60] Both Baugh and Maxwell identified a crucial aspect of post-national thought—work from around the Caribbean could be informed by Africa, the national or island origin of its creator notwithstanding. Maxwell lauded Baugh himself for "the perception and empathy with which... [he] approached a book as significant as *Mumu*... most of our critics are blinkered by their European orientation and education and are not concerned with listening to the drum."[61] Furthermore, Maxwell acknowledged the work of Harris and Carpentier alongside Lamming and Brathwaite, who at that point were working in both Caribbean and British contexts and in English and other literary traditions. They were thus unbound by islands, nations, or oceans.

Members of CAM's Jamaica chapter conceptualized alternative futures in the postcolony and former colonial centers. Maxwell cited Fanon's notion of the "zone of occult instability" in "Toward a Revolution in the Arts." She reiterated Fanon's argument that "it is not enough... to free oneself by repeating proclamations and denials... [nor] to get back to the people in that part our of which they have already emerged; rather we must join them in that fluctuating movement which they are giving shape to"[62] The burden on the newly liberated black masses was to create cultures and persevere through the difficult terrain of the "zone of occult instability" for that was where, "souls are crystallized."[63] Maxwell argued that conditions facing West Indies were knowable only through reckoning with the innumerable ways in which Caribbean people exercised and innovated ingenious responses to displacement and alienation. She contended that "our writers and artists sought exile to exist... and... along with the wide swath of migrants, have shipped home disillusionment with Europe."[64] Despite leaving the region, Maxwell noted the close and ever-reproducing relationship between migrants in Europe and their cohorts in the Caribbean. Migrants articulated the realities of their experiences, contributing to a disavowal of Europe and the search for alternate futures. Maxwell referenced Fanon and Brathwaite at length, suggesting her solutions for the problems of Europe had been identified and argued by thinkers who grounded their resistance and sensibilities not only in a rejection of Europe but also in an embrace of Africa, the Caribbean, and the historical phenomena of displacement, characterized by Maxwell as "schizophrenia." She insisted that "because the society is in this alienated and schizoid state

I cannot see how art in the West Indies can ever be separate from politics, social involvement, and commitment to the West Indies reality."[65]

Maxwell recognized Fanon's contemporaneous significance and to his chapter "On National Culture" from *The Wretched of the Earth* when he articulated the struggle for new national cultures was the fight for the liberation of the nation. She added, "we begin . . . this surrealist phase our time of protest literature, protest theatre, protest poetry, protest: period."[66] Maxwell offered a radical view of the possibilities of rebellious artistic practice in forging new alternatives to the white supremacist societies dominating Caribbean life. She encouraged CAM conference attendees to recognize their position as "cultural guerillas"[67] and move away from the psychological subordination she argued pervaded black societies. Maxwell's view advocated for the overlapping vigor of black power activism and art.

In addition to CAM, other West Indians, who were neither formally artists nor intellectuals, made significant contributions to novel epistemologies and Caribbean self-consciousness. The Huntleys attributed the increased verve for black history and knowledge of black peoples to the Rastafari Movement in Jamaica as well in the United Kingdom and the United States.[68] Rastafarians, according to the Huntleys, inherited from Marcus Garvey the thirst for knowledge of black history and accomplishment. For Jessica, Rastas inaugurated a celebration of blackness and young people were particularly impacted by the Rastafari worldview that provided an important conceptual and theoretical space for the young black West Indians in Britain to thrive. She explained that Rastafari black pride was necessary for those who had been personally afflicted by the power and influence of white supremacy in their lives. The Rastafari provided an alternative epistemology that could be harnessed, Huntley explained, into revolutionary fervor and lasting social change.[69] Rastafari consciousness, promoted and publicized[70] by local mobilizations in Jamaica, offered new solutions and visions for blacks in Britain and throughout the diaspora. Jessica Huntley lauded the Rastafari movement because in her estimation, "the fundamental thing they gave you was a sense of pride."[71] Groups like the Universal Rastafari Improvement Association organized within Britain and "trod" far beyond the United Kingdom, extending their efforts to Jamaica, Ethiopia, and Tanzania.[72]

The Rastas and Black Power personalities represented analogous potentials to the Huntleys. Jessica Huntley explained that the Rastas took over from Black Power Movement in Britain after the United States government destroyed that burgeoning movement. Without the influence of the radical American Black Power activists, British youth began to view Rastafari as the primary mode of rebellion and self-determination. The Huntleys considered the rise of Rastafari consciousness a continuation of a movement that emboldened black people.

In addition to the novel conceptualizations of cultural significance in political radicalism offered by the Huntleys and their cohorts, other activists and politically mobilized Caribbean residents began to make claims over public space in the context of late imperial London. Despite independence and sovereignty in the Caribbean, black people in Britain nevertheless reckoned with realities of racialized existence in the former mother country. Specific groups of radical activists rejected white supremacy outright and articulated a new politics of black power.

BLACK EAGLES

The Black Eagles were a West London-based Black Power group led by Prime Minister Darcus Owusu [Howe]. Michael X, earlier known as de Freitas, contributed to the organization's activities including editing its periodical, *Black Dimension*. In 1968, *Black Dimension* opened with an epigraph from Biafran leader Colonel Chukwuemeka Odumegwu Ojukwu, "if the price is death for all we hold dear, then let us die without a shred of fear."[73] Howe and Michael X announced the intent and perspective of the Black Eagles, linking the struggles of black people in Britain to the contemporaneous civil war in Nigeria.

The Eagles' demands situated their politics firmly within the radical activist milieu of late 1960s Britain. They insisted on full employment for black people in the United Kingdom, better housing conditions and a role in determining housing allocation, an end to police brutality, freedom for imprisoned black people, black criminal defendants tried in courts of their peers, and education that exposed the true nature of the racist society in which they lived.[74] The Eagles did not envisage abstract goals, their politics where shaped by the relevant contemporaneous social and political context in Britain.

As a core member of the Black Eagles, Michael X transitioned from an early career as strongman for Poland-born Notting Hill slumlord Peter Rachman to a black power advocate.[75] In November 1968 police entered Michael's home after receiving a tip that he had perpetrated a string of robberies. According to the Eagles, once inside, the police wrecked the house, herding Michael's "children . . . from room to room."[76] They moved through the house until an officer produced "a peice [*sic*] of cannabis half the size of one's little finger, claiming he found it in . . . Michael's coat pocket."[77] Under the leadership of Howe, the Eagles rejected drug use as it countered their position of "the creation of a new Black man" arguing that "the taking of any drug as the path to the ruin of Black minds."[78]

The Eagles suggested the inextricable links between racial struggles in the United Kingdom and similar movements around black racial justice around the world. They championed the rise of black nationalism through "becoming increasingly aware of their political power" claiming that "the Americans are taking a spanking from our Brothers in Black America."[79]

The Eagles offered a radical ethos for London's black community through their conceptualization of social justice activism as an ongoing struggle in Britain abroad. They framed the exploitative power of white dominant English culture in four stages. They insisted that "whitey" firstly "pacifies . . . secondly, he contains . . . thirdly, he punishes, silences, or imprisons . . . finally, he exterminates."[80] Drawing on the notoriety of Enoch Powell, the Eagles referred to Powell's advocacy for "repatriation" as the final stage in the elimination of black power mobilization. By arguing for the cessation of colored migration and the expulsion of black and brown Commonwealth citizens, the Eagles determined Powell wished to say "Nigger go home, we don't need you [anymore]."[81] Whereas typical discourse regarding the Commonwealth Immigrants Act perpetuated or refuted stereotypes of African and Asian laborers and arrivants, the Black Eagles instead rejected the civil political notions that predominated. By characterizing Powell in more severe terms—that of an unabashed and selfishly colonial-minded racist—the Eagles articulated a more radical sensibility regarding racial uplift and representation. They castigated Powell in no uncertain terms, despite his position having been reflected in the politics and articulations of more mainstream Conservative figures.

Howe and Michael mobilized around British affairs and also engaged with the black power and civil rights movements in the United States. When *Black Dimension* asked "What ever Happened to H. Rap Brown?" The Eagles cited Maryland Governor Spiro Agnew's public denouncement of Brown during 1967 as proof of how in "American politics it is a good recommendation to be a racist."[82] Noting that in 1968, Agnew was newly elected U.S. vice president, the Eagles criticized the seemingly inextricable link between power and racial prejudice in American society.

Through consideration of the ways racialized restrictions on movement reflected a changing dynamic in British society, the Black Eagles also drew connections to U.S. government response to Brown's politically charged rhetoric. Howe reported that "on several occasions during my stay in the United States, Rap applied for permission to leave Manhattan [where he was under house arrest] for Washington, Montreal, Philadelphia, and California . . . Brother Rap has also been banned from entering Britain and so again Black people have been deprived of a valuable information on their Afro-American brothers."[83] The Eagles' critiques of racial regimes extended across the Atlantic and they supported black liberation across the world.

Stokely Carmichael was banned from entering both Britain and Trinidad in July 1967.[84] Trinidad's banning of Carmichael along with his South African wife Miriam Makeba was particularly egregious for the Eagles because Trinidad was "the land of his birth."[85] *Black Dimension* referred to Trinidad and Tobago Prime Minister Eric Williams as "the bespectacled demon" for refusing Carmichael's application. On behalf of "West Indians in England" the Black Eagles demanded Carmichael and Makeba be admitted. Since they argued "the Queen can go to Trinidad," Carmichael also had every right.

Black Dimension located its wide-ranging perspective through detailed accounts of developments across the African diaspora and through articulating support or disavowal of various political projects. For instance, the Eagles reported on news from Cuba, and heralded Fidel Castro's claim that the coming American election was "nothing more than a dispute among economic clans."[86] "Radio Havana" received praise for broadcasting "criticism of African foreign and domestic policies . . . [and] a series of indictments of racism in the United States."[87]

The Eagles propagandized through columns and messages of encouragement in *Black Dimension*. In addition to positive dispatches of black power and self-sufficiency, they offered artistic renderings of black beauty, achievement, and community bonds. Embedded in these messages was a commitment to solidarity and well-being. *Black Dimension* wanted black peoples to believe they were "masters at survival . . . the greatest warriors that ever walked this Earth."[88] What distinguished the Eagles from earlier iterations of black racial justice activists in Britain were militant expressions of liberatory dreams. Howe and Michael believed in the possibilities of militant resistance and linked their ongoing struggles in Britain and across diaspora with longer historical antecedents in Africa and affecting Africans across the world.

Mythologizing the durability of black people figured significantly into Black Eagles propaganda. African peoples were lauded for their "philosophy of survival," in particular the ability to "feel for each other . . . exist on very little," the Eagles explained, "we are the only people who know how."[89] In contrast to activists working for inclusion, acceptance, and camaraderie with English neighbors before the 1962 Commonwealth Immigrants Act, the Black Eagles rejected the acceptable notions of British interracial collaboration and friendship. Instead, they offered a radical perspective that highlighted their singular experience of suffering and unique capacity to survive to their historical and contemporaneous racial subordination. Rather than hoping to be seen as British, the Eagles made claims on how their African identities were fuller, more humanistic, and rooted in the intellectual and affective condition of blackness.

Similar to the Huntleys and La Rose, the Eagles also mobilized the formation of a classically trained black political base. In *Black Dimension*, the Eagles provided a reading list that encouraged readers to "know yourself, buy and read" a list of titles including, *From Michael de Freitas to Michael*

X, Autobiography of Malcolm X, Fanon's *Wretched of the Earth,* and Elijah Muhammad's *Message to the Blackman.*[90] Whereas earlier black activists in Britain, such as Dominican Edward Scobie and the staff of *Checkers* magazine, promoted literature that idealized the possibilities of interracial collaboration, by the end of the 1960s, radical black thinkers pivoted toward radical tomes that questioned the legitimacy of European colonialism and posited race conscious alternatives to postcolonial realities.

Black radical political culture in Britain was not monolithic and the Black Eagles' militancy raised the skepticism of other similarly aligned groups. In the *Trinidad Guardian,* September 29, 1968, Andrew Salkey was quoted as criticizing black British organizers for "aping the Black Americans." According to the paper, Salkey found an unnecessary affinity in that "they [Americans] had Malcom [sic] X- we got Michael X. They have Black Panther—we get BLACK EAGLES." Furthermore, Salkey rejected some of the transatlantic dissemination of black power political rhetoric. He suggested "Black Islam and Black Power have some meaning in the American context. Here they're just pure fantasy . . . closer to Hollywood than either Chicago or Notting Hill."[91] However, Salkey himself rejected the claim that he provided any of those quotations to the paper.

The Black Eagles supported Salkey in refuting "the statements attributed to [him]" based on the idea that "the two quotations . . . describing the hopelessness of the principles of Black Power in Britain and . . . the harmful parallels between the Black Revolutionary scene in America and . . . of the one here, in England, are maliciously imaginary."[92] The Black Eagles and Salkey suggested that the establishment papers in the United Kingdom and their allies across the Commonwealth had plotted to undermine the political consciousness they developed—despite Salkey and Howe working in different organizations. There was public pressure to mitigate strains of black activist thought and action in Britain.

Particularly insulting for the Eagles was the rejection from the *Trinidad Guardian* as a paper of the Caribbean. The paper suggested that Trinidadian Eagle Stafford Howe looked to defect "from the Eagles' nest" along with "Michael X and Junior Telfer." Stafford responded that he was "proud to be a Black Eagle . . . defection from the Eagle's nest will come only with my possible death" and Telfer reprimanded the paper for hiding "behind a powerful publishing company . . . [to] print what is libelous." Telfer recommitted to, "the solidarity of the Black Brothers in England . . . we are united and we have our way of letting the Brothers in the Caribbean know."[93]

Jamaican Locksley Comrie, President of the Oxford Union and interlocutor of the Eagles, renounced the *Guardian*'s coverage of a 1968 seminar he arranged entitled "The Realities of Black Power" in London. According to the paper, a black American Panther named Rico disrupted the meeting alleging that "there is no parallel at all between your situation here and ours in the United States" only for Comrie to respond that "Rico . . . [was] not a Black Panther . . . [but] one of the Chiefs of the Black P-Stone Nation in Black Chicago . . . go to the West Indian Students Centre to listen to the tapes . . . he had only good things to say about the Eagles."[94]

Black power in the late 1960s extended beyond political marches and public responses to racialized violence and the push toward decolonization in London. The historical basis for black power activism illustrated the novel intellectual and historical-consciousness-based perspectives of London actors. "The Realities of Black Power" was held to coincide with Marcus Garvey's birthday. Through a blend of artistic and intellectual contributions, CAM offered a multifaceted rendering of black power, beginning with an address from the Tanzanian High Commissioner. Brathwaite and La Rose read poems which were followed by addresses on "Black Organizations in Britain," "The Road to Awareness of Being Black in Britain," and "The Development of W.I. Standing Conference in Relation to the Changing Racial Scene in Britain." Fitting with CAM's commitment to the intersections of politics and arts the conference also featured a "soul session" by the Gamblers and the staging of noted African American Black Panther and playwright Ed Bullins's *The Electronic Nigger*.[95] These ambitious presentations reflected CAM's situating solutions to racial inequality firmly within the frameworks of black power.

Howe and Michael X were enmeshed in the crucible of British racism and therefore particularly suited to levy claims against racialism in various aspects of society. The Eagles decried the appointment of General Secretary of the Transport and General Workers Union, Frank Cousing as the leader of a Community Relations Committee. Because Cousing led "a Union whose white workers refused to support strike action against the racial policy of London Transport,"[96] he was unfit for a position fostering interracial community relations.

Unlike popular press coverage of racial tensions and the optimistic view that interracial cooperation would ameliorate negative feelings, the Black Eagles criticized the motivations of white community activists and workers. In addition to decrying Cousing's appointment, the Eagles asked their readers if "any one ever heard of Mrs. Anna Chataway . . . she has been appointed a member of the [same] Commission."[97] This was a grassroots movement reflecting the lived experiences of racial subordination and innovative strategies for freedom.

THE BLACK HOUSE

After the Notting Hill Riots, Conservatives charged nonwhite migrants with criminal activity and insinuated that they were responsible for rising levels of racial tension in Britain. At the 1958 Conservative Party Conference, Norman Powell moved a resolution calling for the deportation of so-called undesirables. Almost a decade later, in 1967, the Home Office issued a circular to all Chief Constables entitled *The Police and Coloured Communities*, in recognition of the bitterness nonwhites felt toward the police and persistent policing tactics.[98] However, within the next two years, another pamphlet was issued, *Coloured School Leavers*, pathologizing the problems black and brown youth had in Britain as a cultural deficiency which inadequately prepared them to finish school and justifiably marked them as "second-class citizens."

People of color were criminalized while police surveillance and harassment became common practice of areas of black and brown settlement (i.e., Handsworth, Brixton, Tottenham). The public nature of police interactions was important in the way people of color understood and conceptualized their place in British society. Black youths wished to stake claims over their neighborhoods as an articulation of their belonging to that community. For that reason, they dubbed the Handsworth police station, "Babylon House," or reflecting its precise geographic location, "the pigs on Thornhill Road." The squat house of Michael X became the Black House, and the Calypso Club and Mangrove Restaurant in Notting Hill remained central to London black identities. Africans, South Asians, and Caribbean-born or descended residents were innovating a black radical politics and making claims over space within London—Britain's imperial laboratory.

Michael X operated the Black House commune in North London, where similarly minded radicals devised a politics of resistance intertwining various strains of black power consciousness. De Freitas adopted the "X" designation after meeting Malcolm X in London and later "Abdul Malik" after his conversion to Islam. During Malcolm's tour of Britain in 1965, Michael traveled alongside him. Michael X was emblematic of the gray area of black British identities in the mid-twentieth century. Before mobilizing various fringe personalities at the Black House, de Freitas served as an enforcer for London slumlords such as Peter Rachman. He was in this way, quintessentially British.

Central to the organization of the Black House was a novel political orientation, rooted in practical solutions to racial inequities and the concept of political change. Combining the literal occupation of abandoned space in London with the founding of Racial Adjustment Action Society (RAAS), Michael made claims in Britain and developed a public program of resistance and social justice. Names of dozens of visitors and residents adorned the outside of the House including Trinidad-born filmmaker Horace Ové, African American entertainer Sammy Davis Jr., African American actor and political activist Dick Gregory, and Nigerian percussionist and bandleader George Folunsho "Ginger" Johnson.[99] According to its organizers, RAAS began "one sultry morning" and before long they held "enthusiastic meetings the length and breadth of the country . . . attended by large numbers of black and white people . . . we planned for the future . . . the wonderful and heart-longing things we wanted to create."[100]

RAAS began in 1963 when "a number of black people led by Michael Abdul Malik[101] realised the onslaught of racism in Britain." By 1969 "an area of North London . . . [had] been obtained" to hold seminars, educational projects, a restaurant, and a supermarket. RAAS engaged with black power movements and organizations from around the world. Sister Elva arrived in Addis Ababa to represent the group during the meeting of the Organisation for African Unity in September 1969 and reported on developing black-oriented projects RAAS spearheaded in Britain.[102] In their publicity materials, RAAS identified its core principle of encouraging "fraternal association and mutual support between the coloured peoples in the United Kingdom and abroad both in their native lands and in the countries where the coloured population constitutes a minority."[103] Within London, RAAS volunteers showed solidarity with London School of Economics students who organized a sit-in against the administration, delivering rice and other foodstuffs to the students.[104]

The desire for RAAS to create their own spaces was rooted in rejecting the racial status quo and the plan to "sweep our angry youth from the street corners into creativity."[105] RAAS envisioned the establishment of social centers and resources appealing to communities of color including "a commercial outlet which will act as a reservoir to provide for . . . much needed projects like a playschool for our little children." In order to fulfill the substantial lacunae in typical British education regarding the former colonies, RAAS hoped to organize "a workschool where we can teach various languages [and] history which will bring us nearer to Africa." Reflecting the radicalizing perspectives among black communities in London, RAAS noted, "Blacks in England . . . are newly and deeply aware of a relationship with the whole black, and especially the African world."[106] Centering the necessity of informing and propagating the relationship between black people in Britain, the diaspora, and Africa, RAAS developed a black political sensibility extending beyond the confines of individual nation-state citizenships or notions of belonging.

RAAS considered the status of black residents of Britain as part of the struggles of black people around the world. RAAS leadership took "pride and purpose from the array of independent Caribbean and African states . . . and [advocated] the need of Britain itself to project an image of racial peace."[107] Hoping to extend their role because of the "grave and heavy responsibility" of communal uplift, RAAS planned to do "so many other things" including operating a supermarket, "a restaurant with our own exotic foods, a boutique with our own clothing designs."[108] Through their early efforts at articulating the need to "eradicate the causes of friction between white and coloured communities in the United Kingdom and elsewhere, and to bring about a healthy and well balanced partnership between the races," RAAS were by the turn of the 1970s, able to "put into physical realization . . . a centre of our own . . . the BLACK HOUSE."[109]

Located at 95 Holloway Road in North London, RAAS founded the Black House as a place "where we could meet . . . talk . . . laugh . . . dance . . . argue . . . discuss."[110] RAAS occupied this local space, but also sought to implement plans for "developing Afro-Asian-Caribbean countries" such as "crash and long term programme[s] of study, diligence and application" in advanced technical skills.[111] By focusing on education and training in technology as well as a "language laboratory where . . . Swahili, Arabic and English will be taught . . . by black linguists," and courses led by "black historians [who] . . . interpret both the ancient and modern histories of these countries and the former 'mother' countries" RAAS envisioned rectifying the persistent problem of pedagogical silences around black people and their histories as well as a programmatic approach to equipping black people will skills for employment and progress in Britain and abroad.[112] Michael X and his cohorts committed to a policy of improving their station through the creation of black-oriented institutions of study. RAAS insisted on internationalist black-oriented discourse through, "research . . . not only . . . [for] the black people of Britain . . . but . . . also . . . the schools, universities and libraries of Africa, the Caribbean and Asia."[113]

The proposed Cultural Centre was designed to be "a store house crammed with the material to satisfy a great hunger grown from generations of deliberate deprivation," a vessel linking "cultural activities . . . and all . . . other fields of development."[114] RAAS were concerned with facilitating black education as well as publicizing problems of racialization in Britain. In addition to education measures, they intended to host a "theatre, a library of black writers, a museum . . . film presentation . . . festivals, exhibitions and concerts" at the Cultural Centre.[115]

To mobilize educational and cultural efforts, RAAS insisted on the intermingled intellectual work and the arts. Trinidadian steel band and black theatre in Britain and the Caribbean were highlighted by RAAS as essential components of radical politics of resistance. RAAS credited Martinican poet and politician Aimé Césaire with breaking "with all sorts of cant and . . . produc[ing] the plays we need today."[116] For RAAS black theatre was revolutionary art performed in front of "an audience of militants . . . particularly concerned with black people."[117] RAAS considered "Black theatre . . . a counterpart of political Black Power . . . creating a new language permitting self-identification. . . .a challenge to civilization as a whole."[118] Their pamphlets extolled culture as "the prologue to revolution proper . . . like revolution it moves the masses to action."[119] Focusing on grassroots and participatory actions highlighted their unique notion of social change.

RAAS did not limit their conception of culture to the stage or music studio—they considered the culinary background of West Indian and African peoples to be central to a positive self-image and a "community spirit of homeliness and satisfaction."[120] At the proposed Black House Communal Table, guests would eat in a complex that was "both creative and relaxing . . . [and] . . . charges will be low."[121] RAAS argued for a radical politics of inclusion predicated on expanding their audience and publicizing black power through democratizing access to facilities and broadening the potential for widespread collaboration.

Despite the reactionary politics of British public figures who opposed migration of West Indians and Africans and who contested their continued presence in Britain, RAAS offered recourse for representation and support. Reporting for the *Tribune* in June 1969 Ben Mallalieu recognized "Michael Malik [X] . . . working with Nigel Samuel on a new project in the Holloway Road."[122] Samuel was a wealthy white university dropout who donated substantial financial support to the commune. This project would become the Black House and Malik and Samuel intended to further rebuild "a series of derelict shops from 121 to 126 Holloway Road . . . into a supermarket, a restaurant, an art gallery, a theatre/cinema/lecture hall . . . offices and flats."[123] Mallalieu considered the value of the Black House project as ending the black community's exploitation in areas such as "Notting Hill, Moss Side, Tiger Bay and Brixton . . . [where] ghetto environment[s] and ghetto mentality . . . tends to be excessively restrictive and aggressive."[124] He noted that rather than perpetuating social ills, the "project . . . is a place where others can learn about and learn from black culture . . . a multi-racial project."[125]

REPURPOSING THE MASTER'S TOOLS

Celebrities such as Muhammad Ali and Yoko Ono visited the Black House and increased the squat's public profile. In April 1970, a black American actor named Leroy House complained to Michael X that he had received reduced pay at the cleaning company where he was then employed. Michael and three members of the Black House traveled to proprietor Marvin Brown's "Clean-A-Flat" offices, removed stacks of Brown's files, and informed him that if he wanted to reclaim them, he would have to pick them up at the Black House. Brown called the police and traveled to Holloway Road. Upon arrival, Brown was met by a thirty-person court (made up of black men and black and white women) that demanded he make amends for the mistreatment of blacks throughout history. Brown protested on account of his Jewish heritage, he was a persecuted minority, and was then marched around the room with a spiked "slave collar" around his neck. After this ordeal, Michael X took

£13 from Brown, gave him £8 in change and a copy of his autobiography *From Michael Freitas to Michael X*. A week later fifty police descended on the Black House and arrested all who raided Brown's office. De Freitas had spent about thirteen years in Britain before fleeing to Trinidad after his arrest in the Marvin Brown affair.

The Black House's "court proceedings" undermined and commandeered the otherwise unquestioned assumptions of fairness and the ubiquitous notion of the centrality of the rule of law in British culture. Instead, the shackling of a rumored exploitative white British businessman was a novel iteration of justice unique to radical racial thinkers and emergent in the particular context of postcolonial and post-*Windrush* Britain. Imbued with centuries of meaning, the slave collar placed on a white man's neck represented usurping the symbolic power of slavery and racial violence in the context of modern Britain. Furthermore, the "slave collar," like the tufts of hair clipped from Ono and John Lennon's heads and auctioned off for charity to raise funds for the Black House were the possession of Michael—an unapologetic and brash agent of black power.

Beyond the symbolic nature of the slave collar squeezing Brown's throat, RAAS attempted to reorient and radicalize the potential of embracing black identification through the reclamation of control over their own affairs and institutions. The Black House exemplified the repossession of the material aspects of racial subordination in the metropole. Squatting and occupying space and remaking it in the image of Michael and his cohorts were central to the possibilities of charting a different path for radical-minded activists.

BEYOND THE BLACK HOUSE

British Black power developed through the mélange of black experiences from across the former empire and through engagements of ex-colonial subjects in the center of empire. Within radical political circles of postwar Britain and independent Africa, Caribbean, and South Asian societies, influential figures arrived from numerous corners and articulated a blend of ideas, images, and political qualms wherever they went. Obi Egbuna, a Nigerian born novelist, playwright, and black power activist penned *Destroy this Temple: The Voice of Black Power in Britain*, in 1971. In July 1968, Egbuna was arrested and charged with writing a letter conspiring to murder white police officers. According to *Destroy this Temple*, Egbuna was "dragged out of bed in the dead hours of the morning" and "never saw . . . [his] flat again till after six months of grueling detention in Brixton Prison."[126] While his bail application was rejected five times, Egbuna endured twenty-three hours of solitary confinement for the duration of his incarceration. His radical politics allow insight into the development of race-first mobilization.

Egbuna realized the potential of black power politics through the arrival and provocations of Carmichael in particular. Egbuna remembered how Carmichael's address that roused a crowd at Speakers Corner in Hyde Park in summer 1967 exposed the black community in London to the rhetoric and consciousness of black power. Egbuna remarked that "by the time [Carmichael] finished speaking, it had become evident that, if he was lucky enough to get away from Britain without being arrested, he was destined to be banned from coming back."[127] Carmichael had articulated an unspoken sentiment among black people in British communities—Egbuna noted that the divisions among black people—from Africa, the Caribbean, the United States, or British born—were substantial and caused consternation between respective groups. Egbuna lauded Carmichael's approach to the inclusivity of black power as opposed to many active extant civil rights groups of the time. Egbuna regarded RAAS as a Muslim group due to Michael Abdul Malik's leadership, CARD as modeled too closely to nonviolent resistance groups like the American Southern Christian Leadership Conference, and criticized the view that "it was the climax of absurdity to call a 'West Indian' African"[128] in Britain. Through the converging of these distinct groups who shared a racial background, Egbuna argued for the mobilization of a militant black power.

While the Eagles and RAAS created space for a radical politics of black power, other organizations such as the Universal Coloured People's Association propagated positive black images in the pursuit of black political and economic solvency. Similar to the cultural work of CAM, UCPA noted the aesthetic potential of black self-images and popular iconography. They commended the "Negro woman [who] no longer burnt her hair to 'whiten' herself" and the black American cultural schools emerging in the late 1960s to teach "Swahili and other African and Asian languages with pride."[129] Black Americans adopted cultural representations including wearing the djellabah and UCPA noted "in Watts, culture-voracious SNCC youths were chanting 'Odinga Odinga' with gusto . . . in Chicago, Phillip Cochran [sic] . . . staggered the White world when he declared that White classical music is 'unnatural' and profane."[130] It is important to note that the UCPA strove to remain informed of the events and specific examples of black pride and power in multiple locations in the United States. They were deeply committed to understanding the specificity and particular details of black and African pride and expressions in sites other than the United Kingdom.

Just as members of the Black Unity and Freedom Party and Eagles cited Carmichael's visit to London as formative for the development of black power in Britain, UCPA credited the efforts of "black cultural nationalists" in America with bringing a whole "generation of Carmichaels to the fore."[131] The new cohort of black power activists boasted of their broad noses, thick lips, and beady hair that they too were beautiful.[132] UCPA engaged with international and non-British iterations of black power in a direct manner that recognized the specific influence of cultural knowledge in various expressions of black belonging and positive racial identity.

UCPA were exceedingly critical of white supremacist politics, politicians, and policies in the U.S. and assailed the "fascist Reagan . . . who wants emergency measures to prevent [black power].[133] UCPA situated the policies of California governor Ronald Reagan within a white backlash against social justice, likening him to British secretary of state for the Colonies Duncan Sandys who preached a "complete blockade" of colored immigration. Sandys supported Ian Smith and the U.D.I. in Rhodesia and was a son-in-law of Winston Churchill. An important figure in the Conservative establishment, Sandys represented the apotheosis of white supremacist rhetoric and political action in Britain and abroad.

UCPA skewered the alliance between Sandys and Smith and recognized the way each attempted to stymie the potential political power of black people in Britain and Rhodesia. They contested Sandys' notion that "the less the number of blacks, the less likely they are to resort to violence" and suggested that "BLACK POWER is not a quantitative entity . . . it . . . is not a number . . . it is a degree of anger which the oppressed Black man feels in his guts."[134] UCPA were unmoved by attacks on their movement through blocking migration because they believed, "it takes a single match-stick to burn London down . . . [and] one angry Black man to light that match."[135] Through mobilizing a small, clandestine movement of committed activists UCPA would progress toward their ultimate goal, "a revolutionary conspiracy of Black people."[136] Full of swaggering pro-black bravado, UCPA were unafraid to confront their enemies, especially when couched in the rhetoric of defense. They believed, "the only way to neutralize violence is to oppose it with violence. We are no initiators of violence. But if a White man lays his hand on ONE of us, we will regard it as an open declaration of war on ALL of us. If the White man does not want a Black steamroller coming his way, he will be well advised henceforth to put his hands where they belong. In his pockets."[137] UCPA rhetoric targeted the status quo in Britain, contesting typical modes of dissent by projecting an aggressive and bellicose black power.

While integration and assimilation marked the tenor of black and brown activism in Britain before the *Windrush*, by the late 1960s, rebels and revolutionaries moved toward a politics of racial identification and located their resistance in the logic of historical injustices. UCPA considered the black [wo]man in Britain as "only a speck in the wind of history"[138] swept up by the Englishman and forced to seek opportunities in Britain. UCPA understood the reality of the black presence in the midcentury as they recognized "we are not here of our choosing. We do not enjoy slotting shillings for heat. We do not enjoy the tyranny of landladies, We do not enjoy the taunts and insults by fascist teddy boys hiding in police uniforms."[139] UCPA were hyperaware of the historicized nature of their subjugation and the depth of British-based racialization. They argued that "the attitude of the collective White man in Britain . . . is that the collective Black man should be grateful for being allowed immigration into the country. This . . . ignores the basic fact of history. Every collective person in England is an immigrant. It is arrogant impertinence that one immigrant should demand entry gratitude from another."[140]

Black power vanguards contested with the intersecting exploitation of class and race, particularly in ways that white working classes could not and were unwilling to engage. UCPA suggested that white workers contributed directly to the problems of nonwhite workers because whites wanted "to create an aristocracy of labour . . . White first and worker afterwards, he would rather form a racial pact with his kith-and-kin capitalist exploiter and go to distant lands with guns, bayonets, and naphalm [sic] to decimate, rob and rape the workers and peasants of other races to whom he feels superior."[141] UCPA bemoaned the perpetual state of racial animosity with race as the primary factor in social relationships—superseding class. When white allies offered to collaborate, UCPA critiqued them, characterizing the typical white liberal as believing in, "justice, equality and liberty for the Black man as long as this remains within the realm of abstraction . . . in the fruits of revolution but disapproves of the revolution that brings them about."[142] UCPA critiqued a moderate liberal perspective that articulated progressive and inclusive ideals while unwilling to substantively change the structure of the systems of oppression.

Claudia Jones and many other black women played a central role in black power activism as well. Olive Morris, Barbara Beese, and Althea Jones-LeCointe all contributed in tangible ways to movements of black power. Morris was seventeen in 1970 when she was in Brixton protesting a Nigerian diplomat's arrest for a parking ticket. During a confrontation with police, Morris kicked a police officer and hit him in the jaw.[143] While the Eagles and others promoted a masculinist image publicly, black women were also frontline combatants against police and racist aggression.

The Mangrove Restaurant in Notting Hill, run by Trinidadian civil rights campaigner and activist Frank Crichlow, was an informal club and meeting place for West Indians and was under scrutiny and surveillance from Scotland Yard through the late 1960s. Between January 1969 and July 1970 police raided the restaurant a dozen times. On August 9, 1970, the Black

Panthers led a protest demanding, "hands off the Mangrove" only to be met by police resistance. Protesters carried a banner reading "Black oppressed people all over the world are one."[144] At the front of the phalanx was a young man carrying a pig's head. The collective marched past the police stations in Notting Hill and Notting Dale before violence broke out in Paddington between police and protesters. The police arrested nine protesters, known as the "Mangrove Nine" including Crichlow, Beese, and Jones-LeCointe. Jones-LeCointe and Beese were charged with criminal possession of weapons and assaulting police officers. The women participants mobilized in crucial ways and were the vanguard of black radical resistance.[145] The Nine were eventually acquitted of all charges of incitement.

BLACK POST-NATIONAL EPISTEMOLOGY

The Institute of Race Relations (IRR) facilitated social justice activism through civic mobilization and the production of new concepts and ideals rooted in non-Anglocentric notions of justice and knowledge. In the IRR's *Race* newsletter, Gordon K. Lewis, the Puerto Rico-based Welsh expert on Caribbean thought and politics, offered a scathing rebuke of British attitudes toward social difference and charged metropolitan ignorance as willing and deplorable. In the July 1969 edition of *Race*, Lewis presented, "three general observations . . . about a specifically Caribbean view of the presence of the new coloured micro-cultures in post-war English society."[146] He historicized the "West Indian migrant-person" as "not simply . . . symbolizing the movement of the West Indian colonial unemployed and underemployed but just another stage . . . of the circulatory migratory movements of the Caribbean folk-peoples over the last 60 years."[147] Intra-Caribbean migration contributed to regional dynamism since the end of slavery across the area in the nineteenth century and Lewis castigated the "English observers . . . [who]have usually failed to see this because of their characteristic incuriosity about the ancestral background of the new immigrants."[148] Lewis rejected the common "negrophobic" response of Britons who "had reacted from the very beginning with hostility . . . panic fear, to the 'unarmed invasion.'"[149] A core component of the West Indian imaginary Lewis explained was recognizing the limited nature of Eurocentric and in particular British conceptualizations of West Indian identity, place, and belonging.

Despite writing two decades after the arrival of the *Windrush*, Lewis noted that "British political leadership, including Labour, managed to see it not as a free movement of voluntary labour but as a sort of slave transportation engineered by evil agencies somewhere in the Caribbean,"[150] as if West Indians arrived in Britain as part of a conspiracy to overtake the metropolitan British state. Lewis instead identified the influx into Britain as another example of the historic West Indian diaspora and its "uprootedness . . . a feature of West Indian society since the 17th century . . . unforgettable experiences . . . through the wilderness, through a land of drought and the shadow of death, through a land that no white man had passed through . . . where no white man had dwelt . . . the misery and loneliness . . . is still with them."[151] Black radical politics therefore emerged as a response to the historical displacement and alienation of West Indians even before reaching metropolitan Britain. Lewis explained various strains of black political responses to continued exclusion including the "emergence of black Zionism . . . 'black capitalism' . . . movement[s] seeking to apply the historic virtues of economic Calvinism to the neo-ghetto economies."[152]

Lewis recognized the basis for the revival of "Garveyism, emphasising . . . less the idea of the physical return to Africa and more that of the psychological return."[153] He argued that the strains of black radical politics had roots in the historical condition of diaspora and rootlessness. This condition was regarded as "nonbelonging" in the British context. Furthermore, Lewis suggested Garveyism was reborn not in advocating repatriation to Africa but rather by psychologically training and orienting politics around notions of black African race pride. Lewis recognized that the postwar migrant generation had to reckon with the reality of their racialization in British society and the textures of their West Indianness did not resonate—only race mattered. In Britain, there was not conceptual space for the intersection of ethnic, island, religious, or other social differentiations alongside matters of race. Lewis suggested that West Indians in England needed to "confront its [English society] quasi-racialist reality . . . are less and less West Indians in English society, more and more black men in white society."[154] In this way Britain was less distinct from "white society" and racialized Others consequently existed in a fixed state of black inferiority.

Lewis regarded metropolitan anti-black antagonism within the English tradition of exclusion, skepticism, and objection to perceived foreigners. He cited the "anguished white liberal" who explained to his "confused West Indian friend, on a recent BBC programme: 'The song is we shall overcome, not we shall come over.'"[155] Lewis identified the problem of multiculturalism not to the strangeness of the West Indians but rather the refusal of white Britons to accept them in any appreciable way. By mocking "we shall overcome" the Briton placed the onus on the West Indian—overcoming and improvement was his responsibility, not the duty of the British state or of British citizens in the metropole. Additionally, the Briton suggested the foolishness and ignorance of the West Indian who, he believed, misunderstood the song and actually arrived in Britain. This was a stunning perspective on the enormous fissure between conceptualizing the relationship between white and black and colony and metropole.

While West Indian and African cultural production flourished in metropolitan British spaces, Lewis noted that these articulations were varied and did not always advocate a progressive spirit. Lewis criticized how the seeming permanence of "colonial loyalty . . . [that] dies hard . . . like Braithwaite's *To Sir, With Love* . . . still manage[s] to purvey to the myth that well-dressed appearance and polite behavior . . . can transform English prejudices."[156] Lewis criticized Braithwaite's appeals for moderation in *To Sir, With Love*, noting that the expression of good manners did not automatically endear West Indians to the British. Furthermore, Lewis argued that most West Indians were not Anglophilic nor deferential to traditional English values and mores, certainly not after independence and the earlier patterns of exclusion and discrimination among colonial migrants after World War II.

Lewis found the contemporaneous Caribbean political milieu frustrating—largely a byproduct of what he characterized as hackneyed notions of sovereignty rooted in English traditions. From Puerto Rico, Lewis wrote that "island politics . . . are at best fifty years behind the contemporary English times, whether it be the crowd-hero politics of the smaller islands . . . or the Fabian politics of the Peoples National Movement in Trinidad, where Dr. Williams brought the traditional Fabian values into power in 1956 at the very moment when they were on the decline in Britain itself."[157] Lewis saw Caribbean political development as slow in responding to the contemporaneous times, due to unwarranted deference for English traditions that had become moot even in England. Lewis instead advocated that West Indian leaders embark on a transformative politics, more reflective of their particular realities. He critiqued the notion that West Indian perspectives were culturally "akin to British outlooks" arguing instead, "West Indian society, for all of its deceptive anglicisation, is *sui generis* . . . read . . . *Wide Sargasso Sea* . . . to see how from the beginning even the white groups in that society, always the most pro-English, developed a distinctive psychological separatism, the famous Creole identity, divorcing them, by everything in their island life, from English prides and prejudices."[158] Lewis noted that West Indians came to Britain from societies that already operated a racialism that was distinct from metropolitan forms. Although blacks made up the majority, they nevertheless were dominated by groups who saw themselves as superior not only to the black West Indians but peerless in the absence of the white English in the British Isles. The *sui generis* quality of Caribbean culture did not dissolve because West Indians arrived in Britain. It became the specific mechanism of their political configurations harnessed in the cauldron of the declining empire.

Even before decolonization, the position of leading intellectual middle-class figures was impossible to ignore. In 1954 Jamaica, the People's National Party published a commemorative pamphlet on the life of its founder and leader Norman Manley entitled *Man of Destiny*.[159] This pamphlet was hagiographic despite debuting while Manley was developing his Jamaican nationalist platform and almost a decade before the nation became independent. Manley's qualifications were manifold and represented the apotheosis of British metropolitan and colonial tradition:

> When the adolescent Norman was through at J.C., he worked and taught at J.C., Hope Farm School and at Tichfield School until the news came that he had won the Rhodes Scholarship . . . He entered Jesus College Oxford University to read for the Bar. But his studies were interrupted by World War I when he joined the ranks of the Royal Field Artillery as a gunner and saw three years' active service in France and Belgium where his brother was killed beside him and where he refused to be made an officer, preferring to live and fight in the ranks.[160]

PNP heralded Manley as an elite intellectual in the metropole—a Rhodes scholar who also dared the ultimate sacrifice on behalf of Britain, noting his service in France and Belgium during World War I. Manley seemed to be the ideal "liberating father" to forge a path for Jamaican sovereignty.[161]

Black Power featured in multiple iterations by the close of the 1960s and Lewis criticized migrant political theory as "nothing much more than. . . variations on the imported American slogan of Black Power."[162] Because the Black Eagles and Egbuna for instance, credited Carmichael with bringing the language of "black power" to Britain, Lewis may have viewed these articulations as lacking a unified, coherent platform. Lewis critiqued the "self-appointed messiahs, leaders of committees without rank and file memberships"[163] who offered a vision that saw "English white society . . . in the same way as . . . the Book of Revelation saw . . . Roman imperialism but, relying on the external magical agency to release its victims from the tyranny."[164] Lewis located his frustrations in the lack of an intellectualized activist articulation among the groups. He did not, however, note the specific character of different organizations and their perspectives.

Lewis wrote against postcolonial liberal notions of the West Indies that he characterized as myth. He explained that both, "West Indian nationalist and English liberal alike" applauded the West Indies as "a successful multi-racial society."[165] The reality in the region, according to Lewis was that "West Indian life is . . . a multi-layered pigmentocracy suffering from its own private disease of subtle 'shade' prejudice . . . the migrant . . . moves from a classificatory system based on the fine detective recognition of 'shade' to an English classificatory system that has taken over the American black-white dichotomy, so much more brutal and insulting."¹⁶⁶ Lewis noted the problem of English ignorance of the West Indies and the racial system in both places. He suggested that West Indians were surprised by their first encounters with the *brutality* of strict white-black racial bifurcation. Reflecting on postcolonial possibilities, Lewis identified the enemy in West Indian life was, "the perpetuation, by the new middle-class elites of the successor-states of empire, of the 'white bias' of the society; and in English life of a potent negrophobia so ingrained that it produces a 'left wing racialism' as easily as the neo-Fascism of the National Front."¹⁶⁷ Lewis recognized that changing dynamics in British society remained oriented around a racial exclusion and remade in the vestiges of empire.

CAM in Britain reaffirmed its objectives during its 1968 convening. While working as the first editor for the Caribbean at Longman Publishing, Anne Walmsley attended the conference to witness talks on the role of the Caribbean artist in political affairs. During a session on the "Purpose and Future of CAM," Locksley Comrie insisted on the political potential of art and culture suggested, "all art that does not contribute to revolution is invalid."¹⁶⁸ Comrie admonished the elite scholarly perspective of some, telling "CAM members to get off intellectual backsides."¹⁶⁹ He specifically took issue with the, "WI Students Centre, and the attitude of the students there." Comrie wished to distance CAM from the formal relationship developed with WISC and instead take it "to Ladbroke Grove and Brixton."¹⁷⁰ While CAM emerged from efforts of intellectuals, the group also reassessed its meaning and mobilization strategies through looking toward the grassroots possibilities of engaging laypeople in the neighborhoods of black settlement in London.

John La Rose argued that "structureless organization" of CAM contributed to its dynamism but also implored conference attendees to establish "intercommunication, discussion of ideas ... [and a] plunge into public activity."¹⁷¹ Comrie supported La Rose's notion and suggested "CAM ... bring to Brixton people what they're missing."¹⁷² Comrie focused on neighborhoods like Brixton because of the higher concentration of black residents and reiterated CAM's aim to engage with intellectuals and artists but also with the working classes from Africa and the Caribbean who were sometimes scattered across different London areas.

Walmsley noted how Guyaanese broadcaster, critic, and poet Ivan van Sertima was frustrated by the lack of access Caribbean people had to the history of the region. Van Sertima recently returned to Britain after visiting Guyana for the first time in nine years. Walmsley describe van Sertima's vexation regarding the Caribbean being portrayed as "historyless ... an illumination ... not ... knowledge and facts ... void of ... national identity."¹⁷³ Van Sertima suggested, in Walmsley's notes "that writers must work in another dimension to absorb indigenous tradition."[174] Like other CAM members, van Sertima was convinced of the necessity of creating traditions anew—thinking outside the realms of possibility determined by Europe in order to create institutions and societies reflective of the African and indigenous roots of Caribbean societies.

RASTAFARI AND REASONING

While West Indians countered the political and social strife in late-1960s Britain through creative artistic and scholarly endeavors, some radical thinkers and agitators also engaged in the work of reconceptualizing spirituality. Rastafarians in Jamaica were critical to the radicalizing perspective of influential black Atlantic thinkers such as Walter Rodney who engaged them in Kingston. Rodney was drawn to the Rastafarians because of their spiritual and social ingenuity and because their initial activities were surveilled by the police in Jamaica. Authorities believed Rastafarians were a threat—upsetting the status quo of decolonizing and newly independent civil society. *The Ras Tafari Movement in Kingston, Jamaica*, known as the *Rastafari Report* was compiled by M. G. Smith, Roy Augier, and Rex Nettleford under the auspices of the University College of the West Indies in Mona. Published in 1960, Augier, Nettleford, and Smith responded to reports of and interest in the activities of the little-known Rastafari movement in Jamaica in the final years of British rule. The Rastas themselves appealed to the faculty by asking that they publish work revealing the true principles and aims of the movement.

The authors located origins of the movement in the mountains of Jamaica and noted that Rastafarians were informed by race pride and reconciliation with the African past. Most central was the deification of Haile Selassie. They noted as early as 1935 reports from local papers such as the *Jamaica Times* published articles referring to the "the so-called Niyabingi Order in Ethiopia and the Congo . . . both Ethiopia and Haile Sellassie [*sic*] were in the news . . . the Ethiopian Emperor was head of the Niyabingi Order, the purpose of which was the overthrow of white domination by racial war."[175] Early accounts suggested "violent note had already been struck by [Leonard] Howell, and Niyabingi was defined in Jamaica as 'Death to black and white oppressors.'"[176]

The *Report* identified transnational dimensions of Rastafari, despite Jamaican government assaults on the movement. The authors emphasized the government raid on "Pinnacle . . . in 1954" as contributing to the "the increase in the number of dreadlocks men in Kingston . . . [and] a very large expansion of the activities of the Ethiopian World Federation in Jamaica."[177] The situation in Jamaica inspired, "commencement of large scale emigration to Britain, the decline of revivalism in Jamaica, and the activities of the political parties" which, "all gave a fillip to the movement, which has since grown very rapidly."[178] Because of *Windrush*-era migration, the decline of religious revivalism, and the aggression of the police, Rastafari grew as a uniquely Jamaican diasporic mode of resistance.

Nettleford et al. noted "in 1955 the Jamaican migration to Britain assumed major proportions . . . and in the same year the executive of the Ethiopian World Federation Inc . . . [in] New York 27, wrote to the Executive Committee of Local 31 . . . that the Emperor Haile Selassie I had granted '500 acres of very fertile and rich land . . . to the Black People of the West, who aided Ethiopia during her period of distress.'"[179] The researchers concluded that "with the migration to Britain underway, and the opportunity for migration to Ethiopia apparently open, the Messianic cult which Professor [George] Simpson had studied in 1953 became a full-blown belief in mass migration."[180] Migration to Britain, therefore, inspired Jamaican Rastafarians that migration to Ethiopia was also possible. Rastafarian notions of repatriation were rooted in what they considered an indelible connection to Africa and a loyalty and faith in Selassie.

Critical to Rastafari's rise as a revolutionary movement were spiritual awakenings and official response by the government of Jamaica, which regarded Rastas as a disruptive force in the newly postcolonial society. The researchers found that the general public was weary of "a stereotype Ras Tafarian, who wears a beard, avoids work, steals, smokes ganja, and is liable to sudden violence."[181] This image of Rastafarians marginalized them within Jamaican society. They were outcast because of the lack of information about them and general social standards about public appearance and behaviors. Despite their ostracization and targeting by the authorities, the *Report* noted, "how . . . meetings . . . began and ended with the recitation of psalms and the singing of hymns . . . were punctuated by frequent interludes of religious observance."[182] The investigators explained that Rastafari was a "movement which is so deeply religious [it] need not become a menace to society."[183] The authors concluded that Rastafarians had a depth of social, political, and spiritual faith and their rejection of many standards represented a rebellious approach to addressing society's ills. Rastafari reasoning provided a platform for the expression of different conceptualizations of power, justice, and salvation rooted in specifically resistance-based Afrocentric notions of epistemology. These foundations were important to the political articulations of post-national West Indian agitators in Jamaica, London, and also Tanzania.[184]

Rastafarians concerned themselves with creating alternative modes of thought in Britain to counter the conceptual and educational struggles of West Indians in the metropole. Grenadian Bernard Coard published *How the West*

Indian Child is Made Educationally Subnormal in the British School System for the Caribbean Education and Community Workers' Association with New Beacon in 1971. After delivering a paper at the CECWA Conference in 1970, Coard researched and wrote the manuscript that summer. CECWA approached fifty-seven organizations for assistance including the Oxford West Indian Association and the Black Panther Association. New Beacon initially printed 10,000 copies of the report and it became the publisher's first bestseller.

Horace Campbell has credited the vision of Rastafari doctrine in Britain with "spurning the technological rationality . . . materialism and the degenerate mass media promoting the celebration of commodity fetishism . . . as an alternative to the corrupt spirit of Europe."[185] Rastas in Britain organized a branch of the Ethiopian World Federation (Local 33) in Notting Hill, another component of black resistance in the metropole. EWF Local 33 issued *Rasta Cry* from Portobello Road as the organ of their resistance in the early 1970s. Rastafari was posited as the "only solution for black youths because it is unique . . . collective . . . fundamental. It is not Marxism, Maoism, nor Black Powerism. It is the only instrument that can destroy the yoke of imperialism and colonialism in the West Indies and African."[186] In the former imperial capital, Rastafarians designed and articulated a path of resistance rooted not in rectifying their relationship to Britain or imperial legacies but instead in forging forward a new vision of possibility. Through educating and engaging youth, EWF Local 33 offered a unique tool of empowerment for diasporic Africans in Britain, the Caribbean, and Africa.

ABENG AND DEVELOPMENTS "BACK HOME"

After the Rodney Riots in Jamaica, the potential for black power activism came to the fore as multiple segments of Jamaican society mobilized simultaneously to resist the restrictive anti-black policies of the postcolonial state. Barrymore Bogues has illuminated the particular phenomenon of the emergence of the *Abeng* newspaper, its editorial board, and the movement that coalesced around it.[187] Its editorial committee was made up of Rupert Lewis, Robert Hill, George Beckford, and Horace Levy. Born in Jamaica, Beckford returned in 1964 to lecture at UWI Mona in economics. He previously lectured in agricultural economics in St. Augustine, Trinidad, after earning an undergraduate degree from McGill in Canada in 1958, followed by an MA and PhD at Stanford. Lewis was director of the Guild Press at UWI Mona, as well as editor of *Scope, Impact, Social Scientist,* and *Bongo Man* publications. Hill became interested in Garvey and the UNIA due to his uncle Frank

Augustus Hill's labor activism and pursued research in London, Toronto, and Mona. As a criminologist and community activist, Levy also moved between multiple spaces in the newly independent Jamaica. Through their life histories, the initial *Abeng* group exemplified radical politics beyond the limited scope of the postcolonial Jamaican nation-state.

Abeng's February 1969 debut announced the central task of the newspaper, "to help us discover ourselves—not just the past, but . . . what we are today and what we can be tomorrow if we can move forward together."[188] Named after the Jamaican Maroon communication tool—the horn of a cow that could be blown as a signal—*Abeng* intended to "have a 'particular call' for each and every Jamaican."[189] *Abeng* tapped into a logic of historical continuity—basing their radical rebel perspective in postcolonial Jamaica on the historical legacy of resistance in the island dating to colonialism and slavery. The paper claimed that as late as 1956 the "Abeng is still blown in Westmoreland as a summons when there is some communal job to be done."[190]

Abeng situated its politics in the independent Jamaican political milieu but also regarded the ideas and contributions of other West Indians moving through the Caribbean and Britain as critical to their platform. C. L. R. James penned "Capital" for *Abeng* in February 1969 and decried the "slavish dependence on foreign capital and foreign enterprise" present in postcolonial Caribbean societies who nevertheless were "dressed in a national flag and beating an independence drum."[191] *Abeng* also reprinted articles from Garvey's *Blackman* and *Negro World*—placing the contemporaneous problems of Jamaican society into a longer historical pattern of exploitation and racial inequality.

Similar to radical activists and organizations in Britain, *Abeng* took interest in the possibilities of postcolonialism in the Caribbean and Africa. Omo Ogun chronicled ongoing struggles of newly independent African nations against their former European colonial occupiers. Ogun characterized the entire historical relationship between Europe and Africa as theft. He argued Europeans "stole the brothers and sisters of the African to use as his slaves . . . the African's land . . . his culture . . . his mind."[192] He argued for the protection and production of Afro-centric culture in the postcolony as central to the independence project, similar to the efforts of CAM and Black Eagles in London. Ogun lauded the Tanzanian government when it "attacks miniskirts, hair-straightening, and rock and roll (white man's corruption of the black man's music)" and worked instead toward, "making the African proud of himself again."[193] *Abeng* forwarded the notion that culture was central to directing the possibilities of the postcolony in Africa and the Caribbean. Ogun recognized the Fanon-prophesized problems of "black men who have been so completely brainwashed that they think . . . the only really culture comes from the white man . . . these black men are the rulers of the new African states."[194] Ogun identified West Indians and diasporic Africans alongside their continental counterparts when suggesting "the African will never be truly free until these house-slaves of the white man have been swept away along with his rule."[195] The possibilities of deliberate coordinated action rooted in educating black masses in Britain and abroad were objectives that Rastafarians, black nationalists, grassroots activists, and postcolonial statesmen rallied around by the enactment of the highly restrictive 1971 Immigration Act in Britain.

NOTES

1. Edward Brathwaite, "The Caribbean Artists Movement," *Caribbean Quarterly* 14, no. 1/2 (March–June 1968), 57. See also *Caribbean Voices* program.

2. Ibid., 58. In addition to Williams, fellow Guianese Frank Bowling and Jamaican sculptor Ronald Moody (Harold Moody's younger brother) were his contemporaries in the world of visual and plastic arts. Interestingly, Bowling maintained a loose affiliation with CAM, never participating in their exhibitions.

3. Ann Walmsley, *The Caribbean Artists' Movement, 1966–1972: A Literary and Cultural History* (London: New Beacon Books, 1992).

4. From Edward Brathwaite to Bryan King (November 30, 1966) Correspondence between members of the Caribbean Artists Movement, and with associated bodies or individuals (November 30, 1966 to February 13, 1973); George Padmore Institute Archives Reference: GB2904 CAM/3/1.

5. Ibid.

6. From Bryan King to Edward Brathwaite (December 2, 1966) Correspondence between members of the Caribbean Artists Movement, and with associated bodies or individuals (November 30, 1966 to February 13, 1973); GPI: GB2904 CAM/3/2.

7. From Edward Brathwaite to Edward Lucie-Smith (December 12, 1966) Correspondence between members of the Caribbean Artists Movement, and with associated bodies or individuals (November 30, 1966 to February 13, 1973); GPI: GB2904 CAM/3/3.

8. Ibid.

9. From Edward Lucie-Smith to Edward Brathwaite (December 17, 1966) Correspondence between members of the Caribbean Artists Movement, and with associated bodies or individuals (November 30, 1966 to February 13, 1973); GPI: GB2904 CAM/3/4.

10. Letter from Edward Brathwaite to Dr. Reinders (November 2, 1967) Correspondence between members of the Caribbean Artists Movement, and with associated bodies or individuals (November 30, 1966 to February 13, 1973); GPI: GB2904 CAM/3/268.

11. Brathwaite, "The Caribbean Artists Movement," 58.

12. Ibid.

13. Ngugi changed his name to Ngugi wa Thiong'o in 1967.

14. Letter from Edward Brathwaite to Kenneth Ramchand (December 28, 1966) Correspondence between members of the Caribbean Artists Movement, and with associated bodies or individuals (November 30, 1966 to February 13, 1973); GPI: GB2904 CAM/3/6.

15. See chapter 3.

16. From Kenneth Ramchand to Edward Brathwaite (January 4, 1967) Correspondence between members of the Caribbean Artists Movement, and with associated bodies or individuals (November 30, 1966 to February 13, 1973); GPI: GB2904 CAM/3/7.

17. Ibid. Credit is also due to Lewis Gordon for his work on "disciplinary decadence" which is apt here.

18. Ibid.

19. From Andrew Salkey to Edward Brathwaite (January 14, 1967) Correspondence between members of the Caribbean Artists Movement, and with associated bodies or individuals (November 30, 1966 to February 13, 1973); GPI: GB2904 CAM/3/12.

20. From Gordon Rohlehr to Edward Brathwaite (March 16, 1967) Correspondence between members of the Caribbean Artists Movement, and with associated bodies or individuals (November 30, 1966 to February 13, 1973); GPI: GB2904 CAM/3/33.

21. From Edward Brathwaite to Frank Collymore (April 11, 1967) Correspondence between members of the Caribbean Artists Movement, and with associated bodies or individuals (November 30, 1966 to February 13, 1973); GPI: GB2904 CAM/3/42.

22. From Edward Brathwaite to Antonio B. de Castro (August 21, 1967) Correspondence between members of the Caribbean Artists Movement, and with associated bodies or individuals (November 30, 1966 to February 13, 1973); GPI: GB2904 CAM/3/144.

23. From Edward Brathwaite to the editor of *The Observer* (September 7, 1967) Correspondence between members of the Caribbean Artists Movement, and with associated bodies or individuals (November 30, 1966 to February 13, 1973); GPI: GB2904 CAM/3/178.

24. Extract from *The Star* of Dominica (September 16, 1967) Correspondence between members of the Caribbean Artists Movement, and with associated bodies or individuals (November 30, 1966 to February 13, 1973); GPI: GB2904 CAM/3/189.

25. From Chalmer St. Hill to Edward Brathwaite (November 17, 1967) Correspondence between members of the Caribbean Artists Movement, and with associated bodies or individuals (November 30, 1966 to February 13, 1973); GPI: GB2904 CAM/3/286.

26. Letter from Locksley Comrie (Discussion Officer, Union of West Indian Students, Great Britain and Ireland) to Edward Brathwaite (July 1968) Correspondence between members of the Caribbean Artists Movement, and with associated bodies or individuals (November 30, 1966 to February 13, 1973); GPI: GB2904 CAM/3/442.

27. Ibid.

28. From Oliver Clarke to Edward Brathwaite (August 14, 1968) Correspondence between members of the Caribbean Artists Movement, and with associated bodies or individuals (November 30, 1966 to February 13, 1973); GPI: GB2904 CAM/3/442.

29. Brathwaite, "The Caribbean Artists Movement," 59.
30. Ibid., 5.
31. From Edward Brathwaite to the editor of the *Daily Telegraph* (September 1967) Correspondence between members of the Caribbean Artists Movement, and with associated bodies or individuals (November 30, 1966 to February 13, 1973); GPI: GB2904 CAM/3/213.
32. Ibid.
33. From Francis Pike (Faber and Faber Limited) to Edward Brathwaite (September 21, 1967); GPI: GB2904 CAM/3/199.
34. From Edward Brathwaite to Anne Walmsley (October 6, 1967); GPI: GB2904 CAM/3/228.
35. Letter from Don Wilson to Edward Brathwaite (September–October 1967); GPI: GB2904 CAM/3/251.
36. Stuart Hall, "West Indians in Britain," "First day of Conference: talks and discussions," Caribbean Artists Movement (August 31, 1968), 3; GPI: GB2904 CAM4/2/2.
37. Ibid.
38. Ibid., 4.
39. Ibid., 11.
40. Ibid., 12.
41. Ibid., 20.
42. Ibid.
43. Edward Lucie-Smith, from "First day of Conference: talks and discussions," Caribbean Artists Movement (August 31, 1968), p. 21; GPI: GB2904.
44. Brathwaite, Ibid., 22.
45. La Rose, Ibid., 36–37.
46. Richard Small, Ibid., 40.
47. Ibid., 41.
48. Marina Maxwell, "Towards a Revolution in the Arts," CAM (Jamaica) *Newsletter*, March 1968, 1. GB2904 CAM1/13.
49. Ibid.
50. Ibid., 2.
51. Ibid.
52. Ibid.
53. Ibid.
54. Ibid.
55. Ibid., 3.
56. Ibid.
57. Ibid.
58. Ibid., 4.
59. Ibid.
60. Edward Baugh, *Caribbean Quarterly* 13, no. 4 quoted in Ibid. 4.
61. Ibid.
62. Ibid., 4.
63. Ibid.

64. Ibid., 5.
65. Ibid., 6.
66. Ibid., 7.
67. Ibid.
68. Harry Goulbourne, Interview with Jessica and Eric Huntley, Tape No. 5. LMA4462/C/01/04.
69. Ibid. See Campbell, *Rasta and Resistance*.
70. Marley and the Wailers certainly were important figures as they attained worldwide fame though whether most of their fans absorbed, considered, or understood the messages of Rastafari in their music is not conclusive.
71. Goulbourne, Interview with Eric and Jessica Huntley, Tape No. 7. LMA4462/C/01/04.
72. Monique Bedasse, *Jah Kingdom* is an excellent study of repatriation, racial politics, and "trodding diaspora(s)" for West Indians, Americans, Britons, and Africans in the era of postcolonialism.
73. *Black Dimension*, Official Newspaper of the Black Eagles, 1968. Institute of Race Relations Ref. Code: 01/04/04/01/04/01/03.
74. Ibid.
75. Rachman was notorious as one of the most prominent and domineering landlords in Notting Hill who simultaneously rented rooms to nonwhites and also constantly threatened his tenants with retribution for failure to pay.
76. Ibid.
77. Ibid.
78. Ibid.
79. Ibid.
80. Ibid.
81. Ibid.
82. "Whatever Happened to H. Rap Brown," *Black Dimension*.
83. Ibid.
84. Ibid.
85. Ibid.
86. *Black Dimension*.
87. Ibid.
88. Ibid.
89. Ibid.
90. Ibid.
91. *Black Dimension*.
92. Ibid.
93. Ibid.
94. Ibid.
95. "Provisional Programme for Seminar, 'The Realities of Black Power'" (August 16–18, 1968); GPI: GB2904 CAM2/25.
96. Ibid.
97. Ibid.
98. John Solomos, *Race and Racism in Britain*, 122.

99. *The Black House: A Self-Help Community Project in the Making*, published by the Racial Adjustment Action Society, London. BCA: Ansel Wong Papers (front cover).
100. Ibid., 2.
101. Michael Abdul Malik was the name Michael X took after his conversion to Islam.
102. "Excerpt from a TV Speech by Sister Elva." OAU, September 1969, Ansel Wong Papers.
103. *The Black House*, 41.
104. Ibid.
105. Ibid.
106. Ibid.
107. Ibid.
108. Ibid.
109. Ibid., 3.
110. Ibid.
111. Ibid., 5.
112. Ibid.
113. Ibid.
114. Ibid., 8.
115. Ibid.
116. Ibid., 13.
117. Ibid.
118. Ibid.
119. Ibid., 14.
120. Ibid., 18.
121. Ibid., 19–20.
122. "Planning for the Black Community," *Tribune*, June 13, 1969.
123. Ibid.
124. Ibid.
125. Ibid.
126. Obi Egbuna, *Destroy This Temple*, 10.
127. Ibid., 16.
128. Ibid., 17.
129. "Black power in Britain." A Special Statement, by Universal Coloured People's Association 1967 (British Library Shelfmark: YD.2009.a.3412), 6.
130. Ibid.
131. Ibid.
132. Ibid.
133. Ibid., 8.
134. Ibid., 9.
135. Ibid.
136. Ibid.
137. Ibid., 12.
138. Ibid., 10–11.

139. Ibid.
140. A special thanks is due here to Guy Ortolano who teaches a course at NYU entitled "Multinational Britain" that argues for the extremely long history of migration and awkward "nation" building in the British Isles over a millennium.
141. Ibid., 7.
142. Ibid.
143. "Girl's sentence changed," *Times* April 17, 1970, 5.
144. "19 held in clash with police," *Times* August 10, 1970, 1.
145. See W. Christopher Johnson, "'The Spirit of Bandung in 1970s Britain': The Black Liberation Front's Revolutionary Transnationalism," in *Black British History: New Perspectives*, ed. Hakim Adi (London: Zed Books, 2019).
146. Gordon K. Lewis, "Race Relations in Britain: A View from the Caribbean," *Race Today*, July 1969, 79. British Library Shelfmark: P.523/84.
147. Ibid.
148. Ibid.
149. Ibid.
150. Ibid.
151. Ibid.
152. Ibid.
153. Ibid.
154. Ibid.
155. Ibid.
156. Ibid.
157. Ibid., 80.
158. Ibid.
159. This seems to be in the tradition of early twentieth century Jamaican hagiography. See chapter two and the work on Harold Moody entitled *Negro Victory*.
160. *Man of Destiny* (On Norman Manley), published by the People's National Party, City Printery Ltd. 2 Torrington Road, Kingston, Jamaica 1954; 19. British Library Shelfmark: 10864. n. 8.
161. Gordon K. Lewis, "The Trinidad and Tobago General Election of 1961," *Caribbean Studies* 2, no. 2 (1962).
162. Gordon K. Lewis, "Race Relations in Britain: A View from the Caribbean," *Race Today*, July 1969, 80.
163. Ibid.
164. Ibid.
165. Ibid.
166. Ibid.
167. Ibid.
168. Locksley Comrie, "Purpose and Future of CAM," "Second Caribbean Artists Movement Conference" (Contemporary notes taken by Anne Walmsley) August 31 to September 2, 1968; GPI: GB2904 CAM4/2/11.
169. Ibid. Ghana-born Margaret Busby is incredibly important as Britain's youngest and first black woman book publisher. Allison and Busby launched in 1967 and published work by James, Buchi Emecheta, Rosa Guy, and Salkey among other

African and Caribbean writers. See Carole Boyce Davies, "Women and Literature in the African Diaspora," in *Encyclopedia of Diasporas: immigrant and Refugee Cultures Around the World*, eds. Melvin Ember and Ian Skoggard (New York: Springer, 2005).

170. Ibid.

171. Anne Walmsley, Contemporary Notes on "Purpose and Future of CAM" "Second Caribbean Artists Movement Conference"; GPI: GB2904 CAM4/2/11.

172. Ibid.

173. Anne Walmsley, Contemporary Notes on Ivan van Sertima, "The Void of History in the Caribbean," "Second Caribbean Artists Movement Conference"; GPI: GB2904 CAM4/2/11.

174. Ibid.

175. *The Ras Tafari Movement in Kingston, Jamaica*, by M. G. Smith, Roy Augier, Rex Nettleford. University College of the West Indies, Institute of Social and Economic Research, 1960, 11.

176. Ibid.

177. Ibid., 15.

178. Ibid.

179. Ibid., 16.

180. Ibid. The likely reference is: George Eaton Simpson, "Political Cultism in West Kingston," *Social and Economic Studies* 4, no. 2 (1955).

181. Ibid., 27.

182. Ibid.

183. Ibid.

184. See Bedasse, *Jah Kingdom*.

185. Horace Campbell, *Rasta and Resistance*, 186.

186. Quoted in *South London Press*, October 8, 1976. From Campbell, *Rasta and Resistance*.

187. Barrymore Anthony Bogues, "The *Abeng* newspaper and the radical politics of postcolonial blackness," in *Black Power in the Caribbean*, ed. Kate Quinn (Gainesville: University Press of Florida, 2015), 81.

188. "Why Abeng," *Abeng* 1, no. 1 (February 1, 1969), 1.

189. Ibid.

190. "People Still Remember the Abeng," *Abeng* 1, no. 1 (February 1, 1969), 3.

191. C. L. R. James, "Capital," *Abeng* 1, no. 2 (February 8, 1969), 2.

192. Omo Ogun, "African Battleline: Stolen Culture," *Abeng*, February 8, 1969, 4.

193. Ibid.

194. Ibid.

195. Ibid.

Conclusion
Beyond Britain: Black Liberation Dreams

Over more than three decades, West Indian thinkers in Britain and moving through imperial geographies configured a radical politics through the ingenious construction of racialized radical conceptual space *and* the development of material public spaces reflecting these radical politics.[1] The Black House, Florence Mills Social Club, the *West Indian Gazette*, CAM, *Abeng*, and *Black Dimension* all served as material representations of radical black politics in Britain and abroad. The radical politics of the late 1960s can be described as *black post-nationalism* because the aims and methods of figures of West Indian backgrounds eclipsed typical political mobilization and stretched far beyond the confines of the nation-state model.

As shown by Priyamvada Gopal, radicalization within British metropolitan discourse on anticolonialism was not a phenomenon only emergent from leftist British circles but was substantially influenced by patterns of radical anticolonialism devised by peoples from across empire. Gopal noted the 1945 Pan-African Congress in Manchester as a moment of historical significance because "the cast of characters it brought together . . . and . . . for apotheosizing the currents of black self-assertion and radical anticolonialism that had emerged so powerfully in the previous decade [1930s]."[2] Because black people in Britain contested the validity and practice of empire for decades, it is unsurprising that they remained important figures in resistance efforts through the postcolonial era.

In contrast to the legacies of assimilation and acceptance of earlier influential West Indians in London like Harold Moody and Edward Scobie, by the time of the passage of the 1971 Immigration Act, black power politics advocated for a revolutionary program of resistance reflecting a black postnationalist perspective. The Act severely restricted the migration of citizens from the Commonwealth of Nations and received support from the historical white dominions of Canada, Australia, and New Zealand.³ The Act superseded the Commonwealth Immigrants Act 1962–1968 and introduced the concept of *right of abode* which gave a person the unrestricted right to enter and live in the United Kingdom. This right was held by citizens born in the British islands, those born to or adopted by a CUKC born in the British islands, or others who met an incredibly restrictive set of guidelines, excluding West Indians.

By 1969, Gordon Lewis offered a critique of a number of West Indians who hoped to "make a career out of the English public service structure," following the example of "Lord [Learie] Constantine and Dr. David Pitt."⁴ Lewis argued that Enoch Powell was the "self-appointed archpriest of an unreformed House of Lords" and mused that "it would be interesting to read an imaginary conversation . . . between himself and Lord Constantine on the virtues of the second chamber as a vehicle of political locomotion."⁵ Lewis identified the absurdity of the House of Lords and the illusion of the righteousness of British political heritage. Both Constantine and the virulent racist Powell were in the House of Lords, an institution bound by English tradition—begging the question of how much progress had indeed been made. The institutions reformulated including people of color but otherwise remained essentially unchanged. Lewis noted the traditional lionization of British ideals and institutions, even indicting "Garvey [who] . . .in his London speech of 1928, could still repeat the ancient legend that Queen Victoria herself had freed the slaves in 1834" and a contemporaneous "West Indian high official . . . in London . . . [who] insist[ed] that the 'race problem' might be solved if only the Queen could be persuaded to appoint a black equerry to the Royal Household."⁶ Lewis recognized the allure of British cultural dominance and noted how earlier radicals like Garvey appealed to the sensibilities of British justice and fairness. However, Lewis regarded the perpetuation of these "hereditary" excuses for Anglo-supremacy as counter to the possibilities of the psychological and material struggles against the old colonial order. Borrowing from the figure of the black sycophant in the United States, Lewis argued, "In England as much as in the Caribbean . . . the metropolitan Uncle Sam generates, in response, the creole Uncle Tom."⁷ Lewis critiqued the notion of assimilation and the efforts of some West Indians to inculcate good feelings merely by reproducing the political institutions and values of the exploitative and hegemonic British state.

Lewis's emphasis on the transformative nature of migration for West Indians located the particular dynamism of the metropole, especially when compared to the home societies of the Caribbean. He argued that if the West Indies could be regarded as English they must be understood as reflective not of "modern England, nor . . . England of the Enlightenment, but by . . . mid-Victorian England of Thackeray and Dickens."⁸ Lewis explained that West

Indian society was marked by "mid-Victorian values of social snobbery, plutocratic wealth and mass cultural illiteracy [that] still live on in the post-independent societies."[9] Lewis continued arguments made by C. L. R. James in *Beyond a Boundary* that recognized the particular influence of Victorian era cultural residues that resonated in the West Indies into the twentieth century. Lewis furthered this contention by suggesting, unlike James who was writing about the colonial period, that even after Federation and later island-based independence and sovereignty, West Indian societies were still dominated by the values of social condescension and discord, plutocracy and minority wealth accumulation, and mass cultural illiteracy. Most citizens were tuned out of the dominant cultural milieu despite being foundational to these societies.

Through the jarring exclusion and alienation in the metropole, Lewis argued that West Indians nevertheless met "the English realities of 1969 with the outmoded values of 1869."[10] West Indians produced a voluminous literature of disillusionment in response to the cold British reception and the dissolution of the "image of a liberal England."[11] Considering West Indian attitudes outdated, Lewis admonished the "Victorian background [that] equips him to understand the new, virulent forms of English social snobbishness . . . the English disqualify [their enemies] . . . and what the black immigrant meets is a series of English disqualification exercises, implemented with all the massive ingenuity of English hypocrisy."[12] Lewis contended that West Indians were doubly unprepared for British society because they were conditioned to romanticize it and were also repressed by the social exclusion that bludgeoned them on a systematic and quotidian basis.

By distinguishing the interior culture of Caribbean societies from the colonial and metropolitan realities of public Caribbean life as well as conditions in London, Lewis suggested the essential role the West Indian background played in informing the sensibilities of migrants and in turn influencing what this work has referred to as black post-nationalism.

BLACK POST-NATIONALISM AND PUBLIC SPACE

Resistance to the racial status quo in Britain derived from ingenious reconceptualization and reformations of black activists and thinkers who moved away from their assumed status as loyal colonial subjects and later citizens toward more revolutionary transgressive patterns of identification and mobilization. Whereas cultural nationalists in the United States, the independent Caribbean, and postcolonial Africa were sometimes complicit in their acquiescence to the strict confines of nation-state models, white supremacy functioned as the connective tissue between the colonial and postindependence eras in many Global South societies. Willing to accede control and sovereignty over the futures of their nation-states to the parameters of global capital and the retention of financial, economic, and political ties to former colonial masters, some postcolonial leadership was guilty of reformulating typical modes and institutions of exploitation after independence. Because of postcolonial states' tethered relationships to Europe and the United States, West Indians and Africans who resisted, challenged, and reconceptualized the potential of the nation-state phenomenon have been the topic of this study. Their specifically racialized black post-nationalism emerged from a refashioned and altogether revolutionary conception of political and spiritual freedom informed by Caribbean and African backgrounds and exploding in the crucible of British empire. This work suggests that cultural nationalists were shortsighted in attempts to better themselves by yielding to paradigms that structurally disempowered their racial group while benefitting them individually. This is contrasted to the black power post-nationalist vanguard that was willing to forgo "national belonging" for freedom.

Blackening Britain has focused on Afro-Caribbean thought and the emergence of political blackness that included other racialized subjects who were not phenotypically black. The thought and philosophical genealogy of these Afro-Caribbean writers, authors, thinkers reflected concern with historical and contemporaneous notions of blackness and Africa. The Black Liberation Front founded in 1971 including Zainab Abbas, Tony Soares, and Ansel Wong among others, figures in later developments around a coalescing black power movement in Britain. After 1971, their organ *Grassroots* publicized a dynamic unbound notion of blackness and the potentialities of activism. Trinidad-born Wong led WISC in the early 1970s where his notions of blackness were drawn from the Caribbean background and the mentorship of Brathwaite, La Rose, and Salkey. From 1974 to 1976, Wong, son of a Chinese-Trinidadian father and African, Carib, and Spanish mother, was the founding Education Coordinator of the Ahfiwe School, the first black supplementary school that was funded by the Inner London Education Authority.

Particular to the radical activities of West Indian thinkers was a unique perspective on the possibilities of organizing outside of the nation-state. Rebel theorists and activist-intellectuals and their artistic interlocutors forwarded racial identification at the expense of the nation-state model. Finding inspiration and potentiality in the *notion* of political blackness empowered Jones, Brathwaite, Jones-LeCointe, Salkey, James, Michael X and others to collaborate and devise strategies of resistance in Britain and the Caribbean that was unbound and unaccountable to nation-state political infrastructures. The conceptual space of black resistance—articulated through organs such as the *West Indian Gazette* or *Black Dimension*—reflected the carving out of public discursive space operating beyond the realm of nation-state discourse.

By primarily addressing concerns of black political solvency and liberation, these periodicals rejected conventional debates around politics, belonging, and race. Instead, they echoed a changing dynamic across the Global South, with Afro-Caribbean revolutionary thinkers at the forefront. These developments took place in Britain but did not belong to Britain. These periodicals, penned by non-belongers instead blackened British society.

Rather than mobilizing political campaigns in order to acclimate to and persevere within British society, by the 1970s, radical black thinkers instead envisioned and created innovative epistemologies of black achievement, resistance, and futures. Through owning, occupying, and maintaining control over public spaces in London, Caribbean radicals articulated domain over public discourses regarding race, citizenship, and identity in Britain and abroad. This articulation radicalized earlier visions of integration that had dominated the learned Afro-descended classes and their activism before World War II. Collaborations between intellectuals and artists, engaged outside of the restrictive confines of singular practices or disciplines, offered a novel and imaginative politics forged in multiple sites—Britain, the Caribbean, and Africa—that ultimately upset the conventional nation-state project in favor of post-national revolutionary epistemologies.

NOTES

1. It is also worthwhile to consider the Anti-University of London at 49 Rivington St operated in 1968. Egbuna, James, and Hall utilized the space as a critical center of a radical countercultural network that included feminist psychoanalyst Julie Mitchell, Carmichael, and others.
2. Gopal, *Insurgent Empire, Anticolonial Resistance and British Dissent* (London; New York: Verso, 2029) 389.
3. Immigration Act, 1971 c. 77.
4. Gordon K. Lewis, "Race Relations in Britain: A View from the Caribbean," *Race Today*, July 1969, 79.
5. Ibid.
6. Ibid.
7. Ibid.
8. Ibid.
9. Ibid.
10. Ibid., 80.
11. Ibid.
12. Ibid.

Coda [Crisis]: *Windrush* at 70
The Hostile Environment

During the seventieth anniversary of the arrival of the *Windrush* in 2018, Britain was embroiled in contestations over citizenship, national belonging, and the racialization of contemporary society. Rather than celebrating the contributions and influence of Caribbean, African, and Asian communities in Britain, the Home Office had initiated a program of denaturalization of these populations. Beginning in 2010, when Home Secretary Theresa May introduced methods to make Britain "hostile to immigrants," the Home Office destroyed or discarded innumerous entry cards and travel documents of *Windrush*-era migrants. The lack of official documentation was coupled with the Home Office's mandate that businesses, leasing agents, unions, and the National Health Service require extensive documentation for residents in Britain in order to access social services. British citizens have died because of the lack of recourse to the healthcare services in Britain or after their deportation to nations from which they never held citizenship.

In 2013, May engineered a program codenamed "Operation Vaken" which dispersed advertising vans with slogans recommending undocumented immigrants "go home or face arrest" in areas with significant immigrant populations. These "Go Home" vans toured six London boroughs for an entire month—July 22 until August 22.[1] A government evaluation claimed sixty voluntary departures directly resulted from Operation Vaken.[2] Through blatant intimidation, the Home Office succeeded in establishing and perpetuating hostilities toward people of color in Britain.

Jamaican-born Hubert Howard legally landed in London at the age of three in 1960 and had not left Britain since his arrival. In 2005, his employer, the Peabody Housing Association, requested Howard prove his right to remain in the United Kingdom. After attempting to acquire a passport in 2006 to visit his ailing mother in Jamaica, the Home Office informed Howard that they held no record of him and cautioned that if he left Britain he might not be able to return. Howard did not visit Jamaica before his mother's death. He applied again for a passport and in 2012 was made redundant by Peabody because he could not prove to them his legal stay. Indebted after losing his job, Howard was diagnosed with leukemia. His daughter Maresha lamented that Howard "was a fighter, but the way he was living caused his illness." Her father had been preoccupied by naturalization complications and neglected his health in pursuit of verifying his citizenship. He spent the majority of his final two months pursuing British citizenship which was granted at the end of October, only three weeks prior to his death. The hostile environment orchestrated by the Home Office's predatory tactics contributed to the unlawful disenfranchisement and ultimately death of a number of British citizens.[3]

RACIAL PATHOLOGIES OF CRIME AND DISORDER

Through the 1980s, British police units harassed and intimidated young people of color under premises that they were exhibiting suspicious behaviors. The *sus* laws that targeted black power activists since the 1960s were useful for police to excuse and legitimate their surveillance of nonwhite youths. Despite the decades since the arrival of the *Windrush*, some white Britons continued to harbor anti-black and anti-immigrant sentiments even in areas of diverse demographics across Britain. A disproportionate number of black families lived in poverty in London and were criminalized as a result of having little resources and poor access to legal recourse. The presence of black people in some areas instigated a racist backlash from their white neighbors and other interlocutors. Southeast London, for instance, was home to a substantial Afro-Caribbean community but also an area in which far-right groups including the National Front had been active. In January 1981, a fire erupted during a house party in New Cross, southeast London, and thirteen black youths died. Believing the fire to have been a racially-motivated arson, in the aftermath Darcus Howe organized a mass protest against the Metropolitan Police response. On March 2, 1981, Howe led the "Black People's Day of Action" march for seventeen miles from Deptford to Hyde Park. Between 5,000 to 25,000 participants have been estimated to have marched together passing Fleet Street and the Houses of Parliament.

In April 1981, the Metropolitan Police began a program called *Operation Swamp 81*. The project increased the presence of plainclothes officers and uniformed patrols throughout south London. Within five days, 943 people were stopped and searched and 82 people were arrested through this evocation of the "sus law." Later in 1981, between April 10 and 12, the Brixton Uprising erupted between members of the local Afro-Caribbean community and the Metropolitan Police. Leslie George Scarman, Lord Scarman, was commissioned by Home Secretary William Whitelaw to complete an inquiry into the riots on April 14, two days after the disorder subsided. The Scarman Report was completed and released on November 25, 1981. Among black people in Brixton, Scarman found "a widespread and dangerous lack of public confidence in the existing system" because "people do not trust the police to investigate the police."[4] Scarman argued that "complex political, social and economic factors [created a] disposition towards violent protest."[5] Through racially pathologizing serious societal ills, Scarman noted the propensity for nonwhites to mistrust police but also concomitantly charged them with inciting violence. In the official reckoning with overeager policing, Scarman found black and brown citizens justifiably skeptical of police while *also* being driven to disorder, violence, and destruction.

ENGLAND AND THE WORLD

In July 2019, England hosted and won its maiden Cricket World Cup, featuring Pakistani, West Indian, Indian, Irish, and South African-born and descended players in crucial roles in the team. Theresa May was filmed dancing a jig desperately devoid of the flavor, rhythm, and melody of the former colonies which had been so instrumental in bringing the cup "back home." Decades of intolerance and British national discourse targeted and criminalized nonwhites, characterizing them as unwelcome foreigners, charging them with living "on the dole," and taking advantage of social services reserved for citizens, forcing the post-*Windrush* generations to withstand threats to their presence in Britain from conservative and reactionary political discourses. West Indian cricketers—Barbados-born Jofra Archer for instance—who had a choice to play for the West Indies via his Barbadian-birth or England through a residency requirement, reflect the transformative power of black post-national identification. His choice represented his ability to elect his professional destiny—his place of birth and racial classification notwithstanding. The postcolonial realities in Caribbean nation-states as well as in the former imperial metropole continue to have ramifications for racialized subjects and citizens on each side of the Atlantic.

CLADDING IN KENSINGTON

Windrush anniversary recognition and celebrations were preceded by the horror of the Grenfell Tower disaster in 2017. On June 14, a fire erupted in the 24-story block of flats in North Kensington just prior to 1:00 a.m. and killed

72 people. Grenfell was a part of the Lancaster West Estate, a council housing complex completed in 1974. Like many tower blocks across Britain, Grenfell implemented a "stay put" policy in the case of a fire. The building's thick walls and fire doors were thought sufficiently dense to contain a fire long enough for fire services to arrive. British regulations only required a single central staircase, severely limiting the emergency exit protocol for residents. The exterior cladding of Grenfell was combustible but significantly cheaper than noncombustible alternatives. Specifically, the tower was clad in panels composed of an aluminum composite over a polyethylene (plastic) core which melted, enflamed, and sent flames and rivulets down the building's sides. Emergency and infrastructural oversight would prove disastrous when a freezer-refrigerator unit caught fire and flames spread throughout the building. Grenfell did not have sprinklers, fire alarms, or fire escapes. Apartment doors were not self-closing, in violation of residential codes.

The victims of the Grenfell fire were overwhelmingly persons of color. Of the seventy-two deaths, seven were white Britons. More than half of the adult victims arrived in Britain after 1990. Residents settled from a total of nineteen nations including Afghanistan, Sudan, Dominica, Egypt, Lebanon, and Eritrea. An almost 900-page report was released more than two years after the fire, in October 2019. The public inquiry's first phase focused on the flammable materials in the building's exterior and criticized the response of the London Fire Brigade. While the inquiry's leader, retired appellate court judge Martin Moore-Bick, emphasized a lackluster response by emergency personnel, the building itself abounded with hazards. Grenfell's cladding materials are banned for use in high-rises in a number of countries including the United States. A separate, independent report was completed six months after the fire and found Britain's building safety rules relatively lax when compared with other rich nations. Judith Hackitt, a chemical engineer who previously worked as a health and safety regulator, compiled the study that called for a better accreditation system for those working in construction or inspection of high-rise buildings, closer communication with fire services, more frequent risk assessments, and for penalties for fire safety violations severe enough to discourage the savings from cutting corners.[6] Rather than addressing the issues that contributed to the Grenfell fire, the government instead placed blame on responders to mitigate the role their inaction and inadequate safety standards played in even allowing the tower to be occupied. The lack of attention to construction and maintenance at Grenfell was regarded by working class and nonwhite Londoners and residents across Britain as a purposeful neglect. Vulnerable communities seemed to be discarded and the specifically lenient guidelines and protocols allowed for the tragedy to happen. In the second decade of the twenty-first century, racialization in Britain remained a matter of life and death—the life of the British nation coincided with the death of the African other—who may have been British.

NOTES

1. The vans traveled through Barking and Dagenham, Barnet, Brent, Ealing, Hounslow, and Redbridge.
2. U.K. Home Office, "Operation Vaken: Evaluation Report," October 31, 2013.
3. Amelia Gentleman, "Windrush Victim Dies without Compensation or Apology," *The Guardian,* November 12, 2019.
4. D. G. T. Williams, "The Brixton Disorders," *The Cambridge Law Journal* 41, no. 1 (April 1982), 3.
5. "The Scarman Report: The Brixton Disorders 10–12 April 1981: Report of an Inquiry" (Harmondsworth: Penguin, 1982).
6. David D. Kilpatrick, "Grenfell Fire Inquiry Finds U.K. Construction Rules Dangerously Lax," *New York Times,* December 18, 2017, Section A, p.11.

Select Bibliography

ARCHIVES AND LIBRARIES

United Kingdom
Black Cultural Archives, London
British Library
George Padmore Institute Archive
Institute of Race Relations
London Metropolitan Archives
National Archives, Kew
New York
Schomburg Center for Research in Black Culture
Port of Spain, Trinidad
Alma Jordan Library, University of the West Indies

PERIODICALS

Black Voice
The Guardian
Manchester Guardian
Black Dimension
Caribbean Times
Daily Worker
Daily Mail
Flamingo
Link
Grass Roots
Port-of-Spain Gazette

Times of London
Caribbean Artists Movement Newsletter
West Indian Gazette and Afro-Asian News
West Indian Students' Union Newsletter

PUBLISHED PRIMARY SOURCES

Banton, Michael. "The Economic and Social Position of Negro Immigrants in Britain." *Sociological Review*, New Series I (1952): 2.
———. *The Coloured Quarter: Negro Immigrants in a British City*. London: Jonathan Cape, 1955.
———. *White and Coloured*. London: Jonathan Cape, 1959.
———. "Social Distance: A New Appreciation." *Sociological Review*, New Series 8 (1960): 2.
Drake, St. Clair. "Value System, Social Structure and Race Relations in the British Isles." PhD Diss., University of Chicago, 1954.
Glass, Ruth. *London's Newcomers: The West Indian Migrants*. Cambridge: Harvard University Press, 1961.
Hill, Clifford S. *West Indian Migrants and the London Churches*. London; New York: Oxford University Press, 1963.
Hinds, Donald. *Journey to an Illusion: The West Indian in Britain*. London: Heinemann, 1966.
Holton, James. "The Status of the Colored in Britain." *Phylon (1960)*, Vol. 22, No. 1 (1st Qtr., 1961): 31–40.
Jacobson, Dan. "After Notting Hill." *Encounter*, December 1958.
Jephcott, Pearl. *A Trouble Area: Notes on Notting Hill*. London: Faber and Faber, 1964.
Lamming, George. *The Emigrants*. London: Michael Joseph, 1954.
Little, Kenneth. "The Position of Colored People in Britain." *Phylon (1940–1956)*, Vol. 15, No. 1 (1st Qtr., 1954): 58–64.
MacInnes, Colin. *City of Spades*. New York: Macmillan, 1958.
Malcolm, Jean. "Nightfall at Notting Hill: A Study in Black and White." *The Phylon Quarterly*, Vol. 19, No. 4 (4th Qtr., 1958): 364–366.
Morrisson, Majbritt. *Jungle West 11*. London: Tandem Books, 1964.
Patterson, Sheila. *Dark Strangers: A Sociological Study of the Absorption of a Recent West Indian Migrant Group in Brixton, South London*. Bloomington: Indiana University Press, 1964.
Peach, Ceri. *West Indian Migration to Britain: A Social Geography*. New York: Oxford University Press, 1968.
Richmond, Anthony H. *The Colour Problem: A Study of Racial Relations*. Harmondsworth, Middlesex: Penguin Books, 1955.
Rodney, Walter. *The Groundings with My Brothers*. London: Bogle-L'Ouverture Publications, 1969.
Salkey, Andrew. *Caribbean Essays: An Anthology*. London: Evans, 1973.

Selvon, Samuel. *The Lonely Londoners.* London: Allan Wingate, 1956.
Wickenden, James. *Colour in Britain.* London: Oxford University Press, 1958.
Williams, Eric Eustace. *Inward Hunger: The Education of a Prime Minister.* Chicago: University of Chicago Press, 1971.

Secondary Scholarship

Adi, Hakim, editor. *Black British History: New Perspectives.* London: Zed Books, 2019.
Ahmed, Sara. *Uprootings/Regroundings: Questions of Home and Migration.* Oxford; New York: Berg, 2003.
Anderson, Benedict. *Imagined Communities: Reflections on the Origins and Spread of Nationalism.* London: Verso Press, 1983.
Baker, Houston A., Manthia Diawara, and Ruth H. Lindeborg. *Black British Cultural Studies: A Reader.* Chicago; London: University of Chicago Press, 1996.
Baucom, Ian. *Out of Place: Englishness, Empire, and the Locations of Identity.* Princeton, NJ: Princeton University Press, 1999.
Beckford, George. *Persistent Poverty: Underdevelopment in Plantation Economies of the Third World.* New York: University of the West Indies Press, 2000.
Bedasse, Monique A. *Jah Kingdom: Rastafarians, Tanzania, and Pan-Africanism in the Age of Decolonization.* Chapel Hill: University of North Carolina Press, 2017.
Bell, Wendell, and Ivar Oxaal. *Decisions of Nationhood: Political and Social Development in the British Caribbean.* Denver, CO: University of Denver, 1964.
Benedict, Ruth. *Race and Racism.* London: George Routledge, 1943.
Bhabha, Homi. *The Location of Culture.* London: Routledge, 1994.
Bolland, O. Nigel. *Struggles for Freedom: Essays on Slavery, Colonialism, and Culture in the Caribbean and Central America.* Kingston: Ian Randle, 1997.
———. *The Birth of Caribbean Civilisation: A Century of Ideas About Culture and Identity, Nation and Society.* Kingston: Ian Randle, 2004.
Brah, Avtar. *Cartographies of Diaspora: Contesting Identities.* New York: Routledge, 1996.
Brathwaite, Edward. *The Development of Creole Society in Jamaica 1770–1820.* Oxford: Clarendon Press, 1971.
Brereton, Bridget. *Race Relations in Colonial Trinidad: 1870–1900.* Cambridge: Cambridge University Press, 1979.
Brock, Colin. *The Caribbean in Europe: Aspects of the West Indian Experience in Britain, France, and the Netherlands.* London: F. Cass, 1986.
Brown, Jacqueline Nassy. *Dropping Anchor, Setting Sail: Geographies of Race in Black Liverpool.* Princeton, NJ: Princeton University Press, 2005.
Byron, Margaret. *Post-War Caribbean Migration to Britain: The Unfinished Cycle.* Aldershot, England: Avebury, 1994.
Campt, Tina. "The Crowded Space of Diaspora: Intercultural Address and the Tensions of Diasporic Relation," *Radical History Review*, Vol. 83 (2002): 94–111.

———. *Other Germans: Black Germans and the Politics of Race, Gender, and Memory in the Third Reich*. Ann Arbor: University of Michigan, 2004.

Carby, Hazel. *Cultures in Babylon: Black Britain and African America*. New York: Verso, 1999.

Carter, Trevor, and Jean Coussins. *Shattering Illusions: West Indians in British Politics*. London: Lawrence & Wishart, 1986.

Chamberlain, Mary, editor. *Caribbean Migration: Globalized Identities*. London: Routledge, 1998.

Chatterjee, Partha. *The Nation and Its Fragments: Colonial and Postcolonial Histories*. Princeton: Princeton University Press, 1993.

Clifford, James. "Diasporas." *Cultural Anthropology*, Vol. 9, No. 3 (Aug., 1994): 302–338.

———. *Routes: Travel and Translation in the Late Twentieth Century*. Cambridge, MA: Harvard University Press, 1997.

Collins, Marcus. "Pride and Prejudice: West Indian Men in Mid-Twentieth-Century Britain." *Journal of British Studies*, Vol. 40, No. 3 (Jul., 2001): 391–418.

Comaroff, Jean, and John Comaroff. *Of Revelation and Revolution: Christianity, Colonialism, and Consciousness in South Africa*, Vol. 1. Chicago: University of Chicago Press, 1991.

Crichlow, Michaeline, and Patricia Northover. *Globalization and the Post-Creole Imagination*. Durham, NC: Duke University Press, 2009.

Cronin, James E. *The Politics of State Expansion: War, State, and Society in Twentieth-Century Britain*. London: Routledge, 1991

Darwin, John. *Britain and Decolonization: The Retreat from Empire in the Postwar World*. New York: St. Martin's Press, 1988.

Davies, Carolyn Boyce. *Left of Karl Marx: The Political Life of Black Communist Claudia Jones*. Durham, NC: Duke University Press, 2007.

Deakin, Nicholas, E. J. B. Rose, Julia McNeal, and Brian Cohen. *Colour, Citizenship, and British Society*. London: Panther Books, 1970.

Dean, D. W. "Conservative Governments and the Restriction of Commonwealth Immigration in the 1950s: The Problems of Constraint." *The Historical Journal*, Vol. 35, No. 1 (Mar., 1992): 171–194.

Drake, St. Clair. *Black Folk Here and There: An Essay in History and Anthropology*. Los Angeles: Center for Afro-American Studies, University of California, 1987.

Dworkin, Dennis. *Cultural Marxism in Postwar Britain: History, the New Left, and the Origins of Cultural Studies*. Durham, NC: Duke University Press, 1997.

Edwards, Brent Hayes. "Uses of Diaspora." *Social Text*, Vol. 19, No. 1 (Spring, 2001): 45–73.

———. *The Practice of Diaspora: Literature, Translation, and the Rise of Black Internationalism*. Cambridge, MA: Harvard University Press, 2003.

Etoke, Nathalie; trans. Bill Hamlett. *Melancholia Africana: The Indispensable Overcoming of the Black Condition*. London: Rowman & Littlefield, 2019.

Farred, Grant. "You Can Go Home Again, You Just Can't Stay: Stuart Hall and the Caribbean Diaspora." *Research in African Literatures*, Vol. 27, No. 4 (Winter, 1996): 28–48.

Foner, Nancy. "Male and Female: Jamaican Migrants in London." *Anthropological Quarterly*, Vol. 49, No. 1 (1976): 28–35.

———. *Jamaica Farewell: Jamaican Migrants in London*. Berkeley: University of California Press, 1978.

Foot, Paul. *Immigration and Race in British Politics*. Harmondsworth: Penguin, 1965.

Fryer, Peter. *Staying Power: The History of Black People in Britain*. London: Pluto Press, 1984.

———. *The Politics of Windrush*. London: Index Books, 1999.

Giddens, Anthony. *Modernity and Self-Identity: Self and Society in the Late Modern Age*. Cambridge: Polity Press, 1991.

Gilroy, Paul. "It Ain't Where You're From, It's Where You're At: The Dialectics of Diaspora Identification." *Third Text*, Vol. 13 (Winter, 1991a): 3–16.

———. *There Ain't No Black in the Union Jack: The Cultural Politics of Race and Nation*. Chicago: University of Chicago Press, 1991b.

———. *The Black Atlantic: Modernity and Double-Consciousness*. New York: Harvard University Press, 1993.

Gmelch, George. *Double Passage: The Lives of Caribbean Migrants Abroad and Back Home*. Ann Arbor: University of Michigan Press, 1992.

Gomez, Michael. *Reversing Sail: A History of the African Diaspora*. Cambridge: Cambridge University Press, 2005.

Gordon, Lewis. *Fanon and the Crisis of European Man: An Essay on Philosophy and the Human Sciences*. New York: Routledge, 1995.

Goulbourne, Harry. *Caribbean Transnational Experience*. London: Pluto Press, 2002.

Gramsci, Antonio. *Selections from the Prison Notebooks*. Edited by Quintin Hoare and Geoffrey Nowell-Smith. New York: International Publishers, 1971.

Guild, Joshua Bruce. "You Can't Go Home Again: Migration, Citizenship, and Black Community in Postwar New York and London." PhD Diss., Yale University, 2007.

Gullace, Nicoletta F. *The Blood of Our Sons: Men, Women, and the Renegotiation of British Citizenship During the Great War*. London: Palgrave Macmillan, 2002.

Habermas, Jurgen. *Theory and Practice*. Boston: Beacon Press, 1973.

Hall, Kim. *Things of Darkness: Economies of Race and Gender in Early Modern England*. Ithaca: Cornell University Press, 1995.

Hall, Stuart. "Race, Articulation and Societies Structured in Dominance." In *Sociological Theories: Race and Colonialism*. Paris: UNESCO, 1980.

———. "Cultural Identity and Diaspora." In *Identity: Community, Culture, Difference*, edited by Jonathan Rutherford. London: Lawrence & Wishart, 1990.

———. "On Postmodernism and Articulation." In *Stuart Hall: Critical Dialogues in Cultural Studies*, edited by David Morley and Chen Kuan-Hsing. London; New York: Routledge, 1996.

Hampshire, James. *Citizenship and Belonging: Immigration and the Politics of Demographic Government in Postwar Britain*. New York: Palgrave, 2005.

Harney, Stefano. *Nationalism and Identity: Culture and Imagination in a Caribbean Diaspora*. Kingston: University of West Indies Press, 1996.

Harris, Clive, and Winston James. *Inside Babylon: The Caribbean Diaspora in Britain*. London; New York: Verso, 1993.

Hebdige, Dick. *Cut 'n' Mix: Culture, Identity, and Caribbean Music.* London; New York: Methuen, 1987.
Hernon, Ian. *Riot! Civil Insurrection from Peterloo to the Present Day.* London: Pluto Press, 2006.
Hewitt, Roger. *White Backlash and the Politics of Multiculturalism.* Cambridge; New York: Cambridge University Press, 2005.
Hine, Darlene Clark, Tricia Danielle Keaton, and Stephen Small. *Black Europe and the African Diaspora.* Chicago: University of Illinois Press, 2009.
Hiro, Dilip. *Black British, White British.* New York: Monthly Review Press, 1973.
James, C. L. R. *Beyond a Boundary.* Durham: Duke University Press, 1993.
Jennings, James, editor. *Race and Politics: New Challenges and Responses for Black Activism.* London: Verso, 1997.
Johnson, W. Christopher. "Guerilla Ganja Gun Girls: Policing Black Revolutionaries from Notting Hill to Laventille." *Gender & History,* Vol. 26, No. 3 (Nov., 2014): 661–687.
Katznelson, Ira. *Black Men, White Cities: Race, Politics, and Migration in the United States, 1900–30, and Britain, 1948–68.* Chicago: University of Chicago Press, 1976.
Knight, Franklin. *The Caribbean, the Genesis of a Fragmented Nationalism.* New York: Oxford University Press, 1978.
Knight, Franklin, and Colin Palmer. *The Modern Caribbean.* Chapel Hill: University of North Carolina Press, 1989.
Kushner, Tony. *We Europeans?: Mass Observations, 'Race' and British Identity in the Twentieth Century.* Aldershot, England: Ashgate, 2004.
Lamming, George. *The Pleasures of Exile.* Ann Arbor: University of Michigan Press, 1992.
Lawrence, Daniel. *Black Migrants, White Natives.* London: Cambridge University Press, 1974.
Lefebvre, Henri. *Critique of Everyday Life Vol. 2 Foundations for a Sociology of the Everyday.* New York: Verso, 1991.
Levine, Barry B. *The Caribbean Exodus.* New York: Praeger, 1987.
Mason, David. *Race and Ethnicity in Modern Britain.* New York: Oxford University Press, 2000.
Matera, Marc. *Black London: The Imperial Metropolis and Decolonization in the Twentieth Century.* Berkeley: University of California Press, 2015.
McKittrick, Meredith. *To Dwell Secure: Generation, Christianity, and Colonialism in Ovamboland.* Portsmouth, NH: Heinemann Press, 2002.
Miles, Robert, and Annie Phizacklea. *White Man's Country: Racism in British Politics.* London: Pluto Press, 1984.
Moore, Robert. *Racism and Black Resistance in Britain.* London: Pluto Press, 1975.
Mullard, Chris. *On Being Black in Britain.* Washington: Inscape Publishers, 1975.
Neptune, Harvey R. *Caliban and the Yankees: Trinidad and the United States Occupation.* Chapel Hill: University of North Carolina Press, 2007.
Nettleford, Rex. *Mirror Mirror: Identity, Race, and Protest in Jamaica.* New York: Morrow, 1972.

Northrup, David. *Africa's Discovery of Europe: 1450–1850*. New York; Oxford: Oxford University Press, 2002.
Oxaal, Ivar. *Black Intellectuals and the Dilemmas of Race and Class in Trinidad*. Cambridge, MA: Schenkman, 1982.
Padmore, George. *The Life and Struggles of Negro Toilers*. London: R.I.L.U. International Trade Union Committee of Negro Workers, 1931.
———. *Africa: Britain's Third Empire*. London: Dennis Dobson Ltd., 1949.
———. *Pan-Africanism or Communism*. New York: Doubleday & Company, 1971.
Palmer, Colin. *Eric Williams and the Making of the Modern Caribbean*. Chapel Hill: University of North Carolina Press, 2006.
Palmer, Ransford W. *In Search of a Better Life: Perspectives on Migration from the Caribbean*. New York: Praeger, 1990.
Paul, Kathleen. *Whitewashing Britain: Race and Citizenship in the Postwar Era*. Ithaca, NY: Cornell University Press, 1997.
Perry, Kennetta Hammond. *London Is the Place for Me: Black Britons, Citizenship, and the Politics of Race*. New York: Oxford University Press, 2015.
Phillips, Charlie, and Mike Phillips. *Notting Hill in the Sixties*. London: Lawrence & Wishart, 1991.
Phillips, Mike. *London Crossings: A Biography of Black Britain*. London: Burns & Oates, 2001.
Phillips, Mike, and Trevor Phillips. *Windrush: The Irresistible Rise of Multi-Racial Britain*. London: HarperCollins, 1999.
Pilkington, Edward. *Beyond the Mother Country: West Indians and the Notting Hill White Riots*. Boston: I. B. Tauris & Company Limited, 1990.
Post, Ken. *Arise Ye Starvelings: The Jamaican Labour Rebellion of 1938 and Its Aftermath*. The Hague: Martinus Nijhoff, 1978.
Procter, James. *Dwelling Places: Postwar Black British Writing*. Manchester: Manchester University Press, 2003.
Putnam, Lara. *Radical Moves: Caribbean Migrants and the Politics of Race in the Jazz Age*. Chapel Hill: University of North Carolina Press, 2013.
Reeves, Frank. *British Racial Discourse: A Study of British Political Discourse About Race and Race-Related Matters*. Cambridge; New York: Cambridge University Press, 1983.
Rex, John, and S. Tomlinson. *Colonial Immigrants in a British City: A Class Analysis*. London: Routledge & Kegan Paul, 1979.
Rich, Paul. *Race and Empire in British Politics*. Cambridge; New York: Cambridge University Press, 1986.
Richmond, Anthony H. *Colour Prejudice in Britain: A Study of West Indian Workers in Liverpool, 1941–1951*. Westport, CO: Negro Universities Press, 1971.
Robinson, Cedric J. *Black Marxism: The Making of the Black Radical Tradition*. London: Zed Press, 1983.
Rowe, Michael. *The Racialisation of Disorder in Twentieth Century Britain*. Aldershort: Brookfield, 1998.

Sandhu, Sukhdev. *London Calling: How Black and Asian Writers Imagined a City*. London: HarperCollins, 2003.

Schwarz, Bill. "'Claudia Jones and the *West Indian Gazette*': Reflections on the Emergence of Post-colonial Britain." *Twentieth Century British History*, Vol. 14, No. 3 (2003a): 264–285.

———. *West Indian Intellectuals in Britain*. Manchester: Manchester University Press, 2003b.

Scott, David. *Conscripts of Modernity: The Tragedy of Colonial Enlightenment*. Durham: Duke University Press, 2004.

Sherwood, Marika. *Claudia Jones: A Life in Exile*. London: Lawrence & Wishart, 1999.

Solomos, John. *Race and Racism in Britain*. New York: St. Martin's Press, 1993.

Tabili, Laura. *"We Ask for British Justice": Workers and Racial Difference in Late Imperial Britain*. Ithaca, NY: Cornell University Press, 1994.

Von Eschen, Penny M. *Race Against Empire: Black Americans and Anticolonialism, 1937–1957*. Ithaca: Cornell University Press, 1997.

Wallace, Elisabeth. *The British Caribbean from the Decline of Colonialism to the End of Federation*. Buffalo, NY: University of Toronto Press, 1977.

Walmsley, Anne. *The Caribbean Artists Movement, 1966–1972*. London: New Beacon Books, 1992.

Walvin, James. *Making the Black Atlantic: Britain and the African Diaspora*. London; New York: Cassell, 2000.

Wambu, Onyekachi, editor. *Hurricane Hits England: An Anthology of Writing About Black Britain*. New York: Continuum, 2000.

Waters, Chris. "Dark Strangers in Our Midst: Discourses of Race and Nation in Britain, 1947–1963." *Journal of British Studies*, Vol. 36 (Apr., 1997): 207–238.

Waters, Mary C. *Black Identities: West Indian Immigrant Dreams and American Realities*. New York: Russell Sage Foundation, 1999.

Waters, Rob. *Thinking Black: Britain, 1964–1985*. Berkeley: University of California Press, 2018.

Watkins-Owens, Irma. *Blood Relations: Caribbean Immigrants and the Harlem Community, 1900–1930*. Bloomington: Indiana University Press, 1996.

Western, John. *A Passage to England: Barbadian Londoners Speak of Home*. Minneapolis: University of Minnesota Press, 1992.

Whitfield, James. *Unhappy Dialogue: The Metropolitan Police and Black Londoners in Post-War Britain*. Portland: Willan Publishing, 2004.

Wild, Rosalind. "Black Was the Colour of Our Fight': Black Power in Britain, 1955–1976." PhD Diss., University of Sheffield, 2008.

Williams, Eric Eustace. *The Negro in the Caribbean*. Manchester: Panaf Service, 1945.

Williams, Raymond. *The Sociology of Culture*. Chicago: University of Chicago Press, 1995.

Index

Abbas, Zainab, 212
Adams, Grantley, 7, 35–36, 81, 118, 134
Adams, Robert, 32
Adi, Hakim, xxix, 41nn13, 15, 42n24, 207n145, 223
Afghanistan, 218
African American history, xvii
African American(s), xvii, xxi, xxv, 22, 30, 40, 55, 73, 118, 137, 149, 154, 171–72, 181–82, 188, 190; exceptionalism of, xxi
Africans, xii, xx–xxi, xxv, xxxn36, 2–3, 17–18, 22, 24, 32, 35, 40–41, 58–60, 81, 85–87, 101, 125–26, 130–31, 139, 148, 153–54, 159, 170, 182, 185, 188, 200, 202, 205, 212; diasporic, ix, xviii, xix, xxi, xxv, xviii n15, xxixn22, xxxn28, 20–22, 24, 29–33, 35–36, 39–41, 94, 116, 149, 156, 171, 175, 182, 186, 200, 202; discrimination and repression against, xii, 148, 152–54, 159–60, 186; in the French army in WWI, 32; Indigenous, 22
Afro-Caribbeans, *passim*, but see especially, xii, 22, 29, 62, 80, 96, 102, 107, 111, 114, 116, 136, 181, 187, 201, 216; "blackening" Britain, 212; revolutionary thinkers, 213

Agents of Interracial Friendship Co-ordinating Council, 80–81, 83
Akinsanya, Gbola, 130, 163n72
Ali, Duse Mohamed, 24
Alma Jordan Library, University of the West Indies, 221
American Southern Christian Leadership Conference, 190
Anderson, Benedict, xxviin7, 223
Anderson, Tryphena, 51, 63n34
apartheid, 73, 103, 110, 137, 140, 145, 154, 165n123
Atkins, Virgil, 112n7
Australia, 138, 154, 165n123, 171, 173, 210
Azikiwe, Nnamdi, 76–77

Baker, Baron, 67, 69, 79, 88n8
Baker, Houston A., Manthia Diawara, and Ruth H. Lindeborg, xxxn26
Baldwin, James, 118
Banton, Michael, xxviiin14, xxviin18, 113, 121–22, 161nn27–29, 222
Barbados, xiii, xv, xxxviiin12, 35, 84–85, 116, 118, 120, 145; Public Library in, 172
Barbados Labour Party, 8, 118
Barbados Workers' Union, 35
Bassey, Hogan Kid, 112n7

229

Baucom, Ian, 12, 15n42, 223
Bearden, Romare, 118
Beckford, George, 200, 223
Bedasse, Monique A., 205n72, 208n184, 223
Beese, Barbara, 192–93
Bell, Wendell and Ivar Oxaal, 223
Benedict, Ruth, 223
Bhabha, Homi, xxixn23, 223
Birmingham University, 171, 173–74
Black Cultural Archives, ix, 43n45, 112n1, 113n44, 163nn72, 74, 79; 221
Black Dimension, 166n162, 180–82, 205nn73, 82, 86, 91, 209, 212, 221
Black Eagles, 146, 180–84, 190, 192, 196, 201, 205
Black Power, xii, xxvi, 88n26, 117, 146–49, 153–57, 166n169, 167n199, 172, 176–77, 179–92, 209, 212, 216–17
Black Voice, 155–56, 167n215, 221
Bogle, Paul, 51, 100, 102, 148
Bogle-L'Ouverture Publications, 102, 148, 166
Bogues, Barrymore A., 200, 208n187
Bolland, O. Nigel, xxviiin13, 14n21, 223
Brah, Avtar, xxixn23, 223
Brathwaite, Edward Kamau, 2–3, 13n2, 14n6, 48, 168–78, 184, 202–204, 212, 223
Brazil, xx, 137, 177
Brereton, Bridget, xxviin6, 13n2, 223
Briggs, Cyril, 30
British Caribbean Association, 83, 134–35, 151, 164–67
British Caribbean Welfare Service (BCWS), 47, 103, 105, 108–109, 114n54
British Communist Party, 29–30, 40–41, 95, 106, 139–40
British Conservative Party (Tory), 103
British Empire, *passim*, but see especially: xiii–xviii, xix–xxii, xxviiin11, xxx, 1–3, 5, 10, 12–13, 18, 22–23, 27–28, 31, 33–34, 46, 48, 54, 60–61, 82, 87, 105, 108, 110, 119, 125, 127, 137, 143–44, 175, 189, 195, 197, 209, 212–13; citizenship in, 37–41; declining of, 54, 110, 127, 158, 195; geographical spread of, 175; Policy Committee of the League of Empire Loyalists, 82
British Guiana Freedom Association, 114n47, 140
British Labour Party, 124, 140, 156
British Library, ix, 221
British Union of Fascists, 66, 74, 89n44, 99, 103, 108, 138
Brock, Colin, 223
Brockway, Fenner, 142
Brown, Christopher Leslie, 3, 14n7
Brown, H. Rap, 156, 181
Brown, J. Dillon, 162nn50, 54
Brown, Jacqueline Nassy, xxviiin19, 223
Brown, Joe, 112n7
Brown, Marvin, 188–89
Bullins, Ed, 184
Bustamante, Alexander, 6–8, 38, 44n80
Butler, R. A., 81
Butler, Uriah, 9
Byron, Margaret, 223

Cambridge University, 55, 129, 169, 173
Campbell, Horace, 166n161, 200, 205n69, 208n185
Campt, Tina, xxixn25, 223
Carby, Hazel, xxviiin19, 224
Caribbean Artists Movement (CAM), 149, 169–76, 178–79, 184, 190, 197–98, 201–205, 207–209
Caribbean Education and Community Workers Association, 114, 146, 200
Caribbean Labour Congress, 8, 35
Caribbean Philosophical Association, ix
Caribbean Times, 133, 221
Caribbean, The, *passim*, but see especially: xi–xxx, 1–18, 20–87,

93–80, 183–89, 195–98, 200–204, 207–29
Carmichael, Stokely (Kwame Ture), 116–17, 147–48, 176, 181–82, 190–91, 196, 213n1
Carter, John, 33–34
Carter, Trevor and Jean Coussins, 224
Catlett, Elizabeth, 118
Chamberlain, Mary, 224
Christian, Euton, 12, 15n40, 49
Cleaver, Eldridge, 116
Clifford, James, 224
Collins, Marcus, 224
Collymore, Frank, 172
Colour bar, 18–20, 50, 80, 104
Coloured People's Progressive Association, 80, 108
Comaroff, Jean and John Comaroff, xxiv, xxxn35, 224
Communist Party USA, 40
Communists, 29–31, 40–41, 43n44, 82, 95, 106, 110, 112n9, 137, 139–40
Compton, J. Egyptien, 93–94, 112n1
consciousness, xi–xxviii, xxx, 3, 8, 11–12, 21–23, 25–26, 29–33, 35, 40, 48–50, 58–61, 69, 72, 78–79, 95–98, 100, 102–103, 105, 126, 129, 131, 141, 149, 155, 173–76, 179, 183–85, 190; Black Power, 185, 190; class, xxii, 22, 24–27, 29, 31, 95, 126, 155, 174–75; collective, xv, 22; colonized, xxi–xxiii; cultural, xv, 173–74, 190; diasporic, xiii; double-, 61, 69, 129; imperial, 60; political, xvi, xxii; post-nationalist, xx; racial, xiv–xv, 6, 126; revolutionary, xii, 155; self, 58, 72, 79, 179, 185
Conservative Political Center in Birmingham, 157
Constantine, Learie, 34, 210
Crichlow, Frank, 69, 76, 89n55, 160, 192–93
Crichlow, Michaeline, and Patricia Northover, 224

cricket (the sport), 26–27, 34, 52, 96, 99, 118, 120, 136, 217
Cronin, James E., 224
Cuba, 26, 30, 145, 182
Cummins, Hugh, 84–85
Curling, Arthur, 5, 14n12

Daily Mail, 73, 88–90, 221
Daily Worker, 44n98, 164n115, 221
Darwin, John, 224
Darwinism (social), 125
Davies, Carole Boyce, 112n10, 208
Deakin, Nicholas, E. J. B. Rose, Julia McNeal, and Brian Cohen, 224
Dean, D. W., 224
Denniston, Oswald, 24–25, 42n26
Dessalines, Jean-Jacques, 26
Dominica, 36, 130, 172, 183, 203n24, 218
Donaldson, R., 37
Drake, St. Clair, 222, 224
DuBois, William Edward Burghardt, 21–22, 118
Duplan, E. J., 21
Dworkin, Dennis, xxixn23, 224

Edwards, Brent Hayes, 64n69, 224
Edwards, M. R., 132, 163n85
Edwards, Viv, 14n8
Egbuna, Obi, 189–90, 196, 206n126, 213n1
Egypt, 24, 218
employment, xi, xv, xviii, 4, 9, 11, 17, 21, 26, 35–37, 52, 57, 66, 80, 82, 85–86, 88n7, 93, 97–98, 103–104, 107, 109, 115, 123–24, 127, 134, 139, 142, 144, 156, 180, 187; colour bar in, 80; underemployment, 1, 123; unemployment, 36, 82, 103, 123, 159
epistemology, xxiv, xxvi; British-, 24, 27, 155; Caribbean-, 176–79; post-national-, 193, 197–98; revolutionary-, xvi, 183, 187–88
Eritrea, 218
Ethiopia, 21, 148, 179, 198–200

Ethiopian World Federation in Jamaica, 198–99
Etoke, Nathalie, xxi, xxxn29, 224
Ezzrecco, Frances, 69, 80

Family Welfare Association, 134, 164n96
Farred, Grant, 224
fascism, 23, 85, 154–56, 191–92, 197
Flamingo, 130–33, 163nn72–87, 164n93, 221
Foner, Nancy, xxixn22, 14n10
Foot, Paul, 225
France, 24, 26, 32, 69, 106, 196
Freedomways (journal), 118
Freitas, Michael de (Michael X; Michael Abdul Malik), 69–70, 76, 79–80, 88–89, 117, 180, 182, 185, 187–90
Fryer, Peter, 42n26, 225

Garvey, Amy Ashwood, 21, 80, 89n49
Garvey, Marcus, xiv, 14n21, 21, 24, 94, 147, 149, 170, 179, 194, 200–201, 210; relationship to Black power, 184
George Padmore Institute, ix, 202n4, 221
Giddens, Anthony, 225
Gilroy, Paul, xix, xxi, xxviii, xxixn15, xxixn23, xxxn26, 225; lacuna in *The Black Atlantic*, xxxn28
Glass, Ruth, xxviiin18, 222
Global South, xvi, 103, 147, 149, 155, 212–13
Gmelch, George, xxviiin13, xxix, 225
Gomes, Albert, 7
Gomez, Michael, 13n4, 225
Gopal, Priyamvada, xxv, xxxn38, 209, 213n2
Gordon, Garnet, 81, 108, 119, 133, 163nn88–91
Gordon, Lewis R., 203n17, 225
Goulbourne, Harry, 117, 205n68
Gramsci, Antonio, xxiii, xxxn32, 31, 43n47, 225

Grant, Ainsley, 74
Grass Roots, 212, 221
Grenada, xiii, 21, 32, 49, 141, 147, 165n136
Grenadians, 124, 131
Grenfell Tower, 217–19
Guardian, The, xxvi, 138, 142, 183, 221
Guiana (British), 14n21, 32–33, 47–48, 102–103, 111, 114n47, 115–21, 134, 137, 140, 144
Guianese, 34, 96, 116, 140, 171, 197, 202n2
Guild Press, 200
Guild, Joshua Bruce, xxixn19, 112n19, 225
Guinness, Walter, 10
Gullace, Nicolletta F., 225

Habermas, Jürgen, xxviin7, 225
Haiti, 21, 26, 28–29, 51, 128, 177
Haitian Revolution, xxiv, 26–29, 128
Hall, Kim, 15n41, 225
Hall, Stuart, xii, xix, xxviiin3, xxixn23, xxxn27, 48, 60–61, 63n13, 64nn72–76, 68–69, 140, 174–75, 204n36, 224, 225
Hampshire, James, 225
Harney, Stefano, 225
Harris, Clive and James, Winston, xxix, 225
Harris, Wilson, 170, 178
Harrison, I., 161n38
Harvard University, 55
Hebdige, Dick, 64n49, 89n43, 226
Hernon, Ian, 226
Hewitt, Roger, 226
Hill, Clifford S., 222
Hill, Ken, 22
Hill, Robert, 200
Hinds, Donald, 72, 89n35, 96–98, 112n14, 222
Hine, Darlene Clark, xxixn22, 226
Hiro, Dilip, 226
Holt, George, 87
Holt, Thomas, xxviin5, 2–3, 13n5

Holton, James, 222
Howard University, 23
Howard, Hubert, 215–16
Huntley, Eric and Jessica, 102–103, 111–17, 119, 139–42, 146, 148, 160nn1, 5, 165nn132–34, 137, 139–46, 166nn164–65, 179–80, 182, 205nn68, 71
Huntley, Eric, 113n32, 115–16, 137–41, 164n117, 165n120
Huntley, Jessica, 115–17, 140–41, 146–47, 166n166, 179

India, 119
Institute of Race Relations (IRR), 80, 122–23, 129, 139, 193, 221; *Race* periodical, 121, 193
Interracial Friendship Co-ordinating Council, 80–81, 83
Ireland, 119–20, 172, 203n26
Islam, 122, 183, 185, 206n101

Jackson, Esther Cooper, 118
Jackson, Sir Donald, 108
Jackson, V., 16n38
Jacob Lawrence, 118
Jacobson, Dan, 222
Jagan, Cheddi, 102–103, 113n32, 116, 119, 133, 137, 140
Jamaica Trades Union Council, 22
Jamaica, xi–xiii, xv, xxv–xxix, 1, 3–10, 12–18, 20–22, 24–25, 32–33, 36–39, 45–54, 62, 86, 94, 118, 129, 134, 140–43, 146, 148–49, 172; demonstrations in, 29; free elections in, 32–33; High Commissioner of, 136
Jamaican Labour Party, xiii, 8, 145
Jamaican workers, xv, 4, 9–10, 21, 37, 126
Jamaicans, xxv–xxvi, 1, 4, 13, 45, 47, 50, 61–62, 70, 77, 86, 95, 128, 131, 136, 141–46, 159; Association of, 95; diasporic mode of resistance, 199; marked as culturally inferior,

47; Maroon communication tool of, 201
James, C. L. R., xiv–xxv, 20, 26–31, 41n1, 42nn32–34, 42nn37–38, 42n43, 173–74, 201, 207n169, 208n191, 211–13, 226; critique of Britain as the world's leading democracy, 119; George Lamming's tribute to, 128
James, Horace, 173
James, Selma, 146
jazz, 55, 137, 177, 227
Jennings, James, 226
Jephcott, Pearl, 114n59, 222
Jim Crow, xxv, 90n65, 110–11
Johnson, De Graf, 21
Johnson, George Folunsho "Ginger," 185
Johnson, W. Christopher, 207n145, 226
Jones, Arthur Creech, 6, 7
Jones, Claudia, 80, 95, 97–99, 106, 110, 112n10, 114n61, 139, 142, 160n12, 165n129, 177, 192, 212, 224, 228; advocate of "people's art," 177; advocate of Bill to Outlaw Racial Discrimination, 142; black radical activism of, 118–19, 192; decried Commonwealth Immigrants Act, 139
Jones, Evan, 169–70
Jones, Louis, 169, 171
Jones-LeCointe, Althea, 116, 193, 212

Katznelson, Ira, 226
Kenya Land and Freedom Army, 40, 84, 137
Kenya, 23, 40–41, 84, 137, 140, 171
Kenyans, xviii, 41, 171
Kew National Archives, 221
King, Sam, 51, 63n29
Knight, Franklin, xxviiin14, 226
Ku Klux Klan, 73, 82, 85
Kushner, Tony, 226

La Rose, John, 140, 166, 169–70, 176, 184, 197, 212

Lambert, Laurie, 165n136
Lamming, George, 60, 127–29, 131–32, 162–63, 173–74, 178, 222, 226
Lawrence, Daniel, 226
League Against Imperialism, 18, 30
League of Coloured Peoples (L.C.P.), 18–19, 22, 32–36, 41, 43, 83
Lebanon, 218
Lefebvre, Henri, 226
Levine, Barry B., 226
Levy, Horace, 300
Lewis, Gordon K., 13n2, 193–97, 207nn146, 161–62, 210–11, 213n4
Liberia, 21, 29–30, 42n41
Link (magazine), 93–95, 112, 221
Little, Kenneth, 107, 162n38, 222
London Metropolitan Archives, 221
London Missionary Society, 18

MacInnes, Colin, 22
Madoo, Patricia, 58, 64n64
Makalani, Minkah, xiv, 42n42
Malcolm, Jean, 222
Manchester Guardian, 65, 88–90
Manley, Norman, 8, 10, 38, 47, 52, 62, 76–77, 89n51, 118, 140, 196, 207n160
Marvin Brown Affair, 188–89
Mason, David, 161n38, 226
Matera, Marc, xxxn37, 226
McCarran Act, 95, 112n9
McKay, Claude, xiv
McKittrick, Meredith, 226
Mexico, xxvi–xxvii, 177
Miles, Robert and Annie Phizacklea, 226
Ministry of Labour (UK), 97, 144
Moody, Harold A., 18–20, 32–35, 41–43, 202n2, 207n159, 209
Moore, Archie, 112n7
Moore, Robert, 226
Moore-Bick, Martin, 218
Morris, Olive, 192
Morrison, Herbert, 39–40
Morrisson, Majbritt, 222

Mosley, Oswald, 66, 73–75, 82, 89n44; Mosleyites, 145, 159
Mullard, Chris, 226
Munroe, Trevor, 141, 165n135
Musgrave-Wood, John, 38
Muslim(s), 190. *See also* Islam

NAACP (National Association for the Advancement of Colored People), 152
National Labour Party, 82
nationalism, xii–xviii, xx, 66, 155, 207, 209, 211, 212, 223–26; black-, 145, 181; post-, xii–xii, 169, 178, 199, 209; trans-, xx
NATO (North Atlantic Treaty Organization), 119
Neptune, Harvey R., xxviin6, 226
Neruda, Pablo, 118
Netherlands, The, 106
Nettleford, Rex, 198–99, 208n175, 226
Ngũgĩ wa Thiong'o (also known as James Ngugi), 170–71, 202
Nigeria, 23–24, 28, 33, 76–77, 86, 130–31, 149, 153, 173, 180, 185, 189, 192
Nigerians, 77, 130–31, 185, 189, 192
Northrup, David, 227
Nyerere, Julius, 118

Ortolano, Guy, 207n140
Ouseley, Herman, 72, 89n34
Ové, Horace, 185
Oxaal, Ivar, 223, 227
Oxford University, 23, 45, 53–58, 68, 129, 173–74, 196

Padmore, George, xxv, 20, 22–23, 29–32, 35, 41–43, 202, 221, 227
Palmer, Colin, xxviin5, 14n9, 15n34, 26, 227
Pan African Congresses, 20–41, 172, 209
Pan-Africanism, xix, xxv, 17–43, 60, 118, 172, 177, 209, 223, 227
Patterson, Floyd, 112

Patterson, Orlando, 13n2, 169–72, 222
Patterson, Sheila, 104, 123–24, 139, 162, 165n131, 169
Paul, Kathleen, xiv, xviii–xxix, 227
Peach, Ceri, xxviiin14, 222
People's Progressive Party (PPP), 102, 111, 115–19, 140
Perry, Kennetta Hammond, xiii–xiv, xxviin9, xxix, 89n45, 153, 165–66, 227
Phillips, Charlie and Mike, 227
Phillips, Mike and Trevor, lxxviii, 70
Phillips, Mike, xxixn24, 89nn33–4, 90n61, 227
Pike, Francis, 174, 204n33
Pilkington, Edward, xxixn22, 67, 88–89, 114n57, 227
Pixley, F. A., 8
Port-of-Spain Gazette, 221
Powell, Enoch, 156–59, 168, 181, 210
Prescod, Pearl, 80
Procter, James, 227
Puerto Rico, 26, 30, 177, 193, 195
Putnam, Lara, 14n11, 227

Rachman, Peter, 180, 185, 205n75
Racial Adjustment Action Society (RAAS), 185–90
racism, *passim*, but see especially: 20, 73–74, 154–56, 176, 182, 184, 186
radicalism, *passim*, but see especially: xii, xxv–xxvi, 210, 212; black-, 18, 117–18, 152, 156, 176, 183, 185, 193–94, 209; Caribbean-, xiv, 30, 106, 116, 128, 180
Rai, Balram Singh, 111
Ramchand, Kenneth, 56–58, 64, 171, 173, 203n16
Rastafari, Rastafarianism, xxvi, 120, 146, 148, 177, 179, 198–200, 202, 205n70; Universal Rastafari Improvement Association, 179
Red International of Labour Unions (R.I.L.U.), 31, 43n48
Reeves, Frank, 227

Reid, Vic, 178
Reid, Vince, 45, 49–50, 62n3, 63nn23–27, 75, 89n45, 94–95, 112n8
Rex, John and S. Tomlinson, 227
Richmond, Anthony H., 46, 62n8, 222, 227
riots, xxv, xxixn22, 9, 24, 65–80, 82–87, 93–96, 99–109, 122, 124–25, 128, 138, 144, 152, 159–60, 173, 184, 200, 217
Roberts, George, 32
Robeson, Paul, 40–41, 44n98, 100, 110, 114n61, 137, 164nn114–15
Robinson, Cedric J., 42n20, 227
Robinson, Prime Minister A. N. R., 48
Robinson, Sir Roland, 134
Robinson, Sugar Ray, 112n7
Rodney, Walter, 140–41, 145–49, 159, 166nn174, 177, 176, 198, 200, 222
Roper, Trevor, 138
Rowe, Michael, 227

Saint Kitts, 14n21, 169
Saint Lucia, 14n21, 128
Salkey, Andrew, 147, 169–71, 174, 183, 203n19, 207n169, 212, 222
samba, 137
Sandhu, Sukhdev, xxviiin16, 162n50, 228
Scarman, Leslie George, 217, 219
Schomburg Center for Research in Black Culture, 114, 221
Schwarz, Bill, 228
Scobie, Edward, 47, 130, 133, 164n93, 183, 209; in *Checkers*, 36–40, 44nn79, 85 and 88, 183
Scott, David, xxiv, xxxn34, 133, 228
Sealy, T. E., 22
Selassie, Emperor Haile/Tafari Mekonen, 148, 198–99
Selvon, Samuel, 60, 126, 223
Sheppard, Jill, 116, 160n4
Sherwood, Marika, 41n13, 112n20, 228
ska, 177

slave trade(s), xx, xxxn28, 1, 13n4, 27–28, 108, 137
slavery, xxi, xxvi, 4, 13n2, 17–18, 49, 97, 102, 132, 137, 175, 193, 201
Small, Richard, 141, 146, 147, 204n46
Solomos, John, xxix, 205n98, 228
South Africa, xiii, xvi–xiv, xvi, xxiv, xxix–xxx, 21, 23, 34, 50, 73, 103, 110–11, 137, 138, 140, 145, 149, 154, 165n123, 181
Soviet Union (USSR), xxi, 145
St. Luke's College, 18, 41n4
Stepney Coloured Peoples Association (SCPA), 106, 113n45
Stepney Communist Party, 30, 40, 43n45
Sudan, 218
Sunshine Workers Association, 115

Tabili, Laura, 41n14, 228
Tanzania, 179, 184, 199, 201
Tanzanian High Commission, 184
Third Reich, xxvii, 30
Third World, The, 147, 176
Thomas, John Jacob, 23, 42n20
Times of London, 222
Toussaint L'Ouverture, 42, 51, 128
Trinidad and Tobago, xiii–xv, xxv, 14n21, 25–29, 39, 42, 48, 58, 98, 126, 134, 141, 147, 171–72, 177, 181–83, 187, 189, 195, 200; carnival, 98; People's National Movement in, 118, 195
Trinidadians, xxv, 42n20, 96, 128, 132; Indo-, 56, 58, 72, 102, 132
Tswana people, xxiv

UK Interracial Brotherhood, 108
United Kingdom, *passim*.
United States of America (USA), *passim*, but see especially: xiii–xxi, xxiv–xxix, 1–5, 9, 20, 22–27, 31, 40–41, 55–56, 95, 100, 106, 110–11, 117, 119, 127, 137, 147–49, 152, 154, 156, 177, 179, 181–82, 184, 186, 190, 210, 211–12, 218; civil rights movement in, 181; dominates literature on history of migrants, xix
Universal Coloured People's Association (UCPA), 153–55, 190–92
University of Kent, 169–71, 173–74
University of the West Indies at Mona, 145–48, 172, 198, 200–201; students and workers protesting against Walter Rodney's banishment, 134–36, 161n38
University of the West Indies at St. Augustine, 200

Vernon, Ramon, 132–33, 163n88
Von Eschen, Penny M., 226

Walcott, Clyde, 96
Walcott, Derek, 118
Wallace, Elisabeth, 228
Walmsley, Anne, 197, 202n3, 204n34, 207–208, 228
Walvin, James, 228
Wambu, Onyekachi, xxviii, 228
Waters, Chris, 228
Waters, Mary C., 14n10
Waters, Rob, 228
Watkins-Owens, Irma, xxixn25, 14n10, 228
West Indian Federal Labour Party, 118
West Indian Gazette and Afro-Asian News, 95–103, 114n47, 133, 209, 212, 221
West Indian Students' Union Newsletter, 149
West Indian(s), *passim*. *See also* Caribbean, The
West Indies Federation, 6–9, 21, 36, 59, 81, 83, 102, 111, 116–17, 120–21, 140, 145, 147, 171, 211
White Defence League, 82–83
Whitfield, James, 228
Wickenden, James, 223
Wild, Rosalind, 228

Williams, Eric Eustace, xxiv–v, 17, 23–28, 31, 42, 96, 100, 117–18, 147, 172–73, 182, 195
Williams, Henry Sylvester, 18, 20, 172
Williams, Raymond, 15n41, 228
Windrush, The MV Empire, passim, but see especially: xi–xii, xv, xxv–xxix, 1–3, 6, 14–17, 24, 35–36, 42, 45, 49, 62–63, 72, 89–90, 142, 157–58, 189, 191, 193, 199, 215–17
Women's Progressive Organization, 116
Wong, Ansel, 112n19, 206n99, 212
Wood, Donald, 122, 161, 171
World War I, 18, 24, 32, 196
World War II, xi, xiii–xiv, xxi, xxiii–xxviii, 3–17, 20–23, 34–38, 49, 73, 123, 138, 157, 195, 213

X, Malcolm (*El-Hajj Malik El-Shabazz*), 116, 147, 183, 185

Yale University, 55

Author Biographical Note

James Cantres is an assistant professor in Africana and Puerto Rican/Latino Studies at Hunter College, CUNY, where he specializes in migration, black internationalisms, radical politics, cultural formations, and Africana epistemologies. Trained as a historian, Dr. Cantres locates twentieth century black Atlantic upheavals within the broad histories of transatlantic slavery, cultures of resistance, and the historicity of black identifications. His work also explores the ways African diasporic art forms and popular culture—reggae, literature, sports, and the plastic arts—articulate belonging and unbelonging among black peoples in the Black Atlantic through the period of decolonization and independence in Africa and the Caribbean.